MORAL CHARACTER

"Anyone who wants to know what human beings are actually like, as well as those who are interested in how we might become better than we typically are, should read this book. In its combination of philosophical sophistication with careful attention to a genuinely broad and representative selection of data, it provides a model for how naturalistic philosophy can fruitfully address ancient questions."

Neil Levy, University of Melbourne, *Ethics*

"Christian Miller's *Moral Character: An Empirical Theory* presents us with a way of thinking about moral character that is, remarkably, both intuitive and revolutionary ... This book deserves careful analysis and will no doubt provoke attention and debate within the field of moral psychology. It is well-written and engaging; while he covers much territory, Miller makes the structure of his overall argument clear and seamless ... *Moral Character: An Empirical Theory* is empirically-informed moral psychology at its best."

Lorraine Besser-Jones, Middlebury College, *Journal of Moral Philosophy*

"Miller has accomplished a major achievement ... He draws together a very large body of empirical research in support of his insightful account of cross-situationally consistent moral character traits. No one involved in the person-situation debate, psychologist or philosopher, can now afford not to know Miller's account. He has moved the debate forward in a fruitful way."

Don Collins Reed, Wittenberg University, *PsycCRITIQUES*

"Miller uses psychological studies extensively, knows the philosophical literature well, and shows admirable caution about what remains to be known. Highly recommended."

Hans Oberdiek, Swarthmore College, *Choice Reviews*

"let me emphasize that anyone interested in the intersection of empirical psychology and ethics will profit from reading Miller's book ..."

Bradford Cokelet, University of Miami, *Notre Dame Philosophical Reviews*

Moral Character

An Empirical Theory

CHRISTIAN B. MILLER

OXFORD
UNIVERSITY PRESS

OXFORD
UNIVERSITY PRESS

Great Clarendon Street, Oxford, OX2 6DP,
United Kingdom

Oxford University Press is a department of the University of Oxford.
It furthers the University's objective of excellence in research, scholarship,
and education by publishing worldwide. Oxford is a registered trade mark of
Oxford University Press in the UK and in certain other countries

First published 2013
First published in paperback 2015

Published in the United States of America by Oxford University Press
198 Madison Avenue, New York, NY 10016, United States of America

British Library Cataloguing in Publication Data
Data available

Library of Congress Cataloging in Publication Data
Data available

ISBN 978-0-19-967435-0 (Hbk.)
ISBN 978-0-19-874420-7 (Pbk.)

To Jessie Lee Miller, my amazing wife

Contents

Preface

THE THEME OF THE BOOK

Most of our friends, colleagues, and even family members are not virtuous people. They do not have virtues such as compassion, honesty, or courage.

But at the same time, they are not vicious people either. They do not have vices such as cruelty, dishonesty, or cowardice.

The aim of this book is to show that instead most people today have characters which do not qualify as either virtuous or vicious. They have many positive moral features, but also many negative ones too. Our characters are decidedly mixed, and are much more complex than we might have thought.

Consider, for instance, the following case. Suppose someone is walking along in a shopping mall gazing at the different stores. Suddenly a shopper walks across her path carrying a grocery bag with a tear in the bottom from which candy is falling to the ground. Every indication is that the shopper has no idea that the candy is leaking out of the bag. Would you expect most people to let this shopper know about the leak? I think we would expect this. After all, it is clear what the problem is, and the effort involved in solving it is very minimal and would not cause much of a delay. The shopper would also most likely be very grateful. And helping the shopper is clearly what a good person is expected to do, other things being equal.

But it turns out, according to a study performed by Dennis Regan and his colleagues (1972), that most people did not bother to notify the shopper. More specifically, out of twenty female participants, only three made any attempt. The other seventeen simply let the candy continue to fall.

Actually, there is a bit more to their study. These twenty visitors to the mall were control participants who, a few stores earlier, had each been approached by a male confederate of the experimenters asking to have his picture taken using an expensive looking camera. He went on to say that the camera was rather sensitive, and each participant who then tried to take a picture found that the shutter did not work. Fortunately, these control participants were assured that the camera "acts up a lot" and that they did not do anything wrong. The confederate then left the participant, and a few stores away it was a second confederate who walked across the path of the participant with the torn bag of candy.[1]

---

[1] Regan et al. 1972: 43.

Does this earlier event make any difference to our expectations about helping the shopper with the torn bag? It is hard to see how it would. The participant was told that the problem with the shutter was not her fault, and so she had no reason to feel any guilt about that. It was an unfortunate development for the owner of the camera, but not one that should have bothered the participant much if at all. And it certainly does not justify or morally excuse her failing to notify the owner of the candy.

Now consider twenty additional participants in the identical setup as above, with the one difference being that each of them was instead told by the camera owner that she must have done something wrong and jammed the camera, and that it would now have to be fixed (presumably at significant expense to the owner). Did this change in the setup lead to a subsequent change in helping behavior? Indeed it did—55 percent of these participants helped (11 out of 20), as compared to only 15 percent of the controls![2]

What explains this difference? As I will suggest in more detail in chapter two, the most natural explanation is that the participants in this experimental group were made to feel guilty about breaking the camera, which led to the formation of a motive to relieve their guilt. Helping the person with the torn bag immediately presented itself as an opportunity to do so. So they were more inclined to help.[3] Note, though, that if this is the correct explanation, then such helping hardly seems morally praiseworthy, as we should expect it to be from a compassionate person. Note as well that even in this case, 45 percent of these participants still did not bother to perform this simple act of kindness, which we should expect from a compassionate person. Finally, note how such a small change in the situation (what the person was told about the camera) played a very significant role in influencing whether many people chose to help at a later point in time. A compassionate person is not expected to have her helping influenced by such changes, I would think.

Here is another, more recent study by Lawrence Williams and John Bargh (2008). Suppose participants are divided into two groups and have just completed a very simple task. As a reward, they are each told that they will receive either a "gift to treat a friend" or a personal reward to keep for themselves.[4] It turned out that in one group, 75 percent kept the gift for themselves. In the second group, only 46 percent did.[5]

---

[2] Regan et al. 1972: 44.

[3] Of course this is not the only psychological model which could explain the relationship between guilt and increased helping; others will be discussed in chapter two. At this stage of the discussion, I am only mentioning it as a hypothetical model, but one which will turn out to be well supported by other studies on guilt and helping.

[4] The rewards were a Snapple beverage or a $1 gift certificate for a local ice cream shop, but the results did not vary significantly between the two (Williams and Bargh 2008: 607).

[5] Williams and Bargh 2008: 607.

Were there any relevant differences between the two groups? Just one—whether the participants were asked to hold a hot or cold "Icy Hot" therapeutic pad as part of a product evaluation. It turned out that the overall frequency of performing kind actions for a friend dropped 50 percent between the groups based simply upon holding a cold rather than a hot pad.[6] Again, I would not expect a kind person to be influenced in this way.

These results are likely surprising to many of us. They do not appear to reflect what we think we know about other people's characters. While most people may not be moral saints, we would have thought that they at least have stronger characters than this.

But there are plenty of *other* studies which do find people acting quite well from a moral perspective. For instance, Russell Clark and Larry Word (1974) had participants pass by a laboratory on their way to take a written test, and they could see a technician working on some electrical equipment in the lab. On their way back after completing the test, participants had to pass by the lab again, where a (staged) emergency happened. There was a flash of light and the technician seemed to receive a serious shock. Next he, "would stiffen his body while giving out a sharp cry of pain, upset the apparatus and his tools, then collapse in a prone position on the floor."[7] In the experimental condition where there was no risk to the participant of getting shocked if he or she helped, 100 percent of participants did so. The percentage also was 100 percent when participants were assigned to groups of two instead of walking by the lab alone.[8]

Nor is this just an isolated result. In a different study, participants by themselves responded to the sound of a screen crashing on a workman and his painful groans at a very high rate (90 percent).[9] And participants in four different group configurations helped at a rate of 100 percent in a non-ambiguous emergency involving a maintenance worker falling from a ladder in another room.[10] Similarly in 62 out of 65 cases an ill-looking man was helped after he collapsed on the floor of a New York City subway.[11] Hence there are a variety of situations where most people seem willing to readily help others in need.

It is studies such as the ones mentioned above which have led me to believe that while moral character is very important and plays a significant role in shaping our thoughts and actions, it is also much more complex than we typically recognize. For most of us, it seems that we have the capacity to

[6] Williams and Bargh 2008: 607.
[7] Clark and Word 1974: 281.
[8] Clark and Word 1974: 282.
[9] Darley et al. 1973.
[10] Clark and Word 1972.
[11] Piliavin et al. 1969. These studies will be mentioned again in chapter six when discussing the effect of groups on helping.

exhibit both impressive moral excellence and depressing moral failure. My conclusion will end up being that we have moral characters which are simply neither virtuous nor vicious.

WHY CARE ABOUT CHARACTER?

But even if my conclusion ends up being correct, is it worth bothering to gain a better understanding of character? I believe that it is. When we think about how to understand human behavior, one of the first things we tend to mention is someone's character. We often say that our friend was quiet at the party because he is shy, or that one of our colleagues stayed late at the office because she is hard-working. In addition, having a certain kind of character is something that we value greatly. Employers typically aim to hire conscientious and loyal employees, rather than lazy and dishonest ones. Friends tend to value honesty, trust, and fairness in each other, and they question the strength of their friendships when one of these qualities is suddenly in doubt. Similarly, parents often try to raise their children to be compassionate, courageous, and wise, and our society invests tremendous resources into forms of moral education that emphasize character building.

More systematically, character concepts have been thought to be important in advancing our understanding of at least the following:

Societal Problems. Often writers on character point to character flaws as at least part of the explanation for many of our problems in society such as corporate scandals, tax evasion, teenage pregnancy, abuse, and infidelity.

Moral Education. A centerpiece of a good upbringing has traditionally been character education, and parents most immediately (as well as society at large) are typically expected to help foster positive character traits in children.

Normative Ethical Theory. One of the leading ethical theories today in philosophy is virtue ethics, where the character concepts are central to ethical thinking. But most other plausible theories will also ascribe some important role to the virtues and vices, even if it is not a foundational role.

Role Models. The moral exemplars and heroes whom we aspire to emulate in our lives are often those people who have excellent characters. Indeed, it is precisely their traits of character which can attract us to them and make them worthy of being role models in the first place.

Understanding Family and Friends. We want to have a good understanding of our friends and family, so that we can know whether we can trust them, whether they will be there when we need them most, whether they will be honest with us, and so on.

Understanding Ourselves. We also want to understand ourselves better, not just from moment to moment, but also over extended periods of time—what kind of people we are, what we tend to do in different situations, what motivates us and explains our patterns of behavior, and so on.

My goal in this book is not to establish a tight connection between the study of character and these different topics. But *if* thinking more about character can help us to make progress in each of these areas, then it certainly is a worthwhile endeavor.[12]

INTENDED AUDIENCE

This book is intended to be a contribution to our understanding of character which is aimed primarily at scholars working in philosophy and psychology. Philosophers have been thinking about character for thousands of years, but only in recent decades have psychologists performed carefully controlled studies on morally relevant thoughts and behaviors, studies which have important implications for better understanding how our characters are put together.

In addition, this book should be of interest to those whose work significantly overlaps with philosophical and psychological questions about character, such as scholars in the fields of religion, moral education, sociology, history, and literature. I also hope that many people who are simply interested in the topic will find this book to be helpful independently of their professional work.

Hence I have tried to make the writing accessible without at the same time sacrificing clarity and rigor. Because of this, some sections on topics in philosophy might seem overly simplistic for specialists in the area, and the same is true for certain topics in psychology for those who work in that field. I ask that allowances be made given the interdisciplinary audience I have in mind.

Having said this, the book is still an academic study of the topic, and may be challenging for those with no background or training in either philosophy or psychology.

PLAN OF THE BOOK

Part I provides the needed conceptual background for my framework, and in particular clarifies how I will be understanding such terms as 'character traits,' 'dispositions,' and 'virtues.'

---

[12] The primary goal of this book is to outline an empirical account of the kind of moral character traits which, I will argue, most of us possess. Another book would be needed to apply that account to all the different areas outlined above.

Part II consists of five chapters which outline various empirical results and models for thinking about when and why we help others in need. Collectively this discussion serves to point in the direction of my positive framework and offers evidential support for it as well. In addition, the chapters begin to justify the claim that most of us do not have the virtues, in this case the virtue of compassion.

Part III is the heart of the book. Chapter seven offers the outline of an account of our actual moral character as it pertains to helping. Chapter eight then steps back and generalizes this account to other moral domains, while also outlining some basic methodological principles for the empirical study of character.

It would be a disappointing result if the framework for thinking about moral character that I propose only applies to helping. To see that it does not, Part IV briefly turns to two other moral domains—hurting others and lying—and shows how there is initial support for my framework there as well.

For anyone who works on character in either philosophy or psychology, there will be several notable omissions from the table of contents—there is no discussion of situationism, the CAPS models, and the Big Five taxonomy. There is also nothing said about the important philosophical implications for meta-ethics (in particular in supporting an error theory about judgments of character) and normative ethical theory (in particular the challenge raised by Gilbert Harman and John Doris to the empirical adequacy of virtue ethics).

These omissions are all intentional. In the companion book to this one, entitled *Character and Moral Psychology* (Oxford University Press, 2014), I first simply assume that my account of our actual moral character is correct, and then consider these additional topics in light of that account. *Character and Moral Psychology* is written to be independent of this book, and so readers who are more interested in these topics are encouraged to start with that book instead.

Acknowledgements

Earlier versions of chapters one, seven, and eight were discussed as part of the Character Project Research in Progress Group at Wake Forest University. Thanks in particular to William Fleeson, R. Michael Furr, Peter Meindl, and Eranda Jayawickreme for comments.

An earlier version of chapter one was discussed as part of the Wake Forest University Philosophy Department Research in Progress Group. Thanks in particular to Stavroula Glezakos, Win-chiat Lee, Adrian Bardon, Emily Austin, and Patrick Toner for comments.

Material from chapters one and seven was presented at the University of Tennessee, Duke University, and University of Minnesota at Duluth, as well as at a symposium on character at the 2011 American Philosophical Association Central Division Meeting. Many thanks especially to Karen Neander, Allen Buchanan, Walter Sinnott-Armstrong, Gopal Sreenivasan, David Wong, Adela Deanova, Daniel Moseley, Todd Calder, Anne Baril, John Doris, Paul McNamara, Brian Robinson, Sean Walsh, Jason Ford, and Tristram McPherson.

For written comments on chapter one, thanks to Kevin Timpe, Donald Smith, Matt Talbert, Peter Vranas, and Nicole Smith.

With kind permission from Palgrave Macmillan, chapters two and three draw on my paper: "Guilt, Embarrassment, and Global Character Traits Associated with Helping," *New Waves in Ethics*. Ed. Thom Brooks. Basingstoke: Palgrave Macmillan, 2011, 150–87.

With kind permission from Springer Science + Business Media B.V, chapter three draws on my paper: "Social Psychology, Mood, and Helping: Mixed Results for Virtue Ethics," *The Journal of Ethics* 13 (2009): 145–73. An earlier version of this paper was presented at the 2005 University of Denver conference on virtue ethics and social psychology. Thanks to James Taylor, Ralph Kennedy, Adrian Bardon, Avram Hiller, George Graham, Stavroula Glezakos, and Win-chiat Lee for comments.

With kind permission from Springer Science + Business Media B.V, chapter five draws on my paper: "Empathy, Social Psychology, and Global Helping Traits," *Philosophical Studies* 142 (2009): 247–75. Thanks to Nancy Snow and several anonymous referees for their written comments on that paper, and to Dan Batson for written comments on this chapter. A condensed version of this chapter was presented as "Compassion and

Empathy," 2010 Evolution and Ethics Conference, Beijing, China. Thanks to John Cottingham for comments.

With kind permission from the *Journal of Ethics and Social Philosophy*, chapter six draws on my paper: "Character Traits, Social Psychology, and Impediments to Helping Behavior." *Journal of Ethics and Social Philosophy*, <http://www.jesp.org.> 5 (2010): 1–36. Thanks to several anonymous referees for their comments on this chapter. An earlier version of the paper was presented at the 2009 North Carolina Philosophical Society meeting and as a symposium paper at the 2009 American Philosophical Association Pacific Division meeting. Thanks to my commentators at the Pacific, Nancy Snow and Linda Radzik.

Figure 4 in chapter eight is reproduced from: Fleeson, W. (2001). "Toward a Structure- and Process-Integrated View of Personality: Traits as Density Distributions of States." *Journal of Personality and Social Psychology* 80: 1011–27. Figures 5 and 6 in chapter eight are reproduced from: Fournier, M., D. Moskowitz, and D. Zuroff (2008). "Integrating Dispositions, Signatures, and the Interpersonal Domain." *Journal of Personality and Social Psychology* 94: 531–45. Per <http://www.apa.org/about/contact/copyright/index.aspx> (accessed on 13 August 2012), permission is not required for the use of these figures.

Figures 7 and 8 in chapter eight are reproduced with the kind permission of The Guilford Press from: Shoda, Y. and S. LeeTiernan. (2002). "What Remains Invariant? Finding Order within a Person's Thoughts, Feelings, and Behaviors across Situations," in *Advances in Personality Science*. Ed. D. Cervone and W. Mischel. New York: The Guilford Press, 241–70.

I am grateful to Bella DePaulo for checking my use of her studies in chapter ten. Thanks as well to Joshua Seachris for his help at the last minute editing the bibliography.

I would like to thank two anonymous referees for Oxford University Press for their very helpful comments on this manuscript, and Peter Momtchiloff for all of his support.

This book was written during the 2010–11 academic year while I was on a research leave from Wake Forest University. I am very grateful to my department and especially to my chair, Ralph Kennedy, for all their support, and to the Reynolds Leave Program and the Thomas Jack Lynch Funds for funding. For summer support in 2010 and 2011, I am also very grateful to the John Templeton Foundation and their support of the Character Project grant that I direct at Wake Forest (<http://www.thecharacterproject.com>). The opinions expressed in this book are mine alone and do not necessarily reflect the views of the John Templeton Foundation, the Character Project, or Wake Forest University.

On a personal note, I would like to thank my parents, Charles and Joyous Miller, for all their sacrifices and encouragement over many years. This book is dedicated to my amazing wife, Jessie Lee Miller. She is such an incredible blessing.

List of Figures

Part I

Conceptual Background for the Framework

1

Dispositions, Character Traits, and Virtues

The goal of this book is to develop a new framework for thinking about what moral character looks like today. My central claim will be that most people have moral character traits, but at the same time they do not have either the traditional virtues, such as honesty or compassion, or the traditional vices, such as cruelty or cowardice. Rather, most people have what I will call "Mixed Character Traits," with some morally positive features and some morally negative ones too. This is an empirical claim about human beings, and much of the book will be devoted to exploring this claim using experimental results in psychology. But first I need to do some preliminary conceptual work in order to clarify how I will be using such terms as "character traits," "dispositions," and "virtues." Most important of all, by getting clearer conceptually in this area, I aim to show by the end of this chapter that we can make sense of the idea that there are character traits which are neither virtues nor vices. This will then set the stage for the chapters to come which argue that these are precisely the traits that most of us actually possess.

So in this chapter, I aim to do the following:

(i) Clarify the relationship between character traits and dispositions.

(ii) Outline several functional roles of character traits.

(iii) Note that character traits can come in degrees and can exhibit different forms of consistency as well as vary in their generality.

(iv) Focus on the moral character traits and suggest on conceptual grounds that it makes sense to talk about character traits which are neither moral virtues nor vices.

Those readers who are less interested in conceptual distinctions are encouraged to skim this chapter and proceed directly to chapter two where I start to examine some of the relevant psychological research.

1.1 CHARACTER TRAITS AND DISPOSITIONS

There are hundreds of different concepts which we ordinarily use to describe someone's character, such as forgiving, just, compassionate, loving, kind, nefarious, vile, greedy, understanding, and courageous. All of these concepts are used to refer to *traits of character*—to say that someone is a greedy person, for instance, is to say that one of the traits which best describes his character is the trait of being greedy. Thus I think that:

> (1) A person's *character* primarily consists of her character traits and the relationships between them.

To partially describe Hitler's character, for instance, I might mention traits like cruelty and injustice and how the two might have worked together in his mind.[1]

As ordinarily understood character traits are personality traits, and are concerned with the mental life of a creature, that is, the mental states and processes that constitute thinking.[2] These mental states and processes can and typically do influence behavior in all kinds of ways. A shy person, for instance, *wants* to avoid speaking in public, and so may decline speaking invitations because of that. A sociable person, on the other hand, may get *excited* by an upcoming party and spend hours mingling with the crowd.

As character *traits*, they are more than just momentary states of mind, and so just because someone is exhibiting certain thoughts does not mean that he has the underlying trait. Character traits can give rise to characteristic mental *states*, but mental states do not have to depend on character traits.[3] As an illustration, Smith might be in a compassionate frame of mind—he might be thinking about how best to help someone else in need, care a lot at this moment about helping that person, and arrive at the correct answer as to what would be best to do for her. It certainly seems that Smith has compassionate mental states. But if this happens to be the only time in his life when he thinks and feels this way, and otherwise he just tries to promote his own self-interest,

---

[1] See Moody-Adams 1990: 116. This does not capture all uses of "character," such as when we say of a person whom we just met that, "he is quite a character!" Rather I am only interested in the sense of "character" that has been of primary interest in discussions of moral education, ethical theory, and personality psychology, and that is represented in ordinary discourse by expressions such as, "Mother Teresa has a compassionate character" or, "We want our children to grow up to become people of strong character."

[2] It is an interesting and difficult question whether, on the other hand, all personality traits are character traits. I give some reasons for answering negatively in *Character and Moral Psychology*, chapter one.

[3] For the distinction between traits and states in psychology, see, e.g. Mischel and Shoda 1995: 257, 1998: 235, Fleeson 2001: 1012, 2007: 826, Fleeson and Noftle 2008a: 1358, Fleeson and Noftle 2008b, Fleeson and Gallagher 2009: 1099, and Roberts 2009: 140 (and the references cited therein). The distinction is commonplace in philosophical discussions of character.

then I suspect we would also likely not say anything more than this—he does not have a trait of compassion, but just a momentary compassionate state.

The same idea applies to the distinction between character traits and characteristic bodily *actions*. Smith might make a large donation to charity. In most cases we would call that a compassionate action, and would praise him for it. But merely knowing this about his action does not necessarily tell us anything about either the mental states behind the action or the traits (if any) which led to its being performed. For all we know, Smith could have been entirely in a selfish frame of mind, wanting to be recognized by society. That state of mind could have arisen from a trait of selfishness. So a compassionate action does not entail the possession of a compassionate trait. And neither does a compassionate state of mind.[4]

Thus for someone like Tom to have the character trait of shyness, for instance, he has to have some enduring *tendency or disposition* to have shy thoughts and act in shy ways. This disposition is distinct from the shy thoughts and actions, although it can give rise to both. Furthermore, these thoughts need not be active all the time or in every situation; when he is alone, for instance, Tom may not have them at all. Rather, it might only be when he is in certain conditions which are relevant to this trait, such as parties or classrooms, that they kick in and play an active role in his psychology. As philosophers like to say, in these conditions Tom's shy thoughts go from being merely *dispositional* thoughts, to being *occurrent* thoughts.[5]

Similarly, the shy beliefs and desires that he forms in these situations need not be precisely the same *particular* mental states on every relevant occasion— they can be as diverse as wanting to leave a party or wanting to hide behind a large football player in class. What matters is that they are of the same broad

[4] For use of these distinctions, see Foot 1978: 173, Aristotle 1985: 1105b 6–10, 1134a 16, 1135a 5–11, 1135b 20–1136a 4, 1151a 10, Irwin 1996: 47, 54, Wiggins 1997: 99–100, Hursthouse 1999: 123, 134–6, Athanassoulis 2000: 218, Harman 2003: 92, 2009: 239, 241, Swanton 2003: 4, 29, Kamtekar 2004: 486, Hurka 2006, Adams 2006: 3, Appiah 2008: 61, 64, 70, Upton 2009a: 48–9, Russell 2009: 80, 133, 191, and Annas 2011: 8, 44–5, although I depart from Swanton and Hurka in claiming that a person could perform a compassionate action from either a good or bad motive—trait properties of actions are not tied to the motives or intentions behind the actions, on my view, just as they are not tied to any character traits which give rise to them either. Rather I prefer to say that performing a virtuous action just amounts to the person performing that action, whichever it happens to be, which is deemed to be a virtuous action by the correct normative theory, regardless of what motives the person had for performing it. For instance, it might be the action which has the property of being what a fully compassionate person, acting in character, would have also performed in the same circumstances, as Aristotle seems to hold (1105b 6).

[5] Occurrent thoughts, though, need not be conscious. I can have many subconscious occurrent desires which are causally influencing my behavior in all kinds of ways. For instance, Tom might be influenced to leave the party by a desire to avoid crowds of people, without realizing that he in fact has this desire.

type, namely shy thoughts, not that they are mental states with exactly the same content on each occasion.

So generalizing from this example of Tom, I propose that in a preliminary way we can understand a character trait had by a person as roughly:

> (2) A disposition to form beliefs and/or desires of a certain sort and (in many cases) to act in a certain way, when in conditions relevant to that disposition.[6]

A person who is shy is disposed to believe, desire, and act shyly, and can form such thoughts and act this way when, for instance, at a large party. Someone who is sociable is typically disposed instead to form different thoughts and exhibit different behaviors when at large parties.

A quick note about how I will be using "beliefs" and "desires." It is customary in philosophy to divide all mental states into two broad types— cognitive mental states which are labeled "beliefs" and non-cognitive mental states which are labeled "desires."[7] The difference between the cognitive and non-cognitive is notoriously hard to pin down precisely. To use a common metaphor, cognitive mental states are all those states which aim to capture or reflect the way the world is; they are said to have a mind-to-world direction of fit. A belief that Thomas Jefferson was the first president of the United States fails to reflect the way the world is, and so the fault is with the belief, not the world. Non-cognitive mental states have the opposite, world-to-mind direction of fit, and so aim to change the world to bring it in line with the desire. For instance, I might desire to be the next president of the United States, and so aim to make the world reflect this goal. A failure to do so is not a failure of the desire, but of the world from my perspective.[8] Here I will use the term "desire" very broadly to range over a number of different kinds of non-cognitive mental states, such as wishes, wants, tastes, whims, urges,

---

[6] Note that nothing in (2) requires that there be individual differences between how people are disposed to believe, desire, and act in order for there to be character traits. Psychologists often focus on individual differences when studying traits, but I claim this focus should be restricted to *gathering evidence* for their existence, rather than as a conceptual requirement for understanding them in the first place. In principle, there may be no individual differences in a population's possession of a character trait—it is conceivable that everyone could have honesty or courage equally, for instance. Hence individual differences are not constitutive of such traits in the first place (contrary to Funder 2008: 570 and Fleeson and Noftle 2009: 151). For a similar claim, see Doris 2002: 19 n. 23, Kamtekar 2004: 468, Badhwar 2009: 280, and Sosa 2009: 287. For the opposing view, see Johnson 1997: 74, 87.

[7] More precisely, it is customary to divide all mental states *with intentional objects* into these two categories. I am not committing myself to the claim that all of what goes on in our mental lives falls under the heading of either beliefs or desires. As an anonymous reviewer noted, qualia, for instance, are not meant to be part of this discussion.

[8] For more on the direction of fit metaphor and some of the challenges it faces, see Schueler 1991, Humberstone 1992, Zangwill 1998, and Sobel and Copp 2001.

promptings, hopes, and intentions.[9] The objects of desires can include such familiar mental items as my goals, plans, and aspirations.

Returning to (2), then, the idea is that character traits are dispositions to form beliefs and/or desires and potentially to act in relevant ways as well when in the appropriate circumstances. The ambiguity about whether they pertain to beliefs, desires, *and* actions is intentional. Some character traits certainly do seem to involve all of these elements, as in the case of compassion or selfishness. Others, though, could involve desire states without a belief state—perhaps irritability or general anxiousness might be candidates.[10] Still other traits such as foresight or closed-mindedness might only involve belief states without desire states. Finally, note that some character traits do not directly involve action in any ordinary sense pertaining to intentional bodily movement (hence "action" here does not include mental actions). The traits of being analytical and logical, which pertain to a person's reasoning capacities, might be two such examples.[11] While I do not want to commit myself to any of these specific proposals in this paragraph, I also do not want to rule them out from the very start.

So according to my proposal in (2), a character trait is a disposition of a certain kind, or a "trait disposition" as I will call it.[12] Let me make a few additional points about these dispositions in the remainder of this section.

It is a feature of dispositions in general that they are sensitive to certain *stimulus events* or *stimulus conditions* specific to the given disposition. In virtue of being fragile, for instance, a vase might be sensitive to being hit by a baseball, but not to the color of the baseball. Similarly a properly functioning

---

[9] For broad versus narrow uses of "desire," see Schueler 1995: chapter one. Some philosophers of action argue that intentions are best understood as primarily cognitive states (e.g. Velleman 1989). Nothing hangs upon how I classify them here.

[10] To reiterate what was said in n. 5, nothing is assumed here about the desires having to be *conscious*. In some cases, at least part of the effect of a trait can be to lead to the formation of subconscious desires to act in certain ways. Thanks to Kevin Timpe here.

[11] See also Hampshire 1953: 6, Alston 1970: 65–72, 1975: 21, and Adams 2006: 132–8. Richard Brandt even raises the possibility of personality traits that influence a person's (non-intentional) behavior without involving dispositions to form either beliefs or desires (1988: 68).

[12] The link between character traits and dispositions is widespread in philosophical work on character. See, as representative examples, Hampshire 1953: 5, Alston 1970: 65, Brandt 1970: 24, 27, Aristotle 1985: 1105a 34, Butler 1988: 216, 231, Audi 1991: 160, Mumford 1998: 8, Sher 1998: 5, Harman 1999: 317, 2003: 92, Athanassoulis 2000: 218, Sreenivasan 2002: 49, 57, Swanton 2003: 1, 19, Kamtekar 2004: 479, Goldie 2004: 8, 15, Upton 2005: 133–4, 2009a: chapter two, Webber 2006b: 205, Adams 2006: 18, 130–2, Besser-Jones 2008: 311, 316–21, Appiah 2008: 35, Russell 2009: 12, 14, 191, Flanagan 2009: 53, Prinz 2009: 131, Sosa 2009: 279–80, Annas 2011: 8–9, 104 (for virtues but not for vices), and especially the references in Doris 1998: 509 n. 20, 2002: 15 n. 2.

But among psychologists there is a significant divide in the literature on whether character traits, and personality traits in general, are real dispositional properties of individuals. I review this debate and offer some reasons to reject the opposing views in *Character and Moral Psychology*, chapter one.

thermostat is sensitive to the temperature in the room, but not to its smell. It seems that certain events and facts about a situation or environment are relevant to a disposition in a way that others are not.

Stimulus events can *trigger* characteristic *manifestations* of dispositions. A baseball can break a fragile vase, and the temperature of the room can lead to a certain reading on the thermostat. Prior to the stimulus, the disposition might have been latent, as for example the disposition to believe that $2 + 7 = 9$ is latent during most of my day. But with the right kind of stimulus, such as a math test, the disposition can become manifest, say in the form of the occurrent belief that $2 + 7 = 9$. Indeed, all dispositions to believe or desire certain things become manifest directly in the form of occurrent mental states. These occurrent mental states can then lead in many cases to corresponding behavior.[13]

Character traits work in the same way. The trait of compassion can be triggered by what the person sees as ongoing suffering, and can lead directly to compassionate thoughts and ultimately to compassionate behavior aimed at relieving that suffering.[14] Note that the immediate stimuli for character traits do not have to be the actual features of a situation, but can just be the person's *impressions of* those features, impressions which in some cases can be seriously mistaken and yet still activate the relevant trait. Suffering that goes unnoticed in a situation through no fault of the person's own, for instance, will not have an impact on her trait of compassion, even if it is true that if the suffering were noticed, then she would typically help to relieve it.[15]

[13] Things are not so simple, of course. Background conditions also play an important role. A match has the disposition of being flammable and so typically lights (manifestation) when struck (stimulus), but not in an environment without oxygen. A vase has the disposition of being fragile and so typically breaks (manifestation) when knocked off a ledge (stimulus), but not if gravity is much weaker than it is on Earth. And so forth.

Note that these are cases where the background conditions interfere with the ability of the disposition to be manifest, but still allow the disposition to continue to exist. Other background conditions may either prevent or eliminate a disposition from being instantiated in the first place, such as a healthy human being with the disposition of being strong, suddenly passing away from a heart attack. See Mumford 1998: 86.

[14] But not if there are interfering background conditions, i.e., the person is experiencing serious depression or a mental illness which blocks the operation of the trait and precludes the formation of compassionate thoughts even in the presence of obvious suffering. For general remarks about character traits and background conditions, see Brandt 1970: 35 and Upton 2005: 135–6, 2009a: 27–30. In addition, nothing about the above is meant to imply that the compassionate behavior need depend *only* on the trait of compassion—other character traits, for instance, can also play a partial causal role as well.

[15] For this last point, see Alston 1975: 21. Note that nothing about the above implies how *frequently* character traits are actually triggered—that will depend on a number of factors including how strongly the trait is held, the situations the person is in, and even the nature of the particular trait itself. Some traits, such as fairness, perhaps, or modesty, are by their very nature likely going to be highly active during the day for people who have them to a significant extent. With other traits, such as perhaps bravery or integrity, the person may rarely be in the kinds of situations which trigger their activation. Indeed, it seems possible on conceptual

In functioning in these ways, character dispositions are not inert properties in a person's mental life; rather they *causally mediate* between their various stimuli and manifestation events. So if Jones has a compassionate disposition whereas Frank does not, that is not merely an individual difference between them. It is also and crucially a difference in the possession of a property which (together with the relevant stimulus) plays a significant causal role in leading to Jones's compassionate thoughts and behavior.

Because of this causal role, trait dispositions can also create expectations about how a person would likely behave in various situations, thereby serving as a basis for making accurate predictions. If, for instance, George Washington was deeply courageous and Abraham Lincoln highly honest, then we can reasonably predict how they would likely have behaved in different circumstances during the course of their lives. Similarly for compassionate Jones it might be true that:

(3) If Jones were to encounter a person who he notices is in need of a moderate amount of help, he would typically attempt to help, regardless of whether helping is in his self-interest.

Whereas for selfish Frank:

(4) If Frank were to encounter a person who he notices is in need of a moderate amount help, he would typically attempt to ignore the need, unless he thought helping were in his self-interest to a relevant degree.

Of course as stated these predictions are much too simplistic. Background conditions can interfere with dispositions in all kinds of ways—Jones might also be suffering from depression or mental illness, for instance. But the important point here is that the causal activities of trait dispositions can create expectations about the person's future behavior in both himself and others.[16]

Let me summarize what has been said about character trait dispositions so far. Dispositions in general can be stimulated in various ways, and so long as there are no interfering background conditions, they can give rise to their relevant manifestations. If Jones has a particular trait disposition such as compassion then Jones has an actually existing (instantiation of a) property which can causally bring about occurrent compassionate thoughts and, thereby, compassionate behavior. These dispositional properties ground the truth of conditionals about what a person would likely think and do in relevant situations.

---

grounds that a person could have a character trait and yet never have it be triggered at all during her lifetime.

[16] Various attempts have been made in the literature to improve these predictions. For an overview, see Upton 2009a: chapter two.

One last point needs to be made here. I have said something about how character traits *function*, that is, about how they are triggered and can give rise to relevant occurrent beliefs and desires. But what exactly *are* these character trait dispositions themselves? In *Character and Moral Psychology*, I expand on this topic at length, and interested readers are encouraged to consult that discussion. But briefly, my view is that character trait dispositions are, at least to a large extent, made up of interrelated mental state dispositions.[17] Let me explain.

I have said that a trait like compassion is itself a causal disposition. But we can also have very specific mental state dispositions as well that are relevant to compassionate behavior. Some of them might include:

A disposition to form the belief that it is important to help a person in need.
A disposition to form the desire to help another person for his or her own sake.
A disposition to form beliefs about what are and are not appropriate forms of helping.

The question, then, is this—how do these specific beliefs relate to the following disposition:

The disposition of compassion.

One answer could be that they are completely unrelated, so that whether a person has the trait of compassion has nothing to do with whether he has dispositions to form compassionate beliefs and desires. But no one has ever held such a position as far as I am aware, and for good reason. Rather, the standard answer is to say that in general:

A character trait disposition which is had by a person *consists of* some cluster of her relevant interrelated[18] mental state dispositions such that necessarily,

---

[17] For early statements of these ideas, see Alston 1970: 61, 88–90, 1975: 45–6, Brandt 1970: 27, 1988: 66–7, and Butler 1988: 220. See also more recently Trianosky 1990: 97, Audi 1991: 162, McCrae 1994: 152, Johnson 1997: 77, Doris 2002: 66, Solomon 2003: 47, Kamtekar 2004: 479, Sabini and Silver 2005: 546, Upton 2005: 134–5, 2009a: 4–11, 28–9, 49, 2009b: 177, Webber 2006b: 209, Adams 2006: 4, 17, 131–8, Taylor 2006: 6, Russell 2009: 172, 292, and Snow 2010: 90–1.

The qualification "at least to a large extent" is important, as certain abilities, faculties (e.g. willpower if it is a faculty), or skills (e.g. perceptual sensitivities) might also be needed in at least some cases for the possession of a character trait, and perhaps these abilities, faculties, or skills do not themselves entirely consist of mental state dispositions.

[18] That the mental state dispositions are "interrelated" is important. Obviously not just any random collection of mental state dispositions will amount to a character trait like compassion independently of the content of those mental states. But it is also not enough for a person to just *have* the appropriate mental state dispositions. A person does not have the trait of compassion unless she has the relevant belief and desire dispositions, *and* they (or the occurrent states they give rise to) trigger each other when appropriate. The beliefs that someone is in need and that I can help that person, should in relevant cases be related to a desire to devise means of helping him. Otherwise there could be an unrelated bunch of mental states, rather than a character trait. For similar remarks, see Snow 2010: 20.

if she has this cluster of dispositions, then she instantiates that character trait as well.[19]

In other words, having the relevant mental state dispositions *enables* a person to have the corresponding character trait. The trait, to put it differently, is anchored in the specific dispositions to form relevant beliefs and desires.[20] Without those specific dispositions, the relevant trait disposition would not be possessed by a person.

Returning to Jones, his trait of compassion is itself grounded in underlying mental state dispositions in Jones's mind, and specifically in mental state dispositions which are *appropriate* to the virtue of compassion from an ethical perspective. These could include his disposition to *recognize* people suffering in his environment, to *want* to help relieve their suffering regardless of whether doing so would benefit himself, to *weigh* different helping strategies, and so forth. But it would *not* include, for instance, a disposition to want to make people feel guilty after being helped, since from any plausible ethical perspective that would not be a disposition which is an appropriate constituent of the virtue of compassion. Figure 1.1 provides an illustration of the picture I have in mind, with the arrows symbolizing causal influence:

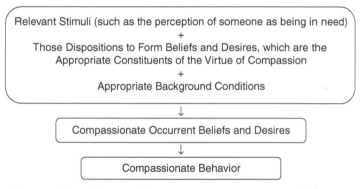

Fig. 1.1. From the trait of compassion to compassionate behavior.

[19] For an important qualification of this claim, see n. 17. As Nicole Smith reminded me, there are uses of the term "cluster" in certain areas of philosophy of language which imply that no single member of a cluster of properties is either necessary or sufficient for, in this case, possessing the trait of compassion, but to have sufficiently many of the properties in the cluster is necessary and sufficient for possessing the trait. I want to make it clear that I am not using the term in this technical sense.

[20] What precisely is this anchoring relation? Is it the relation of identity, or perhaps a non-reductive constitution relation? I remain neutral on this lively debate between trait monists and trait dualists here, but say more in *Character and Moral Psychology*, chapter one.

So when Jones encounters someone in need and the relevant background conditions are cooperative, his trait can be activated. This amounts to the underlying dispositions to form mental states of various kinds that are appropriate to the virtue of compassion being activated. As dispositions, they will have their own stimulus conditions. And as the grounds of compassion, they can be activated by the perception of need. In being activated, they can go from being latent dispositions, to causing the formation of occurrent mental states as their manifestations—beliefs, wishes, hopes, intentions, and so forth of the relevant sort, in this case compassionate—which then in turn can cause the performance of compassionate actions, other things being equal.

1.2. SOME ADDITIONAL FEATURES OF CHARACTER TRAITS

We said that character traits are dispositions to form beliefs and/or desires and potentially perform certain bodily actions. As dispositions, character traits do not need to be activated to still exist or be possessed by a person. Someone can have the trait of compassion, for instance, but not be around anyone who needs help, and thereby not have formed any occurrent beliefs or desires related to helping others.

In this section, I want to mention several other important features of character traits: their function roles, minimal thresholds, degrees, consistency, and generality. All of these features will be important in the chapters to come.

Character traits play various functional roles. I doubt that I can come up with an exhaustive list of these roles, but here are at least five of the central ones:

(a) *Understanding*: Character traits are a basis for understanding ourselves and others by classifying people in various ways which can be important to interpersonal and intrapersonal interaction. When I form an impression of Smith, for instance, my general understanding of him may be framed in terms of character traits and shaped heavily by my perceptions of his honesty, compassion, or generosity. The same could be true, not only about Smith, but about myself as well.[21]

(b) *Explanation*: Character traits are a basis for (partially) explaining why people act the way that they do. Smith may cheat on tests because he is dishonest (either in general or just dishonest in test-taking situations),

---

[21] Thanks to Mike Furr for pointing out to me this role. See also Hogan 1996: 170.

whereas Jones may regularly give money to charity because he is compassionate, other things being equal.[22]

(c) *Prediction*: Character traits are a basis for predicting what a person who has them will likely do in the future.[23] For instance, if I think that Smith is shy, then I can take myself to have a fairly good idea of how he will likely behave in a room full of people at the next work party, other things being equal.

(d) *Evaluation*: Character traits are a basis for normatively assessing a person. So when I say that Smith is dishonest, I am evaluating him as a person in a negative way, at least in that one respect.

(e) *Imitation*: Character traits are a basis upon which to imitate another person and cultivate positive traits while avoiding negative ones. So I might strive to become more compassionate, and model my life after people such as Jesus, Gandhi, Socrates, and Mother Theresa who are said to have had certain virtuous character traits to a high degree.[24]

For example, if I know that Jane is a highly artistic home designer, then I can understand something important about her, be able to partially explain why she behaves in certain ways, predict to some extent what she would likely do in certain contexts, evaluate her when it comes to this domain, and even imitate her if I aspire to excellence in this area of my life.

Character traits have minimal thresholds and come in degrees. In order to possess a character trait, a number of necessary conditions have to be met. For instance, the person must first possess one or more psychological dispositions. That is one of the necessary conditions for even being eligible to have a character trait of *any* kind in the first place, on the proposal I have already offered. But there are additional necessary conditions which must be met in order to have a *specific* character trait of, say, compassion rather than cruelty.

---

[22] This explanatory role is not limited to specific behaviors. Richard Brandt notes that historians, "make free use of trait-concepts in explanations of events (the collapse of a nation may be ascribed to things like the queen's vanity)" (1970: 23).

[23] But only what a person is "likely" to do, since among other things people seem to be able to act out of character as well. In those cases, explanations in terms of character traits would also not be helpful.

[24] Note that the functional roles in (a) through (e) are roles which character traits play, regardless of whether anyone in fact thinks about them in these ways. In other words, a character trait serves as a basis to explain and predict someone's behavior, even if no one realizes that the person has that trait.

For further discussion of one or more of the above functional roles, see Mischel 1968: 6, 9–10, Mischel and Mischel 1976: 208, MacIntyre 1984: 199, Brandt 1988: 64, Newman and Uleman 1989: 165–9, Moody-Adams 1990: 111, 117–18, Funder 1994: 126, Sher 1998: 6, Harman 1999: 317, Doris 2002: 5, 15, Sreenivasan 2002: 52, Goldie 2004: 3–6, 60, 66–7, Kamtekar 2004: 478, Upton 2005: 149, 2009a: 48, 50–1, 56, 61, 2009b: 176, 185, Adams 2006: 3, 18, 132, and Besser-Jones 2008: 314.

Call these specific conditions the *minimal threshold* that a character trait has to meet in order to qualify as that particular kind of trait rather than some other.

This idea should be familiar from the end of the previous section. If character traits are grounded in specific mental state dispositions, then one cannot count as having a given character trait like honesty without first having the specific dispositions to form beliefs and desires relevant to honesty, and also not having the specific dispositions to form beliefs and desires relevant to dishonesty. So a given character trait qualifies as a given virtue provided that its underlying mental state dispositions are of that virtuous kind themselves.

To make this more concrete, consider compassion once again. If a politician reliably helps in a variety of helping-relevant circumstances, then it might seem as if the person has the trait of compassion. But suppose it turns out that he desires to help others only when it makes him look better to the media. Then while this trait might satisfy one of the necessary conditions in the minimal threshold for compassion (it leads to helping behavior), it has not satisfied another one—the motivation is not of the appropriate sort. Note that the claim here is *not* that the trait therefore only qualifies as being weak compassion as opposed to deep compassion. Rather, the claim is that the trait does not (yet) qualify as compassion *at all*. Until his trait satisfies all the necessary conditions for *compassion*, it does not meet the minimal threshold for compassion and so the person does not instantiate the specific trait of compassion to any degree at all.

To use another example, for some character traits there are certain obvious situations in which, other things being equal, one would expect a person with the trait to exhibit trait-appropriate behavior, even if the trait is held to only a weak degree. As Richard Brandt notes for the trait of sympathy, for instance, "[e]ach of us has a conception of what a sympathetic person will do in a situation of a certain kind. For instance, we may think a sympathetic person will interrupt a friendly tennis game to tend to a child who has fallen off his bicycle. If he won't do that, we do not call him sympathetic."[25] So reliable performance of sympathetic actions in these obvious cases seems necessary, again other things being equal, for even qualifying as a person with the trait of sympathy.

Now if a person does not have a trait like sympathy or compassion, it does not follow that he must have acquired an *opposing* trait such as selfishness or cruelty to any degree. She may simply have none of these traits at all. Furthermore, we ordinarily think that character traits are not permanent features of our personalities. We assume, in other words, that we can gain and lose them, at least over an extended period of time, and so while a person might have had the trait of sympathy ten years ago, perhaps he has lost it in the interim.

Once a trait *does* satisfy the conditions for being a particular character trait, then it can come in degrees of more or less. Two people can have the trait of

---

[25] Brandt 1970: 36. For brief criticism of this proposal, see Butler 1988: 237.

compassion, say, but they might each have it to different degrees.[26] How could this difference in degree become manifest in behavior? Here are a few ways:

(i) Higher degrees of trait-possession can be positively correlated with *increased frequency* of trait-relevant behavior in the *same* trait-relevant circumstances. For example, a highly honest person might tell the truth more often at parties than someone who has the virtue to a lesser degree.

(ii) Higher degrees of trait-possession can be positively correlated with *increased frequency* of trait-relevant behavior in *various* kinds of trait-relevant circumstances, on the assumption that the trait in question pertains to more than one kind of situation. In other words, a person with a higher degree of the trait would exhibit it more often in situations X, Y, and Z which are relevant to that trait, as compared to how often he would exhibit the trait in those situations if he had it to a lesser degree. So a highly honest person might tell the truth more often at parties *and* also at home and at the office, than does someone who is honest to only a moderate degree.[27]

(iii) Higher degrees of trait-possession can be positively correlated with increased likelihood of performing *demanding* trait-relevant behavior in the same or different trait-relevant circumstances. Demandingness could be a function of such variables as lack of support from friends and family, financial burdens, societal opposition, risk of pain and suffering, and so forth. So a highly honest person is, for instance, more likely to tell the truth under oath if that is what there is most reason for her to do, even if such an action risks financial ruin.

(iv) Higher degrees of trait-possession can be positively correlated with increased *depth* of trait-relevant behavior in the same or different trait-relevant circumstances. Depth is a function of how much a person is willing to do in performing a trait-relevant behavior. A helping situation may not be very demanding, such as picking up dropped papers,

---

[26] This assumption about character traits is widespread. For representative statements, see Allport 1931: 371, Brandt 1970: 23, 36–7, 1988: 79, Alston 1970: 75–6, 78, Butler 1988: 232, Kupperman 1991: 14, Hursthouse 1999: 145, Taylor 2006: 9, Appiah 2008: 35, 48, Upton 2009a: 15–16, 60, Badhwar 2009: 274, Russell 2009: chapter four, and Sosa 2009: 280. The degree to which a person has a character trait is some complex function of the degree to which he has the underlying mental state dispositions and the relations between them.

[27] The assumption mentioned above is important, since otherwise a person could have a trait like "honesty at parties," and have it to a very high degree, while also not exhibiting it in any other kinds of situations.

Another difference captured by degrees of trait possession could involve the trait-relevant situations in which the person exhibits the trait to any extent. The greater extent to which the trait is possessed, the higher the number of such situations relevant to the trait in which it might be manifested.

but a person with a low degree of compassion could just go through the motions, whereas a person with a higher degree could help pick them up in a courteous and respectful manner and wait until every single paper is accounted for.[28]

So in light of this discussion, there are two distinct questions that one can ask about a person's character: does she have a particular trait, such as honesty, *at all*, and if she does, *to what degree* does she possess this trait?

In my experience, the idea of a minimal threshold for possessing a given character trait is relatively plausible to philosophers working in ethics, but is less plausible to many personality and social psychologists.[29] To use terms common from psychology, my claim is that character traits are both *categorical traits*—you have to meet certain standards to qualify as possessing them—but once you do they are *continuous traits* which can show up anywhere along a wide continuum of more and less. Psychologists, I often find, grant the distinction between categorical and continuous traits, but deny that character traits are categorical ones. So in subsequent chapters, I will go to some length to further develop this idea, beginning at the end of chapter two where I try to articulate some of the conditions in the minimal threshold for the virtue of compassion.

Character traits are consistent. A person's character trait is expected to lead, not just to behavior of the trait-relevant kind, but to *consistent* behavior.[30] This seems like a simple enough point, hardly worth mentioning here. But there actually turn out to be many forms of consistency that are relevant to traits

---

[28] For related discussion of different ways that traits can come in degrees, see Alston 1970: 75–6, 78, 1975: 20 and Upton 2009a: 60. In all four of the above, I assume that other things are being held equal.

[29] This difference becomes apparent especially in *Character and Moral Psychology*, chapter six in the context of discussing the Big Five taxonomy, where character trait labels such as "modesty" are applied to some degree to every human being.

For discussion that is broadly related to my notion of a minimal threshold, see Hursthouse 1999: 149–50, Swanton 2003: 25, Upton 2009a: 7, 49, 53, Kupperman 2009: 245, Eklund 2011, and especially Brandt 1970: 33–7 and Russell 2009: 112–17. As Russell rightly points out (114), there will likely be some degree of vagueness rather than a sharp boundary between whether a trait just barely qualifies as a particular kind of trait and whether it does not qualify.

[30] Absent the influence of background conditions which might hinder either its being triggered or its functioning properly. What follows about consistency of behavior applies to consistency of belief and desire as well, but I have omitted this from the text to simplify the discussion.

The claim about character traits leading to consistent behavior should be taken very broadly. For instance, as Donald Smith pointed out to me, the trait of being mercurial involves unpredictable mood changes over time and across situations. However, there is still a sense in which this trait is consistent, namely that it leads to consistently inconsistent behavior. In other words, a person whose mood was very calm and steady would be exhibiting manifestations of a trait which are not consistent with being mercurial. The claim that there are many ways of thinking about consistency is picked up again in the next footnote.

and that are discussed at length in the psychology literature. Let me briefly mention a few here which will figure prominently in the chapters to come.[31]

Suppose Jones's compassion leads him to donate money to the Salvation Army representative on the street corner one day. And again the next time he comes across this same person. And again the next time. Jones is thereby exhibiting consistency of a certain kind—consistency of a single behavior over iterations of the same (or very similar) situation, which is what can be called:

> *Single-Situation Trait Stability*: A person regularly manifests behavior which is in accordance with the trait in question, over several instances of the same trait-relevant situation. So, for instance, if Jones is deeply compassionate, he might donate to the Salvation Army representative every time he goes to the grocery store this month.

Now consider another form of stability. Instead of focusing on just one situation, consider Jones's behavior over a variety of situations and over the course of a given time period, say a week or a month. And then compare this *aggregate* or collection of specific behaviors to the aggregate of behavior related to the same trait in one or more additional periods of time, say the next week or month. If the average level of his aggregate trait behavior is similar in these two time periods, then he is exhibiting a more general form of stability:

> *Aggregate Trait Stability*: A person regularly manifests similar *levels* of aggregate behavior which is in accordance with the trait in question, over different periods of time. So, for instance, while Jones might have helped in different ways during two different time periods, his average level of compassionate behavior across all these helping situations might still be very similar.

Now return to compassionate Jones and his donating money. That is not the only form of compassionate behavior most people would expect him to exhibit on any given day. Generally and other things being equal, in a situation involving a severe wreck on a deserted road he would be expected to call 911, in one involving dropped papers he would be expected to offer to help pick them up, and so forth. So Jones would be expected to be cross-situationally consistent throughout the day in his compassionate behavior:

> *Momentary Cross-situational Consistency*: A person manifests behavior which is in accordance with the trait in question, while in several different trait-relevant

---

[31] This should not be taken to imply that there are no other kinds of consistency, besides those that follow in this section, which are also important for discussions of character. For instance, Fleeson and Noftle (2008a) distinguish between 36 kinds of consistency which pertain to personality traits in general, and go on to argue that no one kind is necessarily privileged. At the same time, it should become apparent that the four kinds I focus on below both historically have been and indeed deserve to be prominent in both conceptual and empirical discussions of character traits.

situations during a narrow period of time. So, for instance, Jones might offer to pick up dropped papers, help make change for a dollar, and hold the door for a handicapped person, all in the span of an hour.

Of course, we can wonder not only about how cross-situationally consistent Jones is in his behavior during an hour or a day, but also during longer periods of time:

> *Extended Cross-situational Consistency*: A person regularly manifests behavior which is in accordance with the trait in question, while in a variety of different trait-relevant situations during an extended period of time. So, for instance, Jones might perform compassionate actions in many of the situations he encounters during the span of a month.[32]

It is worth stressing that for there to be cross-situational consistency, the actions do not need to be precisely the same ones in the different situations (such as giving five dollars no matter what the helping-relevant circumstances are, which would be absurd), but rather need only be different instances of one broad type of character-based action (such as a compassionate action). In other words, the trait of compassion can give rise to such diverse particular actions as donating to charity, picking up dropped papers, and taking someone to the hospital.

With these four kinds of consistency in mind, it is a mistake to think it essential to character traits that they be both stable *and* cross-situationally consistent. *Local* character traits are ones which require stability in relevant behavior with respect to one kind of situation, but fail to exhibit cross-situational consistency. Unlike Jones, Conrad for instance might repeatedly make a donation to charity when asked, while exhibiting little else by way of compassionate behavior. He might, in other words, have what can be called "donation compassion," whereas Jones has the *global* trait of compassion in general.[33] So cross-situationally consistency is not a necessary feature for qualifying as a character trait, which explains why it was not mentioned in previous sections.[34]

The distinction between global and local traits is clearly not a sharp one. The *generality* of traits, or the range of different situations they apply to, can

---

[32] This is different from aggregate trait stability, which only concerns the similarity of the person's behavior over time, and not whether that behavior is consistent from one situation to the next. Jones might be very stable in the average level of his helping behavior from one month to the next, but only help in certain situations and not others.

[33] For more, see Doris 1998: 507–8, 2002: 23–5, 64–6. Actually this is only one way of construing "local" traits. They could instead be understood, not as local to a kind of situation, but as local to a period of time or to some other criterion. I have chosen the approach above since it is the most common in the philosophy literature on character. Thanks to Will Fleeson for this reminder.

[34] For this point in psychology, see Johnson 1997: 75, 1999: 444, 446, Mischel and Shoda 1998: 235, and Mischel 1999a: 457. For an opposing view, see Buss 1989: 1385.

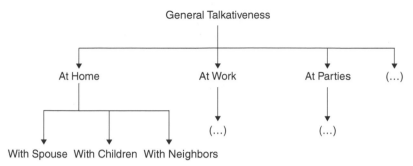

Fig. 1.2. Some levels of talkativeness.

vary across a broad spectrum extending from one extreme of all the situations a person confronts in her life, to the other extreme of only very specific and narrowly defined situations.[35] Figure 1.2, for instance, is a very rough schematic representation of what several degrees of generality might look like for a trait such as talkativeness.

Hence someone might possess a highly global trait of talkativeness if he is disposed to reliably exhibit talkative behavior in all these different situations. But another person might only have the less global trait of being disposed to be reliably talkative at home, while also being fairly quiet at work or at parties. Some might still call this person "talkative," but it would be more accurate in this case to describe him as having a trait of "talkativeness at home." That trait better explains and more accurately predicts his behavior. A third person might only have talkativeness at home with her children. A fourth might have talkativeness at home with her children while the spouse is away. And so forth.

Finally, let me end this section with a very important and widely used distinction for thinking about consistency. When a person is said to be consistent in his compassionate behavior in the same situation on two different occasions, what counts as the "same" situation? Is the "same situation" defined by that person himself, for instance, or by an outside observer? Similarly, when a person is said to be consistent in his compassionate behavior across two different situations, who is deciding that these count as "different" situations?

As indicated, one approach to answering these questions is to use a perspective that is external to the person in question, perhaps involving the beliefs of ordinary independent observers or in the case of psychology experiments,

---

[35] For helpful discussion of degrees of generality, see Alston 1975: 36–42 and Buss 1989: 1384–6. For brief remarks, see Sreenivasan 2002: 66, Kamtekar 2004: 469, and Adams 2006: 125–7. For a recent view which seems to be based on traits which differ in their generality, see Upton 2009a.

the perspective of the psychologists themselves conducting the experiments. Such observers might consider a person's home and workplace, or dorm and classroom, to be two different types of situations, and then go on to test whether her behavior in question is consistent between them. Thus if she ends up failing to act compassionately in both kinds of situations, then she does not exhibit (momentary) cross-situational consistency.

Using standard terminology in parts of the psychology literature, such an approach appeals to the *nominal* features of the situation. But another way of thinking about consistency relies on what features of situations are important to the person in question. These are the *psychologically salient* features or, "the features of the situation that have significant meaning for a given individual."[36] Note that these features are *not* to be defined as those which the person thinks or consciously takes to be salient. That is too restrictive of an understanding of this category.[37] Rather these are features which cause relevant psychological states to activate in the person's mind, whether she is conscious of their impact or not. Thus racial features, for instance, could trigger implicit stereotypes without the person even realizing what is going on, and nevertheless these features would still count as "psychologically salient" in the sense that is relevant to this book.[38]

---

[36] Mischel 2004: 15. The distinction between nominal and psychologically salient features of situations is especially prominent in social-cognitive approaches to personality, which are discussed in *Character and Moral Psychology*, chapter five. See, e.g. Mischel 1968: 190, 1973: 259–61, 263, 1999b: 43–4, 46, 2004: 15, 2007: 266, 2009: 284, Mischel and Peake 1982: 749, Shoda et al. 1993: 1024–5, 1029, 1994: 685, Mischel and Shoda 1995: 248, 1998: 247–8, 2008: 218, Shoda and Mischel 1996: 421–2, Shoda 1999a: 163, Cervone 1999: 323–6, Mischel et al. 2002: 51, Mendoza-Denton et al. 2007: 215, Zayas and Shoda 2009: 280–1, and especially Shoda et al. 1994: 675–6 and Shoda and LeeTiernan 2002. See also Ross and Nisbett 1991: chapter three, Vansteelandt and Van Mechelen 1998: 758, Funder 2008: 571–3, Eaton et al. 2009: 210, 212, Orom and Cervone 2009: 230, 234, 238–9, and van Mechelen 2009: 180. For philosophers who have discussed this distinction, see Brandt 1988: 78, Flanagan 1991: 291, Sreenivasan 2002: 50, 57–60, Doris 2002: 76–85, Solomon 2003: 52, Kamtekar 2004: 470–3, Upton 2009a: 12–13, 2009b: 178, Lukes 2009: 293, Russell 2009: chapters eight to ten, Snow 2010: chapter one, and Alfano 2011: 127.

[37] Thanks for Rachana Kamtekar for helping me to see this.

[38] Hence when we think about a person's cross-situational consistency with respect to the psychologically salient features of various situations, there is a sense in which the person will always be trivially consistent in her behavior. In other words, if she is performing an intentional action in the first place, then she will always be acting in a way that is consistent with her relevant psychological states. So it becomes unclear what "inconsistency" would amount to on this approach. Thanks for Win-Chiat Lee for raising this point, and to Emily Austin for discussion.

We could still develop a notion of behavioral "inconsistency" which has to do with acting in accordance with the person's *conscious* values or *reflectively endorsed* values or some proposal along those lines which draws on resources from the action theory literature. Since subconscious psychological states and processes can lead to behavior which is not in line with a person's endorsed values, in those cases the person can still be said to be acting inconsistently.

These two ways of thinking about consistency can lead to significant differences. Two situations might seem to have nothing to do with each other, but to the person in question they might both have similar psychologically salient features which end up leading to consistent behavior. Or in the opposite manner two situations might, according to the psychologists conducting a study, seem to be quite similar in their relevance to a given trait, but they end up having very different psychologically relevant features for the participant who experiences them. This can lead the experimenters to conclude that the participant does not exhibit cross-situational consistency in his behavior in this area, even when he is indeed being highly consistent relative to his own mental life. Bem and Allen offer a nice example of how this might happen in an actual study: "an individual who regards himself as extremely conscientious might not consider his casual attitude toward personal hygiene as pertinent to that trait. The fact that the investigator's concept of conscientiousness might include personal hygiene within it is not relevant."[39]

Given this distinction, it turns out that much care will have to be paid to how global and local traits are to be understood. For instance, Figure 1.2 does not clearly specify whether what counts as "home," "work," and "parties" are defined by the person who is said to be talkative in one of these ways, or instead by using more generic nominal labels supplied by an experimenter. This could end up making a significant difference. Observers might study someone who seems to be talkative at home but not at work. So on the basis of the nominal features of her situation, they conclude that she has the local trait of talkativeness at home. But perhaps in reality the person has a strong disposition to talk to those whom she considers trustworthy, and at the present time she does not have any trustworthy friends at work. Then the observers could mistakenly predict her behavior and be surprised to find her being quite talkative with a close roommate at a college reunion, or with a new colleague at work who has just earned her trust. So for this person, a more helpful understanding of the different degrees of generality associated with talkativeness could be represented in Figure 1.3.

Again, while some people might be generally talkative, it would be more accurate to describe this particular person as only talkative with those whom she considers trustworthy. The disposition could lead to cross-situationally consistent behavior *across* nominally different situations such as her home, work, and parties.

I will make much use of the idea of nominal versus psychological salient features of situations in later chapters.

---

[39] Bem and Allen 1974: 511. As Eaton et al. note, "the situations that interact with personality dispositions are not relegated only to the externalities with which one is in contact. Instead, features of situations can be *created* by an individual's thoughts, mood states, fantasies, and so on" (2009: 212, emphasis theirs).

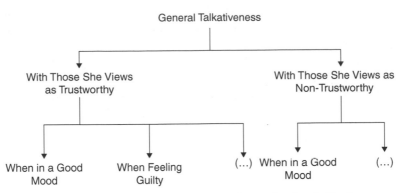

Fig. 1.3. Psychologically salient features and some levels of talkativeness.

1.3 MORAL VIRTUES AND VICES

Let me end with two final conceptual points about character traits. First, there might seem to be a striking omission up to this point—nowhere have I specifically mentioned the idea of morality. After all, isn't the concept of a character trait a *moral* one?

At times this seems to be assumed in the psychology literature.[40] And of course psychologists are free to define the terms "character" and "character trait" as they wish. But if they are also trying to capture ordinary and widespread views about character, then the answer to this question is no. Many character traits are indeed moral traits—consider honesty, compassion, and justice to name a few. But what about this list:

> Talkative, expansive, artistic, dry, jovial, formal, clever, calm, nervous, extraverted, shy, sociable, imaginative, logical, and witty.

All of these seem like they are character traits. While they function to evaluate the person who has them—to say that someone is "witty" seems to be at once to describe *and* to assess that person—the kind of evaluation that is involved here certainly need not involve *moral* evaluation. We do not morally praise someone just for being logical or witty.[41]

Another way to see this point is to note that if anything is a character trait, certainly a *virtue* would be (and the same with a vice). But there are plenty of non-moral virtues and vices; just take examples from the epistemic (e.g. being

---

[40] See, e.g. Narvaez et al. 2006: 967. For this same assumption in philosophy, see, e.g. Goldie 2004: 27, 31, 33 and Russell 2009: xii, 292–3, 330.

[41] As Kupperman remarks, "Someone can be a weak and depressing oaf without ever behaving immorally" (1991: 8).

logical), prudential (e.g. being clever), and aesthetic (e.g. being artistic) realms of the normative, for instance. Someone who has the virtue of artistry when it comes to home designing would indeed have a character trait but not a moral one.[42]

So I think there is good reason to not put all character traits under the heading of morality.[43] It would be nice to have some plausible and informative criterion to use to distinguish the moral from the other normative domains. But unfortunately I do not have such a criterion, and neither does anyone else as far as I know. Philosophers have been hard pressed to come up with any rigorous way of properly distinguishing the moral, typically relying instead on their intuitions.[44] So while I can provide the following test for distinguishing a moral character trait from a non-moral one:

(5) Vary the degree to which the person possesses the trait, and see whether our moral assessment of the person in this regard alone also changes.

it obviously relies upon a prior familiarity with what counts as moral assessment. Fortunately for my purposes, it does seem as if there are clear intuitions in this area, as the examples above were intended to illustrate. And I will not need anything like a rigorous criterion for the scope of morality in what follows. So for the remainder of this book, my focus will be on the moral character traits, and any reference to "character traits" should be assumed to apply only to the moral ones unless otherwise noted.

The mention of virtues takes me to the second point. Much of the recent philosophical interest in character traits has centered specifically on the virtues. Virtue ethicists take the virtues to be among the central ethical concepts and often use them to ground an account of morally right actions. But even consequentialists, Kantians, moral pluralists, and advocates of other competing views have realized the importance that the virtues should play in their overall normative ethical theories, even if it is not at the foundational or grounding level.[45]

I see no reason why these various accounts of the virtues cannot accept my approach to character traits and simply add additional conditions in order to narrow the focus to the virtuous ones. While trying to remain neutral on

---

[42] Brandt 1988: 79. For an opposing view, see Swanton 2003: 69–76.

[43] For similar remarks, see Brandt 1970: 23, Butler 1988: 215, and Kupperman 1991: 7–9. Gordon Allport made the same observation long ago (1931: 371).

[44] For relevant discussion, see my 2011c, section one. For a review of different proposals, see Gert 2011.

[45] Thus we can distinguish between virtue theory and virtue ethics; most of the leading ethical theories today are virtue *theories*, since they each offer their own accounts of the virtues and ascribe some normative role to them. But at the same time, many of these ethical theories are best understood as broadly consequentialist or Kantian views, and their advocates also tend to reject some of the central claims of virtue *ethics*. For more on this distinction, see Swanton 2003: 5, 28 and Snow 2010: 1–2.

disputes between these different approaches in normative theory, one general proposal would be to add the following:

(6) The virtues are all and only those good traits of character which are such that, other things being equal, when they directly lead to action (whether mental or bodily), the action is (typically) a good action and is performed for the appropriate reasons.[46]

Compassion clearly counts as a virtue on this proposal, whereas greed would not. And note again that the virtue terms can also be properly applied to actions and states of mind, independently of their connection to an underlying virtuous disposition. Certain actions can still be "compassionate" even if they happened to be performed for primarily selfish reasons such as to avoid guilt or seek public recognition. Similarly, a state of mind can be "compassionate" and morally praiseworthy even though it happens to only be fleeting in a given person's psychology and not tied to a deeper psychological structure.[47]

Virtues make up only one subset of the character traits, and parallel remarks to the above apply as well to the vices. They both are to be found in all of the various normative domains,[48] but again I want to focus just on the moral domain and suggest here that the virtues and the vices do not exhaust *all* of the character traits.[49] I will try to illustrate this in detail in the Part III, but for now here are a few examples:

A character trait which partially consists of a disposition to desire to tell the truth even at significant cost to myself (and, let us suppose, for what are in fact morally

---

[46] This leaves it open whether the trait is intrinsically or only instrumentally good. On some approaches, for instance, certain virtues like courage fall into the latter category. For relevant discussion, see Foot 1978: 174–6 and Adams 2006: 33–4. Hurka (2006) sketches a view which would allow virtuous dispositions to have only instrumental value.

The proposal also leaves it open as to what makes the action good and the reasons appropriate. The goodness of the action could be grounded in facts about virtue or in something else altogether such as good consequences. Hence no claim is being made about the dependence relation between the goodness of the dispositions and the goodness of the action that is caused by the activation of the disposition (for helpful discussion, see Hurka 2006).

Nevertheless, this very broad proposal still might be too restrictive to capture all the accounts of virtue in the literature. Some, for instance, may not require the last clause about appropriate reasons (see Driver 2001). It does, however, capture most of the leading proposals so far as I am aware, especially in the literature on Aristotelian forms of virtue ethics.

[47] For discussion of this way of applying the virtue concepts to actions and states of mind, and for some of the controversy that arises here, see n. 4.

[48] While it might have been commonplace in the past to dwell on the moral virtues, the epistemic virtues are receiving a great deal of attention for instance (see, e.g., DePaul and Zagzebski 2003), and there are plenty of candidates for virtues in the aesthetic, prudential, legal, political, religious, and athletic domains.

[49] For brief remarks along these lines, see Kupperman 1991: 10, Zagzebski 1996: 112–13, Sreenivasan 2002: 62, Swanton 2003: 25, 206–7, Kamtekar 2004: 482–4, Besser-Jones 2008: 326, and Annas 2011: 103, 105. Brandt 1970, Goldie 2004: 26, Adams 2006: 36, and Winter and Tauer 2006: 75 seem to hold the opposing view.

appropriate reasons), except when by lying I can improve a negative mood, in which case I am strongly disposed to desire to lie instead.

A character trait which partially consists of a disposition to desire to help others even at significant cost to myself (for what are in fact morally appropriate reasons), except when I anticipate feeling embarrassed or shamed if I try to help, in which case I am strongly disposed to desire to ignore the need for help instead.

A character trait which partially consists of a disposition to desire to thank others (for what are in fact morally appropriate reasons) for doing something kind towards me, except if they happen to belong to one particular ethnicity, in which case I am strongly disposed to desire to ignore them instead.

Now clearly (to me at least) none of these dispositions is compatible with the virtues of honesty, compassion, and gratitude, respectively, at least as they are ordinarily understood. But in my view neither are they vices such as dishonesty, selfishness, or ingratitude. Indeed, I think we would be glad that someone has one of these dispositions, *if* the person does not have the relevant virtue, and *especially* if the only alternative is to have the relevant vice. For instance, I think we should be glad that the person with the first trait is disposed to tell the truth in so many different situations, even if he also consistently lies in certain cases when he is experiencing a bad mood—as opposed to being someone who, for instance, is looking for opportunities to lie whenever it would be in his self-interest.

So while they are neither virtues nor vices, there is no reason to preclude these dispositions from counting as character traits. They are dispositions to feel and (subsequently) act in certain ways. They play the five functional roles outlined for character traits. They obviously consist of clusters of mental state dispositions. They can lead to behavior which is both stable and cross-situationally consistent.

The claim that there are numerous character traits which are neither virtues nor vices, is not meant to be a merely academic observation. It will form the heart of the positive account of our actual character to be developed in Part III.

1.4 CONCLUSION

I have covered a lot of ground in this chapter in order to develop the conceptual framework needed for what is to come. So let me summarize the central observations made about character traits:

(a) They are trait dispositions which manifest as beliefs, desires, and/or actions of a certain sort appropriate to that trait, as a result of being stimulated in a way appropriate to that trait.

(b) They are grounded in the interrelated mental state dispositions specific to the given trait.

(c) They play functional roles associated with understanding, explanation, prediction, evaluation, and imitation.

(d) They each have their own unique criteria in their minimal threshold, come in degrees, can exhibit different kinds of consistency, and can vary in their generality.

(e) Some of them are virtues and vices, but it makes sense to say that there could be character traits which are neither virtues nor vices.

I ended by discussing the concepts of moral virtue and vice, the most famous concepts associated with character. But do these concepts really reflect the character traits that most of us *actually* possess?

Part II

Developing the Framework

2

Guilt and Helping

Having outlined the conceptual framework for thinking about character traits in chapter one, I now turn to the central project of this book, which is to offer a picture of the moral character that most people actually possess today. More specifically, I want to address the following questions:

Do most people actually have character traits which pertain to moral thought and action?

If most people have such traits, what do they consist in and how do they tend to function?

If most people have such traits, what tends to enhance and inhibit their operation?

If most people have such traits, how consistent are they in leading to relevant behavior both over time and across situations?

If most people have such traits, are they moral virtues or are they moral vices?

Now obviously these are ambitious questions to try to address, and I will not take them up directly until chapter eight. In the meantime I will do several things to make the discussion more manageable.

First, rather than talking about character traits in general, I will focus on just one area of morality, namely helping other people, and try to get clearer on what most people's character looks like there. This will serve to make the discussion more concrete. It will also provide a template from which to generalize to other character traits.[1] Secondly, I will not try to exhaustively canvas the various psychological processes most of us have which bear on helping (what a daunting task that would be!). Rather here in Part II I narrow the focus to processes associated with guilt, embarrassment, positive moods, elevation, activated moral norms, empathy, negative moods, and embarrassment avoidance. This will provide more than enough data, in my opinion, to begin to draw important implications about our actual character in this area.

---

[1] The same pattern of focusing on helping, drawing conclusions about traits associated with helping, and then generalizing to all character traits, is followed in most recent philosophical work about our actual character. See, e.g. Harman 1999, 2000 and Doris 2002: 27–9.

The discussion in these chapters will follow a similar pattern. I review studies which examine the relationship between one of the above variables, such as guilt, and both helping behavior and helping motivation. These results will then be used to try to infer what the underlying psychological relationship is between, say, guilt and helping. For instance, do people who experience guilt, help more so as to try to make amends for their particular wrongdoing, or just to try to stop feeling guilty? Such a discussion can hopefully shed some light on what mental dispositions most of us have in this area—are we in fact disposed, say, to help others so as to eliminate feelings of guilt? Finally, once the nature and functioning of these dispositions has been clarified, then they will be morally assessed. In particular, are they the kind of dispositions one would expect of the virtuous (or the vicious) helper? I will argue that they are not.

So as I now turn to the experimental literature, I begin in this chapter with guilt. Researchers have typically found a robust positive correlation between feelings of guilt and helping,[2] and it will be important to carefully examine the leading psychological models they have developed to explain this relationship. In section one, I briefly distinguish between guilt and shame. Section two looks in detail at research on guilt and helping, while section three examines the relationship between these results and the virtue of compassion.

2.1 CHARACTERIZING GUILT

It is customary in the psychology literature to find guilt listed under the heading of a self-conscious emotion. In contrast to more basic emotions such as anger, fear, and disgust, these emotions involve the self in their evaluations. More precisely, self-conscious emotions typically involve an implicit awareness of normative standards, of the self's responsibility for living up to those standards, and of the self's standing in relation to those standards. Success or failure in living up to these norms can elicit guilt, shame, pride, and/or embarrassment, among other self-conscious emotions.[3]

Concerning the concept of guilt,[4] let me start with the commonsense observation that typically a person feels guilt when he (i) performs an action (or omission) that violates one or more of his normative standards for

---

[2] In psychology it is common to instead find the expression "prosocial behavior." I follow Estrada-Hollenbeck and Heatherton (1998) in understanding prosocial behavior as, "actions that are voluntary and that specifically benefit another person" (1998: 219), and will treat "prosocial behavior" and "helping behavior" as interchangeable.

[3] For more, see Caprara et al. 2001, Tangney et al. 1996: 1264, 2007a, 2007b, Tracy and Robins 2007, Basil et al. 2006, Menesini and Camodeca 2008, Lewis 2008, and Hosser et al. 2008.

[4] Here I am not concerned with legal guilt, where we say that a criminal is guilty of having broken the law. My focus is on the negative subjective experiences of guilt for actions we have

behavior, (ii) those standards have some significant degree of importance to him, and (iii) the action is one that he sees himself as being personal responsible for performing in the first place.[5] For instance I periodically feel guilt over not donating more money to famine relief because such an omission violates my moral standards (and I care about those particular standards), and it is an omission for which I am responsible.[6]

How can guilt be distinguished from the other self-conscious emotions, and specifically from shame? Unfortunately there is no consensus in the literature about how to do this,[7] but a promising approach makes use of the self-action view initially developed by Helen Block Lewis in her 1971 book *Shame and*

---

performed that go against our normative standards. For different uses of the term "guilt," see Baumeister et al. 1994: 245.

[5] For similar claims see, e.g. Kugler and Jones 1992: 318, Baumeister et al. 1994: 245, Lindsay-Hartz et al. 1995, Eisenberg 2000: 667, Sinnott-Armstrong 2005: 199–202, and Basil et al. 2006.

These are not offered as anything like strictly necessary and sufficient conditions but rather as useful generalities that are adequate for my purposes in this chapter. For instance, concerning their necessity, the phenomenon of collective guilt for the moral failures of others does not fall neatly under heading (iii) (see Baumeister et al. 1994: 251–2, Estrada-Hollenbeck and Heatherton 1998: 216, and Tangney et al. 2007a: 358–9, 2007b: 28. Sinnott-Armstrong (2005: 202) proposes a nice revision to accommodate these cases.). Similarly, there is some evidence that guilt can arise just as strongly in response to accidental transgressions, which again is not in line with (iii) (Baumeister et al. 1994: 249). See Baumeister et al. 1994 for a thorough discussion of the complexities involved here.

Nor are these conditions proposed as jointly sufficient. Some psychologists, for instance, stress the role of punishment in guilt (Kugler and Jones 1992: 325, Caprara et al. 2001, and Zemack-Rugar et al. 2007: 929; for criticism see Baumeister et al. 1994: 245). Others claim that regret over wrongdoing plays a central role (Kugler and Jones 1992: 325 and Eisenberg 2000: 667).

[6] Note that when talking about guilt in this way, I am referring to a *state* of guilt, or an occurrent feeling of guilt which arises as a result of performing a particular action, forming a certain intention, or omitting a specific behavior. As with character traits, we should distinguish between the state of guilt and a general trait of guilt or proneness to guilt, which is a disposition to experience a state of guilt in a wide variety of guilt-eliciting circumstances specific to that person's own evaluative standards. For discussion compare Kugler and Jones 1992, Jones et al. 1995: 308, and Tangney et al. 2007a: 347, 2007b: 22.

[7] Three approaches can be quickly dismissed:

  (i) One approach uses the types of situations which elicit guilt. Unfortunately, studies have found that the very same situations involving lying, failing to help, stealing, and so forth can elicit guilt in some participants and shame in others (and both guilt and shame in still others). For discussion, see Tangney 1998: 4, Eisenberg 2000: 668, and Tangney et al. 2007a: 348, 2007b: 25.

  (ii) Another approach is to claim that guilt is a more "private" emotion involving painful feelings of conscience, whereas shame is a more "public" emotion involving public disapproval. Again though, the empirical data points in the other direction. Participants have been found to experience both guilt and shame in public contexts, and shame can be experienced in just as solitary and private a way as guilt. See Tangney et al. 1996: 1257, 2007a: 348, 2007b: 25, Tangney 1998: 4, Sinnott-Armstrong 2005: 201, and Lewis 2008: 748.

  (iii) A third approach claims that guilt is a strictly moral emotion, whereas shame arises in both moral and non-moral contexts. However, just our ordinary experience alone suggests that people can feel guilty as a result of committing certain non-moral transgressions as well, such as violating certain rules of etiquette or breaking laws which are not clearly part of morality. See Tangney 1995: 116 and Tangney et al. 1996: 1262. For a contrary view, see Eisenberg 2000: 668 and Sinnott-Armstrong 2005: 201.

Guilt in Neurosis.[8] The heart of this approach is that guilt involves a focus on a specific action or series of actions, whereas the object of shame is the self in general. Hence I feel guilty for having *done* something, such as lying to a friend, whereas I might be ashamed of *myself* for having lied to my friend. As Jennifer Manion writes, "one's feeling of guilt concerns a rule or rule-like constraint that one has broken, the harm that has ensued and the people affected by the harmful act . . . the feeling of shame indicates a profound disappointment in the kind of person one thought one was."[9]

This basic conceptual point has a number of implications for the role that shame and guilt play in our psychological lives, some of which are mentioned briefly here:

(a) Shame often produces feelings of worthlessness as one "shrinks" from the world and tries to avoid public condemnation. A person's self feels exposed, even if there is no actual public observing the perceived deficiency. Guilt typically does not produce these particular feelings and reactions.[10]

(b) Because of the connection to the self, shame can inspire feelings of helplessness and an inability to do anything about one's condition, whereas a similar connection has not been found with guilt.[11]

(c) Closely related to the previous two consequences, shame tends to lead to avoidance of the shame-eliciting circumstances and more generally to social withdrawal, whereas guilt tends to lead to a focus on the action and correlates positively with attempts at reparation.[12]

(d) By focusing on the self, shame impedes empathetic feelings, whereas guilt typically has the opposite effect.[13]

---

[8] For employment of this approach, see among many others Tangney et al. 1992, 1996, 2007a: 349, 2007b: 25–6, Baumeister et al. 1994: 245, Barrett 1995: 28, Tangney 1995, Quiles and Bybee 1997, Bybee and Quiles 1998: 274, Estrada-Hollenbeck and Heatherton 1998: 216, Tangney 1998: 5, Eisenberg 2000, Caprara et al. 2001, Manion 2002, Sinnott-Armstrong 2005: 200, Amodio et al. 2007: 528, Lewis 2008: 748, Menesini and Camodeca 2008, and Hosser et al. 2008. For an opposing view, see Roberts 2003: 223.

[9] Manion 2002: 76.

[10] Tangney et al. 1992: 469, 1996: 1257, 2007a: 349, 2007b: 26, Lindsay-Hartz et al. 1995: 278, 283, 295, Barrett 1995: 41, Tangney 1998: 5, Manion 2002: 76, 80, Amodio et al. 2007: 529, Menesini and Camodeca 2008: 184, Lewis 2008: 748, and Hosser et al. 2008: 139.

[11] Tangney 1998: 7, Bybee and Quiles 1998: 274, Caprara et al. 2001: 221, Tangney et al. 2007a: 349, 353, Amodio et al. 2007: 528, and Hosser et al. 2008: 139.

[12] Barrett 1995: 41, Tangney 1995: 119–20, 1998: 7–8, Tangney et al. 1996: 1257, 2007a: 350, 2007b: 26, Estrada-Hollenbeck and Heatherton 1998: 216, Eisenberg 2000: 668, Sinnott-Armstrong 2005: 201, Menesini and Camodeca 2008: 184, Lewis 2008: 748, and Hosser et al. 2008: 139.

[13] Baumeister et al. 1994: 254–5, Tangney 1995: 129–33, Lindsay-Hartz et al. 1995: 296, Eisenberg 2000: 668, Manion 2002: 81, and Tangney et al. 2007a: 350, 2007b: 26–7.

(e) As will be discussed in the next section, guilt is positively correlated with subsequent helping behavior. In addition, proneness to guilt is also related to decreases in the likelihood of problematic behaviors such as theft, drug abuse, unsafe sex, using risky needles, and inmates' post-release recidivism. Fewer such correlations have been found in the case of shame.[14,15]

In sum, both guilt and shame are self-conscious or regulative emotions which are significantly different in a variety of respects. With this brief clarification in mind, let me put further discussion of shame to one side and focus solely on guilt.

2.2 GUILT AND HELPING

In this section I want to do two things: (i) highlight some of the empirical studies on the relationship between guilt and helping, and (ii) carefully distinguish between competing motivational explanations for this relationship.

Over forty years of work on guilt and helping has consistently found a strong positive correlation between the two. Participants who are induced to feel guilty in both laboratory and natural settings reliably help at statistically

---

[14] Bybee and Quiles 1998: 270, Tangney et al. 2007a: 354–5, Hosser et al. 2008, and especially Stuewig and Tangney 2007. For cautionary notes about this claim, see Manion 2002 and Menesini and Camodeca 2008.

[15] In addition, shame is typically considered to be the more painful of the two emotions, precisely because it is focused on the self rather than on just an instance of behavior (see Tangney et al. 1992: 469, 2007a: 349, 2007b: 26, Tangney 1995: 117, 1998: 5, Eisenberg 2000: 667–8, Manion 2002: 77–8, Sinnott-Armstrong 2005: 201, and Lewis 2008: 748).

Both externalization of blame and feelings of anger have been positively correlated with trait shame and occurrent shame, and externalized blame has been found to mediate the anger. Neither of these has been positively correlated with guilt (see Tangney 1995: 120–9, 1998: 7, Lindsay-Hartz et al. 1995: 296, Eisenberg 2000: 669, Tangney et al. 2007a: 351–2, 2007b: 27, and Hosser et al. 2008: 139).

Proneness to shame has also been correlated with a number of psychological deficits, such as low self-esteem, depression, anxiety, and posttraumatic stress disorder. Indeed many psychologists consider shame to be maladaptive (see Tangney et al. 1992, 1995, 2007a, 2007b: 27. For cautionary notes about this claim, see Manion 2002 and Menesini and Camodeca 2008.). The case of guilt is more complex. On the one hand, ordinary occurrences of guilty feelings, which stem from a guilt predisposition, have been found to correlate with lower hostility, reduced depression, and other signs of mental health. On the other hand, a recurring condition of chronic guilt, which is detached from the immediate actions performed by the person, has been found to correlate positively with symptoms of depression and psychopathology. This has led some psychologists to distinguish between two distinct kinds of guilt, chronic and predispositional, and in the remainder of this chapter I set chronic guilt to one side.

For helpful discussion of these two kinds of guilt, see Estrada-Hollenbeck and Heatherton 1998: 224, Eisenberg 2000: 669–70, and especially Quiles and Bybee 1997, Bybee and Quiles 1998. And for guilt and mental health in general, see Tangney et al. 1992 and Tangney et al. 2007a: 351–4.

higher rates than control participants. Recall, for instance, the study by Regan et al. (1972)—55 percent of guilty participants let the confederate know about the candy falling out of her bag, as compared to only 15 percent of controls.[16]

In a similar experimental design, Vladimir Konečni (1972) studied the behavior of participants on the streets of Toronto. In the guilt condition, a confederate walked towards the participant carrying three expensive-looking books. After absent-mindedly running into the participant and dropping the books, the confederate exclaimed, "They are not mine, and you have to do this," and walked away. Fifty to seventy-five yards later, the participant came across another person walking out of a doorway who had forty computer-punched cards drop out of a folder. This confederate, while bending down to pick up the cards, said to the participant, "Please don't step on them." Control participants did not have the guilt manipulation but just came across the confederate and the dropped cards. The dependent variables were the number of participants who collected cards and how many they collected:[17]

	% of participants who collected cards	Mean number of cards collected
Control	16	1.29
Guilty	42	4.77

Once again a significant difference in helping is correlated with prior feelings of guilt, provided that it was guilt which was effectively manipulated in this case.[18]

The above only scratches the surface of the empirical work on guilt and helping—literally dozens of other studies show similar relationships between the two.[19] So I will assume the existence of this relationship, and claim that it

[16] Regan et al. 1972: 44.

[17] Konečni 1972: 32.

[18] While guilt seems to foster helping behavior, it has also been associated with avoidance behavior in certain instances. In particular, feelings of guilt can inhibit the very action which prompted them in the first place. See Freedman et al. 1967, Baumeister et al. 1994: 258, and Amodio et al. 2007. Note that these cases involve actual occurrent feelings of guilt, rather than the desire to avoid feeling guilt in the future, which could also inhibit helping if that behavior was thought to make a person feel guilty. Guilt avoidance will be mentioned in chapter six.

As Amodio et al. (2007) argue, this phenomenon makes sense intuitively and is not incompatible with a robust motivational relationship between guilt and helping. On their view, the *initial* experience of guilt, "functions to halt the interpersonal damage being caused by the transgressive behavior" and to, "survey the damage, and learn from mistakes" (525). So if I feel guilty for saying mean things behind someone's back, I might stop doing so and take the conversation in a new direction. Helping behavior, on the other hand, could be a *subsequent* effect of guilty feelings aimed at addressing my guilt and promoting one or more of the motivational goals described below. Amodio and his colleagues used electroencephalograph recordings of cortical activity to study racial prejudice and guilt reactions, and even found empirical support for this proposal.

[19] See, e.g. Freedman et al. 1967, Carlsmith and Gross 1969, Donnerstein et al. 1975, Harris et al. 1975, Harris and Samerotte 1976, Cunningham et al. 1980, Baumeister et al. 1994: 257,

is *because* participants are feeling guilty that they are exhibiting such behavior at higher rates than controls. Note that in the studies in question, all other variables were kept as constant as possible, with the guilt manipulation being the only new causal factor which distinguished controls from members of the experimental group. So with this causal claim, we have the following:

Guilt over a particular perceived wrongdoing
↓
Activation of a helping mechanism
↓
Elevated helping motivation and behavior

where the arrow is intended to symbolize causal influence. Naturally other things are being held equal since if, for instance, there are no opportunities to actually help, or if something else besides the guilt feelings is playing a larger motivational role at the moment, then there is no reason to expect increased helping to result.

What psychological processes might best account for this relationship? More precisely, what motivational state(s) does guilt give rise to which in turn often fosters helping behavior?[20] Here the psychology literature is less clear, as a number of different proposals have been offered, and in many cases with little care in stating them. In the remainder of this section, I mention some of the leading candidates.

Desire to Repair the Specific Wrong. On this proposal, a state of guilt causes the formation of a desire to repair the specific perceived wrong performed by the person, which in turn can motivate helping aimed at repairing the wrong. Thus if I feel guilty for having stolen something from you, this could lead to the formation of a desire to atone for this wrong in some way. There might be a variety of ways of doing so, such as financial compensation or buying a replacement, and these would not naturally be described as acts of helping. But it might turn out that the best way I can see to make restitution for this wrong is to help you in some specific way. In those cases, and holding other things equal, we would expect the person to help at a significantly higher rate than otherwise. Diagrammatically this leads to the following:

Quiles and Bybee 1997, Estrada-Hollenbeck and Heatherton 1998, Zhong and Liljenquist 2006, and Basil et al. 2006. For a helpful list of early studies, see Salovey and Rosenhan 1989. Even participants high in guilt proneness who were primed with subliminal guilt adjectives helped more than both (i) similarly primed participants who were low in guilt proneness and (ii) sadness primed participants (Zemack-Rugar et al. 2007).

It is important to stress that these studies do not pertain to chronic guilt, which as noted in n. 15 is a different kind of guilt which would not be expected to correlate positively with helping behavior. See Quiles and Bybee 1997: 122.

[20] To simplify the discussion, in the remainder of the section I focus mainly on (i) consequential guilt upon performing an action deemed wrong rather than anticipated guilt, and (ii) states of guilt rather than guilt traits.

Guilt over a particular perceived wrongdoing
↓
Desire to repair the specific wrong

Perceived helping task(s) →   ↓   ← *Absence of other means of*
which contributes to   *repairing the specific wrong*
repairing the specific wrong   *which are perceived to be*
                                                   more effective

Activation of a helping mechanism
↓

Potential additional →   *Increased helping motivation*
motives to help   ↓

Increased helping behavior

Thus one consequence of this model is that participants who are experiencing guilt would *not* help at increased rates when the helping task does not have any connection to repairing the specific wrong committed.

Despite this model's simplicity and elegance, it is clearly too simplistic as stated. As we saw in Regan et al. (1972), 55 percent of guilty participants helped even though the task clearly had no bearing on atoning for the specific action of breaking the camera. Even more striking is a series of studies by Jonathan Freedman and his colleagues (1967). In one study, they had a room set up so that participants would likely knock over some index cards that seemed carefully arranged by a graduate student in his office. Half of participants in this guilt condition were later asked to volunteer for an experiment by the same graduate student, whereas the other half were asked to volunteer for an experiment run by an unrelated student. In general 75 percent of participants who knocked over the cards volunteered, whereas less than 39 percent of controls did. Strikingly, though, a significant difference emerged only for the request to assist the unrelated graduate student.[21]

Desire to Repair Wrongdoing as Such. The problem with this first model can be easily addressed if we switch to a more general desire to repair having done something wrong in general. Manifestations of such a desire might include confessing the wrong action, attempting to offer adequate reparation, making amends in some other way if reparation to the one wronged is not possible, punishing oneself, committing to refrain from doing such actions in the future, pleading for forgiveness, offering some form of penance over and

---

[21] Freedman et al. 1967: 122. An advocate of this first model could respond by positing a second desire to avoid confronting someone whom the person has harmed. Indeed, Freedman et al. suggest this very possibility (1967: 123). However, this response would still leave unexplained the host of studies like Regan's which showed increased helping in unrelated subsequent tasks. See also Carlsmith and Gross 1969, who found that, "guilt can lead to compliance even when there is no opportunity to make amends to the injured party" (238). Also relevant are Darlington and Macker 1966 and Harris and Samerotte 1976.

above reparation, and so forth.[22] Thus in the Regan study, by notifying the confederate about the hole in her bag, participants would be taking a step towards atoning for the fact that they earlier broke someone else's camera. The diagram for this model would have to be adjusted as follows:

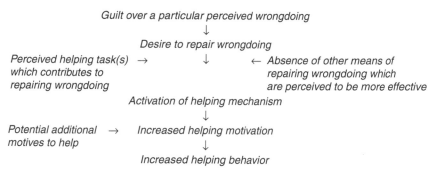

Guilt over a particular perceived wrongdoing
↓
Desire to repair wrongdoing

Perceived helping task(s) →   ↓   ← *Absence of other means of*
which contributes to   *repairing wrongdoing which*
repairing wrongdoing   *are perceived to be more effective*

Activation of helping mechanism
↓

Potential additional → *Increased helping motivation*
motives to help   ↓

Increased helping behavior

Such a model generates a number of testable predictions. One is that actions which serve to eliminate the person's guilt without contributing in any way to repairing wrongdoing, should not significantly decrease helping. Another is that whether a guilt-induced subject is independently experiencing a positive mood should have little to no bearing on helping rates since the positive mood would not satisfy the desire to repair the wrongdoing.

The above model seems to have a strong following in the literature on guilt and helping.[23] At the same time, a number of studies have results which appear to be incompatible with its predictions. Let me briefly mention one study with respect to each of the predictions just noted. Chen-Bo Zhong and Katie Liljenquist (2006) asked participants to recall an unethical action they performed in their past. Next participants were divided into two groups, one of which used an antiseptic wipe to cleanse their hands or one of which did not. After completing a survey about their emotional state, they were given an opportunity to be an unpaid volunteer for a desperate graduate student in another study. The results were that 74 percent of participants who did not use the wipes volunteered to help, whereas only 41 percent who did use the wipes volunteered.[24] Note that the cleansing involved here was not a moral cleaning such as going to confession, which might be considered a means of trying to repair wrongdoing; rather it was simply an act of physical cleansing to eliminate germs.[25] Thus it seems that some participants might have otherwise volunteered were it not for their performance of an action which had no

[22] See Lindsay-Hartz et al. 1995 for related discussion.
[23] See, e.g. Freedman et al. 1967: 117, Baumeister et al. 1994: 257, Tangney 1995: 120, Roberts 2003: 225, Amodio et al. 2007, and especially Lindsay-Hartz et al. 1995.
[24] Zhong and Liljenquist 2006: 1452.
[25] For the effect of confession on helping behavior, see Harris et al. 1975. For more on the relationship between physical and moral cleanliness, see Zhong et al. 2010.

bearing on repairing their prior unethical behavior, thereby clearly contradicting what the above model implies.

Regarding the second prediction, Michael Cunningham and his colleagues (1980) examined the relationship between positive mood, guilt, and helping. Positive mood was manipulated by having participants find a free dime in the coin return slot of a pay phone. Guilt was manipulated by following the same broken camera technique developed by Regan. And the helping task was assisting a confederate pick up papers which had been dropped in front of the participant. The results were as follows:[26]

	Guilt	No guilt
Positive mood	33%	73%
No positive mood	80%	40%

Hence whereas merely guilty participants helped at much greater levels than controls, when participants felt both guilty and in a positive mood they did not. So contrary to the second prediction of this model, experiencing a positive mood does have an important bearing on helping behavior among individuals experiencing guilt.

Desire to Improve One's Own Standing. The previous model posited a desire which is not directly concerned with the person in question, but rather with morality itself and the importance of repairing a failure to live up to his moral standards. In order to help explain the relationship between guilt and helping, we could instead posit a desire that the person might have to improve his (actual or perceived) moral purity, worth, virtue, social image, social attachments, social and communal relationships, moral standing in the community, or the like.[27] The diagram here would look like this:

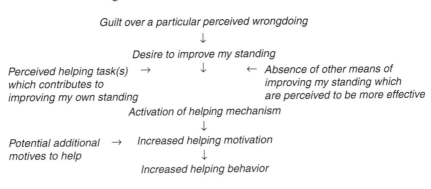

Guilt over a particular perceived wrongdoing

↓

Desire to improve my standing

Perceived helping task(s)   →   ↓   ←   *Absence of other means of*
which contributes to   *improving my standing which*
improving my own standing   *are perceived to be more effective*

Activation of helping mechanism

↓

Potential additional   →   *Increased helping motivation*
motives to help   ↓

Increased helping behavior

[26] Cunningham et al. 1980: 184.

[27] See Carlsmith and Gross 1969: 239, Jones et al. 1995, Zhong and Liljenquist 2006, and especially Baumeister et al. 1994.

This model would generate some of the same predictions as the previous one: (i) actions which eliminate guilt without improving moral or social standing should not significantly diminish helping, and (ii) since positive moods would not improve the person's standing, they should have little bearing on helping rates. Thus the studies which are troublesome for the previous model should cause problems for this one as well. For instance, using antiseptic wipes has no bearing on my actual or socially perceived standing, and yet they served to significantly reduce volunteering among guilty participants.[28]

Desire to Alleviate One's Guilt. The fourth and final motivational model to be mentioned here holds that guilt often causes the activation of a standing disposition to desire to eliminate or reduce the person's guilt. Since helping is one very common way of making oneself feel better and no longer guilty about a prior wrong act, it is only to be expected that guilt would be positively correlated with helping, other things being equal. Thus we get the following:

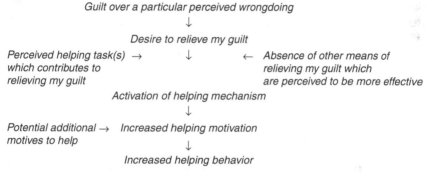

Guilt over a particular perceived wrongdoing
↓
Desire to relieve my guilt
Perceived helping task(s) →   ↓   ← Absence of other means of
which contributes to   relieving my guilt which
relieving my guilt   are perceived to be more effective
Activation of helping mechanism
↓
Potential additional → Increased helping motivation
motives to help   ↓
Increased helping behavior

Such a model would imply, among other things, that whether a person experiencing guilt helps others is in part a function of whether the helping task would be more costly than the benefit derived from relieving the guilty feelings.[29]

Such a guilt-relief model is perhaps the leading proposal in the psychology literature today,[30] but even this view has met with some opposing data. For instance, Yael Zemack-Rugar and colleagues (2007) compared the helping behavior of participants who were high in guilt-proneness and who had been subliminally primed with guilt adjectives, with that of similarly primed participants low in guilt-proneness and also participants primed with sadness

---

[28] Advocates of this model could focus on certain specific variants of the desire to improve one's standing, such as a desire to restore one's moral purity, and argue that there is a psychological association between such a desire and a desire for physical cleansing. Thus by physically cleaning one's hands, one is also in the process undergoing an indirect form of moral cleansing. See Zhong and Liljenquist 2006 for discussion.

[29] For related discussion, see Batson et al. 1986.

[30] See, e.g. Donnerstein et al. 1975, Cunningham et al. 1980, Baumeister et al. 1994: 255–6, Quiles and Bybee 1997: 104, Estrada-Hollenbeck and Heatherton 1998: 221, and Lindsey 2005.

adjectives. After the priming procedure and emotion measures were administered by a computer, participants were told of another study that involved, "an
array of annoying, boring, and repetitive tasks designed to assist a charity in
formulating its research questionnaires." Participants were asked how much
time (between 0–20 minutes) they would like to volunteer to help the charity as
unpaid volunteers.[31] The mean number of minutes volunteered was as follows:[32]

High guilt proneness, guilt prime:	8.4 minutes
High guilt proneness, sadness prime:	3.9 minutes
Low guilt proneness, guilt prime:	3.1 minutes
Low guilt proneness, sadness prime:	2.2 minutes

But it is unclear why guilty participants would be so much more inclined to
become dedicated volunteers for what seems to be a very costly task if helping
is being influenced by cost-benefit assessments pertaining to guilt-relief and if
there would likely be plenty of subsequent opportunities available to relieve
guilt in other ways.[33]

Let me conclude this section with some comments about these models. First,
they clearly each need to be developed more carefully than has been done
above, although even this presentation is more detailed than one typically
finds. Furthermore, each of the models is really just a label for a family of
closely related proposals. For instance under the heading of the desire to
improve the person's standing, we can distinguish a desire to improve his
actual moral standing given his personal set of norms, versus a desire to
improve his *socially perceived* moral standing. Clearly these two desires can
lead to the performance of different actions in certain cases. In addition, while
conflicting empirical results were mentioned for each of the four models, they
should not be taken as decisive problems but rather as initial concerns that
further experimental work needs to address. Finally, these models need not be
treated as exclusive. It might turn out that a person forms one of these desires

---

[31] The study was also cleverly rigged to supposedly last sixty minutes but proceeded quickly
enough so that participants could volunteer to help for the entire twenty minutes if they wanted
to without scheduling conflicts.

[32] Zemack-Rugar et al. 2007: 935.

[33] An advocate of the guilt-relief model could suggest that there is no incompatibility once
temporal distance is taken into account. Given that we seem to ascribe greater importance to
costs and benefits in the immediate as opposed to the distant future, the participants in the first
group might have been attracted to the likelihood of immediate guilt relief despite the annoying
nature of the tasks, rather than the mere prospect of distant guilt relief. Thanks to an anonymous
referee for this suggestion, which strikes me as plausible.

For another study involving guilt and an unpleasant helping task, see Darlington and Macker
1966. For critical discussion of this fourth model, see Zemack-Rugar et al. 2007: 934 and
especially Lindsay-Hartz et al. 1995.

in some situations when he feels guilty, and another one of them in other situations—or even two or more of them at the same time!

2.3 GUILT AND CHARACTER TRAITS

With this brief overview of the psychological literature on guilt and helping, let me draw six implications, each of which will point in the direction of the picture of character that I develop more systematically in Part III.

(a) *Many people do not perform even simple helping tasks*. Recall that control participants in these studies typically did not help. Regan found that only 16 percent of controls notified the woman with the leaking bag, and Konečni found that only 15 percent of controls would stop to help pick up dropped computer cards. These findings would not be surprising if the helping tasks were very demanding or time consuming, but note how trivial the tasks are. Indeed, not only do many control participants not help, an omission which can often be morally problematic in its own right, but they sometimes go further than that. For instance in the Konečni study, "the control subjects tended to make a fairly large and unnecessary semicircle around the pile of cards, and hardly ever commented on what had happened."[34] Thus the first implication is that, apart from the boost provided by guilt, many people in various situations tend to not help even with relatively simple tasks.

(b) *Guilt as an enhancer*. A typical study reviewed earlier involved one helping task which is monitored on a single occasion. It is natural to complain that such a study really tells us very little about someone's moral character, and I entirely agree with this complaint.

However, when these studies are examined *cumulatively*, important motivational and behavioral patterns may begin to emerge. In this case, the experimental literature involves a wide variety of different situations which caused feelings of guilt (such as breaking a camera or knocking over books) as well as many different opportunities to help (such as volunteering for an experiment and notifying someone about a torn bag).

What becomes clear is a remarkably consistent pattern—participants experiencing guilt help in general significantly more often than do participants not experiencing guilt, other things being equal. In other words, guilt seems to function as an *enhancer* of helping, which can increase the frequency with which a person would otherwise help in helping-relevant situations.

Furthermore, given that these studies used random samples of participants and given that they were conducted in various locations and time periods,

---

[34] Konečni 1972: 32.

their results can be applied more broadly than just to the participants themselves. In other words, we can infer that *most people* are such that occurrent feelings of guilt serve as enhancers for helping.

What about *anticipated guilt*, or the emotion which results from a person's belief about how guilty he would feel in the future if he does or does not perform a given task? For instance, I can anticipate feeling guilty if I choose to not call my parents on their birthday, or ignore a request from a student to meet about a paper. The natural hypothesis is that anticipated guilt will also serve as an enhancer for helping, provided that the helping is perceived to be a means to avoid future feelings of guilt. Otherwise, if the helping task would only maintain or worsen the feeling of guilt, then anticipated guilt will function as an *inhibitor* of helping.[35]

What little work there is supports this hypothesis. Lisa Lindsey (2005), for instance, found a strong positive correlation between anticipated guilt over not helping those in need of a life-saving bone marrow donation, and both the intention to and actual compliance with requests to be tested as a possible donor. One hundred and forty-six undergraduate students were brought into the lab twice with seven to ten days in-between their visits. Participants who were given a high anticipated guilt message had correlations of 0.63 between the message and anticipated guilt, 0.84 between anticipated guilt and behavioral intent, and 0.42 between behavioral intent and actual behavior.[36]

(c) *Some of the mental state dispositions responsible for helping.* Not only are there many studies which demonstrate consistent patterns of helping related to guilt, but these patterns also allow psychologists to theorize about the mental states which best account for them. Recall that the leading account is one according to which a feeling of guilt can activate a disposition to desire to alleviate one's guilt. This can then motivate a search for means to do so. Note that helping has not entered into the motivational story yet. Indeed, I might think that there are no helping opportunities available at the moment, or that the available helping opportunities are impossible for me to perform, and so not help at all.

But if I also believe that there are some helping opportunities available to me, then together with my desire to alleviate my guilt, another set of mental state dispositions can then be triggered:

(a) Beliefs concerned with the relationship between helping others and various personal costs for me, such as lost time, money, alternative activities, and so on.

(b) Beliefs concerned with the relationship between helping others and various social reactions to me, such as approval, gratitude, praise, and so forth.

---

[35] I will say much more about inhibitors in chapter six.
[36] Lindsey 2005: 469. See also Basil et al. 2006 on anticipatory guilt and charitable donations.

(c) Beliefs concerned with the relationship between helping others and various moral consequences for me, such as living up to my norms, improving my moral standing and purity, and so forth.

(d) Beliefs concerned with how these various personal costs, social reactions, and moral consequences contribute towards alleviating my guilty feelings.

(e) Desires concerned with helping when doing so will contribute towards alleviating my guilty feelings, and more so than any reasonable alternative means of doing so which is thought to be available.

(f) Desires concerned with not helping when doing so will contribute towards perpetuating my guilty feelings, or will not alleviate them as effectively as some reasonable alternative means of doing so which is thought to be available.

The above make up part of the "helping mechanism" that was represented in the diagrams in section two, again provided that this guilt-relief model is correct. To this I also need to add one more factor:

(g) The absence of any other means of alleviating my guilty feelings which are perceived to be even more effective in doing so than helping.

If all of these mental states in (a) through (f) align properly, then together with (g) the upshot can be that I am significantly more motivated to perform some particular helping task, other things being equal.

To make this a bit less abstract, imagine what might be going on for participants in the guilt condition of Regan's study who actually did notify the shopper of the hole in her bag. Suppose, in fact, that I am one of these participants. I have just been made to feel guilty for having broken an expensive camera. If we accept the leading model in the research literature, then these feelings of guilt can trigger a desire to alleviate my guilt. Soon thereafter I notice someone whose bag is leaking candy and whom I can easily help. This (in most cases subconsciously) leads to the activation of various beliefs—beliefs that helping her would not delay me very much, that it would likely promote positive social reactions such as gratitude from the shopper and admiration from onlookers, that it would be in accordance with my moral standards for being a good person, and so forth—all of which by my lights contribute to alleviating my guilt. It is also important that there is not anything else I can see that is worth doing at this moment and which could serve as an even better means of combatting my guilt, such as perhaps donating money to the Salvation Army volunteer. All of this then leads to the formation of my desire to help the shopper, so long as it will prove to be effective in relieving guilt by my lights. Hence while otherwise I might have ignored the shopper, given the causal influence of these mental states, I end up saying something to her.

(d) *Helping which is significantly influenced by guilt seems to be consistent.* There is very little longitudinal research which examines the relationship between guilt and helping for the same people in multiple situations over time. Nevertheless, once the underlying beliefs and desires have been identified, plausible assumptions can be made about what that research might show. With regards to stability, for instance, we can assume that most people would continue to exhibit increased helping when feeling guilty in the same situations. When it comes to cross-situational consistency, there is every reason to expect the same behavioral trends to show up when the same people encounter different circumstances and helping tasks. For instance, psychologists could design a study comparing controls and guilt-induced subjects as to their willingness to volunteer to clean up beaches, and then several days later to donate five dollars to Worldvision.

The kind of cross-situational consistency is one which depends on what features of the situations are salient to the person in question, and when they are, to what degree. It demonstrates the impressive subtlety that people show in adjusting their behavior from one situation to the next. Two situations might seem very similar as helping opportunities, but in one the person is experiencing guilt and in the other not, and so he helps in the former and not the latter. Or the person is experiencing guilt in both of them, but still behaves differently because due to various subconscious calculations, one of the helping tasks is thought to not alleviate guilt while the other is thought to do so. From the outside this behavior can look highly fragmented, as the same person may help in one situation and not help in what to observers may seem to be a near identical one. But from the inside it makes perfect psychological sense.

This consistency across time and situations allows for what should be fairly accurate predictions about the helping of individuals experiencing guilt. Or rather, such would be the case once we have a better idea of what the correct model is of the relevant motivational states. Suppose for now, as I have been doing, that the guilt-relief model is correct. Then one prediction is that:

(P) Other things being equal, if participants are experiencing guilt as a result of something they think they have done wrong, and:

  (i) are presented with a moderately demanding opportunity to help
  (ii) take themselves to be able to help
  (iii) take the benefits of helping in terms of guilt-relief to outweigh the costs associated with helping
  (iv) do not take there to be any more effective means available for relieving the guilt

  then many of these participants will probably attempt to help.

Note that this is stated in terms of what these people will "probably" do—none of the studies showed that all of the participants in the guilt condition helped, just as none of them showed that all of the participants in the control condition did *not* help. So the claim is not that each individual will always try to perform some helping task when experiencing guilt and when the conditions in (P) obtain. Rather, the claim is that if we monitor that person's behavior and guilt levels over time, we could expect to find a significant difference in the frequency of his helping which positively correlates with his experience of guilt, other things being equal.

(e) *Helping motives which arise from guilt are not altruistic.* Genuine altruistic motivation to perform an action is motivation concerned with what is (thought to be) good for another person, regardless of whether the action would directly benefit the one performing it or not. Given this formulation, the motives to help which are brought about by guilt do not appear to be altruistic. To see this, let me proceed carefully.

The two central concepts here are *altruistic* and *egoistic* motives. What they have in common is that they are both *desires*.[37] What divides them is something about the propositional content of these desires which they aim to bring about. Furthermore, in this discussion the focus is on *ultimate* desires, rather than derivative or instrumental ones.[38] For instance, I might have this desire:

(i) My desire that I help John with his homework.

On the surface, this appears to be altruistic, since it is primarily concerned with doing something good for John. But it could turn out that it was caused in part by this prior desire (together with relevant beliefs about John and his popularity):

(ii) My desire that I help other people with their homework so that I will become popular.

And that desire itself could be derived from a still more fundamental desire such as:

(iii) My desire that I become popular.

---

[37] By saying this, I am not taking a stand on controversial debates about the Humean theory of motivation. In fact, as I argue in my 2008a, I think the Humean theory is false. Rather, talk of "desires" is only intended to facilitate the presentation, and anything which follows can be easily adapted to bring it in line with various theories of motivation. For a similar switch to talking about desires, see Sober and Wilson 1998: chapter six, and May 2011b.

[38] Ultimate desires are sometimes labeled "irreducible desires" or "desires which are ends in themselves." For proposals about how to formally distinguish ultimate and instrumental desires, see Sober and Wilson 1998: 217–19 and 218: n. 15 and Stich et al. 2010: 151–2.

This ultimate desire is clearly egoistic.[39]

So I claim that we should focus our attention primarily on the propositional content of desires, and more specifically on the content of ultimate desires. But even this category is too broad for my purposes. What I am really interested in are ultimate desires which are concerned with what *benefits* the self or others, rather than desires such as:

(iv) My desire that I count grains of sand.

It seems possible that I could desire this, not for the sake of whatever pleasure I might derive from counting the grains, but simply as an end-in-itself (let us suppose). But this desire does not count as altruistic just because it does not contribute to my benefit even by my own lights. Or to take a better example, consider this ultimate desire:

(iv*) My desire that another person fail, be injured, or die.

Since it is an ultimate desire, it is not concerned with how I might be benefitted by another's failure or take pleasure in it. It is a malevolent ultimate desire which is, intuitively, neither egoistic nor altruistic.[40]

So my concern will be with (a) desires, which are (b) ultimate, and which, (c) in the process of being satisfied, someone is benefitted according to what counts as being benefitted by the person who has the desire.[41] Examples include (iii) above, where the only way the desire can be satisfied is if I am benefitted in this way by my own lights. Similarly with:

(v) My desire that you get better from your illness.
(vi) My desire that I no longer experience guilt.

These are both desires concerned with what benefits a person.

With these preliminary remarks in mind, I claim that *egoistic* desires are those ultimate desires which are primarily concerned with benefitting the person who has them, whereas *altruistic* desires are those ultimate desires which are concerned with benefiting another person in such a way that is not dependent on whether the person with the desire would be benefitted. Here are more precise characterizations of these central concepts which, although still rough, are sufficient for my purposes:[42]

---

[39] Some desires may be both ultimate and instrumental, such as a desire for pleasure or the avoidance of pain (Stich et al. 2010: 151–2). If there are desires like this, then they will be included under the heading of ultimate desires in what follows.

[40] For similar remarks, see Sober and Wilson 1998: 225, 229–30.

[41] Talk of desires being "satisfied" is not intended to mean what it often does in ordinary thought and language, such as being content or pleased. Rather, this is a technical notion in philosophy whereby a desire is satisfied so long as what the desire represents comes about or, equivalently, where the proposition which is the content of the desire is true. For helpful discussion, see Sober and Wilson 1998: 212.

[42] In what follows I have been helped by Sober and Wilson 1998: 217–19, 224–31 and May 2011b: 40–3. See also Adams 2006: 65, 74 and Batson 2011: 20–9.

(E) A person's ultimate desire is *egoistic* just in case:

> (i) It concerns what she thinks benefits (at least) herself.
>
> (ii) The desire cannot be satisfied unless she would be benefitted in her eyes, *regardless* of whether anyone else would be benefitted. If the content of the desire does include what benefits another person, then it does so only because the other person's benefit is seen as an instrumental means to benefitting herself.

(A) A person's ultimate desire is *altruistic* just in case:

> (i) It concerns what she thinks benefits (at least) one person who is not herself.
>
> (ii) The desire cannot be satisfied unless someone other than herself would be benefitted in her eyes, and benefitted in such a way that is independent of what would subsequently benefit her.[43]

A desire like (vi) clearly counts as egoistic on this framework, since it only concerns what benefits me. Similarly, the desire in (v) would count as altruistic, since it is concerned with what is good for my friend regardless of whether I would derive any benefit from his getting better. What about a case like this:

> (vii) My desire that you and I both get better from our illnesses.

This desire would not be egoistic, since it cannot be satisfied independently of whether my friend also gets better. Rather it seems intuitively to be an altruistic desire, since I am thinking (in part) about what is good for someone else, and in such a way that does not require that I benefit from his recovery from the illness. The proposal in (A) rightly classifies it as such.[44]

Finally, consider this desire:

---

[43] This is formulated narrowly in terms of what benefits another *person*. But as Sober and Wilson rightly note (1998: 229), a formulation of altruistic desires should be broadened to include ultimate desires which are concerned with, e.g. the environment, particular animals, a group of people, and so forth. My concern in this book is with moral behavior directed towards other persons, but the proposal in (A) can be easily adjusted to have a broader focus.

In addition, I understand "benefits" broadly so that it includes, for instance, protection of rights and intellectual and aesthetic pursuits. It can even include helping to advance another person's project which itself is self-sacrificing for that person. Hence as Adams remarks, "Being *for your good* is only one of the ways in which I may be *for you*" (2006: 69, emphasis his). For related discussion, see Adams 2006: 20, 69.

[44] Cases like this—involving desires which are concerned with both the person with the desire and at least one other person who is not treated simply as a means—are problematic cases for many formulations of egoistic and altruistic desires. Sober and Wilson, for instance, realize this and simply deny that they count as either egoistic or altruistic, instead inventing a third category of "relational" desires (1998: 225–6). But at least many of these desires seem fairly clearly to be either egoistic or altruistic on intuitive grounds, as in the example of (vii) above as well as the examples provided by Sober and Wilson themselves (1998: 225) and May 2011b: 44–5. My framework has the ability to categorize them as such. Stephen Stich and his colleagues instead use these cases to argue that egoism and altruism are vague concepts (2010: 152–3). See also May 2011b: 43–5 for related discussion.

(viii) My desire that you get better from your illness so that you can help me with
        my homework.

Leaving aside for the moment the question of whether this is an ultimate
desire, intuitively it seems egoistic as I only seem to care about your health
insofar as it would help me. The proposal in (A) would agree—while it is true
that the desire is concerned with what benefits someone else and while it is
also true that it cannot be satisfied unless that person would be benefited, this
benefit for the other person is purely *instrumental* to what would be in my
own self-interest.

With this background on egoistic and altruistic desires in place, let me
return to the desires to help which can arise from guilt. Here are the desires
posited in two of the leading models:

> *Desires to help to improve my own standing*
> *Desires to help to alleviate my guilt*

Despite the differences in detail, these models share at least one thing in
common—they posit purely egoistic desires. If I do end up helping, then to
the extent that my behavior results from one of these motives, the person
whom I am helping is being treated merely as a means to providing me with
some kind of benefit. In other words, in acting from such desires, I do not
really care about a person in need for her own sake.

Now it can certainly be a very good thing in many cases that I still do help
someone, rather than ignoring her. But consider the following principle:

(ME) If a person performs a morally appropriate and helpful action, but does so
      only as a result of one or more ultimate desires whose main concern is with
      his own self-interest (such as a desire to promote his own pleasure or to
      relieve his feelings of guilt), then the action does not result from virtuous
      motives.[45]

Michael Stocker's classic hospital visitation example nicely illustrates the
intuitive support for (ME).[46] Suppose, to embellish the example a bit and
also to adapt it to the discussion here, that you have been stuck in the hospital
for weeks when your best friend comes to visit you. You are very glad that your

---

[45] I would also claim that it is not deserving of any moral worth or moral esteem, where
"moral worth" is used in roughly the way that Kant does, namely as a form of high moral esteem
for the psychological processes that were responsible for bringing the action about (4: 398). For
support for such a claim about moral worth, see Kant 4: 397 and Baxley 2010: 34–9. As Robert
Adams claims, "we think not caring for the good of other people, for its own sake, is morally
bad—in extreme cases, even wicked. If it is a settled motivational pattern, it is a *vice*" (2006: 76,
emphasis his).
[46] See Stocker 1976: 74. Stocker's main focus in this paper is whether certain forms of
motivation, including egoistic motivation, are compatible with, "love, friendship, affection,
fellow feeling, and community" (70). But he does note that the same concerns he raises about
these motives also apply to, "moral merit and demerit, moral praise- and blameworthiness, the
moral virtues and vices" (74).

friend is there, but in the course of the conversation it emerges that she is only visiting you to help eliminate her guilt over some unrelated action earlier in the day. As she leaves, she reports that she no longer feels guilty any more, and even thanks you for this. While it was highly beneficial for her, it seems apparent that her visit is deserving of no moral esteem or praise whatsoever. The action by itself might have been virtuous—in the sense that it might happen to correspond to what a virtuous person, acting in character, would also have done in the same circumstance. But clearly the motivation behind it is not virtuous. It is purely selfish, and calls into question the extent to which she really is your best friend. Of course, more could be said about this case, and properly examining it and the plausibility of (ME) more generally are beyond the scope of this chapter. Here I will content myself with having clarified why the desires mentioned above are not altruistic desires to help.

I also mentioned two other models which instead involve more impersonal, normative forms of motivation:

> *Desires to help to repair the specific wrong*
> *Desires to help to repair wrongdoing as such*

Here the primary concern is with what morality (or some other set of norms) demands by way of making reparation, rather than with the interests of a particular person in need. Those interests can certainly become important motivationally as well, but only because caring about them is a *means to* satisfying these demands for reparation. When either desire gives rise to actual helping behavior, the helping is thereby instrumental to satisfying certain normative standards. Hence because these desires are not *ultimately* concerned with helping in order to benefit someone else in need, they turn out to be *neither egoistic nor altruistic desires*.[47]

What should be said in morally evaluating them? Again, it can certainly be a very good thing in many cases that they turn out to lead to helping, especially if the alternative is that someone in need gets ignored. But my own view is that as a general matter:

> (MD) If a person performs a morally appropriate and helpful action, but does so only as a result of one or more ultimate desires whose main concern is with the satisfaction of impersonal moral requirements (such as a desire to do the right thing or to repair past wrongs in general), then the action does not result from virtuous motives.[48]

---

[47] I will say more about what I will call "moralistic" motives in chapter four, section three.

[48] For related discussion, see Foot 1972: 164–7, Stocker 1976, 1981, Wolf 1982: 83, 90, Smith 1994: 75–6, Hursthouse 1999: 132, Adams 2006: 76, and Baxley 2010: chapter one.

Here I also think that the above claim applies to the question of the moral worth of an action, a question that is familiar from the literature on Kant (see in particular Kant 2002, 4: 397–9. For a helpful overview of the issues, see Baxley 2010: chapter one). I do not take a stand on whether Kant's own view is committed to ultimate desires of the sort mentioned in (MD). Baxley, for

Thus to adapt Stocker's example to the second model of guilt-induced helping, if your friend comes to visit and is primarily motivated by her desire to use the visit to help atone for some moral damage she has done earlier in the day, then such an action does not show any special attachment towards you and your needs and concerns. Rather it seems cold and impersonal, as you are treated merely as a means to help her atone for her own moral wrongdoing. Since the primary concern is not with your needs, if certain other means had presented themselves earlier in the day which she thought more appropriate in bringing about this atoning, such as confessing the wrongs or aiding the wronged party directly, then your friend likely would not have come to the hospital at all.[49] This is not, I think many of us would say, the kind of motivation for helping other people that is deserving of our highest moral esteem and is associated with a virtuous person.[50]

But (MD) is controversial, and I do not want to devote space to arguing for it here. Even without it, the conclusion I have reached is still important, namely that guilt-induced motivation to help on all of the leading models is not altruistic, and at least on most of them it is not virtuous either.

(f) *Most people do not possess the virtue of compassion.* For the sixth and final implication, I want to turn explicitly to the topic of moral character. When it comes to helping others, the moral virtue which is commonly mentioned is compassion.[51] What the corresponding vice is supposed to be is less clear. Possible candidates include cold-heartedness, selfishness, indifference, and callousness.

---

instance, agrees that *if* Kant were so committed, then this form of motivation might be problematic, but she argues that Kant does not in fact hold this kind of view (2010: 21–9).

[49] This point would apply to the first model of guilt-induced helping as well.

[50] Perhaps one reason for this is that the reasoning involved seems to exhibit what Bernard Williams famously called "one thought too many" (Williams 1976: 18). A desire to help had by my friend that was primarily responsive to concerns about what is good for me would be a virtuous desire that could lead to actions having moral worth. But a desire to help that was caused by a prior thought about what action would best contribute to repairing some past wrong, or to use another example, about what action would best contribute to being a good person or doing the morally right thing, shows that my friend has "one thought too many." The mere fact that I am her best friend should have provided her with ample motivation to come and visit me. As Michael Smith writes in a related context, "If any further motivation were required then that would simply indicate that [s]he doesn't have the feelings of direct love and concern for [me] that [I] rightly want and expect. [Sh]e would be alienated from [me], treating [me] as in relevant respects just like a stranger" (1994: 75; see also Wolf 1982: 90). However, the literature on Williams's general claim and on Smith's specific use of it (in the context of criticizing motivational externalism) is vast and complicated, and it is not necessary for me to pursue these issues further here.

[51] Some discussions of virtue use "benevolence" here rather than "compassion." See, for instance, Adams 2006 and Russell 2009: 84. There may be some subtle differences between the two concepts, but I have not seen any in the literature that would matter for my purposes. The same holds for "kindness" as opposed to "compassion" (Adams 2006: 190), as well as for "charity" (Hursthouse 1999: 97, 100).

The discussion in this chapter suggests a number of respects in which most people do not have the virtue of compassion. To see this, I will briefly focus here on four such respects in which the standards for being a compassionate person do not seem to be met. To use the language from chapter one, these are four criteria in the *minimal threshold* for compassion, the set of necessary conditions which must be satisfied before a character trait can qualify as the virtue of compassion.[52] Here and in the remaining chapters of Part II I will just discuss these criteria briefly, saving the more thorough discussion for Part III. They are also summarized in the Appendix.

Before looking at the requirements individually, though, I want to flag a possible misinterpretation of my reasoning here, a misinterpretation that I have often seen when presenting this work previously. The misinterpretation is that I am reasoning as follows:

(i) A particular study, such as Regan et al. (1972), found that participants behaved in one particular situation in a way that is incompatible with one of the requirements for possessing the virtue of compassion.

(ii) Therefore, there is good reason to think that most people in general do not have the virtue of compassion.

Now clearly we should not be impressed with such an argument—no broad conclusion would be warranted on the basis of one such study. Rather, my reasoning is instead as follows:

(i*) Dozens of studies have observed the behavior of participants in different helping-relevant situations.

(ii*) On the basis of these studies collectively, we can arrive at plausible accounts of the underlying dispositions to form beliefs and desires which are responsible for the patterns of behavior that were observed.

(iii*) When compared to various requirements for possessing the virtue of compassion, both the patterns of behavior that were observed as well as the underlying mental state dispositions that were inferred, are incompatible with these requirements.

(iv*) Therefore, there is good reason to think that most people in general do not have the virtue of compassion.

This line of reasoning seems compelling to me, and it is the kind of reasoning I will use not just in this chapter but throughout the book. But it naturally invites the question—what are these requirements supposed to be?

---

[52] To be clear, these are just four of many such conditions. I will never claim in this book to have exhaustively characterized any given moral virtue or vice.

.   To begin, here is a behavioral requirement:

> (a) A person who is compassionate, when acting in character, will typically attempt to help when in moderately demanding situations relevant to helping.[53]

But this was not found to be the case for many of the control participants, as already noted earlier in this section. Even when the need for help was obvious and the effort involved was minimal, many of them did nothing.

Here is a second requirement:

> (b) A compassionate person's trait of compassion will not be dependent on the presence of certain enhancers (such as moderate guilt, embarrassment, or good mood) in leading him to perform helpful actions, such that if these enhancers were not present, then his frequency of helping would significantly decrease in the same nominal situations.

The thought here is that a compassionate person would be expected to help another person in need at roughly the same rate *regardless of whether* he is feeling moderate guilt about something or not. If instead the person often helps when guilty, but not in situations that are otherwise the same in terms of their nominal features, then that is a fairly reliable sign that he has not yet developed a compassionate character. But as we have seen, both helping motivation and behavior seem to significantly fluctuate as a result of the enhancing effects of guilt.

Third, here is a motivational requirement:

> (c) A compassionate person's trait of compassion will typically lead to helping which is done at least primarily for motivating reasons that are morally admirable and deserving of moral praise, and not primarily for motivating reasons which are either morally problematic or morally neutral.

Just reliably helping another person is not enough to qualify as compassionate. Someone could act this way and at the same time have completely crass or selfish reasons for doing so, such as to win community service awards. A compassionate person not only behaves in certain ways but also does so as a result of the work of compassionate motives.

But we have just seen how this requirement may not be met by motivation to help which arises from guilt. On at least some (if not all) of the leading models, any such helping would not be done for virtuous motives.

This concern about motivation can be put more forcefully by strengthening the requirement in (c). In the case of compassion, it is not just that the motives should be morally praiseworthy ones, but also that:

---

[53] For this and the remaining requirements both in this chapter and in the subsequent ones, it is assumed that other things are held equal. I have omitted this to help make the presentation less cumbersome.

(c*) The virtue of compassion gives rise to compassionate motivation to help another person, and that motivation is *altruistic* motivation to help. Indeed, it is the fact that it is altruistic which grounds the moral praiseworthiness of this motivation.

This should be intuitively compelling. When thinking about paradigm examples of compassionate people, I suspect most of us would see them as being fundamentally concerned with the good of those in need when they help. If we learn that in fact their helping was simply motivated by their own self-interest, for instance, then we would typically revise our evaluation of them as compassionate. Similarly, although more controversially I admit, if we find out that they were helping simply out of duty or a desire to respect general moral principles, then I also suspect we might similarly revise our evaluation. Back to guilt:

(C) On all the leading models of guilt-induced helping, the motivation to help which is derived from this emotion is *not* altruistic motivation.

Hence, (c*) and (C) together provide another reason for thinking that most people do not have the virtue of compassion.

Thus by way of summary, it seems that many people will often not help with such simple tasks as picking up dropped computer cards, and even when they help, they might do so as a result of feeling guilty, thereby making the helping behavior at least partially if not entirely dependent on motives which are not altruistic like a desire to alleviate their guilt. None of this is what should be expected from a compassionate person.[54]

Before concluding, here is an important objection. It might be granted that the motivation to help *which is connected to guilt* is not deserving of moral praise nor has any moral worth. But at the same time this need not be the *only* motivation which led many participants to tell the shopper about her leaking bag, for instance. In fact, in section two I was careful to note the potential for "additional motives to help" in all of the diagrams. Suppose this additional motivation is altruistic. Then according to the objection, so long as a *significant portion of* one's motivation is altruistic, that is enough to satisfy the

---

[54] A qualification should be noted here. Researchers have repeatedly found a positive correlation between guilt and empathy. If it turns out that (i) by focusing the person on the harm caused to others by his wrong action, feelings of guilt will in some instances *give rise to* empathetic feelings for another's suffering or misfortune, and if (ii) empathetic motivation is genuinely altruistic (a claim which will be examined in chapter five), *then* motivation to help which arises from empathy for the other person's situation, rather than directly from one of the four guilt-produced desires in section two, would typically be altruistic and so be compatible with compassionate motivation. But even here it is highly unlikely that *all* cases of guilt-influenced helping are mediated by empathy, rather than just some. And even if all were, that would still not call into question the incompatibility with claims (a) and (b) above. For more on guilt and empathy, see Tangney 1995: 131–3 and Tangney et al. 2007a: 350–1.

motivational requirement for possessing genuine compassion, and so is sufficient to block the incompatibility with claims (c) and (c*) above.[55]

I certainly grant the existence of mixed motives, and also the psychological
possibility of actions jointly arising from some motives which are altruistic
and others which are non-altruistic. I even grant that a person could be
compassionate and still act from mixed motives, some of which are self-
interested.

But on the other hand, I maintain that a compassionate person does not
depend on the presence of egoistic motives in order to have sufficient motivation to help others in various situations. In cases where such motives are not
present, the altruistic motives of a compassionate person should be sufficient
by themselves to still bring about reliable helping.

Suppose, for instance, that we observe someone who regularly helps at a
nursing home, food bank, and homeless shelter. On the surface this certainly
appears to be a compassionate person. Upon closer examination, suppose we
find that she is helping both because she cares about the people in need for
their own sake, and also because she has some deep-seated guilt for certain
actions in her past and views these opportunities as reliable means to alleviate
her guilt. With this new information, it still could be that she is a compassionate person overall. So says the objection, and thus far I agree with it.

But now suppose it turns out that she eventually eliminates her guilt, so that
it no longer continues to make any motivational contribution to helping at all.
If she were genuinely compassionate, that should not matter with respect to
her helping—perhaps it might drop off a little, but we should expect her to still
reliably appear at these places, other things being equal. Yet in fact she stops
appearing, and not because she has found other helping opportunities which
she thinks are even more worthwhile. Rather, it turns out that the altruistic
motivation by itself proved to not be nearly strong enough to carry her
forward.

In this case I think we have good reason to conclude, on the basis of this
information alone, that she really was not compassionate all along. In other
words:

(d) A compassionate person, when acting in character, does not regularly help
from egoistic motives which are often powerful enough that, were they not
present, he would not continue to reliably help, as his altruistic motives are
not strong enough to motivate reliable helping by themselves.[56]

---

[55] A version of this objection was suggested to me by John Cottingham. See also Webber
2006b: 208, Adams 2006: 78, and Snow 2010: 103.
[56] A parallel (although perhaps more controversial) set of principles could be formulated for
motives to obey general moral principles.

This is another necessary condition in the minimal threshold for the virtue of compassion.

Given the large drop-off in helping rates between participants who helped when feeling guilty versus control participants, and given the truth of any one of the leading egoistic models for guilt-induced helping, I again think there is good reason to conclude that most people do not possess the trait of compassion, *even granting* the existence of mixed motives for helping. Recall, for instance, the Zhong and Liljenquist (2006) study in which 74 percent of guilt-induced participants who did not use antiseptic wipes volunteered to help a desperate graduate student, whereas only 41 percent who did use the wipes volunteered. If these results are representative of the population at large, then note how such a minor thing as using hand wipes was able to deflate egoistic motivation to help and divert so many people from otherwise helping.[57]

Thus despite the objection from mixed motives, I still maintain that the results I have surveyed in this chapter give us good reason to reject the claim that most people are compassionate. Having said this, the experimental data is also compatible with the existence of a *few* people who might have the virtue of compassion to some degree. For instance, it turned out that 15 percent of controls still stopped to help pick up the computer cards in Konečni's study, and 16 percent of controls called attention to the torn bag in Regan's study. Longitudinal studies of these participants as they encountered other helping situations would have been very useful.

---

[57] Yet another necessary condition in the minimal threshold for compassion is that:

> (e) A compassionate person, when acting in character, does not regularly help from egoistic motives which are often powerful enough that they would lead him to pursue another non-virtuous course of action besides helping, if that alternative is thought to be more conducive to the satisfaction of the egoistic motives.

If one of the egoistic models of guilt-induced motivation to help is correct, then it suggests that most people could be egoistically motivated in this way, regardless of whether a person is in need of help or not.

To see why this is a requirement of the virtue of compassion, consider the same example again, but now suppose that the volunteer has not yet eliminated her deep-seated guilt after all. In fact, it is still playing a significant motivational role in leading her to volunteer, along with the altruistic motives too. Suppose as well that one day she starts gambling regularly to address her guilt (perhaps by, subconsciously, avoiding having to think about it), and she begins to use the time devoted to volunteering to gamble instead. In this case, her behavior suggests that she was not primarily motivated to helping the people in need, but rather was ultimately searching for a means to assuaging her guilt. This new opportunity came along, and it now looks to her like a more effective means of doing so than volunteering. This would be a sign, I think we should say, that she is not genuinely compassionate.

2.4 CONCLUSION

In this chapter I have surveyed some of the empirical work on guilt and helping in order to ultimately advance both a negative and positive claim. The negative claim is that the experimental results can be plausibly interpreted to suggest that most people do not have the virtue of compassion. The positive claim is that instead most people seem to be (i) disposed to help more frequently when feeling guilty, and (ii) when they do help because of this emotion, they do so in certain consistent ways across time and situations, as a result of (iii) the casual activity of mental state dispositions which are not altruistic. All of these assertions will end up playing an important role in my account of Mixed Traits in Part III.

Of course examining the experimental work on just this one emotion does not tell anything like a complete story about helping motivation and behavior. But it has provided what I hope is an interesting and important place to start.

3

Embarrassment, Positive
Moods, and Helping

In the previous chapter I was able to draw a number of implications from research in psychology on guilt, implications which begin to point in the direction of the picture of Mixed Traits that will be outlined in Part III of this book. Here I turn to two other enhancers for helping—embarrassment and positive moods—and see whether similar implications can be drawn. The first section distinguishes between embarrassment and shame, while the next two sections discuss what, for the moment, are the leading psychological models of the relationship between embarrassment and positive moods on the one hand, and helping on the other. Section four then turns to some of the consequences that these models seem to have.

3.1 EMBARRASSMENT AND SHAME

Often feelings of embarrassment arise when the following conditions obtain: (i) a person has a particular public image, persona, or self-presentation of herself and her behavior for some set of circumstances, (ii) she cares about maintaining that public image in those circumstances, (iii) when actually in the circumstances, she does not think she lives up to this self-image—her thoughts, behavior, character, or other potential objects of embarrassment conflict with that image in a way that she does not want them to, and (iv) she thinks (or imagines) that this failure has been detected by other people to whom she wants to maintain the image, thereby causing her unwanted social evaluation.[1] To take an example, most people are embarrassed when they trip

---

[1] See also Edelmann 1987, 1990, Babcock and Sabini 1990, Szabados 1990, Harré 1990, Gonzales et al. 1990, R. Miller 1995, 1996, 2007, Sabini and Silver 1997: 11, and Purshouse 2001. As with guilt, these conditions are not proposed as strictly necessary or sufficient, but rather as useful generalities meant to cover central cases of embarrassment. In stating them, I follow the leading approach in the psychology literature to conceptualizing embarrassment,

and fall in public because such behavior goes against the image of themselves they want to project to others. Even if no one is actually around at the time, the mere likelihood of someone coming on the scene soon is often enough to feel embarrassed. On the other hand, tripping and falling on a deserted island might make a person annoyed or angry, but not likely embarrassed without anyone else present.[2]

Other situations which give rise to embarrassment also fit this picture.[3] For instance, a student who is being teased by a bully in front of his friends might become embarrassed because the bully is making him appear to his friends in a much worse way than he wants himself to appear publically. Or when a person forgets the name of a good friend when introducing her, he can easily become embarrassed because he is presenting an image to his friend and to the others present which does not reflect the public image he had aspired to. Similar points could be made about cases involving unintended nudity, or wardrobe malfunctions (as with Janet Jackson), or failures to control various noises or gases.[4]

I think we naturally associate embarrassment with negative actions by the person or others in the circumstances. But speakers can experience embarrassment when they are given long and generous introductions, and it is hard to see anything negative about either the content of what was said about them or the manner in which the introduction was delivered. My proposal understands such cases as arising from a concern on the part of the speaker that she might be coming across as potentially prideful, arrogant, immodest, or in some other way out of line with the image that she wants to project. Hence many speakers

namely the social evaluation model. For discussion of this approach and criticism of rival views, see Harré 1990, R. Miller 1995, Purshouse 2001, and especially Edelmann 1987 and R. Miller 1996: chapter seven.

One difficult kind of case for the above conditions involves embarrassment felt as a result of the behavior of others, such as a drunken friend who makes a fool of himself at a wedding. One way to handle such cases might be to broaden the notion of a public image to include not only the person's own behavior, but also that of others in situations he is in where he cares about their behavior. Thus I might be embarrassed by the drunken person at the wedding, even if we have never met before, because of the way in which he is violating the public image I wanted *all of us* to conform to. On this proposal, everyone is made to look bad to a certain extent in my eyes as a result of his actions. For relevant discussion along similar lines, see R. Miller 1995: 330, Purshouse 2001, and Roberts 2003: 232–3.

[2] What about cases where a person is currently embarrassed for actions he performed earlier in life, even if there was no one there to observe them at the time? While he might not have been embarrassed at the past time, note that he is embarrassed now precisely because a new audience is present, namely his *present self* who is judging the public image his prior self was projecting. For related discussion, see Szabados 1990: 346 and Purshouse 2001: 534–6.

[3] For an extensive taxonomy of circumstances which give rise to embarrassment, see Edelmann 1987: 47–54 and R. Miller 1995, 1996: 46–70.

[4] For related discussion, see Harré 1990: 187–9, Lewis 1995: 211, 2008: 750, and R. Miller 1996: 34, 126–7.

will begin with a humorous or self-deprecating remark which alleviates their embarrassment by, they hope, appropriately restoring their public image.

How then should embarrassment be distinguished from shame?[5] The characterization of embarrassment above suggests a natural starting point. Embarrassment, I said, involves a concern about what *others* are thinking about the person. Someone who is experiencing feelings of embarrassment is concerned that others are taking him to be behaving in a certain undesirable way which is inconsistent with what he wants his public image to be. Shame, on the other hand, involves what the person thinks about himself. In the liar example, he might be ashamed with himself for being a liar, even if the lie goes undetected and helps to bolster his public image.[6]

This simple conceptual distinction also has a number of implications for the roles that shame and embarrassment play in our lives, some of which are briefly mentioned below:

(a) Embarrassment tends to be both shorter in duration and milder in intensity than shame, which follows naturally from the difference

---

[5] Here several approaches seem unpromising:

  (i) One attempt is to claim that actions which give rise to feelings of shame are intentional, whereas embarrassing actions are unintentional. This might be true in many cases, but there are many counterexamples. For instance, some people are ashamed of their height or skin acne, whereas others are embarrassed when caught intentionally misbehaving. When two lovers are discovered where they should not be by a group of tourists, they might immediately blush and run off in embarrassment. See also Edelmann 1987: 44–7 and Babcock and Sabini 1990: 162–6. For an opposing view, see Harré 1990: 186–7.

  (ii) According to Robert Solomon, embarrassing actions are ones in which the person judges herself to be innocent, whereas shameful actions are ones for which we bear responsibility (1976: 305. For criticism see Szabados 1990: 342 and Purshouse 2001: 521–2). But again some people are ashamed by their height, while our naughty lovers were embarrassed about being discovered doing something for which they were clearly responsible and can understand being justifiably criticized.

  (iii) Perhaps the most intuitive approach of the three would be to claim that shame involves some kind of moral failing, whereas embarrassment involves a breach of norms pertaining to social conduct, such as norms of etiquette, poise, and so forth. But I have already said that shame ranges more widely than morality. And it is easy to come up with cases involving embarrassment and morality. For instance, a person might be telling a lie at a party and could feel guilt immediately afterwards for doing so and be ashamed of himself for being a liar, but he can *also* experience embarrassment once the lie is pointed out by someone in the audience. For related discussion, see Tangney et al. 1996: 1262. For an opposing view, see Harré 1990.

With the failure of these attempts, one might wonder whether there really is a significant difference between shame and embarrassment. Indeed, it is common to find psychologists treating them interchangeably, or at most claim that embarrassment is simply a milder former of shame. See, e.g. Lewis 1971 and Kaufman 1989: 24. Michael Lewis (1995, 2008) distinguishes between two types of embarrassment—embarrassment as mere exposure, and embarrassment as less intense shame. The latter category includes negative self-evaluations, and so includes most of the paradigm cases of adult embarrassment.

[6] For similar remarks, see Babcock and Sabini 1990, Szabados 1990, R. Miller 1996: 21–7, Tangney et al. 1996, and Sabini and Silver 1997: 11.

between self-condemnation versus a concern about what others are thinking about you.[7]

(b) Embarrassment tends to arise from more surprising and accidental events than shame, perhaps because such events are the ones which increase the risk of something going wrong with our intended self-presentations.[8]

(c) Embarrassing situations are typically viewed by the person as more humorous and light-hearted than shameful ones, since they often do not strike as close to how we fundamentally view ourselves as people. The same is true for how audiences often respond to embarrassed people (laughter, amusement, sympathy) versus shameful people (seriousness, disgust, avoidance).[9]

Hence despite their superficial similarity, shame and embarrassment differ in a number of crucial respects.

Having disentangled the emotion of shame from the emotion of embarrassment which is central to this chapter, I set shame to one side for my purposes here. But by having discussed shame as well, I hope to have clarified how embarrassment arises when my behavior publically violates, in an undesirable way, the image I am trying to convey to others.

3.2 EMBARRASSMENT AND HELPING

This section follows the same pattern as the previous chapter by briefly mentioning some empirical work on the relationship between embarrassment and helping, before distinguishing between competing explanations for this relationship. Fortunately, since many parallel claims apply to embarrassment as were made about guilt and helping, I will proceed much more briefly here.

In comparison with guilt, far less experimental work has been done on embarrassment and helping. Nevertheless, the studies that we do have show a significant positive relationship between the two. For instance, Arnie Cann and Jill Blackwelder (1984) had an undergraduate student confederate approach participants who were alone and within three feet of a lavatory door after they had gone to the bathroom. Each participant was asked by the confederate: "I am in a big hurry and I have a friend who needs these notes. I wonder if you could take them to her?" If the participant agreed, he or she was instructed where the friend would be, which was approximately 40 meters

---

[7] R. Miller 1996: 26, 2007: 246, Tangney et al. 1996, 2005: 45, and Eisenberg 2000: 666.

[8] R. Miller 1996: 26, Tangney et al. 1996, 2005: 45, and Eisenberg 2000: 667.

[9] R. Miller 1996: 24, 2007: 246, Babcock and Sabini 1990: 155, and Tangney et al. 1996, 2005: 45.

away. Participants in the control condition were approached in the same way on another floor of the building, but this time they were not coming out of the bathroom but merely walking down a hallway. The results were as follows:[10]

	Agreed to deliver notes
Lavatory condition	80%
Control condition	45%

So according to Cann and Blackwelder's interpretation of the results, there is a dramatic difference in compliance with a minor helping request as a function of the embarrassment people feel after using a public restroom.[11]

What motivational state(s) does embarrassment give rise to which in turn causally influences helping?[12] Let me briefly mention some of the leading candidates, while omitting the diagrams for each proposal in the interest of space:

Desire to Correct One's Damaged Image in the Situation. On this proposal, being embarrassed in a given situation because of a public misstep causes the formation of a desire to repair the damage that has been done to one's image in that situation, which in turn motivates helping. When Jones forgets his friend's name when introducing her at a party, he could form a desire to repair his image in the eyes of his friend and the other people around him, and thereby show that he is a good friend after all. There might be a variety of ways of doing so, such as offering an excuse, providing a justification, diverting everyone's attention, and so forth. But it might turn out that the best way he can see to save face is to help in some significant way. In those cases, and holding other things equal, we would expect the person to help at a significantly higher rate than otherwise. Parallel to the first model of guilt-induced helping, one consequence of this model is that participants who are experiencing embarrassment would *not* help at increased rates when the helping

---

[10] Cann and Blackwelder 1984: 224.

[11] Cann and Blackwelder 1984: 225. For additional studies of embarrassment and helping, see Foss and Crenshaw 1978, Edelmann et al. 1984, and Gonzales et al. 1990. These studies indicate that while actual feelings of embarrassment might serve to enhance the frequency of helping behavior, anticipated embarrassment has an opposite, inhibitory effect. For instance, Foss and Crenshaw (1978) found that 72 percent of participants would help in some manner if a confederate seemed to unknowingly drop a box of envelopes, whereas only 47 percent helped when what was dropped was instead a box of Tampax tampons (244). See also Edelmann 1987: 137–9, Edelmann et al. 1984, and R. Miller 1996: 161–4. The role of anticipated embarrassment as an inhibitor for helping will be discussed in chapter six.

[12] To simplify the discussion I focus mainly on (i) consequential embarrassment rather than anticipated embarrassment, and (ii) states of embarrassment rather than embarrassment traits. Furthermore, I assume a causal relationship exists between embarrassment and helping, rather than just a positive correlation, for the same reason given in the previous chapter with guilt.

task would not have any connection to repairing their image in the specific situation.[13]

As before, this kind of model is too simplistic as stated. In the main study designed to test this hypothesis, Robert Apsler (1975) had participants in the high-embarrassment condition perform a range of tasks including singing the "Star Spangled Banner" while a confederate was known to be watching from another room. In the low-embarrassment condition, participants were watched performing tasks such as reading a book. Controls were not asked to perform any task. Afterwards the confederate asked the participant to help with his class project by filling out a daily questionnaire for anywhere between 0–20 days. The compliance scores were as follows:[14]

	Mean number of days volunteered
High embarrassment	14.9
Low embarrassment	8.7
Control	5.0

Most importantly for this first model, similar results were found when the confederate making the helping request was known by the participant to have *not* previously observed the embarrassing tasks.[15]

Desire to Correct One's Damaged Image. Again the easy revision is to posit a general desire to improve one's image and show people that you are after all a normal, or respectable, or coordinated, or some other kind of person in line with your intended public self-presentation.[16] One implication of this model is that, other things being equal, we should not expect embarrassed participants to show a significant increase in activities which do not pertain to correcting their damaged image, and certainly not activities which might make their images even worse. And yet Rowland Miller and colleagues (1996) found that the leading response to embarrassment among 257 reports was evasion at 28 percent. Flight came in fifth at 9 percent.[17]

Desire to Raise One's Self-Esteem. Another proposal to explain what mediates embarrassment and helping is a self-esteem management hypothesis,

---

[13] Apsler 1975 (146) interprets Goffman (1959) as advocating this model.

[14] Apsler 1975: 149.

[15] Apsler 1975: 150.

[16] See Gonzales et al. 1990, R. Miller 1996: 127, 169–75, and Roberts 2003: 233.

[17] R. Miller 1996: 173. Of course more needs to be said here. For instance, we saw in chapter two, n. 18 that guilt has been associated with avoidance behavior in some instances, perhaps in order to prevent any further damage from being done and to learn from one's mistakes. At the same time, this is compatible with increased helping behavior being a subsequent effect of these guilty feelings which is aimed at promoting one or more of the motivational goals outlined in the previous section. A similar idea could apply here—evasion and flight could be initial defensive mechanisms in many embarrassed participants, but this is compatible with subsequent helping behavior aimed at improving the participant's image.

whereby embarrassment reduces a person's self-esteem, causing the formation of a desire to improve his self-esteem.[18] Helping will sometimes be one such way of making oneself feel better, provided the cost-benefit calculations for self-esteem come out correctly. Unfortunately for this view, however, studies have repeatedly found that reduced self-esteem plays only a marginal role in cases of embarrassment.[19]

Desire to Alleviate One's Embarrassment. Finally we have the hypothesis that embarrassed participants are disposed to desire to eliminate their feelings of embarrassment, which can lead to all kinds of behavior including flight, evasion, providing excuses, offering justifications, using humor, and, if the circumstances are right, helping. Indeed, one might help to correct one's damaged image in the situation or in general, but note that on this view correcting one's image would only be a *means* of alleviating feelings of embarrassment. Of the four proposals sketched in this section, this is the one which seems to have the most support in the psychology literature at the present time.[20]

As with guilt, the same caveats apply to these accounts of what mediates embarrassment and helping. They are all just sketches of more detailed models. They each encompass several more precise proposals. The problematic studies mentioned above are not intended to be decisive. And the four approaches can also be combined with each other in various ways.

3.3 POSITIVE MOOD AND HELPING

In the recent philosophical literature on character, much has been made about certain positive mood studies, in particular the dime helping experiment by Alice Isen and Paula Levin (1972).[21] In that study, forty-one adults were observed making phone calls at particular public telephone booths, and a randomly selected half of the unsuspecting participants would find a dime if they checked the coin return slot. Participants who were not alone or who did not check the slot were excluded from the study. Once a participant left the phone booth, a confederate started moving, "in the same direction as the subject and, while walking slightly ahead and to the side of him or her, dropped a manila folder full of papers in the subject's path. The dependent

---

[18] For discussion, see Apsler 1975: 152.

[19] For a review, see R. Miller 1996: 118–21.

[20] See, e.g. Apsler 1975, Cann and Blackwelder 1984, Edelmann 1987: 142, and R. Miller 1996: 4.

[21] See, e.g. Doris 1998: 504, 2002: 30, Snow 2010: 101–3, and Miller 2009a.

measure was whether the subject helped the female confederate pick up the papers."[22] The results? According to Isen and Levin:[23]

	Helped	Did not help
Found dime	14	2
Did not find dime	1	24

The basic idea is that finding a dime put participants in a good mood (or enhanced their already existing one), which in turn increased their willingness to help.

However, it turns out that this is perhaps not the best study to cite on moods and helping, as other psychologists have failed to replicate the results. Thus Gregory Blevins and Terrance Murphy employed similar experimental conditions and recorded the following results:[24]

	Helped	Did not help
Found dime	6	9
Did not find dime	15	20

Thus they concluded that there is, "no relationship between finding a dime and helping."[25]

In a later study, Levin and Isen (1975) varied their phone booth case in the following way. Instead of potentially helping a confederate pick up dropped papers, participants were given the opportunity to mail a stamped addressed envelope that seemed to have been inadvertently left behind in the phone booth. Thus participants noticed the letter before they checked the coin return slot.[26] Here were the results:[27]

	Mailed letter	Left letter
Found dime	10	1
Did not find dime	4	9

---

[22] Isen and Levin 1972: 387.

[23] Isen and Levin 1972: 387.

[24] Blevins and Murphy 1974: 326. Note that rather than dropped papers in Isen and Levin's experiment, participants in this study had the chance to pick up dropped packages.

[25] Blevins and Murphy 1974: 326.

[26] The purpose of this variant of the experiment was to test the alternative explanation that, "increased helpfulness could be seen as a reflection of their having been more likely to notice the person in need, rather than as a function of their mood state" (Levin and Isen 1975: 142).

[27] Levin and Isen 1975: 146.

But again others had difficulty with replication. James Weyant and Russell Clark, using five different locations and over four times as many test participants, recorded the following:[28]

	Mailed letter	Left letter
Found dime	12	42
Did not find dime	15	37

Given these findings, they concluded that, "subjects who found a dime did not mail an apparently lost letter more often than did subjects who did not find a dime."[29]

Thus the central mood effect study in the recent philosophical literature will not be my focus in this chapter. However, it does not follow that we should set aside all of the mood effect studies in general.[30] After all, there are dozens of other experiments in the psychology literature which exhibit the same trends as were found in these two studies by Isen and Levin. To take just one example, Robert Baron (1997) studied the effect of pleasant fragrances on helping in shopping malls. More specifically, he varied (i) the presence of odors, (ii) the gender of shoppers, and (iii) the order in which shoppers were first asked to fill

---

[28] Weyant and Clark 1977: 109.

[29] Weyant and Clark 1977. Schellenberg and Blevins 1973 also could not duplicate the results of a different helping experiment in Isen and Levin 1972.

In their 1979 study, Daniel Batson and his colleagues varied the dime case in such a way that, upon completing their calls, students at the University of Kansas were presented with the opportunity first to acquire information about the state of Kansas, and then soon afterwards help a female confederate who dropped a large folder of papers. The results were as follows for forty test participants:

	Acquired information	Did not acquire
Dime	18	2
No dime	12	8

	Helped	Did not help
Dime	13	7
No dime	6	14

Naturally it would be important to see if the data can be duplicated, especially given the small sample size. But even if it can be, the results of this study are not nearly as dramatic as those obtained by Isen and Levin 1972. After all, 30 percent of participants helped and 60 percent acquired information even without the mood elevation of finding the dime in the coin slot. For more, see Batson et al. 1979: 176–9.

[30] In a footnote (2002: 30 n. 4), Doris does acknowledge the replication trouble for Isen and Levin's experiments. Given the wealth of other similar experiments, it is not clear why he did not appeal directly to them instead.

out a survey on both their current mood and the air quality in the mall, or instead were first asked to make change for a dollar bill. Pleasant fragrances were those located outside stores like Cinnabon and Mrs. Field's Cookies, whereas clothing stores and the like were chosen as control sites. A participant helped only if she stopped and made change for the dollar bill, and only individuals of the same gender as the accomplice were approached. Here were the percentages of people who helped out of 116 shoppers surveyed:[31]

	No fragrance		Fragrance	
	Helping first	Mood first	Helping first	Mood first
Males	22%	25%	45%	61%
Females	17%	12.5%	61%	59%

Similar significant increases in helping (including self-reported willingness to help, commitment to help, and actual helping behavior) have been linked to positive moods brought about by, for instance, pleasant weather, being on a winning team, and imagining oneself taking a vacation to Hawaii.[32] Overall, there is now strong empirical evidence for a causal connection between positive moods and helping.[33]

My main focus in the remainder of this section is on the leading explanations for this connection. Psychologists typically conceptualize the impact of an environmental variable like fragrance on helping in the following way:

(i) The environmental variable is construed positively and produces positive affect in the person.

(ii) Positive affect significantly increases the activation and/or the functioning of a helping mechanism.

(iii) The helping mechanism in turn brings about relevant helping motivation and behavior.

Let me take each of these claims in turn:

(i) *Positive affect.* The standard terminology in the relevant literature here is not "positive moods" but rather "positive affect." While "affect" is typically used as a synonym both for "feelings" or "moods" on the one hand and for "emotions" on the other, the focus of the experimental work on affect and helping has been primarily on the role of elevated mood. These moods are temporary ones, of the kind that we typically experience on a daily basis and

---

[31] Baron 1997: 501. For more on the effect of fragrances on helping behavior, see Baron and Thomley 1994.

[32] See Cunningham 1979, Berg 1978, and Rosenhan et al. 1981 respectively.

[33] For overviews, see Carlson et al. 1988 and Schaller and Cialdini 1990.

often without giving them a second thought. In addition, the moods in the studies of interest here are only of moderate strength, rather than being intensely felt. As Joseph Forgas writes, these moods are, "low-intensity, diffuse and relatively enduring affective states without a salient antecedent cause and therefore little cognitive content (e.g. feeling good or feeling bad)."[34] Positive emotional states of joy or elation are not included under the heading of "positive affect" as they are comparatively rare in their occurrence and have an intensity that often grabs our attention immediately. Thus for my purposes in the remainder of this chapter, I will follow the standard practice in the relevant psychology literature and focus mainly on the influence that temporary and moderate positive affect has on helping.[35]

The first claim of this section, then, is that something in the environment which is construed positively by the person often generates an increased degree of positive affect in him.[36] We do not need psychology studies to tell us this; it is a commonplace that what we take to be good things happening to us tend to put us in better moods.

(ii) *Positive affect and increased activation.* In those cases where a positively construed environmental variable leads to increased helping, psychologists typically attribute this change to the role of positive affect in triggering or augmenting the activity of a relevant helping mechanism:[37]

Positive affect

↓

Activation of helping mechanism

where as usual the arrow is intended to symbolize causal influence. Unfortunately there has been a great deal of disagreement in the literature as to exactly how positive affect has this influence.[38] Given limitations of space, I will only examine the two leading models: *the mood maintenance hypothesis* and *the concomitance hypothesis.*

According to the first model, positive affect generates or triggers a distinct motive in a person to maintain the good mood she is experiencing. There might be a variety of ways of trying to maintain this mood, but helping other people is typically perceived as one such means because of the social rewards and gratification that are often experienced from doing so. Thus we have the following:

---

[34] Forgas 1995: 41.
[35] For related discussion, see Isen 1987: 205, Schaller and Cialdini 1990: 266, Forgas 1995: 41, and Isen 1999: 522.
[36] See, e.g. Schaller and Cialdini 1990: 271.
[37] For representative examples from the literature, see Isen 1987, Carlson et al. 1988, and Schaller and Cialdini 1990.
[38] For a helpful overview, see Carlson et al. 1988.

Positive affect
↓
Motive to maintain good mood
↓
Activation of helping mechanism

So the starting point of this first model is that positive affect increases helping because helping can prolong the positive affect.

This model has a number of important implications. One is that people in good moods should show different degrees of helping when the task is perceived to be pleasant as opposed to painful, depressing, or ungratifying. If their positive affect really does generate a motive to maintain their good mood, then other things being equal they should be resistant to helping tasks which are so costly or painful that they threaten their good mood. Secondly, as already noted, helping is only one way whereby a person might maintain a good mood. But if there are other actions available which by his own lights are also mood conducive but at the same time are much less costly, then in those cases we should *not* expect positive affect to lead to increased helping.[39]

These two implications can be incorporated into our diagram as follows:

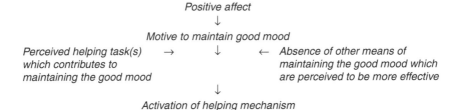

Similarly if the mood maintenance model is correct, then statement (ii) can be revised as follows:

> (ii*) Positive affect significantly increases the activation and/or the functioning of a helping mechanism, provided that the person does not take there to be other, more effective means of maintaining his good mood, and provided that the perceived helping task(s) itself is not thought to threaten his good mood.

The above, then, captures the basic idea behind the mood maintenance model.[40]

None of this implies that in all cases of positive affect and helping, the person helps for the *sole* or even the *dominant* motive of maintaining the good

---

[39] For related remarks, see Manucia et al. 1984, Carlson et al. 1988, Salovey et al. 1991, and Wegener and Petty 1994.

[40] Note that there are obvious similarities between this model and the guilt and embarrassment relief models from earlier.

mood. Rather, all that follows is that such a motive is making *some* contribution to the initial and continued performance of the behavior, perhaps in conjunction with other motives unrelated to mood maintenance. Such a partial contribution can still account for the fact that many participants experiencing positive affect tend to help more than controls. Thus at times the motive to maintain a good mood might be making a significant but weaker motivational contribution than other helping motives, while at other times it may be so strong that it outweighs those other motives to help when the target of the helping might contribute to developing a bad mood.[41]

Several studies seem to offer support for the mood maintenance model. Isen and Stanley Simmonds (1978) performed a variant of the dime-helping experiment but this time rather than helping pick up papers, participants were asked to read a series of statements which were described as designed to put people in a good or a bad mood. The results were that among participants who found a dime, the ones reading positively characterized statements would spend a longer time doing so than would those reading statements which allegedly put people in a negative mood. Participants who did not find a dime, on the other hand, showed no difference in their willingness to read either set of statements. The natural inference to make from these results is that participants who were put in a good mood by the dime read few negatively characterized statements because doing so threatened their good mood.[42]

The other leading model of the relationship between positive affect and helping is the *concomitance model*. As background to this model, it is important to appreciate the significant role that positive affect has to play in our psychological lives quite apart from its bearing on helping. Studies have shown that positive affect can influence all sorts of cognitive processing—among other things, it can lead to increased information acquisition, enhanced task performance, higher self-reward, increased cooperativeness, great optimism about the future, better recall of positive events in memory, and higher efficiency in some problem-solving tasks.[43]

The concomitance model makes use of these observations and holds that increased helping is merely a causal byproduct of one or more of these cognitive changes brought about by positive affect. Thus it could be that, for example, positive affect increases optimism about the future which in turn indirectly leads to more generosity in the present,[44] or that it triggers memories

---

[41] Similarly Isen notes that in certain cases it also might turn out that, "the motive to help another might outweigh one's desire to maintain one's own pleasant feelings if the other's need were very great or somehow more 'important'" (Isen 1987: 208). For helpful discussion of these issues, see Isen 1987.

[42] For related studies, see Forest et al. 1979 and Harada 1983. See also the discussion in Isen 1987: 207–9, Carlson et al. 1988, Salovey et al. 1991, and Wegener and Petty 1994.

[43] See, respectively, Batson et al. 1979, Baron and Thomley 1994, Mischel et al. 1968, Batson et al. 1979, Masters and Furman 1976, Isen et al. 1978, and Isen and Means 1983.

[44] Masters and Furman 1976.

of past helping which indirectly dispose the person to help more now.[45] The central idea, however, is the following:

Positive affect

↓

One or more cognitive changes

→ *Indirect activation of helping mechanism*

Hence the concomitance model is committed to denying that maintaining a good mood is the means by which positive affect increases helping.

The concomitance model itself is not so much a detailed proposal about the relationship between positive affect and helping, as it is a methodological approach to understanding this relationship, an approach which can then be fleshed out in a variety of ways such as the two noted in the previous paragraph.[46] Nevertheless, the model has several important implications of its own. One is that since helping is just a causal byproduct, as far as the participant's positive mood is concerned helping should not vary depending on her estimates of the costs associated with helping (barring cases of very high costs). Second and for the same reason, we should not expect to see participants bypassing opportunities to help when other less costly opportunities are available to maintain a good mood. Thus if the concomitance model is correct, then statement (ii) can be revised as follows:

(ii**) Positive affect significantly increases the activation and/or the functioning of a helping mechanism irrespective of whether the person takes there to be other, more effective means of maintaining his good mood, and irrespective of whether the perceived helping task(s) itself is thought to threaten his good mood.[47]

Statements (ii*) and (ii**) thus seem to provide clearly incompatible approaches to modeling the relationship between positive affect and helping.

There are studies which allegedly support the concomitance model as well. For example, in James Weyant's well-known 1978 study some participants had their affect levels raised by being made to believe they had performed well on a fake anagram test. After learning the results of the test, they were presented with an opportunity to donate their time to charity work. Of the 252 participants, random assignments were made as to which of them would be presented with one of the following opportunities:

American Cancer Society (high benefits) and door-to-door work (high costs)
American Cancer Society (high benefits) and desk work (low costs)
Little League Baseball (low benefits) and door-to-door work (high costs)
Little League Baseball (low benefits) and desk work (low costs)

---

[45] Isen et al. 1978.

[46] For a similar observation, see Carlson et al. 1988: 215.

[47] For related discussion, see Manucia et al. 1984, Isen 1987, and Carlson et al. 1988.

The percentage of participants who volunteered came out as follows:[48]

	Positive affect	Controls
High benefits/high costs	57%	33%
High benefits/low costs	62%	33%
Low benefits/high costs	52%	29%
Low benefits/low costs	62%	33%

Thus in light of these results it seems that positive affect served to augment helping regardless of the perceived costs and benefits, thereby supporting one of the implications of the concomitance model.[49]

Gloria Manucia and her colleagues' much debated 1984 study offers what is perhaps even more compelling support for the concomitance model. Mood was varied by asking participants to recall and reminisce about past happy experiences. They were then given a drug which unbeknownst to them was merely a placebo. Half were told that the drug has the effect of "freezing" their present mood state, while the other half were not told this. Finally, as participants were leaving the experiment, they were presented with an opportunity to donate their time to make calls for a local nonprofit blood organization. If the mood maintenance hypothesis were correct, then presumably participants whose mood states were "frozen" would help less than participants whose mood states were more liable, since helping would not be needed as a means in order to help maintain their moods given the freezing effect of the drug. However, it turned out that the amount of help volunteered was the same for happy participants with both frozen and liable moods. And this is exactly what the concomitance model would have predicted.[50]

Trying to adjudicate the debate between advocates of the mood maintenance and concomitance hypotheses would require more space than I wish to devote to the topic here. Indeed, before we are in a position to reasonably attempt to decide between them, it seems that far more experimental work needs to be done in the first place both to replicate existing studies and to more carefully test these leading models. By way of conclusion, let me again

---

[48] Weyant 1978: 1173.

[49] Note that there may be a way to plausibly reconcile Weyant's results with the seemingly incompatible results obtained by Isen and Simmonds in their dime-helping experiment. For one way of interpreting experiments such as Weyant's is as involving the stimulation of the agent's perceived moral obligations and the generation by those moral obligations of motivation to help. The motivation from this separate augmentation process in turn might have been strong enough to explain why participants volunteered for the unpleasant options even though no motivation was coming from the mood maintenance system. On the other hand, in Isen and Simmonds' study there was no clear appeal being made to the participant's sense of moral duty or obligation when he was asked to read a list of mood statements. The same is true of many other experiments offered in support of the mood maintenance hypothesis. For a similar proposal, see Carlson et al. 1988: 224.

[50] See Manucia et al. 1984. For a response on behalf of the mood maintenance hypothesis, see Wegener and Petty 1994. For related studies and general discussion of the concomitance model, see Cialdini et al. 1982, Shaffer and Graziano 1983, Manucia et al. 1984, Carlson et al. 1988, Cunningham et al. 1990, Schaller and Cialdini 1990, Wegener and Petty 1994, and Isen 1999.

stress that neither of these models purports to tell the whole story about what motivates people in good moods to help. In the case of the concomitance model, positive affect may have as one of its byproducts the strengthening of an already existing helping motive or the production of a weak motive that combines with others to lead to helping behavior.[51]

(iii) *Helping mechanisms and helping behavior.* When positive affect activates the person's helping mechanism, that mechanism in turn, whatever it might be, can cause the formation of motives to help. More precisely, it can do so, other things held equal—if the mechanism is malfunctioning or if the person is temporarily incapacitated, then we should not expect to see her come to the aid of others in need.

In conclusion, by combining statements (i), (ii), and (iii) together with either the mood maintenance or concomitance hypotheses, and holding other things equal, we get the following two diagrams for cases of helping in which positive affect has a role to play in motivating that behavior:

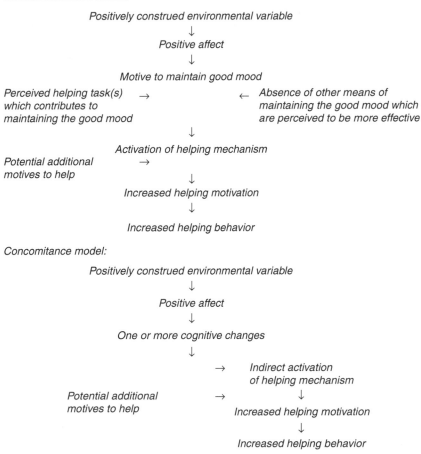

Mood maintenance model:

Positively construed environmental variable
↓
Positive affect
↓
Motive to maintain good mood

Perceived helping task(s)   →   ←   Absence of other means of
which contributes to   maintaining the good mood which
maintaining the good mood   are perceived to be more effective

↓
Activation of helping mechanism

Potential additional   →
motives to help
↓
Increased helping motivation
↓
Increased helping behavior

Concomitance model:

Positively construed environmental variable
↓
Positive affect
↓
One or more cognitive changes
↓

→   Indirect activation
of helping mechanism

Potential additional   →   ↓
motives to help   Increased helping motivation
↓
Increased helping behavior

---

[51] For related discussion, see Isen 1987: 208.

No doubt these diagrams oversimplify each of the two views, but they provide enough detail for my purposes in this chapter.

3.4 EMBARRASSMENT, POSITIVE MOODS, AND CHARACTER TRAITS

In the previous chapter, I examined six different implications of psychological work on guilt and helping. There is no need to revisit those implications in similar detail for the factors examined in this chapter, and so I will treat them much more briefly here, focusing especially on positive moods since the discussion of embarrassment would parallel so closely what was already said about guilt.

(a) *Many people do not perform even simple helping tasks.* As we have seen, many control participants will not make change for a dollar, among other simple helping tasks. While it is true that in their study of embarrassment, Cann and Blackwelder (1984) had 45 percent of controls help, even here a majority would not agree to take some papers 40 meters down a hall. Note as well that the tasks in question are often not particularly strenuous ones like making sizable donations to charity or forgoing a lucrative career to care for sick relatives. Furthermore, there were typically no other obvious helping opportunities in the immediate situation which might have been thought to be more significant than the experimental helping opportunity. Finally, many of the studies that have been done involved opportunities where something of moral significance was clearly at stake. For instance, mood studies have looked at helping tasks such as giving money to help South American children[52] and volunteering to donate blood.[53]

(b) *Two more enhancers, consistent behavior, and causally relevant mental states.* It should be clear why embarrassment and positive moods can be considered enhancers for helping in the right conditions. Other things being equal, we should expect the frequency of helping by a given person to increase when these factors are present along with the appropriate background conditions and moderately demanding helping opportunities.

Furthermore, many people should also exhibit increased helping as they encounter helping-relevant situations which have not yet been experimentally

[52] Cunningham et al. 1980.
[53] O'Malley and Andrews 1983. Hence I disagree with Snow (2010), who suggests that mood effect studies mainly involve "trivial forms of helping behavior" (103). I similarly disagree with Sabini and Silver 2005: 539–40, 561 n. 57 and Webber 2006a: 653, 2006b: 196. See also Prinz 2009: 124–5, who makes similar critical points of Sabini and Silver. Note as well that other effects, such as those associated with guilt and embarrassment, were not limited to trivial forms of helping.

studied, thereby supporting a form of cross-situational consistency. On the basis of these expectations, we can make predictions such as the following for positive moods using the mood maintenance hypothesis:

(P) Other things being equal, if people are experiencing at least intermediate levels of increased positive affect, and:
> (i) are presented with a moderately demanding way of helping someone thought to be in need
> (ii) take themselves to be able to help
> (iii) take the helping task to be effective is preserving their good mood
> (iv) take there to be no other alternative available actions which are more effective in preserving the good mood

then many of them will probably attempt to help.

Of course, there will be individual differences in what people regard as helpful for the person in need, how able they are to perform a given helping task, and what they consider to be conducive to maintaining their good mood. So as much as possible, these predictions need to be tailored to each individual's own idiosyncrasies.

Lastly, this discussion has suggested some of the mental states which seem to be at work in psychologically mediating the link between the enhancer and increased motivation to help. For positive affect and the mood maintenance hypothesis, for instance, I said that a positive mood can give rise to a motive to maintain that mood, which in turn can activate a helping mechanism. This helping mechanism is not mysterious—it would consist of an interrelated collection of beliefs and desires such as:

(a) Beliefs concerned with the relationship between helping others and various personal costs for me, such as lost time, money, alternative activities, and so forth.

(b) Beliefs concerned with the relationship between helping others and various social reactions to me, such as approval, gratitude, praise, and so forth.

(c) Beliefs concerned with the relationship between helping others and various moral consequences for me, such as living up to my norms, improving my moral standing and purity, and so forth.

(d) Beliefs concerned with how these various personal costs, social reactions, and moral consequences can impact my good mood.

(e) Desires concerned with helping when doing so will contribute towards extending my good mood, and more so than any alternative reasonable means of doing so which is thought to be available.

(f) Desires concerned with not helping when doing so will undermine my good mood, or will not extend the good mood as effectively as some alternative reasonable means of doing so which is thought to be available.

These mental states can, in the right conditions, give rise to increased motivation to help.

(c) *Assessing the motivation*. With the framework for thinking about egoistic and altruistic motivation from the previous chapter, I can quickly classify the motivation caused by a positive mood according to the mood maintenance model—it is egoistic, since the motive is concerned merely with keeping the person in that positive mood.

The concomitance model is less straightforward. There does not seem to be a motive that is directly formed by positive affect, and so it is not clear how to assess this model. Let me focus instead on the specific motive to help which is merely a side-effect of the influence of positive affect on cognitive processing, memory, and the like. It seems to not be altruistic—I would not be concerned about what is good for the other person for her own sake. Perhaps it is egoistic, if for instance the positive memories associated with helping in the past are highlighted and foster a motive to help so as to recreate those memories or the benefits that came along with past helping. Ultimately the way to move forward here will depend on how the concomitance model gets fleshed out. That the increased helping motivation is not altruistic is all I need to highlight here.

(d) *Most people do not possess the virtue of compassion*. Where does this leave most people with respect to the virtue of compassion? Again, a more careful discussion of this question will be reserved for chapter seven. But briefly, it seems to me that most of us are not doing very well with the first requirement from chapter two:

(a) A person who is compassionate, when acting in character, will typically attempt to help when in moderately demanding situations relevant to helping.

Control participants again fared poorly in many such situations, including ones where the need for help was obvious and the effort involved minimal, as was discussed earlier in this section.

What about the second requirement that:

(b) A compassionate person's trait of compassion will not be dependent on the presence of certain enhancers (such as moderate guilt, embarrassment, or good mood) in leading him to perform helpful actions, such that if these enhancers were not present, then his frequency of helping would significantly decrease in the same nominal situations.

But this is precisely what happens with an enhancer such as positive mood. A person whose helping behavior is reliable when he is in a good mood but not in a neutral one, is demonstrating that he is not yet a compassionate person—even if morally speaking it is a good thing that he is being more helpful than normal.

We come, then, to the third requirement:

(c) A compassionate person's trait of compassion will typically lead to helping which is done at least primarily for motivating reasons that are morally admirable and deserving of moral praise, and not primarily for motivating reasons which are either morally problematic or morally neutral.

Nothing like a morally admirable motive seems to be at work in positive mood-induced helping, especially on the mood maintenance model which involves:

Desires concerned with helping when doing so will contribute towards extending my good mood, and more so than any alternative reasonable means of doing so which is thought to be available.

Clearly this is a purely egoistic kind of motive which at the very least is morally neutral. Furthermore, we said that:

(c*) The virtue of compassion gives rise to compassionate motivation to help another person, and that motivation is *altruistic* motivation to help. Indeed, it is the fact that it is altruistic which grounds the moral praiseworthiness of this motivation.

Yet:

(C) On the leading models of positive mood-induced helping, the desires to help which partially constitute the helping mechanism are *not* altruistic desires.

So in addition to what I have already said about the role of guilt in influencing helping motivation and behavior, in this chapter I have supplied additional reasons for concluding that most (but not necessarily all) people do not have the virtue of compassion.

3.5 CONCLUSION

This chapter has repeated much of the work of chapter two with respect to two new enhancers for helping—embarrassment and positive moods. Despite unique and interesting details about the psychological processes associated with each of them, at the end of the day they again lead me to similar conclusions as I try to better understand our moral character with respect to helping.

4

Elevation, Activated Moral Norms, and Helping

This chapter introduces two more enhancers, and follows a similar course as the previous two chapters. The one significant twist, though, is the kind of motivation to which these enhancers seem to give rise. The first section of the chapter focuses on elevation, the second on activated moral norms, and the third on the implications for character.

4.1 ELEVATION AND HELPING

Enhancers of helping such as guilt and positive moods have been studied extensively in psychology for well over forty years. At the opposite end of the spectrum, the emotion of elevation has just barely been examined, and what work there is can be mainly found in several recent papers by Jonathan Haidt.[1] So in this section I will be brief.

In the movie *Pay It Forward*, the main character Trevor is given an assignment by his seventh-grade social studies teacher to create a plan that will make the world a better place. Trevor comes up with the idea of doing a good deed for another person, but with the requirement that instead of paying back the favor, the recipient "pay it forward" to a third party with the same stipulation. In that way the performance of good deeds can multiply, but they can also be done indirectly as others observe what is happening. At the end of the movie, hundreds of strangers come forward to honor Trevor for starting this movement and for how it inspired them to become better people.

The movie illustrates the powerful work of elevation, an emotion which can be felt when we see another person perform an action or have a certain

---

[1] See Haidt 2000, 2003a and Algoe and Haidt 2009.

character which we find to be particularly virtuous or morally admirable.[2] Most of us have had such emotional experiences, I would suspect, perhaps by watching Mother Theresa as she ministered to the poor in India, or by witnessing a friend or family member stand up for what is right in the face of scorn from peers or the community. Nor is elevation limited just to actual people or behavior. One of the many benefits of reading great literature is how it can inspire in us a powerful reaction to acts of self-sacrifice, heroism, virtue, and the like.[3]

Feelings of elevation have a distinctive phenomenology. As we know from our own experience, they are feelings of being uplifted and inspired in which our heart is said to be moved and energized, and we are more likely "to report physical feelings in [our] chests, especially warm, pleasant, or 'tingling' feelings."[4] I will return to the object of those feelings in a moment.

My central concern is whether elevation functions to increase helping. Given the nature of the emotion itself, we should surely expect that it would, and the few relevant studies support that expectation. Here I briefly mention two of them.[5] Dan Freeman and his colleagues (2009) examined the social dominance orientation (a measure of anti-black racism) for white participants who were given a chance to donate to a black charity. In one of their studies, the control group was paid five $1 dollar bills for their participation and given a story to read about a beautiful sunset. They were also provided an opportunity to help by placing any portion of their payment in a container designated to support the United Negro College Fund. The setup for the experimental group was the same except that they were instead given a story about the noble acts of forgiveness, comfort, and financial assistance displayed by several Amish people towards the wife and children of a man who murdered five young girls. The results were dramatic. Among controls, the average donation was $0.75 for participants who scored low on the social dominance orientation scale, but dropped in a linear fashion down to $0.00 for

---

[2] Algoe and Haidt distinguish elevation, which is tied to moral excellence, from admiration, which is tied to forms of non-moral excellence (2009: 107). In their 2009, they provide several studies aimed at showing that elevation, admiration, gratitude, and happiness refer to distinct positive mental phenomena.

[3] Haidt defines elevation in terms of "unexpected" acts of virtue (2000: 1), but I doubt that this is a necessary condition on the having of the emotion. I can be familiar with the life and work of Mother Theresa, and fully expect her to act in helpful ways for the poor, while still being elevated by her charity.

[4] Haidt 2003a: 282. See also Haidt 2000: 3, 2003a: 283, Aquino and Freeman 2009: 384, Algoe and Haidt 2009: 106, and Aquino et al. 2011: 704.

[5] See also Haidt 2000: 4, Landis et al. 2009, and Aquino et al. 2011: 711–14 as well as the additional studies in Freeman et al. 2009 and Schnall et al. 2010. For recent work on the relationship between moral identity and moral elevation, including behavioral studies of helping in a modified dictator game and of donations to a charity, see Aquino et al. 2011.

participants who scored high on the scale. By contrast, participants in the experimental condition averaged $0.75 regardless of how they scored on the scale.[6] Elevation, the reasoning of the experimenters goes, neutralized the effect of anti-black racism, thereby causing a higher level of helping in many of the participants who experienced it.

Given the previous chapter on positive affect, a natural worry is that what seems to be increased helping due to elevation, may really just be a result of participants put in a good mood by the inspiring stories of virtuous behavior. Simone Schnall and her colleagues (2010) have done the only test to date of this hypothesis. They divided participants into three groups—an elevation group which saw an inspirational clip from an episode of the Oprah Winfrey Show, a control group which viewed a deep sea exploration segment, and a mirth group which was shown a British comedy. After watching the relevant film clip and completing a survey, participants then observed the experimenter fail three times to open a computer file needed for the rest of the study. Participants were dismissed, but as what seemed to be an afterthought, they were asked by the experimenter if they would be willing to complete another questionnaire for a different study, which was described as boring but one which they could stop at any point. The questionnaire contained eighty-five math problems, and participants who agreed to help were secretly timed as to how long they worked on the problems.[7]

Thanks to the initial survey, participants self-reported high levels of elevation only in the elevation condition, and high levels of mirth only in the mirth condition. The mean number of minutes spent filling out the questionnaire for the additional study was almost identical in the mirth and control conditions (23.73 versus 19.90 minutes). However, participants in the elevation condition doubled their amount of work—40.64 minutes—and many went far beyond the one-hour time slot which they had signed up for in the first place.[8] If being in a positive mood was primarily responsible for increased helping in elevation cases, we should expect to find roughly similar results in the mirth and elevation conditions. But Schnall did not.

So there seems to be good, albeit preliminary support for an *elevation-helping hypothesis*. How should we characterize the motivation involved in such helping, when it stems directly from prior feelings of elevation? Here there simply are no published results upon which to draw that I am aware of, so I will have to speculate a bit. One possibility that can be ruled out is a desire to perform only the same kinds of virtuous actions which inspired the feeling of elevation in the first place. In the studies above, those virtuous actions had nothing to do with the specific helping tasks—donating money to the United

---

[6] Freeman et al. 2009: 81. [7] Schnall et al. 2010: 317.
[8] Schnall et al. 2010: 318–19.

Negro College Fund and filling out an unrelated questionnaire—which were subsequently performed. Helping is being inspired in general.[9]

Now we can easily come up with egoistic hypotheses for this motivation—perhaps the participants are inspired because of the recognition and rewards that the virtuous actions are bringing others. Or perhaps they see these virtuous actions and infer that by being virtuous too they can atone for their own misdeeds and guilt over past behavior. Still other egoistic hypotheses are conceivable. There are also ways of testing them by, for instance, using cases in which the person who acted virtuously is being scorned and punished by society.

My suspicion, for what it is worth, is that the egoistic hypotheses will prove to be inadequate as a complete account of the elevation-helping hypothesis. Both from our own experience and from the nature of the emotion in question, it seems that many people are drawn to the moral goodness or rightness of the behavior *as such*, and not as a means to getting egoistic benefits for themselves. On this approach, what elevation gives rise to are desires such as the following:

My desire to be a better person morally and to act better.[10]

My desire that I act virtuously or live the life of a virtuous person.[11]

My desire that there be more charity, benevolence, or kindness promoted in the world.[12]

My desire to help people in general.[13]

My desire to love other people in general.[14]

My desire to affiliate myself more closely with and emulate those who are morally virtuous or admirable.[15]

As Haidt notes, his research suggests that, "happiness energized people to engage in private and self-interested pursuits, whereas elevation seemed to open people up and turn their attention outward, toward other people."[16]

---

[9] This is not to deny that elevation can cause desires to emulate, admire, and draw closer to the person who does the virtuous action (Haidt 2000: 3–4, Freeman et al. 2009: 74, and Aquino et al. 2011: 704). The point here is that the scope of the desires which it gives rise to, is far broader than just being concerned with this one person. For a similar claim, see Schnall et al. 2010: 319.

[10] Haidt 2000: 2–3, 2003a: 282, Freeman et al. 2009: 74, Aquino and Freeman 2009: 385, Algoe and Haidt 2009: 108, 116, 119, 123, Schnall et al. 2010: 319, and Aquino et al. 2011: 704.

[11] Haidt 2003a: 276, 283 and Algoe and Haidt 2009: 106, 117.

[12] Haidt 2003a: 284.

[13] Haidt 2000: 2–3, 2003a: 282, 285, Aquino and Freeman 2009: 385, Freeman et al. 2009: 74, Algoe and Haidt 2009: 116, 119, 123, Schnall et al. 2010: 319, and Aquino et al. 2011: 704, 709. As one participant reported, "I felt the desire to be like my grandma, and have the same goodwill and huge heart—I wanted to help!" (Algoe and Haidt 2009: 112).

[14] Haidt 2000: 3, Aquino and Freeman 2009: 385, and Aquino et al. 2011: 704.

[15] Haidt 2000: 4, 2003a: 282, Aquino and Freeman 2009: 385, Freeman et al. 2009: 74, Algoe and Haidt 2009: 112, 123, and Aquino et al. 2011: 704, 715.

[16] Haidt 2003a: 282. See also Algoe and Haidt 2009: 123.

I will discuss how to classify these desires in section three. For now the important point of this section is that, given the preliminary studies that have been done, it seems that elevation is another way of increasing helping, and one which may set itself apart in its motivational upshot from the primarily egoistic motives that have been discussed up to this point in the book.

4.2 ACTIVATED MORAL NORMS AND HELPING

I have been examining enhancers for helping which some—especially those not familiar with contemporary psychology—might find to be rather unusual, such as elevation and embarrassment. Notably absent is an obvious candidate—moral norms and standards. Surely if a person comes to think that helping someone in need is moral obligatory or required, then that typically serves as a powerful way of enhancing helping. Doesn't it?

I do agree that moral norms can enhance helping. But the conditions under which they reliably do so, and the psychological processes involved in leading to helpful actions, are complex and difficult to spell out. In this section, I want to do three things: (i) sketch a model of those conditions and processes, (ii) briefly mention some of the empirical data which supports this model and, thereby, the role of moral norms as enhancing helping, and (iii) try to get clearer on the picture of motivation involved in such cases. This is an ambitious undertaking, and in places I will only be able to gesture at some of the exciting work being done in this area.

(i) *A model of moral norms and helping.* To focus the discussion, I limit the moral norms in question to deontological norms, that is, norms pertaining to what is morally obligatory, forbidden, and optional for a person to do. Furthermore, I just examine those norms which pertain in a direct and obvious way to the person's own helping behavior. Examples include a norm that it is morally forbidden to not help a drowning child in a pond, or that it is obligatory to donate 10 percent of my disposable income to charity. Finally, I assume that each person has a variety of moral norms relevant to helping, some of which are widely held and others of which are specific to that person's society, culture, religion, or individual preferences. The norm about drowning children is an example of the former; the norm about donating 10 percent is an example of the latter.

Here is a rough sketch of at least one central way in which activated moral norms might work as enhancers of helping:[17]

---

[17] In developing this model, I have been helped by Schwartz 1977: 241.

Appropriate background conditions
↓
Activation of one or more moral norms relevant to the person's helping
↓
Motive to comply with these norms
+
Potential beliefs about other actions available to the person besides helping
↓
Activation of the person's relevant helping mechanism
(Cost/benefit assessment and additional motives to support or avoid complying
with these moral norms depending on the assessment)
↓
Increased helping motivation
↓
Increased helping behavior

The key step in this model is the second one. "Activation" of a moral norm refers to its becoming relevant to psychological processing in the situation, such that it can play a central role in leading to motivation and action.[18]

The current literature in psychology suggests that there are two leading approaches for understanding what it is for a moral norm to be activated. One is a rationalist approach, perhaps most famously identified with Kant in philosophy and Kohlberg in psychology, where an activated moral norm is the content of a deliberatively formed and occurrent moral judgment that, for instance, I ought to save the child drowning in the pond.[19] On rationalist models, such judgments are often understood as arising from a prior process of rational deliberation or reasoning, as least part of which occurs at the

---

[18] A common expression that might be used here for activated moral norms is "moral judgments." There are two reasons why I have chosen to avoid it. First, the expression is sometimes used very broadly to encompass a person's standing normative commitments, her past conclusions of moral reasoning, her dispositions to believe that some action is right or wrong, and so forth. In this section, however, my focus is just on recently formed and psychologically active moral judgments pertaining to deontological norms and helping.

To address this terminological ambiguity, "occurrent moral judgments" could be understood as synonymous with "activated moral norms." But there is also a second and more important reason for avoiding talk of moral judgments in this chapter. In philosophy, it is common to find the expression "moral judgments" pertaining to acts of helping which are both third-personal (my judgment of what someone else should do or should have done) and first-personal (my judgment of what I should do or should have done). However, Haidt and Bjorklund have recently highlighted how in at least some areas of psychology the expression "moral judgment" is taken to refer only to third-person moral conclusions, whereas "moral decisions" and "moral decision-making" pertain to the first-person case (2008b: 242–4, 249. For similar usage, see Blasi 2009: 416). Since it is precisely such moral decisions that I am interested in here, this gives me a second reason to avoid using the label of "moral judgments" so as to try to avoid terminological confusion across disciplines. When in rare cases I do slip into this terminology, these qualifications should be assumed to apply.

[19] See, e.g. Kohlberg 1981, 1984 and Rest 1986 as well as Blasi's helpful experimental review (1980).

conscious level. This reasoning might, for instance, involve inferences from more general moral norms—in the example, perhaps a moral norm to help any child who is drowning, or more broadly still, to help another person whose life is in danger if so doing is feasible.

The second approach is the social intuitionist one, most often associated with the work of Jonathan Haidt, where moral norms are activated by relatively immediate gut feelings or intuitions that typically are not based on prior reasoning or deliberation, are formed unintentionally and automatically, and are often operating below the level of conscious awareness.[20] Hence in a particular situation a person can come to immediately feel that saving the child from the pond is the morally correct thing to do, and this norm is activated accordingly.[21] After the fact, a rational and reflective judgment might be formed or reasons given for why the person thought this way, but this often involves post-hoc justification and rationalization rather than an accurate reflection of the psychological processes that were undertaken in the first place.[22]

Neither of these approaches is likely to cover *all* cases of activated moral norms, as their advocates themselves typically admit.[23] Indeed, Haidt and Bjorklund have recently conceded that the social intuitionist view applies only to *third*-person moral conclusions (i.e. what someone else should do or should have done), and not to first-person conclusions (i.e. what I should do or

[20] See, e.g. Haidt 2001, Greene and Haidt 2002, Haidt and Joseph 2004, and Haidt and Bjorklund 2008a, b. Haidt and Bjorklund refine this claim such that the intuition "directly causes, or at least influences, moral judgments" (2008a: 198). In addition, intuitions are "sometimes but not always a part of an emotional response" (200). Rather, they take pains to clarify that intuitions are a type of cognition, and that the moral judgments which are caused by intuitions are a product of a cognitive process—"cognitive in the psychological sense that it involves information processing (mostly unconscious), and cognitive in the philosophical sense that moral judgments report beliefs that can be said to be better or worse, more or less accurate" (2008b: 250–1).

[21] Although on the social intuitionist model, this relation is not one of necessity; there can be cases in which an intuition is formed, but the person's other values resist it, thereby blocking the formation of a corresponding moral judgment (Haidt and Bjorklund 2008a: 188).

[22] For earlier discussions of similar ideas, see Darley and Latané 1970: 100 and Blasi 1980: 2–3, 9.

[23] See, for instance, Haidt 2001: 819–20 and Haidt and Bjorklund 2008a: 193–6. For criticism of the vagueness and scope of social intuitionist claims, see Pizarro and Bloom 2003, Jacobson 2008: 222, Narvaez 2008: 234–6, and Blasi 2009: 411–19. For replies, see Haidt 2003b and Haidt and Bjorklund 2008b. There is even a way for both models to be straightforwardly correct if, for instance, there are two distinct psychological processing systems for arriving at activated moral norms, with one being relatively automatic and relying on intuitions, and the other being more deliberative and relying on reflective moral judgments. Indeed, such a dual-processing approach to thinking in general seems to be widely popular (see, e.g. Chaiken and Trope 1999, Haidt 2001: 819–20, and Haidt and Joseph 2004).

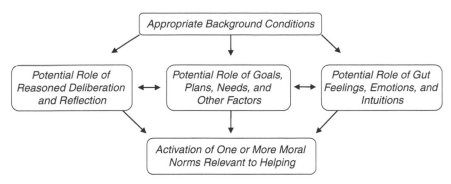

Fig. 4.1. The activation of one or more moral norms relevant to helping.

should have done).[24] In the first-person case, they acknowledge the importance of, "private, internal, conscious weighing of options and consequences,"[25]
that may also involve frequent deliberation by the person and the use of her
goals, plans, needs, memories, and other factors.[26] For my purposes, I can
remain neutral on how these details get worked out, and simply let this step in
the model encompass a much more detailed story about how norms become
activated in Figure 4.1.

With that said, let me return to the model and the background conditions
on the activation of moral norms relevant to helping. Some of these are strict
necessary conditions (such as (a) and (b) below), whereas others are factors
which are directly correlated with activation (such as the remaining conditions):

(a) *Awareness of norm.* Clearly a person has to have a belief about some
    moral norm for it to enhance helping. This belief need not be conscious;
    the condition is only meant to exclude the person's outright ignorance
    of the norm.

(b) *Awareness of need.* The person has to have some belief (whether
    accurate or not) about a need or situation that is relevant to the
    moral norm.[27]

(c) *Personal norm.* A person could be aware of a moral norm and even
    believe that it is a *social* norm, widely held to be important in society
    and bound up with societal rewards and punishments. But for all that
    the person could have little personal attachment to it. So activation is

---

[24] Haidt and Bjorklund 2008b.

[25] Haidt and Bjorklund 2008b: 242.

[26] For these and other factors, see Narvaez 2008: 234–5. As she writes about her own
deliberation, "[i]nstead of intuition's dominating the process, intuition danced with conscious
reasoning, taking turns doing the leading" (2008: 235). See also Pizarro and Bloom 2003.

[27] For some of the variables that impact awareness of need, see Schwartz 1977: 242.

also sensitive to the degree to which a moral norm is a personal norm, that is, a norm which is bound up with a person's self-conception such that conformity with the norm reliably fosters pride, satisfaction, relief, and the like, whereas violation of the norm reliably fosters guilt, regret, self-disappointment, and the like. Personal norms can be general—such as an obligation to give to charity—but when it comes to concrete acts of helping whose motivation stems at least partially from those norms, they are presumably far more specific—such as an obligation to give $50 to Worldvision.[28]

(d) *Background general norms.* Related to the last condition, activation may be sensitive to the presence of more general, personal moral norms relating to helping which, in a given situation, can be used to infer what is morally appropriate with respect to helping behavior in that situation. This can be especially applicable in novel situations where prior judgments about how to act have never been formed.[29]

(e) *Degree of moral identity.* Connected to both of the previous conditions is the degree to which being a moral person and having relevant moral virtues such as honesty and compassion is central to the person's identity or sense of self.[30]

(f) *Sense of responsibility.* Activation is expected to be correlated with the person's sense of responsibility to become involved in the situation or address the need.[31]

(g) *Sense of seriousness of need.* Activation is expected to be correlated with the person's sense of the seriousness of the situation or need in question.[32]

(h) *Sense of personal ability.* Activation is expected to be correlated with the person's sense of individual and collective ability to help address the particular situation or need in question, as well as his more general sense of ability, self-control, and free will.[33]

---

[28] For the contrast between personal and social norms, see Schwartz 1973: 353, 1977: 227, 231–2. For reviews of proposed social norms which are alleged to be widely held, and for critical discussion of their role in explaining helping behavior, see Staub 1974: 296–300, Darley and Latané 1970, Schwartz 1973: 349–51, 1977: 268–72, Pomazal and Jaccard 1976: 317, and Batson et al. 2003a: 283.

[29] See Schwartz 1977: 232–3.

[30] Here I follow the characterization of moral identity in Aquino and Freeman 2009: 376–9. For more, see Aquino and Reed 2002, Blasi 2005, Reynolds and Ceranic 2007, Aquino and Freeman 2009, and Aquino et al. 2011.

[31] For extensive discussion, see Schwartz 1970: 283–5, 1973: 351, 353–5, 1977: 246–50. See also Pomazal and Jaccard 1976: 324 and Bandura et al. 1996: 365.

[32] See Staub 1974: 302–3 and Schwartz 1977: 243.

[33] For recent work on perceived self-efficacy, see Cervone 1999: 318–29, Caprara and Cervone 2000: 118–21, Vohs and Schooler 2008: 49, and Rigoni et al. 2011. For agency and free will, see Bandura et al. 1996: 365, Vohs and Schooler 2008, Baumeister et al. 2009, and Rigoni et al. 2011.

(i) *Sense of consequences.* Activation is expected to be correlated with the person's sense of the consequences of his potential behavior for others.[34]

Other conditions have been proposed in the literature, and this list is certainly not intended to be exhaustive.[35]

Once a moral norm associated with helping is activated, then according to the model it can and typically will generate motivation of some degree to comply with that norm.[36] For now I will remain silent on what this motivation looks like, and will return to the question of whether it is egoistic or not at the end of this section. Next, this motive can activate a helping mechanism which, if all goes well, results in increased motivation to help and, other things being equal, increased helping behavior itself.

This helping mechanism is surprisingly complex. It is concerned, not just with what is the moral thing for the person to do, but also with expected costs and benefits for the person.[37] These include:

(a) The benefits for the person associated with following the moral norm.

(b) The costs for the person associated with following the moral norm.

(c) The benefits for the person associated with not following the moral norm and instead performing another available action.

(d) The costs for the person associated with not following the moral norm and instead performing another available action.

Typically these cost/benefit estimates will have a significant impact on whether the person actually ends up being increasingly motivated to help. If the costs of following the moral norm are sizable enough in her opinion, for instance, then that can overwhelm or undermine any motivation to do so. Not only that, but there can be an additional motive to *deactivate* the moral norm itself, so that it is no longer taken to be psychologically relevant to the person's behavior in this situation.[38] In that way, she can violate a personal norm without having to endure (as many of) the costs normally associated with doing so, such as feelings of guilt and self-criticism. On the other hand, if the cost/benefit assessment comes out in her favor, then that can lead to *additional* motivation to comply with the activated moral norm.

---

[34] See Schwartz 1970: 283–4, 1977: 229, Pomazal and Jaccard 1976: 324, and Bandura et al. 1996: 365–6.

[35] For instance, see recent work on the role of moral conviction (Skitka et al. 2005). For a more systematic treatment of norm activation and moral agency in general, see Bandura et al. 1996.

[36] There is no need to commit the model to anything stronger about this relationship, such as that there is a conceptual or metaphysically necessary connection, as some motivational internalists have claimed. I argue against motivational internalism in Miller 2008b, but can remain neutral on this debate here.

[37] In addition to Schwartz 1977, see Staub 1974: 299–300.

[38] See Schwartz 1973: 353, 1977: 227, 230, 254–5.

Exactly how a moral norm might be deactivated or neutralized is a complex matter. One approach would be by way of the person coming to no longer claim any responsibility for helping someone in need in the situation. Another way would be by denying any ability to help. Still another approach would involve revising the content of the moral norm so that it has an exception clause for cases like this.[39] And there are other approaches that can be imagined—indeed, any one of the background conditions along with any of the other previous steps in the model can be revisited and reconceived in light of the cost/benefit assessment.[40] I will return to this topic of deactivation in more detail later in this section.

It might help to walk through the model with an example. Suppose a friend approaches me, explains his medical condition which requires a bone marrow transplant, knows that I am a suitable donor, and requests that I make the donation. Up until this point, I have obviously never given much thought to this specific action, nor even to bone marrow donations in general. But after some consideration, suppose a moral norm—that it is obligatory for me to help my friend by donating—is activated in this situation. This activation is a function of a number of variables, including my background personal norms about helping friends, an awareness of his need and what it would take to address it, and a sense of responsibility to him as a friend and a donor match.

I have now deliberatively arrived at an occurrent moral judgment that I ought to donate bone marrow to help my friend. This then gives rise to motivation to comply with that obligation. But that is not the end of the story. For there are also plenty of costs involved in donating. Not to mention the anticipated benefits to be had on the vacation I would have to forgo to carry through with helping him. Nevertheless, given how important my friend is to me, the balance of costs over benefits is not significant enough to outweigh my motivation to follow through with the obligation, and so because of the activated moral norm, I am more motivated to help my friend than I would have been otherwise, and do end up going forward with the procedure.[41]

---

[39] As Kant noted in the *Groundwork*, "there arises a natural dialectic—that is, a tendency to quibble with these strict laws of duty, to cast doubt on their validity or at least on their purity and strictness, and, if possible, to make them conform better to our wishes and inclinations" (2002, 4:405 emphasis his). Thanks to an anonymous referee for reminding me of this passage.

[40] For a review of various approaches and the supporting evidence for them, see Schwartz 1970: 284–5, 1973: 354, 1977: 230, 255–62. The process can then become iterated, with new cost/benefit assessments being done in light of the revision of the earlier stages of the process (compare Schwartz 1977: 262–3). These issues will also be examined again in chapter nine when looking at moral disengagement with respect to aggressive behavior. I also consider them briefly in connection with cheating in *Character and Moral Psychology*, chapter three.

[41] Of course there will be important individual differences in this model at every stage, such as what personal norms a person has in the first place, how broad, important, and stable certain ones are to him, how strongly (if at all) he is motivated to comply with a given activated norm, what counts as a cost and benefit for him, how much comparative importance he puts in

(ii) *A few studies which are consistent with the model.* The example of bone marrow donations was not chosen by accident. Shalom Schwartz ran a study in which 148 female clerical workers from Wisconsin returned a questionnaire which had included medical information about transplants followed by a number of questions, the most important of which was, "If a stranger to you needed a bone marrow transplant and you were a suitable donor, would you feel a moral obligation to donate bone marrow?"[42] This question was designed to elicit the degree to which a personal norm about donating to a stranger had been activated. In addition, a 28-item measure of moral responsibility for acting in this situation was included in the questionnaire.

Three months later, 136 of these respondents were mailed a letter with an appeal from a renowned transplant specialist at the University of Wisconsin outlining the bone marrow procedure and its effects, and asking the person to volunteer to join a pool of donors. Each person was given four boxes to choose from, with the strongest commitment being, "I am interested in joining the bone marrow pool. Have your doctor call me for an appointment."[43] Nine percent of the group ended up checking this box.

The interesting result as far as the model is concerned is the relationship between the self-reported moral norm, moral responsibility, and volunteering. Participants who were low on the measure of responsibility had mean volunteering scores which showed almost no variation with how highly they rated their moral obligation to donate bone marrow. In fact, the group with the highest mean volunteering score was the one which gave the lowest rating on felt obligation to donate. However, as responsibility went up, so too did volunteering. Among participants high on responsibility, those with the highest reported degree of felt obligation had a mean volunteering score that was three times greater than the volunteering score for those with the lowest reported degree of felt obligation.[44]

Richard Pomazal and James Jaccard (1976) also used mailed questionnaires, this time to examine blood donations. They were sent to participants a week before an upcoming campus blood drive, and 270 usable copies were returned. Intention to donate was measured on a 7-point scale, as were a number of other variables including the participant's personal moral norm in the form of, "I personally feel I have a moral obligation to donate blood at the upcoming drive."[45] Of those who reported that they intended to donate, fifty-three actually did and 102 did not, with a correlation of 0.46 between intentions

---

following personal norms versus the cost/benefit assessment, and so on. For a similar reminder, see Schwartz 1977: 227.

[42] Schwartz 1973: 356, emphasis removed.
[43] Schwartz 1973: 357.
[44] Schwartz 1973: 358.
[45] Pomazal and Jaccard 1976: 320.

and behavior.[46] Most important for the model, the correlation between the moral norm and behavioral intention was 0.50, and between the moral norm and actual behavior it was 0.43.[47] Here are three other relevant correlations:[48]

	Correlation with behavioral intention
Social responsibility	0.52
Consequences for others	0.38
Cost	-0.34

Of course, all these results are only correlations, and so do not shed light on the causal impact of activated moral norms, but they are in line with what the model would predict.[49]

(iii) *Refining the model.* The discussion of moral norms thus far in this section has primarily drawn from work in psychology dating back to the 1970s. But a recent series of interesting and important studies by Daniel Batson and his colleagues can both refine this discussion and shed some light on the nature of the motivation which arises from norm-activation.

Suppose you are in a situation in which you have to make a choice between acquiring something that is only moderately conducive to your own self-interest, versus making sure that the same thing goes to another person instead. The choice is real, not hypothetical, and we can further stipulate that it is simple and mundane—plus let me add that there is clearly widespread consensus that the morally correct thing to do in this case is to choose in favor of the other person's interests. We can even make this moral principle highly salient to you beforehand (you knew it already going into the situation, but it can't hurt to call it to mind again), and we can follow up by asking afterwards whether you believed it or not. Suppose we do all this, and you do report that you believe the moral principle. Then it looks like a perfect kind of case in which the various background conditions would align in activating this moral norm, and you would be motivated to help out the other person and in fact would do so reliably. Yet in study after study with this setup, Batson found that most people help themselves, not the other person.[50] Something is missing from the model.

---

[46] Pomazal and Jaccard 1976: 321.

[47] Pomazal and Jaccard 1976: 322.

[48] Pomazal and Jaccard 1976: 324.

[49] For additional studies, besides the ones by Batson still to come, that are consistent with at least the broad outlines of the model, see Schwartz 1970, Zuckerman and Reis 1978, Erkut et al. 1981, Ma 2003, and Valdesolo and DeSteno 2008. For a review, see Schwartz 1977. And for a broad and supportive review of the relationship between moral reasoning and moral action with a focus on altruistic behavior, see Blasi 1980, especially 25–35.

[50] For the studies, see Batson et al. 1997a, 1999, 2002a, 2003b. For reviews, see Batson and Thompson 2001 and Batson 2008. For related studies and discussion, see Valdesolo and DeSteno 2007, 2008 and Watson and Sheikh 2008. For criticism, see Fernandez-Dols et al. 2010.

Here is the setup Batson typically used. Participants were told that they were part of a task assignment study. Individually, they were given the choice of whether to assign a positive consequences task or a neutral consequences task to either themselves or another participant, who (they were told) will simply assume the assignment was made by chance. The positive consequences task was such that for each correct response, the participant would receive one ticket for a raffle with a prize of $30 at the store of his or her choice. In the neutral consequences task, there would be no consequences for correct or incorrect responses but, "most participants assigned to the neutral conse- quences task find it rather dull and boring."[51] After making the assignment privately and anonymously, participants were asked about what was the morally right way to assign the task consequences, and to rate on a 9-point scale whether they thought the way they had actually made the task assign- ment was morally right.

What would you have done if you were given this task? Well, if you are like most people, you would have assigned yourself the positive task. Out of twenty participants:[52]

Assigned self to positive consequences task	16
Assigned other to positive consequences task	4

Furthermore, only 1 out of the 16 said that assigning oneself to the positive task was morally correct. Yet even these 16 participants rated the morality of their assignment in the middle of the 9-point scale (4.38).[53]

From here Batson performed many additional studies which were vari- ations of this initial setup. Suppose, for instance, that we make the moral norm at work here salient to participants just before they make their assignment by including a statement that "Most participants feel that giving both people an equal chance—by, for example, flipping a coin—is the fairest way to assign themselves and the other participant to the tasks (we have provided a coin for you to flip if you wish). But the decision is entirely up to you."[54] Ten participants flipped and 10 did not. Eight out of 10 in the first group said flipping was the morally right procedure, and 6 out of 10 said so in the second group. Most importantly:[55]

[51] Batson et al. 1997a: 1339.   [52] Batson et al. 1997a: 1340.
[53] Batson et al. 1997a. Although that was significantly lower than the 8.25 rating for the four participants who assigned the other participant to the positive consequences task (Batson et al. 1997a).
[54] Batson et al. 1997a: 1341.   [55] Batson et al. 1997a: 1342.

Assigned self to positive consequences task out of 10 who did not flip	9
Assigned self to positive consequences task out of 10 who *did* flip	9

This second result is grossly out of line with what the random flipping of a coin would have predicted. At least some of the participants in the second group must have flipped in a way that went in favor of the *other* person, but still assigned themselves the positive task. Self-interest seemed to have crept into their decision-making process in a significant way. Yet, and perhaps most surprisingly, those who flipped rated what they had done much more morally right (7.30 on a 1–9 scale) than those who did not flip (4.00).[56]

Here is another wrinkle—suppose participants are now given the option to have the experimenter assign them one of the two tasks, while also knowing what that assignment is going to be ahead of time. We get the following:[57]

Accepted experimenter's assignment if it would be the positive consequences task	17 out of 20
Accepted experimenter's assignment if it would be the neutral consequences task	11 out of 20
Remaining participants who assigned themselves to the positive consequences task (whether flipped or not)	12 out of 12

So in this experiment, only 22.5 percent of participants ended up with the neutral task. Yet for the 17 participants in the first group, on average they felt they had acted just as morally right (7.06 on a 9-point scale) as the 11 participants in the second group (7.91).[58]

What these results have suggested to Batson is that most of us (at least in these kinds of situations) are disposed towards a kind of *moral hypocrisy*, or appearing to be moral to oneself and others but avoiding the costs of actually being so if one can (try to) get away with it. After all, many participants were typically eager to flip the coin and report after the fact that this was the morally right course of action, but then distorted the process so that the results came out in their favor. Note that it is not the mere fact that they choose the positive consequences task for themselves that is hypocritical by itself—there could be cases where a person thinks of acts like this as being in line with her self-interest, and is not even aware of its moral ramifications. Nor is their hypocrisy captured here by the additional fact that the participants also seemed to believe in the moral principle that flipping the coin is the morally right way to assign the task consequences. For then we would just have a perfectly familiar case of weakness of will, in which you believe that something is right but fail to

---

[56] Batson et al. 1997a: 1341.   [57] Batson et al. 1997a: 1343.
[58] Batson et al. 1997a.

be sufficiently motivated to do it. Rather, their hypocrisy arises when they (i) choose the positive consequences for themselves, while (ii) seeming to believe that flipping the coin and following what it indicates is morally correct *and* (iii) still claiming to themselves and others to have made the morally right task assignment.[59]

How is it really possible for these participants to pull off this combination? In particular, it is one thing to appear to be acting morally to others. But these participants are also appearing to be moral to *themselves* too. How are they able to downplay the costs associated with guilt, regret, and hypocritical behavior for acting immorally by going against what they know to be right, and also experience the self-rewards for moral behavior? Here I can now revisit the issue of how moral norms can be deactivated or have their motivation be undermined or overwhelmed, although the claims in what follows should not be taken to necessarily generalize beyond the specific kinds of cases I am examining here without further experimental evidence. One possibility is that the participants in question have come to deny any moral responsibility in this situation, thereby deactivating the moral norm. Or perhaps they have come to deny that they are able to carry out the task, or that they are no longer aware of the likely consequences of their actions. But there is no evidence to suggest that these background conditions have failed to apply in these particular cases.[60] Another possibility is that these participants have come to think that their behavior is in line with their moral standards, thereby allowing them to not feel guilt and to even perhaps take pride in their behavior. This could be because they have revised the content of the moral principle to create an exception clause for this one kind of situation. Or it might be that they lie to or deceive themselves about what the principle says in the first place.

But the results already cited above cast doubt on these hypotheses as well.[61] Batson also introduced another variety of the setup whereby the moral principle is made salient, a coin is provided, and the coin is clearly marked on one side with "SELF to POS[ITIVE]" and "OTHER to POS" for the opposite side.[62] In those cases when the coin lands on OTHER, it seems very hard to think, in spite of what the moral principle and the coin both say, that a person who still assigns himself to the positive consequences task would take that to be morally acceptable. Furthermore, only 2 out of 40

[59] For more on characterizing moral hypocrisy, see Batson et al. 1997a: 1335–6, 1999: 525–6, 2002a: 330, Batson and Thompson 2001, and Batson 2008, 2011: 222–4.

[60] See in particular Batson 2008: 57. Studies involving other types of situations have found denial of responsibility, for instance, to be an important part of the explanation for a failure to conform to personal norms, as we already saw with the bone marrow study. See, e.g. Schwartz 1973, 1977: 230, 256–62.

[61] Batson et al. 1999: 526. As emphasized in the previous footnote, this is not to say that these hypotheses are not accurate in many other cases of activated moral norms and subsequent moral or immoral behavior, but the focus here is only on understanding the data generated by the Batson studies mentioned above.

[62] Batson et al. 1999: 527.

participants reported afterwards that the most morally right thing to do is to assign themselves to the positive consequences task.[63] Yet of the 28 who chose to flip:[64]

Assigned self to positive consequences task	24
Assigned other to positive consequences task	4

Furthermore, those who assigned themselves to the positive consequences task after flipping the coin again thought that they were being highly moral (7.42 on a 9-point scale), while those who made the same assignment without flipping the coin did not (3.90).[65] So marking the coin and thereby reducing the ambiguity as to what the fair assignment should have been, did nothing to undermine moral hypocrisy. We are still without an explanation for how it seems to work—more on that in a moment.

In terms of my model of moral norms and helping, the studies mentioned above suggest that participants could have had their relevant moral norm activated—in this case, the norm that flipping a coin and conforming to its results is the morally right way to behave—and even be motivated to some extent to do so. But this motivation must have been so weak that, once the cost/benefit analysis was done on an alternative action of secretly ignoring the coin when it went against the person and instead assigning oneself to the positive task, it became fairly easy to outweigh or undercut the motivation to

---

[63] Batson et al. 1999: 529.   [64] Batson et al. 1999: 528.

[65] Batson et al. 1999: 529. A natural thought here is that this result does not distinguish between those participants who flip, win, and then rate the morality of their action, versus those who flip, lose, change the task assignment to favor themselves, and then rate the morality of their action. It could be that the former group (rightly) rates the morality of their action highly, since they are following the fair procedure, whereas the second group rates it low, perhaps around 4.0 as do those who do not even bother flipping the coin and just assign themselves the positive task. If the results came out this way, then we would have evidence for moral weakness of will, to be sure, but not for moral hypocrisy, since the second group would be honest about the moral failure of their action.

In a later study, Batson tested this possibility using secret observations of how each participant who flipped ended up having his or her coin fall (2002a: 334–8). Of the thirty-two who flipped the coin, sixteen got OTHER to POS or otherwise fiddled the coin flip so that it came out in their favor (i.e. repeated flipping). For this group, the mean rated morality of their action was 5.56, which was significantly higher than the 3.89 for the group which assigned itself to the positive task without using the coin. On the other hand, it was also lower than the 7.45 for the group which flipped, won SELF to POS, and assigned themselves to the positive task (336). The upshot is that, "even though the coin had no more effect on their decision than it had on the decision of those who did not claim to use the coin at all, the fiddlers still said they thought the way they made the task assignment decision was more moral. Their sham reference to use of the coin seems to have provided sufficient appearance of morality that they could claim to have acted, if not totally morally, at least moderately so" (337).

do the right thing. So activated moral norms look to have little enhancing power after all, or at least in these kinds of cases.

But all is not lost for moral norms. Batson was able to discover two variables which separately helped to ensure that motivation to comply with the relevant moral norm did win out. The first variable was the introduction of a mirror. The setup was as usual with no labeling of the coin, but now a mirror was propped up against a wall on the only table where participants could fill out their forms. For one group of participants, the mirror was facing them; for the other, it was turned to the wall. This ended up making a significant difference:[66]

	Assigned self to positive consequences task	
	No facing mirror	Facing mirror
Did not flip coin (29)	85%	62%
Flipped coin (23)	85%	50%

Here for the first time we see results in line with what the moral norm requires—for those who flipped the coin and were facing the mirror, the overall results were as chance would predict.

What is the best explanation for the contribution made by the mirror? Batson appeals to research on the psychology of self-awareness, in which objects like mirrors can, "heighten awareness of discrepancies between behavior and salient personal standards, creating pressure to act in accord with standards."[67] In this case, the mirror served to highlight to the person the difference between what he believed was morally correct in this situation, and opposing temptation to act out of self-interest. This heightened awareness seemed to either create extra motivation to comply with the moral norm or lessen motivation to do the self-interested thing (or perhaps both).[68]

In addition to serving as one variable for supporting the role of activated moral norms as enhancers of helping, self-awareness also provides a clue about where to find a plausible explanation for how moral hypocrisy is possible. That clue has to do with a particular form of self-deception.[69] Rather than thinking that participants simply revised their moral standards to make their behavior look acceptable in their own eyes, perhaps instead they were

[66] Batson et al. 1999: 530.

[67] Batson et al. 1999: 529. For more on the psychology of self-awareness, see Wicklund 1975. Self-awareness is also mentioned again in *Character and Moral Psychology*, chapter three when discussing cheating motivation.

[68] Thus the mirror can be said to increase the salience of the self's own personal standards of evaluations. Another hypothesis, though, is that it increases the salience of standards of social evaluation, i.e. how others might judge him. Batson tested this possibility and did not find support for it (2002a: 331–4).

[69] See Batson et al. 1997a: 1336, 1346, 1999: 526–7.

engaging (often unconsciously) in an act of self-deception whereby they avoided comparing their behavior to the relevant moral standards. If the two are kept apart from each other, that mitigates the perceived costs of not acting morally while doing nothing to mitigate the perceived benefits of acting self-interestedly. But with increased self-awareness, the discrepancy between the moral principle and the self-interested option was made especially salient so that it became psychologically difficult for many participants to employ this particular form of self-deception.[70]

The other variable which Batson found to increase motivation associated with activated moral norms had to do with perspective-taking. Take the usual setup, but with the caveat that the default starting point is for the participant to be awarded two raffle tickets for every correct response, while the other participant gets zero tickets. Then the task assignment becomes whether the participant is willing to change the assignment so that it is symmetrical with both people receiving one ticket each. For controls, 38 percent changed the task consequences to symmetrical. However, for the experimental group, 83 percent did.[71] The difference? This group was instructed to adopt the perspective of the other person—"we would like for you to imagine yourself in the place of the other participant."[72] This is different from imagining what the other person is feeling or experiencing—the instructions here are very much in line with the Biblical mandate to, "Do unto others as you would have them do unto you."[73]

So Batson's studies on moral hypocrisy suggest two additional conditions whereby activated moral norms are increasingly likely to give rise to helping. In addition, the studies help to refine the overall (but still too simple) model as follows:

> *Activation of the relevant helping mechanism*
> *(Cost/benefit assessment and additional motives to (i) support norm compliance*
> *if the assessment is favorable to the person or (ii) to not comply if the*
> *assessment is too costly overall, while also as much as possible still*
> *appearing to be moral to oneself and others)*

---

[70] Batson et al. 1999: 527, 529, 531–2, 2002a: 331 and Batson and Thompson 2001: 55. Batson et al. 1999 ran a third study in which they examined whether the motivation involved in self-awareness was still moral hypocrisy as opposed to a motive to care about morality for its own sake, and found evidence in favor of the first option. For very interesting discussion of some of the morally problematic effects of increased self-awareness, see Batson et al. 1999: 535.

[71] Batson et al. 2003b: 1199.

[72] Batson et al. 2003b: 1198, emphasis deleted.

[73] Matthew 7:12. For more on the difference between these two perspectives, see chapter five, section one.

Interestingly, in the familiar variant of the experiment with a positive and a neutral task assignment, participants who adopted this perspective did not assign the other person to the positive task any more than did participants who did not do any perspective taking (25% in each case) (Batson et al. 2003b: 1195). For an explanation of these different results in the two experiments involving perspective taking, see Batson et al. 2003b: 1199–200.

Finally, there is one more issue which I alluded to earlier. In the initial model, I said that activated norms give rise to a "motive to comply with the norms in question." What is the nature of this motive? Is it merely an instrumental motive aimed at a deeper ultimate desire to follow moral norms so as to win egoistic benefits or avoid egoistic costs for myself? Or perhaps it derives from an ultimate desire to be moral or follow moral norms for their own sake? Or perhaps some third account is more promising? One final study by Batson can shed some light on this topic, although much further work is needed.

Consider again those participants who are about to flip the coin. At that point before they see what the outcome is, what is the nature of their motivation? Perhaps for the moment at least some of them want to do the morally right thing (follow the dictate of the coin, however it ends up landing) for its own sake. If the coin lands in their favor, then the outcome also aligns with their self-interest, which is so much the better. But if it lands in the other person's favor, then they might see what being fair would cost them, and their self-interested motives end up outweighing their initial moral motivation. Or perhaps this is all fanciful—perhaps when they are flipping the coin, all they want is what they think is ultimately in their self-interest, which at the moment is just flipping the coin so as to benefit from appearing to be moral.[74]

One way to test these hypotheses, Batson reasoned, is to see if participants cared about whether the flipping of the coin and so the task assignment was done by themselves or by the experimenter. If the egoistic hypothesis is correct, then they should want to flip the coin themselves so that they can rig the outcome. If the other hypothesis involving an ultimate desire to be moral is correct, however, it should not matter who flips. When the experiment was actually run with this choice option, 80 percent of those who used a coin wanted the experimenter to flip it. This initial evidence thus favors postulating a motive to follow the moral norms for their own sake.[75] I will consider what to make of such a motive in the next section.

Suppose this hypothesis about ultimate moral motivation is correct. How strong and psychologically powerful of a force does it typically seem to be? The evidence suggests, at least given the current state of research, that for many of us it is only weak in strength. We can already see this from the studies cited above when so many participants do not actually follow their moral principle about what is a fair task assignment. In addition, Batson varied the previous setup so that the assignment was between a positive and a *negative* task, where

---

[74] More generally, Schwartz suggests that we have a "desire to act in ways consistent with one's values so as to enhance or preserve one's sense of self-worth and avoid self-concept distress" (1977: 226). Such proposals naturally call to mind Kant's claim that, "Out of charity I am willing to grant that most of our actions are in accord with duty; but if we look more closely at the devising and striving that lies behind them, then everywhere we run into the dear self which is always there; and it is this and not the strict command of duty (which would often require self-denial) that underlies our intentions" (2002, 4:407).

[75] See Batson and Thompson 2001: 55–6.

the latter involved receiving "mild but uncomfortable" electric shocks for each incorrect response. With this change, only 25 percent of participants offered to let the experimenter flip the coin, and another 25 percent flipped themselves, with 91 percent choosing the positive task. The remaining 50 percent of participants simply bypassed the pretense of the coin flip and gave themselves the positive task while readily admitting that this was not morally right.[76] The implication is that moral motivation caused by activated moral norms seems to be weak and highly susceptible to being outweighed in cases of this type where the person's self-interest is at stake.

Let me take stock of this section. I have advanced an *activated moral norm-helping* hypothesis, outlined some of the conditions which are conducive to this helping, and provided a sketch of some of the psychological processes at work in giving rise to it. Activated moral norms can thereby serve to increase helping, but the ways in which they do so are far from transparent, perhaps especially to ourselves.

4.3 ELEVATION, ACTIVATED MORAL NORMS, AND CHARACTER TRAITS

What does all of the above have to do with character? Once again, there is no need to go through the same six implications again in detail. Let me run through them briefly, focusing in particular on the story about motivation.

(a) *Failure to help, two more enhancers, consistent behavior, and causally relevant mental states.* Once again, we find that many control participants do not perform simple helping tasks, such as giving another person a chance to win a $30 raffle prize. And it was not as if there were better options available for helping others even more; in laboratory studies such as Batson's, the only alternative to performing the helping task was to actively benefit oneself.

Nevertheless, we have seen that two more enhancers of helping should be added to the list in the form of elevation and activated moral norms. These enhancers can give rise to consistent patterns of motivation and behavior, such as the following:

(P) Other things being equal, the frequency of helping by a person will be a function of the background conditions for positively activating one or more moral norms that she associates with helping, and the subsequent absence of a cost/benefit assessment which favors deactivating those norms. When the conditions for activation are not present, or when there are outweighing costs associated with helping by her own lights, then other things being equal we would expect there to be little to no helping exhibited.

---

[76] Batson and Thompson 2001: 56.

Individual differences along a number of different dimensions (the content of the norms, what counts as a cost and a benefit, and so on) are to be expected here.

And we have seen what some of the mental states are which constitute the helping mechanism connecting activated moral norms with increased motivation to help:

(a) Beliefs concerned with the relationship between complying with the relevant moral norms and various beneficial social reactions such as approval, gratitude, praise, and so forth.

(b) Beliefs concerned with the relationship between complying with the relevant moral norms and various personal costs such as lost time, money, alternative activities, and so forth.

(c) Beliefs concerned with the relationship between not complying with the relevant moral norms and various personal benefits such as increased time, money, alternative activities, and so forth.

(d) Beliefs concerned with the relationship between not complying with the relevant moral norms and various personal costs such as social disapproval, guilt, lost trust, and so forth.

(e) Beliefs concerned with how to weigh these various costs and benefits.

(f) Desires concerned with helping when doing so will contribute towards complying with the relevant moral norms, provided the benefits of doing so are not (significantly) outweighed by the costs.

(g) Desires concerned with not helping when the benefits of complying with the relevant moral norms are (significantly) outweighed by the costs, while also desiring to as much as possible still appear to be moral both to others and to oneself.

(b) *Assessing the motivation.* For both elevation and activated moral norms, I noted that very little empirical evidence is available about the motives they give rise to. But I did claim that preliminary work in psychology gives us some reason to postulate desires such as these:

A desire to help in order to be a better person morally and to act better. (Elevation)

A desire to help in order to affiliate myself more closely with and emulate those who are morally virtuous or admirable. (Elevation)

Desires concerned with helping when doing so will contribute towards complying with the relevant moral norms. (Activated moral norms)[77]

---

[77] Here I ignore the extra complication about the benefits of helping not being (significantly) outweighed by the costs. The omission of this clause does not bear on the main point of the above, which is that such a desire is not altruistic, although it does raise the issue of whether it is egoistic or not.

What should be made of these desires? Both intuitively and on my proposal (E) from chapter two, they are not egoistic desires—their primary concern is not with what benefits me. But at the same time, again both intuitively and on my proposal (A), they also seem to not be altruistic desires—their primary concern is not with what benefits another person.[78] Rather, they belong to a third category of motivation—moralistic motivation—where:

(M) A person's ultimate desire is *moralistic* just in case:

    (i) It concerns the obtaining of (what is thought to be) a moral state of affairs (such as the performance of a moral action, the development of a moral character, and so forth).

    (ii) The desire cannot be satisfied unless (what is thought to be) the moral state of affairs obtains, and obtains even if there are no egoistic or altruistic benefits for those involved.

Even if this way of characterizing moralistic motivation does not capture all the relevant cases, to say that the specific desires above count as moralistic seems highly intuitive. Nor should the existence of a third category of motivation besides egoistic and altruistic motivation be surprising, as I will suggest in more detail in chapter six.

(c) *Most people do not possess the virtue of compassion.* Once again, control participants seemed to not come out very well on the first requirement from chapter two:

(a) A person who is compassionate, when acting in character, will typically attempt to help when in moderately demanding situations relevant to helping.

What about the second requirement that:

(b) A compassionate person's trait of compassion will not be dependent on the presence of certain enhancers (such as moderate guilt, embarrassment, or good mood) in leading him to perform helpful actions, such that if these enhancers were not present, then his frequency of helping would significantly decrease in the same nominal situations.

Let's start with elevation. There seems to be nothing morally problematic about helping more frequently due to being inspired by Mother Theresa's acts of kindness towards the poor, at least other things being equal. So when it comes to (b), at least, elevation and compassion do not seem to conflict. This is in stark contrast to the conclusions of the previous two chapters.

---

[78] However, two of the other desires listed in section one—my desire to help people in general, and my desire to love other people in general—would count as altruistic.

The case of activated moral norms is more complicated. On the one hand, it would seem to be a good thing if people helped more than they currently do thanks to their coming to (occurrently) believe that they have various moral obligations to help. On the other hand, a compassionate person might be expected to be sensitive to other people's needs, even without engaging in deliberation about what she morally ought to do or forming a gut feeling about the deontological status of helping. But for my purposes, I can remain neutral here on whether there is a conflict between this particular enhancer and requirement (b).

Where the most interesting discussion lies is with the third requirement:

> (c) A compassionate person's trait of compassion will typically lead to helping which is done at least primarily for motivating reasons that are morally admirable and deserving ral praise, and not primarily for motivating reasons which are either morally problematic or morally neutral.

How do the motives I just highlighted above fare in connection with elevation and activated moral norms? In chapter two, I already registered my view that:

> (MD) If a person performs a morally appropriate and helpful action, but does so only as a result of one or more ultimate desires whose main concern is with the satisfaction of impersonal moral requirements (such as a desire to do the right thing or to repair past wrongs in general), then the action does not result from virtuous motives.

As Michael Stocker says about such motivation, what is missing is, "simply—or not so simply—the [other] person . . . these ways are dehumanizing."[79] And yet this is precisely what is involved with:

> A desire to help in order to be a better person morally and to act better.

Such a desire can lead to helping, to be sure, but not helping which is ultimately concerned with what would benefit the other person. Rather it is my moral improvement which is the ultimate focus.

Again, though, I do not need as strong a claim as (MD). All I need is the requirement that:

> (c*) The virtue of compassion gives rise to compassionate motivation to help another person, and that motivation is *altruistic* motivation to help. Indeed, it is the fact that it is altruistic which grounds the moral praiseworthiness of this motivation.[80]

---

[79] Stocker 1976: 71–2.

[80] But suppose I am wrong about this, and moralistic motivation is able to count as a form of genuinely compassionate motivation. That still would not render the motives formed by activated moral norms compatible with requirement (c) for compassion. To see why, recall the discussion at the end of the previous section about activated moral norms and how weak and easily overridden this moralistic motivation can be in the face of self-interested costs to the

Yet:

(C) On all the leading models of elevation- and activated moral norm-induced helping, the desires to help which partially constitute the helping mechanism are *not* altruistic desires.

Recall that activated moral norms can give rise to:

Desires concerned with helping when doing so will contribute towards complying with the relevant moral norms, provided the benefits of doing so are not (significantly) outweighed by the costs.

Not only is this not an altruistic desire, it has disturbing consequences for moral behavior. As Batson writes, "A principle that says, 'Do not give your own interests priority...unless there is personal cost,' is tantamount to having no real principle at all. It turns morality into a luxury item—something one might love to have but, given the cost, is content to do without."[81]

4.4 CONCLUSION

One new element we have seen in this chapter is the motivational role that moralistic desires might play in causally influencing us to help. Nevertheless, the prospects for the widespread possession of the virtue of compassion do not yet appear to be any stronger.

In the next chapter, I will examine only one more enhancer, empathy, and the way in which it seems to give rise to altruistic motivation. That might finally give us some reason to be optimistic that the trait of compassion is widespread after all.

---

person. As Batson and Thompson note, "If, as is often assumed, the social role of morality is to keep individuals from placing their own interests ahead of the parallel interests of others, then cost-based justification poses a serious problem" (2001: 56).

[81] Batson and Thompson 2001: 56.

5

Empathy and Helping

Feeling empathy for someone in distress is also known to dramatically increase helping. But unlike the previous enhancers we have seen thus far in Part Two, there is good reason to believe that the motivation to help which arises from empathizing with another is *altruistic* motivation rather than egoistic motivation, moralistic motivation, or motivation of some other kind. This will be an important result, not only for further developing my account of Mixed Traits later on, but also for examining how realistic it is to think that many of us have acquired the virtue of compassion.

In this chapter, I first try to clarify at the conceptual level what empathy involves. Then I turn to the experimental literature on empathy and helping in section two, and to the literature on empathy and altruism in section three. Finally I step back from these empirical details and draw some familiar implications in section four and examine some issues about empathy and compassion in section five.

5.1 CHARACTERIZING EMPATHY

First let me try to clarify what empathy involves. I will not attempt anything like an analysis of the concept here, nor will I be concerned with reviewing the different modes of empathetic arousal which are capable of being experienced by infants, young children, and adults as outlined in the developmental literature on empathy.[1] Rather, my concern will merely be with drawing attention to some of the central features of empathy in paradigm cases. Furthermore, these will be cases involving empathetic *feelings*; one might be able to empathize with how a person came to form certain beliefs or be misled by the evidence, but such cognitive objects of empathy will not be my concern here.[2]

---

[1] For an overview, see the papers in Eisenberg and Strayer 1987a.

[2] In the remainder of this section I have been helped by Snow 2000. For related discussion, see also the papers in Eisenberg and Strayer 1987a, as well as Sober and Wilson 1998 and Darwall 1998, 2011.

It is becoming increasingly common to distinguish three broad kinds of empathy. What they all share is some form of change in one's own emotional life in virtue of particular feelings experienced by another person.[3] But they also exhibit important differences. Let me briefly mention the first two kinds of empathy before turning my attention to the third and, for the purposes of this chapter, central kind.[4]

(a) *Emotional contagion.* Young children can have empathetic feelings caused by emotional contagion in which they "catch" a feeling of a parent directly from the parent's body language, facial expressions, or tone of voice.[5] The phenomenon is not limited to children, though. We are all familiar with automatically picking up the mood of a group of people, for instance when we first walk into a meeting or arrive home to our family. This simplest and earliest form of empathy in human development is unique in that it does not seem to require having the intellectual and imaginative capacity to adopt another person's perspective.

Stephen Darwall highlights two important features of contagion cases.[6] First, while we might pick up the same feeling or emotion through contagion from another person, that acquired feeling need not have the same intentional object as the original feeling did. Even though I might not know what people at the meeting are worried about, I can become worried myself. Or if someone is angry at me, I can catch his anger too, but not in such a way as to also become angry with myself!

Secondly, emotional contagion often occurs under the conscious radar. I might become worried at the party, without realizing I have caught this worry from the people around me. Not only this, but I also might not realize

---

[3] As Stotland famously characterized empathy it is "an observer's reacting emotionally because he perceives that another is experiencing or is about to experience an emotion" (1969: 272). See also Davis 1994: 12.

More precisely, empathy involves a change in one's emotional life in virtue of particular *actual or potential* feelings experienced by another person. The "potential" qualification needs to be added since it seems possible to empathize with, for instance, the distress another person is about to feel, or would likely feel, or would feel if not unconscious. Thanks to Dan Batson for pointing this out to me. Also, the object of empathy does not have to be an actual person at the moment. It could be an imaginary person, a fictional person, a historical person, and so on.

[4] It may be that there are other kinds besides these three, but these are the ones which, by my lights, have figured most prominently in the recent psychology and philosophy literatures on empathy. For similar taxonomies, albeit with differences in the details, see Darwall 2011 and Coplan 2011. Coplan argues that a better taxonomy would only use the "empathy" label for what I am calling the third kind of empathy, since it creates conceptual confusion in her opinion to consider the other two as kinds of empathy. I address this point in Miller 2011b.

[5] For more, see the discussions of infant and childhood emotional development in Eisenberg and Strayer 1987a, Darwall 1998: 264–6, and Coplan 2011. Dan Batson has cautioned me that the jury is still out, in his view, about whether emotional contagion really occurs, and that there is no clear evidence of it from psychology at this point in time. See also Batson 2011: 16 for related discussion.

[6] Darwall 2011: 9–10.

that I *am* worried. So we can "catch" feelings from others without recognizing where they came from or even that we have them in the first place.

(b) *Projective empathy.* Suppose that John is good friends with Jennifer. Jennifer suddenly loses her parents, and is experiencing tremendous distress. John tries to imagine what is going on, and as a result, comes to form similar feelings in his own mind.[7] But what exactly is John supposed to be imagining? In cases of projective empathy, it is the following:

(i) John tries to imagine how he would feel if he were in Jennifer's position.

Note that this perspective-taking is ultimately self-centered—John starts with the situation as Jennifer sees it, but then shifts to imagining how the world would look if *he* were the one to be confronting that situation. Knowing first of all that Jennifer's parents have died, he might ask, for instance, how he would feel if he were to suddenly lose his own parents.

Unlike contagion, an active and relatively sophisticated form of imagination is required for projective empathy. Furthermore, there is a sharing of the intentional object between the two parties, in the broad sense that both John and Jennifer are focused on the deaths of their respective parents. And finally, such an act of imagining is going to typically occur at the conscious level (although it need not), thereby making it easier to diagnose the source of any new feelings that are produced. Interestingly, though, there is no guarantee in cases of projective empathy that there *will* be any new feelings produced, or if there are, that they will be at all similar in kind to those had by the other person. For instance, John might be estranged from his parents, and the result of his act of imagining might be indifference or even relief, in contrast to Jennifer's sorrow.[8]

(c) *Empathy proper.* This third kind has been the central notion in work on empathy in both psychology and philosophy, and will be what I refer to as "empathy" in the rest of the chapter. Return to my example of what John is supposed to be imagining when he is thinking about Jennifer's distress. Here is a second option:

(ii) John tries to imagine what *Jennifer* is feeling in her position.

Here John is trying to step out of his perspective, with his own set of values and concerns, and see the world through Jennifer's eyes with *her* values and concerns. He is trying to imagine what it is like for her to confront the given situation, and what feelings and emotions she is going through. These are clearly two different acts of imagining in (i) and (ii), and can give rise to

---

[7] For a similar example, see Snow 2000: 66.
[8] For related discussion, see Stotland 1969: 289, Batson et al. 1997b, Batson 2009: 7, 2011: 17–19, Darwall 2011: 10–12, and Coplan 2011. This act of perspective-taking is sometimes labeled the "imagine-self" perspective (Stotland 1969: 289).

noticeably different feelings. For instance, Batson, Early, and Salvarani (1997) have found that the act of imagining associated with projective empathy leads to feelings of personal distress in a participant which are not typically found in those who actively imagine as in (ii). Furthermore, it seems clear on intuitive grounds that it is this second kind of imagining which is conceptually tied to paradigm cases of empathy as we normally think of that concept.[9]

Simply imagining what another person is feeling is not enough to have genuinely empathized with her. After all, one might carry out such imagining at a purely intellectual level, and walk away feeling indifferent about Jennifer's distress. So a second crucial component of empathy proper is actually forming certain feelings in one's own mind.[10] Now this is not to say that someone like John has to feel exactly the same way that Jennifer does in order to empathize with her situation; rather he needs to only have felt an emotion which is similar in kind to hers. For instance, John does not have to currently experience quite the degree of distress as Jennifer does, and may only be feeling sadness in comparison to her deep depression. Furthermore, it is important to be clear that the similarity here includes both a similarity of the mental state itself (sadness, distress, etc.) as well as of the *content* of the mental state. In other words, John would be expected to experience sadness, for instance, not with respect to *his* parents dying (we can stipulate that they are alive and well), but rather sadness with respect to the death of *Jennifer's* parents, just as Jennifer herself is upset about the very same thing.[11]

Although the point may be obvious, John forms a feeling empathetically in virtue of *believing* that Jennifer is experiencing a similar feeling. We have already seen that such a belief is not necessary in all cases of empathy, say with emotional contagion. However, focusing as I am on cases involving imaginative contemplation of another's mental life, a person won't be able to empathize with the feelings that another is supposed to have without believing that she has them to begin with.[12] In addition, and here is the important point, whatever John does feel, he must also feel it *because* Jennifer has a similar feeling; in other words, Jennifer's having such a feeling must have been what ultimately gave rise to John's

[9] As has been repeatedly noted in the empathy literature. See, e.g. Wispé 1986, Batson 1987: 93, 2011: 19, Batson et al. 1987: 172, Batson et al. 1997b, Darwall 1998, Snow 2000, Batson et al. 2003b: 1192, and Coplan 2011. This act of perspective-taking is sometimes labeled the "imagine-him" perspective (Stotland 1969: 289) or the "imagine-other" perspective (Batson 1991, 2009: 7).

[10] What could influence whether you form such feelings? One answer is the degree to which, say, John cares about Jennifer and her being in distress. For related discussion, see Batson 2011: 41–6, who in addition emphasizes the importance of valuing the other person.

[11] For similar claims, see Eisenberg and Miller 1987a: 292, 1987b: 91, Eisenberg and Strayer 1987b: 3–5, Barnett 1987: 146, Sober and Wilson 1998: 233–4, Snow 2000: 69, and Day et al. 2010: 205. But it is worth noting that the accuracy condition here—the claim that the feelings formed in the person who empathizes must be roughly similar to those had by the person who is the target of empathy—is controversial (see, e.g. Stotland 1969: 275 and Batson 2009: 10, 2011: 13, 17), and fortunately the central claims about helping in this chapter do not hinge upon the truth of this condition.

[12] See Stotland 1969: 275, Sober and Wilson 1998: 234, 236, and Snow 2000: 68.

affective experience. Otherwise, he could have just formed that feeling by chance, or because of a deviant causal process in his psychology which led him to form a belief about Jennifer's feelings. Such sources would preclude the relevant feelings from counting as genuinely empathetic.[13]

The final point is that it is important to not conflate empathy (in any of its forms, but especially empathy proper) with sympathy. Sympathy is an emotion which involves some form of care or concern for another person. The other person is the object of this state, and so the attitude is third-personal rather than first-personal. As we have seen, empathy proper is rather different—one adopts the first person perspective of the other person, and thinks about the world *with* her, rather than being directly concerned *about* her. Thus in the example, John feels sadness *with* Jennifer. By empathizing with Jennifer, John becomes focused with her on the death of her parents. By sympathizing with Jennifer, John becomes focused on something else, namely Jennifer herself. In order to do so, he need not have adopted her perspective at all in the first place or come to form a belief about what she is feeling in the situation. Perspective-taking is optional for sympathy while I have maintained that it is not for empathy. Yet despite their differences, empathy and sympathy can still naturally occur together—John's empathizing with Jennifer can very quickly give rise to subsequent feelings of sympathy *for* her too.[14]

So empathy and sympathy are different at the conceptual level, I think we can agree. They are also distinct from a third concept, namely personal distress. If I see someone who is sad or depressed, that might cause me to feel bad as well. But if this is a case of personal distress, then I am not feeling bad *for* someone else or *about* someone else's situation, but rather am experiencing negative feelings concerned *just with me*. As we have seen earlier in this section, feelings of personal distress can be closely bound up with emotional contagion and projective empathy, but less so with empathy proper, as Batson, Early, and Salvarani (1997) have demonstrated empirically.[15]

I can summarize these points about empathy proper using my example and Figure 5.1, a diagram of the stages through which the empathetic process works:[16]

---

[13] For additional discussion, see Stotland 1969: 276, Sober and Wilson 1998: 234, and especially Snow 2000: 65–7.

[14] These subsequent sympathetic feelings are also sometimes labeled "compassionate feelings" or feelings of "empathic concern." See, e.g. Davis 1994: 118–20 and Batson 2009, 2011: chapter one.

For similar views about the relationship between empathy and sympathy, see Wispé 1986: 318, Eisenberg and Miller 1987a: 292, 296, 1987b: 91–2, Eisenberg and Strayer 1987b: 5–6, 10, Darwall 1998, 2011: 13, Sober and Wilson 1998: 234–6, Snow 2000: 66, and Slote 2004: 299. For an opposing view, see Batson 2011: chapter one.

[15] For similar claims, see Eisenberg and Miller 1987a: 296, 1987b: 92, Eisenberg and Strayer 1987b: 7, Batson et al. 1987, Shaw et al. 1994: 884, Sober and Wilson 1998: 235, and Batson 2009: 7, 9, 2011: 19.

[16] In the psychology literature, definitions of "empathy" are extremely diverse. Some restrict it to what I call the "Cognitive Component" in the diagram below. Others restrict it just to "Empathetic Feelings." Some even reserve the term just for what I label "Potential

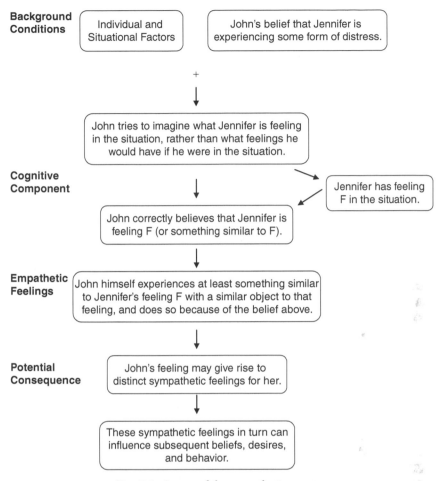

Background Conditions — Individual and Situational Factors / John's belief that Jennifer is experiencing some form of distress.

+

John tries to imagine what Jennifer is feeling in the situation, rather than what feelings he would have if he were in the situation.

Cognitive Component — Jennifer has feeling F in the situation.

John correctly believes that Jennifer is feeling F (or something similar to F).

Empathetic Feelings — John himself experiences at least something similar to Jennifer's feeling F with a similar object to that feeling, and does so because of the belief above.

Potential Consequence — John's feeling may give rise to distinct sympathetic feelings for her.

These sympathetic feelings in turn can influence subsequent beliefs, desires, and behavior.

Fig. 5.1. Stages of the empathetic process.

Clearly much more could be said in defense of the claims made in this section, but they serve their primary purpose of clarifying the phenomenon at issue in the remainder of this chapter.[17] And I am not going to fight about

Consequences" such as sympathetic responding. For helpful summaries of various characterizations of empathy in psychology, see Eisenberg and Miller 1987b: 91–2, Eisenberg and Strayer 1987b: 3–7, Davis 1994: chapter one, and Batson 2011: chapter one.

As should be clear from the discussion above, I reserve the term "empathy" for both the Cognitive Component and Empathetic Feelings. The first stage of the diagram, the Background Conditions, is not representing an actual element of empathy itself. And the Potential Consequences are optional *effects* of empathy, not constitutive elements.

[17] See also Davis 1994: 12–22, which provides an extensive model of the antecedents, processes, intrapersonal outcomes, and interpersonal outcomes associated with empathy.

labels; if the above does not sound like "empathy" then I can give it a different name and still see whether participants who are in this state of mind are more likely to help those whom they think are in need.

Let me expand on this last point about terminology by calling attention to an important body of work in the psychology literature. Daniel Batson is arguably the leading psychologist working on empathy during the past forty years, and much of the rest of this chapter will be concerned with his work. Hence I should note that for him empathy (proper) is, according to his most recent formulation, an "other-oriented emotion elicited by and congruent with the perceived welfare of someone in need."[18] As he goes on to make clear, and has confirmed in personal correspondence, he understands "empathy" as roughly equivalent to what I am calling "sympathy" or "sympathetic feelings" in the last stage of the model. What I have labeled the "Cognitive Component" and "Empathetic Feelings" in the model can give rise to empathy on Batson's view, but neither is necessary for doing so, and neither is a component of empathy itself.[19] As Batson himself is aware, most other theorists in this area, myself included, would prefer to label these feelings "sympathy" or even "compassionate feelings" rather than "empathy."[20] But again, I am not going to fight over labels, and those who prefer Batson's approach can replace my terminology accordingly. We will, however, need to revisit these issues again later in the chapter.

5.2 EMPATHY AND HELPING BEHAVIOR

Before I turn to the literature on empathy and helping behavior, a natural worry that should be addressed from the start is whether the experiments that have been performed by social psychologists are appropriately sensitive to the distinctions mentioned in the previous section and so are careful enough to test for empathy proper (in my sense) rather than, say, projective empathy or other related emotional states. At least in the case of the leading psychologists working in this area, such as Batson and his colleagues, it turns out that the experiments have been appropriately sensitive.[21] In order to induce empathy in the volunteers who served as participants, Batson had them read or listen

---

[18] Batson 2011: 11, emphasis removed.
[19] See in particular Batson 2009: 9–11, 2011: chapters one and two.
[20] Batson 2009: 8, 2011: 12.
[21] For an overview of the different empathetic induction procedures commonly used in psychology, see Eisenberg and Miller 1987a: 308–10, 1987b: 106–10. Clearly not all procedures are equally sensitive to the conceptual distinctions I have made in the previous section. Since in my view Batson's work has been among the most sensitive, it naturally becomes the focus of the discussion in this chapter. Again, though, the terminological differences noted above should be kept in mind.

to accounts of people experiencing some kind of hardship. For instance, one (fictional) case involved a radio broadcast about Katie Banks, a university student whose parents and a sister had been killed in a car crash and who was left to care for her younger brother and sister. The empathy manipulation was achieved beforehand by having participants read a passage such as the following:

> While you are listening to this broadcast, try to *imagine how the person being interviewed feels about what has happened and how it has affected his or her life.* Try not to concern yourself with attending to all the information presented. Just concentrate on trying to imagine how the person interviewed in the broadcast feels.[22]

Note that the aim of these instructions was to directly trigger the perspective-taking involved in empathy, and not to directly trigger an emotional response of sympathy. Furthermore, Batson's experiments were sensitive to whether the participants should imagine their own feelings or those had by Katie in the situation. Indeed he has explicitly distinguished the above set of instructions from these:

> While you are listening to this broadcast, try to *imagine how you yourself would feel if you were experiencing what has happened to the person being interviewed and how this experience would affect your life.* Try not to concern yourself with attending to all the information presented. Just concentrate on trying to imagine how you yourself would feel.[23]

Finally, both of these instructions have been distinguished from those given to control participants whose actions have served as the baseline level of exhibited helping behavior:

> While you are listening to this broadcast, try to *be as objective as possible about what has happened to the person interviewed and how it has affected his or her life.* To remain objective, do not let yourself get caught up in imagining what this person has been through and how he or she feels as a result. Just try to remain objective and detached.[24]

So it seems as if the highly influential experiments in this area by Batson and his colleagues do involve instructions which are sensitive enough to some of the central features of empathy to be able to generate relevant results.

Of course we just noted that Batson himself would not like this way of describing his work. The perspective-taking involved in the first set of instructions would not, on his approach, be a feature of empathy itself, but rather one of potentially several techniques that could be used to causally contribute to the formation of what I have called feelings of "sympathy" and what he would call "empathy" or "empathic concern." Fortunately, though, since this technique is acceptable both on my approach as a way of inducing empathy

---

[22] Batson et al. 1997b: 753, emphasis theirs.
[23] Batson et al. 1997b: emphasis theirs.
[24] Batson et al. 1997b: emphasis theirs. The above instructions all derive from Stotland 1969: 292–3.

(as I understand it) and also on Batson's approach as a way of inducing empathy (as he understands it), I do not see any reason to get bogged down in terminological discussions at this point.[25]

What have these experiments shown thus far? More than fifty different experiments by Batson and his colleagues involving many different feelings of distress, helping opportunities, and helping tasks have shown that as a group, participants who are induced to feel empathy exhibit significantly more helping behavior than control participants towards those thought to be in need. Here is not the place to examine all of these studies, but let me mention two of them.[26]

The instructions above were from a study designed specifically to test whether the two perspectives at work in projective empathy and empathy proper end up causing different feelings in people who adopt them. This was found to be the case, as reported in the previous section. At the same time, this particular study did not also measure actual helping behavior. But Batson employed the same experimental design using the example of Katie Banks in a number of earlier studies. For instance, in Batson et al. 1989, their third study had the empathy manipulation be, "Try to *imagine how Katie Banks feels* about what has happened and how it has affected her life. Try to feel the full impact of what she has been through and how she feels as a result," whereas control participants were told, "Try to *focus on the technical aspects*. Try to assess the effectiveness of the techniques and devices used to make the broadcast have an impact on the listener."[27] Note that in this case the empathy manipulation includes both perspective-taking instructions *and* instructions to form empathetic feelings. So each of the central components of "empathy," as I understand the term, is explicitly mentioned here.

Participants later in the study received an envelope with a letter from the professor and one from Katie herself. She indicated that there were a number of different ways she could use help including, "sitting with her younger brother and sister while she attended her night classes, fixing things around the house, providing transportation, making telephone calls, or stuffing envelopes for a fund-raising project."[28] The envelope also included a response form that asked whether a participant was willing to help, and if so, for how many hours. Here were the results:[29]

---

[25] For another technique of inducing empathy (in his sense), see Batson 2011: 43–5. There he does note that "use of perspective-taking instructions to induce empathy is usually a better research strategy" (44).

[26] For reviews, see Batson 1987, 1991, 2002, 2011, and Batson et al. 2003a. For other related studies, see the references in Stotland 1969: 279–80, Eisenberg and Miller 1987a: 296–310, Eisenberg and Miller 1987b, and Dovidio and Penner 2001.

[27] Batson et al. 1989: 929, emphasis theirs.

[28] Batson et al. 1989: 930.

[29] Batson et al. 1989: 931. The study was actually designed to compare the effect of anticipated mood enhancement on helping for low and high empathy participants. I have averaged the results, which were already very similar in the two mood enhancement conditions to begin with.

	Percent volunteered	Mean number of hours volunteered
Control group	37%	0.60
Empathy condition	76%	1.33

The only relevant difference in the experimental setup was a difference of two sentences in the instructions the two groups were given before receiving the envelope, and yet the different perspectives that were thereby generated led to dramatic differences in actual helping.

Here is another study, from Miho Toi and Batson (1982). Half of the volunteers from an introduction to psychology course were asked to listen to a broadcast and be as objective as possible, whereas the other half were told to imagine the perspective of the person being interviewed. The tape they each heard next contained a (fictional) interview with Carol Marcy, a freshman in the class who had had both of her legs broken in an auto accident and was worried about being able to still pass the course. After listening to the interview and filling out a questionnaire, participants received an envelope with letters from both the professor of the course and from Carol asking for help in going over the missed lecture notes. Furthermore, Carol indicated that she would not be coming back to school but would be studying at home until next semester. Thus Toi and Batson reasoned that participants who did not offer to help would not have to actually see Carol for the rest of the semester and so would not feel (as) guilty. The dependent measure was whether the participants filled out a slip agreeing to help Carol. Here were the percentages who volunteered:[30]

Control group	33%
Empathy condition	71%

Again, the only relevant difference was in the instructions about which perspective to adopt. As indicated above, similar patterns have arisen in dozens of other experiments conducted by Batson and replicated by other social psychologists.

Given these results, let me construct a crude but accurate picture of what seems to be going on in experiments such as the above. Participants are instructed to adopt an empathetic stance at some point in the near future, and when the time comes they actually do empathize with people such as Carol and form empathetic feelings because of what they believe the other person is feeling in her situation. These empathetic feelings in turn generate a sympathetic motive to reduce or eliminate the pain, suffering, distress, or other relevant difficulty that the person is experiencing.[31] Helping is naturally a way of trying to eliminate the problem, and so long as there are reasonable

---

[30] Toi and Batson 1982: 288.

[31] Batson 1987: 95. In personal correspondence, Batson has denied the claim that perspective-taking needs to result in the same or similar feelings being formed in the person who is

opportunities to help which are believed to be available, relevant helping mechanisms are activated and the likelihood that the person will help is increased.[32] Thus diagrammatically we have the following:

Appropriate background conditions and belief about the distress of another
↓
Cognitive component (imagining and forming beliefs about certain feelings of distress in another)
↓
Empathetic feelings
(Desires similar in kind and propositional content to what the other person is feeling)
↓
Motive to reduce or eliminate the other person's distress[33]
+
Beliefs about reasonable opportunities to help the other person in the circumstances and about having the requisite ability to do so
↓
Activation of the relevant helping mechanism
↓
Increased helping motivation
↓
Increased helping behavior

empathizing. Rather on his view, the perspective-taking instead often *directly* results in the production of feelings of sympathy for the other person.

Batson is right that his studies do not provide definitive evidence for whether the perspective-taking manipulation directly gave rise to sympathy, or whether the process was causally mediated by empathetic feelings in the person who was empathizing. However, the empathy-induction instructions in many of his studies at least were designed to promote the formation of similar feelings in the participants (of course, even if these were successful, it would be a further question whether such feelings served as causal intermediaries between the perspective-taking and the sympathy). I noted this already for the Katie Banks 1989 study, and consider as well the following: "Try to feel the full impact of what Jared has been through and how he feels as a result" (Batson et al. 2002b: 1660). Fortunately I can leave this debate open as nothing essential in the chapter hinges upon this particular dispute.

[32] For similar models, see Coke, Batson, and McDavis 1978, Darwall 1998, and Dovidio and Penner 2001: 184.

[33] This formulation of the motive has it be concerned specifically with the other person's distress. More precisely, there is some reason to think that it should be formulated to pertain to the specific problem that the other person is experiencing, rather than other problems which might be going on in his life as well. For instance, Dovidio et al. (1990) compared the helping rates of participants in objective and empathy-induced conditions, when they were provided with either an opportunity to help address the same problem or a different problem that the other person was experiencing. If it was the same problem, 62.2 percent of the participants in the empathy group pledged to help versus 33.7 percent in the objective instructions group. But for the different problem, only 33.7 percent in the empathy group pledged to help, which was actually less than the 45.9 percent in the objective instructions group (Dovidio et al. 1990: 254).

But even formulating the motive so that it pertains just to the other person's reason for distress, cannot be quite right. For Batson et al. (1997d, 2002) found that empathy improved both attitudes and actual helping behavior towards members of a group to which the other person belongs, where group membership was salient to the cause of the distress in the first place. This was true irrespective of whether helping the group would benefit the other person in any way. And Batson and his colleagues also report another study in which empathy towards a person with a need led to increased helping for a second person with a similar need (2002: 1657). So based on these results, it would be a mistake to think that the empathy-induced participants must only be concerned with the good of another person in need or distress.

where again the arrows are intended to symbolize causal influence. In the next section I will say much more about the motive to eliminate the other person's distress. For now the main point to take away from this model is that many participants in the relevant psychological studies are such that feeling empathy for a person thought to be in need significantly increases helping.

5.3 EMPATHY AND ALTRUISTIC MOTIVATION

We have seen that imagining the feelings of another in distress can lead to a motive to relieve that person's distress. But so far nothing in this chapter has indicated whether that motive is egoistic or altruistic (or some third kind). Fortunately there has been a wealth of experimental evidence provided by Batson and his colleagues for what he calls the "empathy-altruism hypothesis," or the claim that, "empathy evokes motivation directed toward the ultimate goal of reducing the needy person's suffering; the more empathy felt for a person in need, the more altruistic motivation to have that need reduced."[34] In chapter two, I characterized altruistic desires as follows:

(A) A person's ultimate desire is *altruistic* just in case:
   (i) It concerns what she thinks benefits (at least) one person who is not herself.
   (ii) The desire cannot be satisfied unless someone other than herself would be benefitted in her eyes, and benefitted in such a way that is independent of what would subsequently benefit her.

While Batson does not provide as detailed a conception, it is clear from the above quote as well as his numerous writings on the subject that he is working with an understanding of altruism that is similar in spirit to (A). So another way to state the hypothesis is to say that empathy can lead to the formation of a desire which is both altruistic and ultimate, and which has as its object the good of the other person, that is, that her suffering, ailment, or distress be alleviated.[35]

---

[34] Batson 2002: 92. This is the "strong" version of the hypothesis. Batson also mentions a weaker version whereby, "empathic emotion evokes both egoistic and altruistic motivation," but he does not focus on this version because it, "has more overlap with egoistic explanations of the motivation to help evoked by empathy, making it more difficult to differentiate empirically from these egoistic explanations" (1991: 87–8; see also 2011: 29). For the most recent statement of the strong and weak versions, see Batson 2011: 29.

[35] Note that when a person actually does help and the helping is causally influenced by such altruistic ultimate desires, it does not follow that the actual behavior must arise *solely* from those desires. There can be egoistic or other kinds of desires which *also* play a partial causal role in giving rise to the behavior as well (for some specific proposals, see Stocks et al. 2009: 664). The empathy-altruism hypothesis is in the first instance a hypothesis about motivation, and not about helping behavior itself. See also Batson 2011: 29–30.

Given what I said about the concept of empathy, this empirical support for the empathy-altruistic hypothesis should not be surprising, provided that people are psychologically capable of realizing genuine empathy in the first place. Recall that empathy proper does not involve the egoistic mindset of imagining how you would feel if you were in the same situation as a person in distress. Rather, it requires stepping outside of your own perspective, and focusing just on what the other person is going through—what emotions and feelings she is wrestling with in the situation, and what those emotions and feelings are about. As Batson's instructions to his participants indicated, "try to imagine how the person being interviewed feels about what has happened and how it has affected his or her life."[36] This kind of focus on another's feelings of distress or sadness can touch a person and cause similar feelings in his own mind directed at the same objects of concern, feelings which can motivate a search for ways to reduce or eliminate that other person's distress for its own sake.[37]

Recall, though, the earlier terminological dispute between myself and Batson. Batson would object to the idea that he supports an "empathy-altruism hypothesis," where "empathy" is empathy proper as I have understood it in section one. Rather I noted that for him "empathy" is roughly equivalent to what I have called "sympathy", and while it can be produced by processes of perspective-taking and feeling what another person is feeling, it does not have those processes as constitutive elements. So using my terminology, Batson would say that he is actually advocating a "sympathy-altruism hypothesis."[38] Again, though, so long as we are clear about how we are each using our terms, I do not see anything of substance that is in dispute here. What matters is not the terms we use but whether there is empirical evidence for the existence of an ultimate motive which is altruistic in its concern. Whether we want to call this motive a motive of "sympathy" that is a causal product of empathy (as

---

[36] Batson et al. 1997b: 753, emphasis removed.

[37] For similar remarks, see Darwall 2011: 13–14. Note that the claim is *not* that the person who empathizes is motivated to help in order to eliminate feelings of personal distress that have formed in him as a result of empathizing with the distress of another person. That would make the motivation to help ultimately egoistic. Rather the claim is that the person who empathizes is motivated to help at least in part in order to try to relieve the distress of the other person, *independently* of whether he would benefit in the process.

[38] In personal correspondence, Batson has confirmed this. For what it is worth, I find it hard to understand some of Batson's earlier writings in light of his current proposal. I quoted the characterization of the empathy-altruism hypothesis as: "empathy evokes motivation directed toward the ultimate goal of reducing the needy person's suffering" (2002: 92). More recently Batson has written that, "Empathic concern activates the desire to reach the goal of eliminating the perceived need of the person for whom the empathy is felt. That is, empathic concern produces altruistic motivation" (2011: 31). But if empathy *just is* sympathetic motivation which is altruistic, then what does it mean to say that empathy "evokes" or "produces" this motivation or "activates the desires" when they are identical?

I would) or we want to call it "empathy" itself (as Batson would), seems to me to be of little importance.

So I will stick with the terminology of the empathy-altruism hypothesis in what remains. In order to defend this hypothesis, Batson has had to examine a number of competing egoistic explanations for the motivational impact that empathy has on helping, and he has cleverly devised experimental approaches for testing most of them. In every case, no empirical support has been found in his studies for any of the egoistic explanations. Clearly evaluating Batson's treatment of each of these explanations is beyond the scope of this chapter, but I can offer some initial appreciation of his results by combining the egoistic explanations into three categories and seeing what a representative experiment looks like for testing each of them.[39]

(i) *Aversive arousal reduction*. According to this explanatory strategy, feeling empathy is thought to be unpleasant or distressful for the person experiencing it, which in turn generates motivation to end such feelings. One such means to do so is to help the person in need and so the participant is motivated to help, but only as a way of making himself feel better.[40] If this explanation is correct, then helping behavior causally brought about in this way would not be altruistic.

One way to experimentally test this proposal is to provide participants with an opportunity to escape being around the person in need. If they are primarily motivated by seeking ways of reducing their aversive arousal, then they will take the opportunity to escape without helping. But this is not what has happened in the experiments. Recall, for instance, Toi and Batson's study in which participants were told to either objectively or imaginatively listen to a broadcast which turned out to be about Carol's auto accident. The study had an additional wrinkle which was not mentioned earlier, namely that only some of the participants were told that Carol would not be coming back to their psychology class. Others were given a more difficult-to-escape scenario in which they were told that Carol would be attending all the remaining classes,

---

[39] The three categories used follow Batson 2002: 94. See also Batson 1987: 84, 105 and Batson et al. 2003a: 281–4. For reviews of the experimental support for the empathy-altruism hypothesis, see Batson 1987, 1991, 2002, 2011, Davis 1994: chapter seven, and Batson et al. 2003a. See also an early study by Krebs 1975. One explanation that does not fit nicely into these categories is the oneness hypothesis advanced by Cialdini et al. 1997, according to which (very roughly) by empathizing with another person, one incorporates one's self in the other, and the division between self and other breaks down. This in turn undermines the distinction between altruism and egoism. For strong empirical disconfirmation of this proposal, see Batson et al. 1997c and the review in Batson 2011: 145–60. For equally strong conceptual worries about this proposal, see May 2011a.

[40] For discussion, see Batson et al. 1981, Toi and Batson 1982, Batson et al. 1983, Cialdini et al. 1987, Schaller and Cialdini 1988, Schroeder et al. 1988, Batson et al. 1989, Dovidio et al. 1990, Batson 2002: 94–5, 2011: 111–14, and Batson et al. 2003a: 284.

and given that she would be in a wheelchair, she would be hard to avoid. Here is how the proportion of participants helping in each condition turned out:[41]

Ease of escape	Objective instructions	Empathy-Inducing instructions
Easy	33%	71%
Difficult	76%	81%

Thus participants feeling empathy for Carol did not appear to be significantly motivated by finding ways to reduce their feelings of distress, unlike participants who took a more detached perspective. Similar results have been produced in variants of this experimental setup.[42]

(ii) *Empathy-specific punishment.* Another family of egoistic explanations maintains that people who feel empathy for those in need are motivated to help primarily in order to avoid one or more punishments for not helping. Such punishments can range from third-person censure such as social or religious disapproval to forms of first-person self-censure involving guilt or shame.[43] Thus again motivation would not be ultimately altruistic towards those in need in such cases since those empathizing would be concerned mainly about themselves and what they can do to avoid the relevant form of punishment.

One way to test at least some explanations which fall under this category is to compare the change in mood experienced by participants when told that their efforts to help someone in need failed. If empathy-specific punishment models are accurate, then there should be a noticeable difference in the mood change between participants who were told that their failure to help was unjustified, and those who were told that it was justified. In particular, if participants were told that their failure was justified, then we would expect them to be greatly relieved, whereas if it was unjustified, then they should be highly distressed. If the empathy-altruism hypothesis is correct, however, there should be little to no mood change between justified versus unjustified failures as the person is concerned only with helping the other in need, and the need still has not been addressed.[44]

Batson and Joy Weeks (1996) carried out a study with just this design. The (fictional) person in need was Julie, who would be receiving a series of mild but uncomfortable shocks. After half the participants were given either the usual set of objective or empathy-inducing instructions regarding an upcoming

[41] Toi and Batson 1982: 288.
[42] See, e.g. Batson et al. 1981, Batson et al. 1983, Batson et al. 1989, Dovidio et al. 1990, and Batson 2011: 111–14 as well as the important recent study by Stocks et al. 2009.
[43] For discussion, see Batson et al. 1988, Batson 2002: 95–6, 2011: 114–21, and Batson et al. 2003a: 282–4.
[44] See Batson et al. 1988: 58–9, Batson and Weeks 1996: 148–9, and Batson 2002: 95–6.

communication, they listened to a tape in which Julie expresses her anxiety about having to receive the shocks. An emotion survey was then filled out, followed by a task which, if performed successfully, could have saved Julie from the shocks. Some participants were told afterwards that they failed the task and it had been "moderately easy," whereas others were told that they failed the task but it was "absolutely impossible." Another emotion survey was then filled out. Using a nine-point mood scale, here is the mean decrease in mood once participants learned of their failure to help Julie:[45]

	Objective instructions	Empathy-Inducing instructions
Failure was not justified	-2.23	-3.17
Failure was justified	-1.25	-2.83

The fact that there was no statistically significant variance to the numbers on the right-hand side strongly suggests that participants were concerned about preventing Julie's suffering rather than about whether they would be punished for not helping her, since if their failure was justified, there would be no grounds for legitimate punishment.[46]

(iii) *Empathy-specific rewards.* The third class of egoistic explanations for empathy-induced helping behavior centers not on punishments but rather on rewards. It claims that people in such cases are ultimately motivated by one or more of the specific rewards attached to helping the person in need with whom they empathize. Such rewards might come in the form of social or religious benefits, or more internal feelings of joy, honor, pride, or pleasure.[47] Once again these would not be altruistic motives for helping.

One way to test these reward explanations is to examine differences in mood based upon whether the problems of the person in need are relieved by the empathizer or by a third party. If empathy-specific rewards are the motivating force behind helping, then comparatively speaking there should be a much higher mood in those who address the need themselves than in those who observe the need relieved by someone else. According to the empathy-altruism hypothesis, on the other hand, it should not matter who is helping the person in need so long as that need is addressed.[48]

Experimental support for this kind of egoistic explanation has not been forthcoming. Batson and his colleagues (1988) devised a study in which participants were initially told that their performance of a helping task

---

[45] Batson and Weeks 1996: 152.

[46] For additional studies which challenge the empathy-specific punishment hypothesis, see Batson et al. 1988 and the review in Batson 2011: 114–21.

[47] For discussion, see Batson et al. 1988, Smith et al. 1989, Batson et al. 1991, Batson 2002: 96–7, 2011: 122–31, and Batson et al. 2003a: 281–2.

[48] See Batson et al. 1988: 53 and Batson 2002: 96–7.

would influence the number of electric shocks someone else would receive. Similar to the previous study, they then heard a recording of the other person expressing concern about being shocked. Two types of experimental manipulations were then introduced—whether participants were told that the other person had been reassigned to a task that did not involve receiving shocks or was still assigned to the same task, and whether as a result the participant would still be performing his or her helping task or it was not required anymore. The general idea was that by performing their helping task well, participants could spare the person from receiving shocks, but if the person is reassigned by those in charge of the experiment, then he would have been prevented from suffering but not through the actions of the participant. Thus if the above egoistic explanation is correct, we would expect significant variations on the mood scores of the participants after the manipulations were done. Instead, the mean ratings on a mood index from 1 to 9 (with 9 being good mood) were as follows:[49]

	Participant performs helping task	Does not perform
Prior reassignment of the other person from shock task	6.29	6.73
No prior reassignment of the other person from shock task	6.56	5.84

The overall conclusion was that "subjects' self-reported mood provided no evidence that high-empathy subjects felt better when the victim's need was relieved by their own action than when it was relieved by other means."[50]

Stepping back from these different egoistic accounts, the general point is this. According to over thirty different experiments carried out by Batson and his colleagues, there is no evidence that high levels of empathy generate egoistic motivation to help; in fact, all the leading egoistic explanations seem to be empirically disconfirmed. At the same time, this conclusion should be taken for what it is. While it is true that a number of particular egoistic hypotheses have been tested, new and more subtle ones continue to be proposed.[51] There is also the possibility that a hypothesis using multiple egoistic motives could

[49] Batson et al. 1988: 56.   [50] Batson et al. 1988: 56.

[51] For instance, Sober and Wilson proposed that a desire to reduce uncertainty could explain the findings in a study by Batson et al. 1991 (Sober and Wilson 1998: 268). See also Batson's reply (2000: 210) and their response (2000: 266). They also proposed that only certain mood enhancements should be mentioned in developing a negative-state relief hypothesis for empathy and helping as a way of responding to a study by Batson et al. 1989 (Sober and Wilson 1998: 271). Here see Batson's reply (2000: 210), Sober and Wilson's response (2000: 267), and the very helpful discussion in May 2011b: 50–4.

For additional egoistic hypotheses, see Stich et al. 2010. They briefly offer a new social version of the empathy-specific punishment hypothesis (188: n. 33), and two versions of the self-administered empathy-specific punishment hypothesis (189–96). For responses see Batson

be true which generates data on helping that overlaps with what the empathy-altruism hypothesis predicts in many cases.[52] Therefore let me wrap up this discussion in the following way. If one or more egoistic hypothesis turns out to be correct, then my discussion of empathy-based motivation to help would simply rehearse what I already said in chapters two and three about the leading models of motivation to help which is associated with guilt, embarrassment, and positive moods. So instead let me *assume* that the balance of evidence, such as it is at the present time, is indeed pointing in the right direction, and that empathy (proper) does give rise to genuinely altruistic motives.

5.4 EMPATHY AND CHARACTER TRAITS

As I have before, I will take these results and draw some implications about motivation and behavior. It is the last implication in particular which will take the discussion in a new direction.

(a) *Many people do not perform even simple helping tasks.* Many control participants do not perform such straightforward acts of compassion as volunteering to tutor Carol at her home, offering to help Katie for an hour with making phone calls, or preventing someone from being mildly shocked.[53] These are not particularly strenuous activities. In addition, there do not appear to be other helping opportunities in the immediate vicinity which might have been thought to be more significant than the experimental helping opportunity. The alternative was simply to ignore Carol's request for help in the class or allow a person to experience electric shocks that he was clearly afraid of. Finally, the helping opportunities in the relevant experiments were clearly morally significant. Recall that participants were given a chance to help someone who had just broken her legs, or whose parents had died and was suddenly responsible for taking care of two younger siblings.

(b) *Empathy as an enhancer, consistent behavior, and causally relevant mental states.* As with guilt, embarrassment, and positive moods, empathy functions as an enhancer which has repeatedly been found to increase helping rates in a wide variety of situations involving different forms of need and forms of helping to address those needs.

2011: 120–1, 135–45. And for yet another hypothesis having to do with anticipatory guilt, see Davis 1994: 140.

[52] For related discussion, see Stich et al. 2010: 201, Batson 2011: 132–4, and May 2011b: 51 n. 12.

[53] For the last helping opportunity, see Batson et al. 1983. I will discuss an experiment with this setup in section five.

Furthermore, because of these results cumulatively I suggest that many people will continue to exhibit these patterns of elevated helping in repetitions of the same situations relevant to helping, as well as in different situations involving moderately demanding opportunities to help which have not yet been empirically studied.[54] Thus, albeit tentatively, I can formulate predictions such as the following:

(P) Other things being equal, if people are experiencing at least intermediate levels of empathy (proper) for someone in need, and:
(i) are presented with a moderately demanding way of helping that person
(ii) take themselves to be able to help
then many of these people will probably attempt to help.[55]

Consider, for instance, a case where participants in a study are asked to imagine what a soldier is feeling who has lost a limb in battle, and are then presented with a chance to donate five dollars to support his rehabilitation. A reasonable hypothesis is that they will donate more frequently and in greater amounts than controls. Plus they would already be expected to help more frequently when feeling empathy in the situations which Batson and other have already studied. So there is a kind of cross-situational consistency to their helping. This consistency should be understood in terms of the psychologically salient features of the situations the people find themselves in—they will have an easier time empathizing with certain individuals rather than others, and even when they do, their empathetic feelings can come in degrees. Further-more, some people have deficits of different kinds associated with empathy, such as with respect to the cognitive component of perspective-taking or the ability to form empathetic feelings. So expectations about consistency over time and across situations should be tailored to each individual's own back-ground attitudes and capacities.[56]

Finally, together with the empathy-altruism hypothesis, these patterns of helping suggest which mental states might be causally at work. I said that empathetic feelings can give rise to a desire to relieve the other person's distress. If the person also believes that there are reasonable opportunities for him to help in the circumstances, then those mental states can trigger the activation of further mental state dispositions:

---

[54] As two psychologists who work on empathy note, "if an empathic response engenders sympathy for the other, one would expect an association between empathy and prosocial behavior across a wide variety of situations" (Eisenberg and Miller 1987a: 296).

[55] After formulating this prediction, I discovered a better version offered by Batson himself: "if (a) a person can provide the needed help, (b) no one else can, and (c) the cost of helping does not exceed the benefit, then the more empathic concern felt, the more likely the person will offer help" (2011: 65).

[56] For more, see Davis 1994: 14, 146–51 and Day et al. 2010: 203–6. I will mention some of these individual differences when highlighting the partiality of empathy in section five.

(i) Beliefs concerned with which means of helping another person would be most effective in relieving her distress.

(ii) Desires concerned with helping so as to relieve the other person's distress.

Once again, these partially constitute the "helping mechanism" from the diagram of empathy and helping in section two, provided that the empathy-altruism hypothesis is correct.[57]

(c) *Most people do not possess the virtue of compassion.* Unlike with the previous enhancers, here we have found empirical evidence that people help, when empathizing, in a way that satisfies one of the requirements of compassion from chapter two:

(c) A compassionate person's trait of compassion will typically lead to helping which is done at least primarily for motivating reasons that are morally admirable and deserving of moral praise, and not primarily for motivating reasons which are either morally problematic or morally neutral.

I also said this principle can be sharpened as follows:

(c*) The virtue of compassion gives rise to compassionate motivation to help another person, and that motivation is *altruistic* motivation to help. Indeed, it is the fact that it is altruistic which grounds the moral praiseworthiness of this motivation.

Given that empathetic motivation to help appears to be altruistic, there is no conflict with the requirements for compassion in this regard.

However, most of us still seem to have a hard time meeting two other requirements for compassion from chapter two:

(a) A person who is compassionate, when acting in character, will typically attempt to help when in moderately demanding situations relevant to helping.

(b) A compassionate person's trait of compassion will not be dependent on the presence of certain enhancers (such as moderate guilt, embarrassment, or good mood) in leading him to perform helpful actions, such that if these enhancers were not present, then his frequency of helping would significantly decrease in the same nominal situations.

I have already addressed (a), so let me say something about (b). Suppose you realize that your good friend has a number of different small projects that need completing around his house, such as taking out the trash and picking up the mail, but due to a recent physical disability he cannot manage these tasks

---

[57] Additional beliefs and desires would need to be added here having to do with a cost-benefit analysis of helping, including the costs and benefits of doing the helping oneself, of having or letting someone else help, and of not helping at all. For relevant discussion, see Batson 2011: chapter three.

anymore without assistance. You are aware of these various needs, but often you ignore them, and not because you have something more pressing to do from a moral perspective. However, suppose it is also true that when you empathize with what your friend is going through and what he must be feeling, then on *those* occasions you are motivated to help, and typically do so.

Your motivation for helping is altruistic, let us suppose, and empathy is functioning as a morally admirable enhancer. Nevertheless, I think many people would have the following reaction—that you are not being a compassionate person in general towards your friend. A genuinely compassionate person *would not need to have* a motive fostered by empathetic feelings in order to reliably help others. *Even without* such a motive, a compassionate individual should be expected, other things being equal, to be able to recognize when someone is in need and try to do what he can to help. It would not count as a legitimate excuse that the reason why someone is not helpful in a given instance is that he could not work himself up into having any empathetic feelings towards his friend who was in need. This excuse should be seen as, quite frankly, rather lame.[58]

This leads to the following refinement of (b) with respect to empathy:

> (b*) A compassionate person's trait of compassion will not be dependent on the presence of even morally admirable enhancers (such as empathy) in leading him to perform helpful actions, if it is also the case that were these enhancers not present, then his frequency of helping would significantly decrease in the same nominal situations.

Now this statement of the requirement will not quite do.[59] For imagine a person who is extremely empathetic, always considering the suffering of those whom she comes across and reliably trying to help them. While it is true that *if* her feelings of empathy were not present, then her helping would decrease, nevertheless that is hardly a strike against her actually having the virtue of compassion. Hence a better refinement of (b) for my purposes is the following:

> (b**) A compassionate person's trait of compassion will not be dependent on the presence of even morally admirable enhancers (such as empathy) in leading him to perform helpful actions, if it is also the case that there are many occasions where these enhancers are not present and he does not help, even though it is true that *if* one of these enhancers were present, then his frequency of helping would significantly increase in the same nominal situations.

This captures what is going on with your friend who is physically disabled. Even though you might reliably help him when you do have feelings of empathy for his situation, the fact that often you do not bother to help him

---

[58] The same point applies in the previous chapter to the enhancers of elevation and activated moral norms.

[59] Thanks to an anonymous referee for pointing this out.

when you don't first have these feelings, is a mark against the possession of the virtue of compassion.

So even despite the morally positive workings of empathy in the respects outlined above, the empirical data at this point does not lead me to support the widespread possession of the virtue of compassion because of the remaining conflicts with the requirements in (a) and (b**). Of course, once again there is the caveat that perhaps a few people actually do possess this virtue. Roughly 33 percent of controls helped Carol in Toi and Batson's study without the empathy manipulation, while 37 percent helped Katie Banks in the Batson et al. 1989 study. Who knows how they might have behaved in other situations?[60]

5.5 FROM EMPATHY TO COMPASSION?

Even if the conclusion of the last section is correct and the experimental literature on empathy at the current time does not yet support the widespread possession of compassion, it might still be reasonable to think that this research has unlocked a key means for people to become *more* compassionate. I have said that compassion gives rise to altruistic motivation, and no other area of psychological research seems to provide significant support for an altruism hypothesis.[61] Furthermore, it seems that most of us are capable of feeling empathy for others on multiple occasions. So perhaps all that is needed to foster compassion is for people to cultivate their empathetic capacities so that they are disposed to empathize to a *greater* degree in the same ordinary situations over time and in some additional new situations. Then the incompatibility with (a) and (b**) would disappear, and we would have an empirically informed route to developing a genuine virtue.

In this section, I want to suggest that this strategy is much more difficult to carry out than it might have initially seemed in four different respects. If these cautionary remarks are warranted, then we have even less reason to suppose that there is much actual possession today of the virtue of compassion.

(a) *Many of us are motivated to avoid empathy.* If empathy is the most promising path to compassion, then we have to reliably *feel* empathy when others are thought to be experiencing some kind of hardship. Yet there is now evidence, not only that we often do not feel empathy in many cases of perceived distress, but also that we may have a motive to actually *avoid* feeling

---

[60] Similarly for some of the participants who did help in the empathy conditions—they could also have the virtue of compassion.

[61] For a similar claim, see Batson et al. 2003a: 287. For brief suggestions of another possibility, see Grusec and Redler 1980: 529 and also Batson 2011: 9.

empathy, so as to bypass the consequences associated with helping that come with empathy. In other words, by implicitly knowing that empathy can lead us to help someone in need, we might be motivated to avoid this feeling in the first place so as to not bear the helping burden.

Laura Shaw and her colleagues (1994) have found evidence for this effect under certain conditions, namely when a person is aware of an opportunity to help and the costs associated with helping are thought to be high in this instance.[62] Their main study involved participants being divided into three groups—one third were unaware that they would be given an opportunity to help a homeless man, and that this opportunity would be highly costly (involving a total of five to six hours of meetings along with the possibility of other helping tasks); another third were aware that they would be presented with this high cost helping task; and the final third were aware that they were going to presented with an opportunity to help him by spending no more than an hour preparing envelopes for potential donors. All participants were then given the option of which of two versions of a taped appeal from the homeless person they would rather hear—a low impact version in which, "the individual presents his needs in a relatively objective manner" or a high impact version in which he presents them in a manner which, "leads listeners to imagine how the individual feels about what he is going through . . . causing them to become empathically aroused."[63] Here were the results:[64]

	Participants choosing empathy-inducing version
Unaware of helping opportunity (high cost)	69%
Aware of helping opportunity (low cost)	69%
Aware of helping opportunity (high cost)	31.5%

The point is that, once they knew that the helping opportunity would be costly, participants were much more likely to choose to hear an appeal for help using objective as opposed to empathy-inducing instructions. And this despite the fact that participants found the empathy-inducing appeal (significantly) more interesting, slightly more useful, more effective in leading to helping, more likely to evoke emotion, and equally informative to the objective appeal.[65] Participants also preferred the empathy-inducing appeal in its own right when not aware of there being an actual opportunity to help (69 percent). The natural conclusion to draw is that many participants seemed to be

---

[62] Shaw et al. 1994: 879–80. As they note, "There is likely an upper limit on this relationship, however; if the cost is too high, cost itself can be used to justify not helping, and one no longer need fear the consequences of becoming empathically aroused" (880).

[63] Shaw et al. 1994: 881.

[64] Shaw et al. 1994: 885.

[65] Shaw et al. 1994: 882–4.

motivated to avoid a situation in which they could feel empathy for the distress of another person which would require a significant investment of their time, resources, or effort to address.[66]

(b) *Empathy-induced motivation is extremely fragile.* Nevertheless, despite this motive to avoid feeling empathy in certain cases, it is obvious that most of us still *do* feel empathy when other people are seen to be in some kind of distress. Yet some of Batson's other work has shown that, once we form these empathetic feelings, they can be extremely fragile such that participants become easily distracted from thinking about what another person in need is feeling. When they are distracted, their altruistic motivation often simply vanishes. Even worse, when made to think about themselves instead, not only will these participants typically lose altruistic motivation to help, but any remaining motivation will ordinarily become self-interested.[67]

We can see this in dramatic form by comparing two studies reported in Batson et al. 1983. Participants were initially supposed to watch another participant perform a series of trials during which he or she would receive electric shocks. In the easy-to-escape condition, participants had to only observe two trials, whereas in the difficult-to-escape condition, they had to watch all of them (between two and ten). However, after the trials began, participants were given a chance to switch places with the shock recipient and receive the shocks themselves. Here is the crucial part of what they were told:

> Before you decide, I should tell you that the shocks Elaine (Charlie) has been getting, and that you would receive if you took her (his) place, are Level 1 shocks. They're the lowest level of shock that would be perceived as at all aversive.[68]

The percentage who agreed to help and the mean number of shock trials agreed to be taken were as follows:[69]

	Distress	Empathy
Easy escape	25% (1.25)	86% (5)
Difficult escape	89% (4.89)	63% (3.75)

[66] Shaw et al. are careful to note that participants did not seem to clearly differentiate between motives to avoid empathy, distress, and sadness, and indeed according to a follow-up study, all three could have been playing a role in generating the results cited above (885). But so long as the avoidance of empathy is at least *part* of the causal motivational story, that is still a significant result for my purposes in this section. At the same time, additional research is clearly needed here. For additional discussion of empathy avoidance, see Batson 2011: 191–3.

[67] Batson 1987: 109. See also Batson 2011: 113–14, 191. For discussion of empathy-induced altruism and the cost-benefit analysis by the person who is altruistically motivated, see Batson 2011: chapter three.

[68] Batson et al. 1983: 714.

[69] Batson et al. 1983: 714.

In the second study, the procedure was the same except that the passage above read:

> Before you decide, I should tell you that the shocks Elaine (Charlie) has been getting, and that you would receive if you took her (his) place, are Level 4 shocks. They are clearly painful, but of course not harmful.[70]

This one change led to a stunning difference in the results:[71]

	Distress	Empathy
Easy escape	50% (3.13)	14% (.29)
Difficult escape	67% (3.89)	60% (3.30)

Compassionate people, on the other hand, would not let their attention to the needs of others be distracted so easily by threats to their own self-interest, or at least not unless the threats were much more severe.

Of course, one could just argue that people need to be better habituated into blocking out other considerations from their minds and focusing solely on what the person in need is believed to be feeling. But there are real practical limitations to how much the psychological lives of most people can be reshaped, and the worry here is that it may be psychologically unrealistic to expect that they both develop a robust disposition to become reliably empathetic, *and* also have their empathetic emotions, once triggered, be strong enough to block these self-interested influences.

(c) *Empathy is highly partial.* A compassionate person's helping should not be sensitive to facts about what group a person in need belongs to, so long as membership in that group is morally irrelevant to whether he should be helped or not. Obviously, if the group in question consists of suicide bombers, Nazis, or the like, that is morally relevant, but in most ordinary cases group membership based upon race, sex, or nationality has no bearing from the moral perspective on helping decisions. Other things being equal, whether a person is male or female, for instance, should not play a role when the need for help is obvious, the problem is easy to address, and the means and opportunity to do so are readily available.

The problem with empathy is that, at least among many participants today, it appears to be highly partial to group membership in morally problematic ways.[72] Here are two examples. Stefan Stürmer and his colleagues (2006) had students read an (alleged) message from a fellow student at the University of

---

[70] Batson et al. 1983: 715.
[71] Batson et al. 1983: 716.
[72] Empathy is also connected to other forms of morally problematic partiality as well. See Batson 2011: 193–5.

Kiel in Germany. The message detailed the student's struggles in finding a room to live in that he could afford. Participants were subsequently given a chance to record their willingness to help this person. Group membership was manipulated by having the student in need introduce himself by saying "Hi, by the way I am Markus (or Mohammed), and who are you?" Participants were forty-seven students of a German cultural background, and forty-seven students of a Muslim background.[73]

While both German and Muslim participants self-reported high levels of empathy for a Muslim student in need, the key difference which emerged was that empathy only correlated significantly with helping intentions by Muslim participants for a Muslim student, but not by German participants for a Muslim student. When the student in need was an in-group member, empathy was a significant predictor of helping intentions (0.62), but when the student was an out-group member, empathy did not predict such intentions (0.09).[74]

From a neuroscientific perspective, Xiaojing Xu and colleagues (2009) used fMRI scans to compare responses by seventeen Chinese and sixteen Caucasian college students to observations of a video of (i) a Caucasian face receiving a painful and a non-painful stimulus, and (ii) a Chinese face receiving the same stimuli. They also asked participants to rate the pain intensity felt by the person, and how unpleasant they were made to feel by observing the video.[75] These ratings turned out to not differ significantly along in-group versus out-group lines. But the fMRI results revealed differences in empathetic responses as measured by neural activity in the anterior cingulate cortex, which is known to mediate empathy for the pain of others. These responses "decreased remarkably when participants viewed faces of racial in-group members relative to racial out-group members. This effect was comparable in Caucasian and Chinese participants and suggests that modulations of empathic neural responses by racial group members are similar in different ethnic groups."[76] Given the divergence between the self-report and neuroimaging findings, it appears that there may be a subconscious racial bias in empathetic feelings for others in distress.

The larger point here is to illustrate another respect in which the gap between our current empathetic capacities and the normative requirements of compassion remains sizable.

---

[73] Stürmer et al. 2006: 945–6.

[74] Stürmer et al. 2006: 948. Similar results emerged in Stürmer's research on sexual orientation, and even on something as benign as whether a person processes information in a "detailed" or a "global" way. For the latter, see Stürmer et al. 2006: 949–54. For the former, see Stürmer et al. 2005.

[75] In another study, Johnson et al. 2002 found that white participants self-reported greater empathy for and would give lesser punishments to white rather than black defendants charged with a criminal act.

[76] Xu et al. 2009: 8528.

(d) *Empathy can lead to immoral behavior*. Compassion understood as a moral virtue disposes a person to act in certain morally appropriate ways. Sometimes empathy does as well. In many of the studies I have mentioned already, empathy led participants to help at higher rates on tasks that were clearly morally acceptable. But empathy can easily lead people away from moral behavior, and *even by their own moral principles*. As such, then, it seems to be, not a moral or an immoral emotion, but a non-moral or morally neutral one.

Batson's research, once again, has been central here.[77] In one study, participants were supervisors who had the ability to assign two workers (also allegedly participants in the study) to either a positive-consequence task (correct responses would be rewarded with a raffle ticket for a $30 gift certificate) or a negative-consequence task (incorrect responses would result in an uncomfortable electric shock). They were told that, "Most supervisors feel that flipping a coin is the fairest way to assign workers to the tasks, but the decision is entirely up to you. You can assign the workers however you wish."[78] Twenty participants then make their assignment. Twenty others were given the usual objective perspective manipulation, and then handed a note from one of the participants (Participant C) describing her relationship difficulties. The final twenty participants were given the usual empathy manipulation before receiving the same note. Here is how Participant C was assigned:

	No communication	Communication (objective)	Communication (empathy)
Positive	10	10	15
Negative	10	10	5

Hence in the empathy condition some participants seemed to knowingly violate the fair procedure for assigning Participant C. Furthermore, ten of the empathy-induced participants used the coin and ten did not. Most interesting, perhaps, is that 90 percent of participants in each group (18 out of 20) said that flipping the coin was the most fair thing to do, and in the empathy group participants who did not follow this principle admitted to having acted less morally even by their own lights.[79]

Batson's experiment involved a principle of procedural justice. What about distributive justice? In a different study, thirty participants each were assigned to the objective perspective and empathy perspective conditions with respect

---

[77] In addition to the studies mentioned below, see also Batson et al. 2003b and the review in Batson 2011: 195–8.
[78] Batson et al. 1995a: 1044.
[79] Batson et al. 1995a: 1045–6.

to the (fictional) story of Sheri Summers, a child with a muscle-paralyzing disease for which there is no cure. They were told that there does exist an expensive drug, not for combatting Sheri's disease, but for substantially improving her quality of life. Participants were then presented with an opportunity to transfer Sheri from the "Waiting List" to the "Immediate Help Group" at a "Quality Life Foundation." The consequence, which was explicitly noted to participants, would be that, "Moving your child up into the Immediate Help Group means that children who are currently higher on the Waiting List than your child, due to earlier application, greater need, or shorter life expectancy, will have to wait longer."[80] Here were the results:[81]

	Low empathy	High empathy
Proportion reassigning	33%	73%

So the vast majority of participants were willing to put a child ahead of others for the distribution of scarce resources even though the others had a greater need or shorter life expectancy.

Again, it is important to stress that empathy also frequently leads to behavior which is in line with commonly accepted moral principles.[82] But the studies above suggest that it can evoke highly partial feelings in certain cases which reflect, not a principle of morality or a moral motive, but a conflict with what is moral.[83] This then is a fourth respect noted in this section in which empathy and the virtue of compassion still seem far apart.[84]

[80] Batson et al. 1995a: 1049.

[81] Batson et al. 1995a: 1050.

[82] For additional results, see Batson et al. 1997d, 2002b. Day et al. (2010) reviewed the literature on empathy and sexual and violent offenders, and in particular the effectiveness of training programs designed to foster empathetic capacities so that empathy will inhibit future re-offending. They raise concerns about the relevant conceptual and methodological issues, and call for more rigorous studies to be conducted.

[83] It can also conflict with what is in the collective good of a group. Batson et al. (1995b) developed two studies in which resources could be distributed to oneself, another individual in the group, or the group as a whole (in which case, the resources have increased value, and if everyone were to distribute to the group, then each individual would be much better off). Empathy-induced participants, as we would expect, distributed more resources to the other individual, at the expense of resources for the group in general. See also the review in Batson 2011: 198–205.

[84] A natural thought here is that empathetic motivation needs to be supplemented with motives of justice or other morally relevant principles. Each can then act as a corrective for the other, with empathy guarding against excessive impersonality and rationalization, and impartial principles of justice guarding against the overly partial tendencies we saw above. For similar remarks, see Batson et al. 1995a: 1053 and Batson 2011: 226.

5.6 CONCLUSION

The observations from the previous section illustrate how much of a challenge it will be to take our empathetic capacities as they seem to be functioning today for most people, and develop them into the virtue of compassion. And these observations do not uniquely pertain to this one virtue.[85] The fact that many of us are (i) motivated to avoid feeling empathy in certain cases, (ii) have empathetic feelings which are extremely fragile and can easily give way to self-interest, (iii) form empathetic feelings that are highly partial in morally problematic ways to group membership, and (iv) allow empathetic feelings to lead to immoral behavior by our own lights, represent significant obstacles to the cultivation of *any* moral virtue using these empathetic capacities. This includes ordinary virtues like kindness, generosity, charity, and selflessness, as well as any potentially undiscovered virtues. At the same time, I want to stress that I have given no reason for thinking that these obstacles are insurmountable, only that this route to virtue will be full of important challenges.

Hence in this chapter I have outlined some of the workings of another enhancer for helping, empathy, and how it lends further support to various claims from earlier chapters. One novel feature of empathy, however, is the altruistic motivation it seems to generate, a feature that can make compassion seem more psychologically realistic. But at the end of this chapter, I suggested some reasons for tempering that optimism, at least for most of us at the present time.

These four chapters have focused on enhancers for helping: guilt, embarrassment, positive moods, elevation, activated moral norms, and empathy. Of course, there are many others besides these; the list has never been presented as complete. But in the next chapter, I turn to the opposite phenomenon—inhibitors.

---

[85] Thanks to Todd Calder for suggesting that I address this point.

6

Negative Moods, Group Effects, and Helping

Over the course of the past four chapters, I have examined a wide variety of what I call "enhancers" of helping motivation and helping behavior. Before going any further, it might be useful to organize these enhancers, and in section one I do so using the nature of the motivation to help to which they seem to give rise. Then I turn to the central topic of this chapter, which are the closely related "inhibitors" of helping. Some general claims about inhibitors are made in section two, and then sections three and four offer two specific examples—negative moods and group effects. This will serve to round out the presentation of work in psychology which has led me to the framework of Mixed Traits to be developed in Part III.

6.1 ORGANIZING THE ENHANCERS

How can we bring some semblance of order to the apparent grab-bag of different variables in chapters two through five that serve to enhance helping motivation and, thereby, helping behavior itself? It turns out that their choice and order of presentation were not an accident, as can be seen once we return to the topic of the different kinds of motives.

While much of the experimental evidence is still preliminary at the current stage of research, I believe enough has been done to take seriously the plausibility of a *pluralistic* theory of motivation.[1] Monist theories hold that all ultimate desires by all people are of only one kind. A monist theory that is egoistic, for instance, would claim that our ultimate desires are always self-directed,[2] while a purely altruistic theory would hold that they are always

[1] Sober and Wilson (1998: 228) also use this label.
[2] Of course this is consistent with there still being many different types of egoistic ultimate desires, such as desires for self-rewards and for the avoidance of various forms of self and social punishment.

other-directed. A pluralistic theory, naturally enough, maintains that for at least some human beings, their ultimate desires are of two or more different kinds.[3]

I have already distinguished between three different kinds of motivation—egoistic, altruistic, and moralistic, the last of which involves ultimate desires to do what is morally right, good, appropriate, or the like for its own sake.[4] For these kinds, I gave a careful formulation of what they involve, and said that there is some preliminary evidence to link certain of the enhancers to each of them. More precisely, and glossing over some of the qualifications that were presented earlier, we have seen:[5]

Egoistic Enhancers
    Guilt
    Anticipated guilt
    Embarrassment
    Positive moods
Altruistic Enhancers
    Empathy
Moralistic Enhancers
    Elevation
    Activated moral norms

Nothing about this taxonomy is intended to be complete. For one thing, there may be other kinds of motivation besides these three. For instance, Batson has also distinguished collective motivation, or motivation not to benefit oneself or another individual person, but rather a group as a whole.[6]

Another obvious reason for why the taxonomy is not complete is that there are plenty of other enhancers besides the ones listed here.[7] One of them, for instance, is negative moods under certain conditions, as I will suggest in section three. In addition, we can expect that beliefs about antici-pated states of positive mood can give rise to helping if that helping is thought to be conducive to attaining that mood. Similarly, beliefs about anticipated states of embarrassment can give rise to helping if that helping is conducive in

---

[3] Or alternatively that for some human beings, they are of one kind, while for others they are of a different kind. For more on pluralistic theories of motivation, see Stich et al. 2010: 153.

[4] For a recent review of work on moralistic motivation, see Batson 2011: 220–4, who calls this motivation "principlism."

[5] For instance, with guilt I said that some of the models of guilt-induced helping might be better classified as involving moralistic motivation rather than egoistic motivation. Similarly in chapter four, n. 78, I noted that elevation might be tied to altruistic motivation.

[6] Batson et al. 2003a: 288 and 2011: chapter nine. There is some evidence that this is a distinct kind of motivation at least in contrast to the egoistic variety. See, e.g. Dawes et al. 1990.

[7] For a helpful overview of relevant variables, see Batson et al. 2003a.

the opposite direction to avoiding that embarrassment. Other possibilities include empathetic joy,[8] empathetic anger,[9] interpersonal warmth,[10] and distress avoidance.[11]

Nevertheless it seems clear both that (i) these three kinds of motives represent three of the most important and psychologically influential kinds for any study of moral behavior, and (ii) the enhancers of helping listed above play a significant role in our psychological lives and are among the most extensively studied variables affecting helping in the psychology literature.

While not the focus of this discussion, it would be important in a longer treatment to consider the various ways in which different enhancers can conflict or cooperate with each other. For instance, an activated moral norm having to do with impartiality might serve to offset to some degree the partiality associated with empathy. Or motives to improve oneself as a result of feeling elevated could lead a person in a good mood to continue to help even when the task becomes unpleasant or difficult. Clearly much important work could be done in this area.

The ways in which each of these different enhancers can increase helping motivation is not mysterious, and I have taken pains to detail some of the mental states which are relevant to each of them. With activated moral norms, for instance, this includes:

(i) Desires concerned with helping when doing so will contribute towards complying with the relevant moral norms, provided the benefits of doing so are not (significantly) outweighed by the costs.

Whereas with respect to positive moods this includes (according to one leading model):

(ii) Desires concerned with helping when doing so will contribute towards extending my good mood, and more so than any alternative reasonable means of doing so which is thought to be available.

And so on for the different enhancers.

Hence helping motivation and behavior are influenced by a number of different mental state dispositions, only some of which may be at work on any given occasion. Furthermore, the enhancers for these dispositions can come in highly diverse forms ranging from feelings of empathy or guilt to reflective moral judgments, and can operate at or below the level of conscious awareness.

---

[8] See Batson et al. 1991.   [9] See Vitaglione and Barnett 2003.
[10] See Williams and Bargh 2008.   [11] See Batson et al. 2003a: 284.

6.2 INHIBITORS OF HELPING

These same points apply in parallel fashion to inhibitors. Because of the obvious similarities, the discussion of inhibitors will be brief. In this section, I make some general observations about their function, before turning to two specific examples of inhibitors in the remaining sections of the chapter.

As with enhancers, I claim that there are certain inhibitors which can decrease the frequency with which a person would otherwise help in moderately demanding situations relevant to helping. Not surprisingly, if a pluralistic theory of motivation is plausible for enhancers, then it is likely going to be for inhibitors as well. Indeed there is significant overlap between enhancers and inhibitors for helping, as the following taxonomy illustrates:

Egoistic Inhibitors
    Guilt
    Anticipated guilt
    Embarrassment
    Anticipated embarrassment
    Positive moods
    Negative moods
    Anticipated empathy[12]
    Anticipated blame
    Perceived situational ambiguity
Altruistic Inhibitors
    ?
Moralistic Inhibitors
    Activated moral norms favoring a helpful action

Once again, neither the kinds of motives nor the list of inhibitors should be taken as exhaustive. For instance, anger has also been found to inhibit helping, and so, presumably, do activated moral norms *opposing* a helpful action.[13]

I will discuss negative moods, anticipated embarrassment, anticipated blame, and perceived situational ambiguity in the next two sections of this chapter. But the overlap between the list of enhancers and inhibitors may seem confusing. What is the point of distinguishing between the two phenomena if the lists end up looking so similar?

The point is that a variable like guilt does not function *only* as an enhancer for helping. I said that guilt directly gives rise to a motive which does not itself pertain to helping, such as a desire to alleviate the feeling of guilt. In *some* conditions—for example, perhaps when I think there is a reasonable helping

---

[12] See Shaw et al. 1994 and the discussion in chapter five, section five.

[13] For anger and helping, see Weiner 1980a, 1980b, Reisenzein 1986, and Schaller and Cialdini 1990: 278. For additional inhibitors, see Schwartz 1977: 242–3 and Shaw et al. 1994: 879.

opportunity which can alleviate my feeling of guilt—helping is enhanced. In *other* conditions—for example, perhaps when I think the only available helping opportunity would serve to make me feel even guiltier—helping is actually inhibited. That is why, when I was detailing the mental states pertaining to the helping mechanism associated with guilt, I listed *both*:

(i) Desires concerned with helping when doing so will contribute towards alleviating my guilty feelings, and more so than any reasonable alternative means of doing so which is thought to be available.

(ii) Desires concerned with not helping when doing so will contribute towards perpetuating my guilty feelings, or will not alleviate them as effectively as some reasonable alternative means of doing so which is thought to be available.

A similar example involves activated moral norms that favor a helpful action and lead to a desire to comply with those norms. In some conditions, this desire in turn will give rise to increased motivation to help, while in others it will work against helping. Which of these outcomes it is often depends on the cost/benefit analysis and the work of either:

(iii) Desires concerned with helping when doing so will contribute towards complying with the relevant moral norms, provided the benefits of doing so are not (significantly) outweighed by the costs.

(iv) Desires concerned with not helping when the benefits of complying with the relevant moral norms are (significantly) outweighed by the costs, while also desiring to as much as possible still appear to be moral both to others and to oneself.

So these examples support the conclusion that some variables, such as guilt and activated moral norms, can serve as *both* enhancers and inhibitors depending on whether other relevant conditions apply.

It is important to be clear about what is being claimed concerning inhibitors. It is not that, when active, they simply lead to the same levels of helping motivation and behavior which are typically found in control participants in studies of helping. Rather, the claim is that they give rise to *motivation to not help* in a certain situation. So inhibitors, when the right conditions obtain, are expected to reduce helping rates *below* those seen in controls, as will become apparent in the results of actual studies presented in the next two sections.

Just as we could consider the interaction of multiple enhancers, so too multiple inhibitors can work together. Even an enhancer and an inhibitor could both be present in the same person at the same time. For instance, she could deliberately form a sincere moral judgment in favor of helping someone, but also believe that there is a good chance she may embarrass herself in front of others if she tries to help. So the motivational boost to help on the one hand could be negated by the motivational boost against helping on the other.

6.3 NEGATIVE AFFECT AND HELPING

In chapter three I was careful to only focus on the impact of *positive* moods on helping. What role do negative feelings or moods have to play? It is easy to think that just as positive mood enhances helping, so negative mood decreases helping as compared to control participants. And that would be right in certain cases.[14] But there is now significant empirical evidence for a connection between negative moods and *increased* helping too (including self-reported willingness to help, commitment to help, and actual helping behavior).[15] So what is often found in the psychology literature on negative moods are claims which directly parallel those for positive affect:

(a) An environmental variable is construed negatively and produces negative affect in the person.

(b) Negative affect significantly increases the activation and/or the functioning of a helping mechanism.

(c) The helping mechanism in turn brings about relevant helping motivation and behavior.

Again let me take each of these claims in turn.

(a) *Negative affect.* As with positive affect, the focus here is on negative moods and feelings rather than on negative emotions. More specifically, "negative affect" will refer to feelings of sadness that are temporary in duration and moderate in strength. As such, negative affect does not include more serious psychological conditions like clinical depression, as well as more intense negative emotions such as fear, anger, or guilt.[16] This is important since these other states also have their own distinct bearing on helping.

The first claim about negative affect should be intuitively compelling—participants confronted with what they take to be negative environmental variables are likely to experience negative affective states.[17] In the experimental literature, the kinds of manipulations designed to produce negative affect have included recalling a sad event, hearing loud noises, and being informed of a poor performance on a test.

(b) *Negative affect and increased activation.* In contrast to what I said might be expected on intuitive grounds, there is strong empirical evidence for the thesis that increased negative affect often significantly increases helping in

---

[14] See, e.g. Mathews and Canon 1975.

[15] See, e.g. Donnerstein et al. 1975. For overviews, see Carlson and Miller 1987, Miller and Carlson 1990, Schaller and Cialdini 1990, Salovey et al. 1991, and Taylor 1991.

[16] See Manucia et al. 1984: 357 n. 1, Cialdini et al. 1987: 750, Cialdini and Fultz 1990: 211, and Schaller and Cialdini 1990: 266.

[17] See, e.g. Schaller and Cialdini 1990: 271.

certain conditions. Thus, for example, in the same study from chapter three, Weyant also used his fake anagram study to induce negative affect in other test participants, and subsequently 71 percent volunteered to help in the high benefit, low cost scenario as opposed to only 33 percent of control participants.[18] So let me start with this initial diagram:

Negative affect
↓
Activation of helping mechanism

As with positive affect, the main focus in the literature has been on how best to model the influence that negative affect has on helping. In this case, a concomitance model has seemed to researchers to be much less promising. For negative moods can impair attention and thinking, fail to enhance the retrieval of negative events in memory, diminish feelings of control, increase time spent on cost/benefit analysis and examination of the situation, and draw focus away from the environment and onto the self.[19] In light of these cognitive influences, it is far from clear why motivation to help others would be produced as a casual byproduct.

Instead, the dominant model for understanding how negative affect increases helping has been a mood management hypothesis.[20] On this view, negative affect generates a motive to relieve the bad mood and return the person to an equilibrium condition. A number of means might be available for elevating mood, and one of them will often be helping others because of the social rewards and gratification associated with such behavior. Thus a preliminary diagram of how this hypothesis works looks something like this:

Negative affect
↓
Motive to relieve the bad mood
↓
Activation of helping mechanism

Not surprisingly, this view has implications which parallel those of the mood maintenance hypothesis for positive affect. One such implication is that other things being equal, people experiencing negative affect will not typically help

---

[18] Weyant 1978: 1173. For other results which indicate a relationship between negative affect and helping, see Cialdini and Kenrick 1976, Cialdini et al. 1982, Manucia et al. 1984, Cialdini et al. 1987, and Cialdini and Fultz 1990.

[19] See, respectively, Ellis and Ashbrook 1988, Nasby and Yando 1982, Alloy and Abramson 1979, Schwarz 1990, and Rogers et al. 1982.

[20] See Weiss et al. 1973, Cialdini et al. 1973, Cialdini and Kenrick 1976, Weyant 1978, Benson 1978, Manucia et al. 1984, Cialdini et al. 1987, Batson et al. 1989, Schaller and Cialdini 1990, and Taylor 1991. For criticism of the mood management model, see Carlson and Miller 1987 and Miller and Carlson 1990. For two alternative models, see Carlson and Miller 1987: 92–3 and Salovey et al. 1991: 222–3.

when the benefits for themselves of doing so are not perceived to outweigh the costs. In other words, if the costs associated with an action are taken to be greater than or roughly equal to the benefits, then that action will often be thought to make no contribution to eliminating a negative mood and hence often not be performed. A second implication is that other things being equal, if there are other actions available which by the person's own lights are also conducive to eliminating a bad mood, but at the same time they are much less costly for him to perform, then in those cases we should not expect negative affect to lead to increased helping.[21]

In light of these implications, I can present a more refined version of the mood management hypothesis as follows:

Negative affect

↓

Motive to relieve the bad mood

Perceived helping task(s)　→　　↓　　←　*Absence of other means of*
which contributes to　　　　　　　　　　*relieving the bad mood which*
relieving the bad mood　　　　　　　　　*are perceived to be more effective*

↓

Activation of helping mechanism

Similarly if this view is correct, then statement (b) can be revised to read:

(b*) Negative affect significantly increases the activation and/or the functioning of a helping mechanism, provided that the person does not take there to be other, more effective means of relieving his bad mood, and provided that the perceived helping task(s) itself is thought to be conducive to relieving his bad mood.

The above, then, captures the basic idea behind the mood management model.

Weyant's study is exactly in line with this model. Thus the breakdown for the proportion of participants who volunteered their time was as follows:[22]

	Negative affect	Controls
High benefits/high costs	29%	33%
High benefits/low costs	71%	33%
Low benefits/high costs	5%	29%
Low benefits/low costs	33%	33%

As expected, it was only in the high benefits/low costs scenario that participants experiencing negative affect exhibited a greater frequency of helping than controls.

---

[21] For related remarks, see Cialdini et al. 1973, Benson 1978, Cunningham et al. 1980, Manucia et al. 1984, Carlson and Miller 1987, and Salovey et al. 1991.

[22] Weyant 1978: 1173.

Similarly, in their 1984 study Manucia and her colleagues also examined the impact of their "freezing drug" on negative affect. First a different group of participants was required to recall and reminisce about sad experiences. They were then given the placebo and again only half of them were told about the drug's ability to freeze mood. Finally as they left the experiment, participants were presented with the opportunity to donate time to make calls for the blood organization. The results? Unlike in the case of positive affect, "sad subjects helped more than neutral mood controls only if they believed their mood was alterable. When sad subjects were led to believe that helping could not improve their mood, they were no more helpful than neutral mood subjects."[23] This is precisely what the mood management hypothesis predicted.

Such a model also helps to nicely explain an important age difference in the experimental results. Young children seem to generally exhibit reduced helping when experiencing negative affect, whereas we have seen that adults will often exhibit increased helping.[24] What best explains this difference? The advocate of the mood management hypothesis has a natural answer, namely that young children have not yet appreciated the social rewards associated with helping. They have not learned how society bestows approval, praise, gratitude, recognition, and the like on those who help others in need. Thus they do not have in place a psychological connection between helping, rewards, and negative mood relief. Adults, on the other hand, have typically been educated in the social rewards connected to helping, and so understand, even if inchoately, that negative affect can be relieved by helping. If this explanation is roughly correct, then one should expect there to be a gradual increase in the relationship between negative affect and helping at various age intervals approaching adulthood. According to a variety of studies, this is what we do in fact find.[25]

As an interesting aside, it is perhaps worth noting that no comparable age difference has been detected in the case of *positive* affect—both young children and adults alike exhibit increased helping.[26] Such a result could be construed as additional support for the concomitance model since the social rewards associated with helping might not be playing a role if young children who do not appreciate such rewards are helping to the same extent as adults when in a good mood.

Finally, by way of conclusion it is important to keep in mind the same cautionary note that was voiced in chapter three. Even if negative affect can

[23] Manucia et al. 1984: 362.

[24] One exception in the case of young children is when the helping would be noticed by an adult. In that case, children in negative moods help more than controls, presumably for the sake of approval from the adult. See Kenrick et al. 1979.

[25] For further discussion, see Moore et al. 1973, Rosenhan et al. 1974, Cialdini et al. 1973, Cialdini and Kenrick 1976, and Manucia et al. 1984.

[26] See, e.g. Moore et al. 1973, Rosenhan et al. 1974, and Barden et al. 1981.

increase helping by treating such behavior as a means to relieving the negative mood, it does not follow from this that the motive of relieving a bad mood is the *only* or even the *dominant* motive when it comes to a particular instance of helping. Instead, that motive might combine with several other independent motives to help, and simply add its own motivational contribution to the mix.

(c) *Helping mechanisms and helping behavior.* The third claim of this section is intended to be straightforward—in cases of helping increased by negative mood, the person's helping mechanism leads her to be increasingly motivated to help due to its having been activated by the output from the mood management system. This claim assumes, though, that other things are equal; increased helping motivation and behavior in these circumstances will not result if, for instance, there are malfunctions in the helping mechanism.

It is now easier to see how negative affect can serve as both an enhancer and an inhibitor of helping. As an enhancer, by combining our statements (a), (b), and (c) together with the mood management hypothesis, and holding other things equal, we get the following diagram:

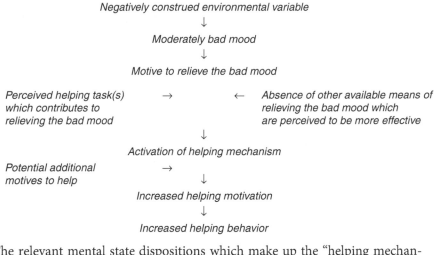

The relevant mental state dispositions which make up the "helping mechanism" would include:

(a) Beliefs concerned with the relationship between helping others and various personal costs for me, such as lost time, money, alternative activities, and so forth.

(b) Beliefs concerned with the relationship between helping others and various social reactions to me, such as approval, gratitude, praise, and so forth.

(c) Beliefs concerned with the relationship between helping others and various moral consequences for me, such as living up to my norms, improving my moral standing and purity, and so forth.

(d) Beliefs concerned with how these various personal costs, social reactions, and moral consequences can impact my bad mood.

(e) Desires concerned with helping when doing so will contribute towards alleviating my bad mood, and more so than any alternative reasonable means of doing so which is thought to be available.

(f) Desires concerned with not helping when doing so will perpetuate or worsen my bad mood, or will not alleviate the bad mood as effectively as some alternative reasonable means of doing so which is thought to be available.

Thus I might have a motive to relieve my bad mood, and a belief that a reasonable helping opportunity is available to me. The first three sets of beliefs in (a) through (c) can lead me to an implicit judgment about what might ensue if I actually helped. And the fourth set of beliefs in (d) might lead me to think about how these various implications relate to alleviating my bad mood. Finally, this all might bring to bear a desire to help in connection with relieving my bad mood.

Similarly a story can be told whereby negative affect functions as an inhibitor. In those cases where I think the helping task would be very costly for me, I could form a desire as in (e) to not help when doing so will perpetuate or worsen my bad mood. So too at least some cases in which helping is perceived to be an advantageous means of relieving the bad mood, but not the most advantageous means, can be understood as follows:

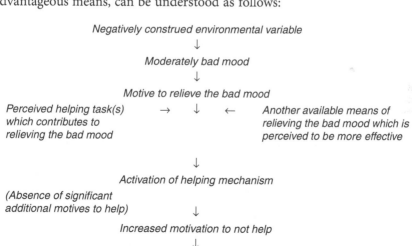

Negatively construed environmental variable
↓
Moderately bad mood
↓
Motive to relieve the bad mood

Perceived helping task(s)   →   ↓   ←   Another available means of
which contributes to   relieving the bad mood which is
relieving the bad mood   perceived to be more effective

↓
Activation of helping mechanism

(Absence of significant
additional motives to help)   ↓

Increased motivation to not help
↓
Absent or reduced helping behavior

Here in this diagram the key contribution is made by my desire to not help when helping would not alleviate my bad mood as effectively as some alternative means of doing so which I think is available to me. Note that helping is actively *inhibited* in these particular cases. In Weyant's experiment, for example, while 29 percent of controls in the low benefits/high costs condition volunteered their time, only 5 percent of participants in the same condition who were also in a negative mood signed up to volunteer. So it seems that the negative mood was actively leading to the *suppression* of their helping, rather than just not enhancing it.

To summarize the discussion of moods, the following three models represent what at present are the most promising ways of understanding the relationship between affect and helping:

> *Positive affect*:
>   Mood maintenance model
>   Concomitance model
> *Negative affect*:
>   Mood management model

It appears that we are psychologically organized to handle positive and negative affect differently in relation to helping and hence, as psychologists have often noted, any model which tries to offer one unified story about both kinds of affect and helping will be overly simplistic. This is true even if the mood maintenance and mood management models end up being correct; sustaining a positive mood is a rather different psychological process from eliminating a negative mood altogether.[27]

6.4 GROUP EFFECTS AND HELPING

Thanks in large part to Bibb Latané and John Darley's pioneering work in the 1960s and 1970s, the inhibitory effect of groups on helping is one of the best known and most reliably documented phenomena in psychology. Yet it is worth noting that there are also plenty of cases in which being in a group does *not* play a significant inhibitory role. So we need to proceed carefully.

In Latané and Judith Rodin's classic 1969 "Lady in Distress" experiment, participants thought they were taking part in a market research survey, and met a female representative in a small room. While they filled out forms, the representative went to the next office and after four minutes:

> if they were listening carefully, [participants] heard her climb up on a chair to get a book from the top shelf. Even if they were not listening carefully, they heard a loud crash and a woman's scream as the chair fell over. 'Oh, my God, my foot,' cried the representative. 'I . . . I . . . can't move . . . it. Oh, my

---

[27] For similar remarks, see Schaller and Cialdini 1990.

ankle. I ... can't ... can't ... get ... this thing off ... me.' She moaned and cried for about a minute longer, getting gradually more subdued and controlled.[28]

The main dependent variable was whether participants exhibited any helping behavior, even if it was just calling aloud to the representative to check on her. The four experimental groups were: just one participant in the room, one participant paired with a confederate who ignored the crash, two participants who were strangers, and two participants who were friends. The percentage helping was as follows:[29]

Alone	70%
Two friends	70%
Two strangers	40%
Participant plus confederate	7%

If we treat the alone participant as the control, then clearly helping is being seriously inhibited by the presence of others,[30] and as I will suggest later, this is not at all what we should expect if the participants had the virtue of compassion to even a moderate degree. Rather, in this study such a character trait seems irrelevant to the psychological explanation of behavior especially in the third and fourth conditions.

Similar helping patterns have been found in a number of different experimental setups,[31] which following Latané and Steve Nida (1981) can be divided into four categories:

Emergencies involving the participants. Here the paradigm experiment involves a stream of smoke coming into the room where one or more participants are seated.[32]

---

[28] Latané and Darley 1970: 58. For the original study, see Latané and Rodin 1969.

[29] Latané and Rodin 1969: 193–5, Latané and Darley 1970: 60–3.

[30] Even in the two friends case, Latané and Darley note that, "While superficially this appears as high as the Alone condition, again there must be a correction for the fact that two people are free to act. When compared to the 91 percent base rate of hypothetical two-person groups, friends do inhibit each other from intervening" (1970: 63).

[31] For reviews, see Latané and Nida 1981 and Latané et al. 1981. In examining forty-eight studies, Latané et al. found that in group effect studies using confederates, 75 percent of alone participants helped, whereas less than 53 percent of participants in groups did. For group effect studies using groups of participants with no confederates, 50 percent of alone participants helped, whereas 22 percent of participants in groups did (1981: 291).

Garcia et al. (2002) even found that actually being in a group context is not necessary for a group effect to result; rather merely priming participants with the idea of being in the presence of others had a significant effect on dollars pledged using a charity-giving measure.

[32] Latané and Darley 1968. For additional studies, see Ross and Braband 1973 and Latané and Nida 1981: 311.

Emergencies involving a victim in danger. Examples include hearing a woman fall off a chair or ladder,[33] a man have an epileptic seizure,[34] a maintenance worker fall off a ladder in another room,[35] and a man cry out in pain from what seemed to be a serious electric shock.[36]

Emergencies involving third party criminal or immoral behavior. Examples include participants watching a thief steal cash from a receptionist's envelope,[37] observing young men steal a case of beer from a discount store,[38] and hearing a bully beat up a child.[39]

Nonemergency settings. Participants in groups have been found to be less likely to help with knocked over discs,[40] accidentally dropped coins in an elevator,[41] and evaluating written work.[42]

Indeed, being in a group can not only inhibit helping others, but it has also been found to inhibit the promotion of the agent's own self-interest.[43]

But matters are more complex than this, as there are group effect studies in which helping is *not* inhibited, or if it is, it is not inhibited to nearly the same extent as the studies above found. Here are some examples:[44]

Group cohesiveness. Friends in a group were significantly faster in responding to a perceived epileptic fit than were strangers in a group,[45] and in another study, participants in groups of four who had been allowed to meet and interact with each other for twenty minutes helped at a much higher rate than did participants who were not so allowed (68.9 percent versus 25.8 percent). Indeed, highly cohesive groups of four helped more than did highly cohesive groups of two, thereby reversing the group effect.[46]

Acquaintance with the victim. Participants helped at the same rate and speed in a group as opposed to alone when they had some prior interaction with a victim of a seizure.[47]

---

[33] Latané and Darley 1970: chapter seven and Staub 1974.
[34] Darley and Latané 1968 and Latané and Darley 1970: chapter eleven.
[35] Clark and Word 1972.
[36] Clark and Word 1974. For additional studies, see Gottlieb and Carver 1980, Schwartz and Gottlieb 1980, Latané and Nida 1981: 311, and Tice and Baumeister 1985.
[37] Latané and Darley 1970: chapter eight.
[38] Latané and Darley 1970: chapter eight.
[39] Latané and Darley 1970: 82. For additional studies, see Schwartz and Gottlieb 1980, Latané and Nida 1981: 311, Chekroun and Brauer 2002, and Fischer et al. 2006: 268.
[40] Karakashian et al. 2006.
[41] Latané and Dabbs 1977.
[42] Petty et al. 1977b. For additional studies, see Petty et al. 1977a, Latané et al. 1979, Latané and Nida 1981: 311, 313, Wiesenthal et al. 1983, and Chekroun and Brauer 2002: 855.
[43] Petty et al. 1977a, for instance, found a decrease in willingness to take coupons for a free burger in group rather than alone contexts.
[44] For some additional examples besides these, see Staub 1974, Latané and Nida 1981: 321, Chekroun and Brauer 2002, and Karakashian et al. 2006: 28.
[45] Latané and Darley 1970: 105–6. See also the discussion of friends versus strangers in groups in Latané and Rodin 1969: 200–1.
[46] Rutkowski et al. 1983.
[47] Latané and Darley 1970: 108–9.

Non-ambiguous emergency situation. Participants in four different group config-urations helped at a rate of 100 percent in a non-ambiguous emergency involving a maintenance worker falling from a ladder in another room.[48] Similarly in 62 out of 65 cases an ill-looking man was helped after he collapsed on the floor of a New York City subway.[49]

Gaze. In an experiment involving dropped coins, 33 percent of participants helped when alone versus 11 percent in the presence of a passive confederate. However, when the victim gazed directly at the participant, 57 percent of those alone helped and 82 percent of those in the presence of the confederate did.[50]

Startle response. Participants facing each other in groups responded to the sound of a screen crashing on a workman and his painful groans at roughly the same rate as alone participants did (80 percent versus 90 percent), whereas non-facing participants in groups responded much less (20 percent).[51]

Future interactions with other group members. Being told to expect future face-to-face interactions greatly increased responses by participants in groups to a choking emergency in which a victim cried for help, and according to the experimenters brought about, "the near elimination of the bystander effect."[52]

A central challenge in this area of research has been to develop a plausible model which helps to explain why group effects on helping have such mixed results. Perhaps the most promising account continues to be the one initially proposed by Latané and Darley, which appeals to the three central psycho-logical processes of diffusion of responsibility, social influence, and audience inhibition.[53] Let us briefly take up each of these in turn.

Diffusion of Responsibility. The more people thought to be present, the more the costs associated with failing to help are not taken to be born just by the one person but rather are partially shared by all the bystanders. By shifting some of the responsibility onto others, the person's fear of being blamed is often proportionally alleviated.[54] Such a process helps to explain why gaze might combat the group effect. By singling out a particular member of a group using a focused gaze, a person in need of help can thereby block diffusion of responsibility by seeming to put more responsibility on that one person's shoulders than on other members of the group.

Social Influence. In ambiguous situations where it is not immediately apparent to the person that someone needs help, she may look to others in a group for

[48] Clark and Word 1972.
[49] Piliavin et al. 1969. For additional studies, see Clark and Word 1974, Schwartz and Gottlieb 1980, and Fischer et al. 2006.
[50] Valentine 1980.
[51] Darley et al. 1973.
[52] Gottlieb and Carver 1980: 258.
[53] For overviews, see Latané and Darley 1968, 1970, Schwartz and Gottlieb 1980, Latané and Nida 1981, Latané et al. 1981, and Cacioppo et al. 1986.
[54] The same applies to the fear of feeling guilty. For additional discussion, see Latané and Darley 1970: chapter ten, Staub 1974: 324, 339, Gottlieb and Carver 1980, and Latané et al. 1981: 298.

guidance to understand what is going on. If they are unfazed and non-responsive, then she is much more likely to conclude that help is not required. Thus a state of what is often called "pluralistic ignorance" can result from the joint presence of a desire for situational clarity, a belief that a potential helping situation is ambiguous, and a belief that others appear to act as if nothing significant is happening.[55] Such a process helps to explain why in the non-ambiguous emergency cases mentioned above, helping did not seem to be significantly inhibited.

Audience Inhibition. The third component of Latané and Darley's model appeals to anticipated embarrassment. The more people thought to be present, the greater the negative evaluation that might ensue if it turns out that I have misconstrued the situation, attempt to help, and yet in fact help is not needed.[56] Such a fear can nicely account for the difference in helping inhibition between groups of friends versus groups of strangers. We are likely to be much more comfortable acting in front of our friends and to fear their negative evaluations less than we would acting in the presence of complete strangers.

By appealing to three separate processes, it might appear as if this model is needlessly complex. But a number of studies in the past thirty years have supported the importance of these processes in accounting for group effects on helping. For example, Latané and Darley ran a study which varied channels of communication.[57] In addition to the alone condition, some participants were in a no-communication environment (to test diffusion of responsibility), a one-way communication environment (to test diffusion of responsibility plus audience inhibition), and a two-way communication environment (to test all three processes). As expected, the highest helping rate was in the alone condition, followed by no communication, one-way communication, and full communication, with a significant percentage drop-off from one condition to the next. Studies such as this one have been taken to show both that (i) even one of these processes can significantly inhibit helping by itself, and (ii) in certain cases all three processes seem to be at work together in jointly inhibiting helping at a rate that is greater than if only one were active.[58]

---

[55] For discussion see Latané and Darley 1968, 1970: 40–2, Latané and Rodin 1969: 198–9, Latané et al. 1981: 298, and Clark and Word 1974. For more on pluralistic ignorance in general, see Miller and McFarland 1991 and Prentice and Miller 1996.

[56] As Latané and Darley note, "The bystander to an emergency is offered the chance to step up on stage, a chance that should be every actor's dream. But in this case, it is every actor's nightmare. He hasn't rehearsed the part very well and he must play it when the curtain is already up. The greater the number of other people present, the more possibility there is of losing face" (1970: 40). For additional discussion, see Latané and Darle 1970: 38–40, Latané et al. 1981: 297, Miller and McFarland 1991, Prentice and Miller 1996, and Karakashian et al. 2006. For more general discussion of the role of anticipated embarrassment, see Sabini and Silver 2005: 557–60 and Adams 2006: 154.

[57] Latané and Darley 1976. See also the summary in Latané et al. 1981: 299.

[58] For additional studies relevant to the importance of each process, see Latané and Darley 1968, 1970: 111, Latané and Rodin 1969: 199–200, Petty et al. 1977a, and Schwartz and Gottlieb 1980.

By now the relationship of these processes to the discussion of inhibitors should be clear. Here, for instance, is one way of partially modeling the effect of audience inhibition on helping in groups:

Belief that this person may (not) need help
+
Belief that I may embarrass myself by helping
↓
Motive to not embarrass myself
↓
Activation of helping mechanism

(Absence of significant
additional motives to help)   ↓

Increased motivation to not help
↓
Absent or reduced helping behavior

The central mental states which are relevant to the above "helping mechanism" would include the following:

(i) Beliefs concerned with the extent to which others are in a position to observe my helping behavior, and about the extent to which they will evaluate and judge me for trying to help.

(ii) Desires concerned with helping when it is thought to potentially earn the approval of those observing me.

(iii) Desires concerned with not helping when helping is thought to potentially earn the disapproval of those observing me.

Similarly for diffusion of responsibility:

Belief that this person may (not) need help
+
Belief that I may be blamed by others if I help
↓
Motive to not be blamed by others
↓
Activation of helping mechanism

(Absence of significant
additional motives to help)   ↓

Increased motivation to not help
↓
Absent or reduced helping behavior

Note that no claim is being made that these are the *only* three processes at work. For instance, Cacioppo et al. have claimed that what they call "confusion of responsibility" also plays a role, where this is not the, "responsibility a potential helper feels for helping a victim, but rather it is . . . the responsibility for harmdoing the potential helper believes others will attribute to him or her should he or she help the victim" (1986: 101). And for additional elaboration of the Latané and Darley framework, see Latané et al. 1981: 300–9.

Here the relevant mental states would include:

(i) Beliefs concerned with the extent to which others are in a position to help as well, and therefore with the extent of my own personal responsibility to help.

(ii) Desires concerned with helping when I bear a significant degree of personal responsibility and so could likely be blamed for not helping.

(iii) Desires concerned with not helping when I do not bear a significant degree of personal responsibility and so would not be blamed for not helping.

Again note that on all of these models helping is being actively *inhibited*, rather than just not enhanced, since the helping rates in such cases are significantly lower than they are for controls who find themselves alone.[59] Indeed, such language is not foreign to psychologists—the group effect literature is replete with talk of the "inhibition of helping."[60]

Thus I claim that the experimental literature supports the widespread possession of mental state dispositions such as those listed above, dispositions which can inhibit helping when a person who has them is in a group setting. I also believe that this is another literature which points to psychological processes which are not compatible with the widespread possession of compassion.

If anything, the functioning of the inhibitors discussed in this chapter is even more antithetical to the virtue of compassion than that of the earlier enhancers. I do not plan on going over the same kinds of reasons for why I think this is the case that were highlighted in previous chapters. For instance, again many participants did not perform obvious and easy helping tasks, and even when they did help, their helping was not for altruistic motives. These points should now be straightforward.

Instead let me take a few of the requirements already stated in Part II, and switch them from talking about enhancers to talking about inhibitors. For instance:

---

[59] This inhibitory effect should not be interpreted as implying that these participants were not motivated *at all* to help (which might be a misleading implication of the diagrams above), or that typically the group effect serves to completely *undermine* helping motivation. Rather, the more plausible interpretation is that the participants are often motivated to help to some extent, and when alone typically do so in emergency cases. But in at least some group effect studies, participants in groups are conflicted by opposing motivation arising from, for instance, anticipated embarrassment. Thus these participants experience motivational tension, and in many instances the motivation to help is outweighed by the motivation arising from one or more of the group effect processes of the kind described above. For related discussion, see Darley and Latané 1968: 382, Latané and Darley 1970: 80, 100, 122, and Ross and Nisbett 1991: 45–6.

[60] See, e.g. Latané and Darley 1970: 38, 126, Latané and Nida 1981: 309, Tice and Baumeister 1985: 421, 424, Garcia et al. 2002, and Chekroun and Brauer 2002: 863.

(a) A compassionate person's trait of compassion will not be dependent on the absence of certain inhibitors (such as anticipated moderate embarrassment or blame, or moderately bad moods) in leading him to perform helpful actions, such that if these inhibitors were not present, then his frequency of helping would significantly increase in the same nominal situations.[61]

Compassionate people are expected to reliably help regardless of whether doing so may increase their bad mood or whether they anticipate being moderately embarrassed. So even if a person who is alone would reliably help in an emergency involving an accident in the next room, a compassionate person would not let anticipated embarrassment get in the way of her helping when a stranger is also in the room with her.

Here are two other requirements adapted from chapter two:

(b) A compassionate person, when acting in character, does not regularly refrain from helping from certain egoistic motives (such as the desire to avoid anticipated moderate embarrassment or blame, or the desire to relieve a moderately bad mood) which are often powerful enough that were they not present, she would reliably help in the same moderately demanding helping situations.

(c) A compassionate person, when acting in character, does not regularly refrain from helping from certain egoistic motives (such as the desire to avoid anticipated moderate embarrassment or blame, or the desire to relieve a moderately bad mood) which are often powerful enough that they *also* lead her to pursue another non-virtuous course of action besides helping, if that alternative is thought to be more conducive to the satisfaction of those egoistic motives.[62]

Yet while a compassionate person might not do these things, they are precisely what most participants did in the standard group effect studies.

6.5 CONCLUSION

This concludes what I want to say in this chapter about inhibitors of helping (although no doubt much more needs to be said). It also concludes the presentation of the some of the experimental evidence from psychology on helping which, in my view, leads us in the direction of the account of Mixed Traits to be developed next (although plenty more evidence could be provided). By now the broad outlines of that framework have been alluded to. In Part III, I turn to laying it out systematically.

---

[61] This requirement exists even if it is *also* happens to be the case that the person regularly attempts to perform helping tasks when the need for help is obvious and the effort involved in helping is very minimal.

[62] It is important to qualify this principle just to *certain* egoistic motives. Someone who does not help when he has a gun being held to his head, and instead does something else that is non-virtuous in order to stay alive, need not thereby be deficient in compassion. Thanks to an anonymous referee here.

Part III

Outlining the Framework

7

Mixed Helping Traits

When I first read various helping studies in psychology, I thought that they challenged the widespread possession of the virtue of compassion. That was a negative conclusion. But I also thought that collectively these studies pointed in the direction of a positive account of character traits related to helping, one that had not been discussed much if at all. The goal of this chapter is to systematically introduce this positive account.

But I am not just interested in moral character as it pertains to helping. Rather, I want to claim that the positive view offered in this chapter can be used as the basis to offer a broader account of the character traits which most people possess *in general*. In chapter eight, I sketch this account, and in Part IV of the book I turn to psychological research in other moral domains such as lying and harming others in order to suggest that my picture seems to be supported there as well.

Returning to this chapter, I said that my positive account is informed by the studies reviewed in Part II. At the same time, it also draws at certain points on ideas from some of the well-known models of (non-moral) personality traits in the psychology literature. In particular, I will borrow in several places from themes developed in both the cognitive-affective personality system (CAPS) model and the density-distribution model, although as far as I know neither model has been extensively applied by psychologists to the topic of moral character. Those who are acquainted with these models should feel at home here, but at the same time I will not presuppose any prior familiarity with them.[1]

Section one of this chapter focuses on introducing the traits I have in mind which pertain to helping others, section two on how these traits can be enhanced and inhibited, section three on their consistency over time and across situations, section four on how they can come in degrees, section five

---

[1] For CAPS see Mischel and Shoda 1995. For the density-distribution model see Fleeson 2001. The CAPS model is discussed at length in *Character and Moral Psychology*, chapter five, and it has recently been used in the philosophy literature in connection with the topic of moral character by Russell 2009 and Snow 2010.

on their generality, section six on how they can function both consciously and subconsciously, and finally section seven on how they are normatively assessed.[2]

7.1 MIXED HELPING TRAITS

Let me dive right into my framework for thinking about character and helping with this first claim:

(C1) Most adult human beings possess a trait of character pertaining to helping, and this trait consists of various interrelated mental state dispositions pertaining to helping.

Of course what counts as "most" is difficult to make precise, and will likely vary by time period, geographical location, and social/cultural influences. Nevertheless, this is intended to be a robust factual claim—the vast majority of people today possess such a trait which plays the five functional roles from chapter one, and specifically can play a significant role in explaining why people act as they do and in predicting their future helping. This includes many of our friends, colleagues, and family members.

Let me qualify this claim right away. Rather than talking about the vast majority of people in general today, I should limit this to the vast majority of people in Western industrial societies. This is simply because the studies that were reviewed in Part II were almost always conducted using participants from either North American or European populations. My picture of character and helping *may* apply more universally than this, but clearly a lot more research would need to be done first before I would feel comfortable making such a claim.[3] So in the remainder of this book, whenever I make claims about "most people" or "our" character traits, they should be assumed to be qualified in this way.

So according to (C1) most people possess a trait pertaining to helping other people who are (at least implicitly) thought to be in need of help in various ways, such as if they drop papers on the ground, request change for a dollar, sound as if they have fallen off a ladder in the next room, and so forth. As a character trait, it is a disposition to form occurrent beliefs and desires of a

[2] When I talk about "character traits," I will continue to use this as shorthand for all and only the traits which are directly related to moral thought and action, and so exclude any personality traits which are not character traits, as well as all character traits which are primarily relevant to athletics, theoretical knowledge, aesthetics, etc., but not to morality.

[3] For relevant discussion, see Prinz 2009: 128–30.

certain sort and (in this case) to also act in a certain way, namely helpfully, and consists of various underlying and interrelated dispositions to form these beliefs and desires pertaining to helping.

If the same kind of trait is widely held in a normal population of human beings, and the trait consists of certain dispositions to form beliefs and desires, then those particular dispositions are going to be widely held as well. In other words, I mean to exclude the following from the scope of this trait:

> *Individually unique mental state dispositions.* Robert Adams offers a nice example: he personally has a policy of giving money to people asking on the street, but only sometimes and when certain factors such as their being non-threatening are at work.[4] If observers knew ahead of time what his specific policy is, they could reliably predict how he would likely behave in many of these helping-relevant situations. But of course many people do not share his same policy. To take another example, a religious person might have a strategy of tithing 10 percent of her income to charity. Or someone might be committed to volunteering at a certain homeless shelter every Friday afternoon.

Instead, what the trait in (C1) consists of are *generic* mental state dispositions. These are certain dispositions common to all individuals who possess the trait. Here are some examples:

(a) Dispositions to form desires concerned with helping when doing so will contribute towards alleviating my guilty feelings, and more so than any reasonable alternative means of doing so which is thought to be available.

(b) Dispositions to form desires concerned with not helping when doing so will contribute towards perpetuating my guilty feelings, or will not alleviate them as effectively as some reasonable alternative means of doing so which is thought to be available.

(c) Dispositions to form beliefs concerned with what is and is not conducive to alleviating my guilty feelings.[5]

Do these sound familiar? They should. These are the dispositions discussed in chapter two in the context of the guilt-relief model of helping. They are what a "helping mechanism" would partially consist of if that model turns out to be correct.

Or consider the following dispositions discussed in the previous chapter with respect to audience inhibition:

---

[4] Adams 2006: 146.

[5] Note that *the specific content* of the beliefs in (c) themselves might vary significantly from person to person, but the claim is that most people have dispositions to form beliefs *of this broad type*.

(d) Dispositions to form beliefs concerned with the extent to which others are in a position to observe my helping behavior, and with the extent to which they will evaluate and judge me for trying to help.

(e) Dispositions to form desires concerned with helping when it is thought to potentially earn the approval of those observing me.

(f) Dispositions to form desires concerned with not helping when helping is thought to potentially earn the disapproval of those observing me.

These were dispositions which I said also constitute part of a "helping mechanism."

In fact, over the course of the previous five chapters I have outlined a number of specific dispositions to form beliefs and desires pertaining to helping and guilt, embarrassment, positive and negative moods, elevation, activated moral norms, empathy, anticipated approval, and anticipated embarrassment. These are all dispositions which I now say partially constitute the character trait I have in mind. Of course, they are not the only ones—as I remarked on several occasions, there are other psychological variables which directly influence helping behavior. But these dispositions give us more than enough to work with in this chapter.

So the upshot of my proposal thus far is that most people have a trait which consists of a variety of dispositions to form beliefs and desires pertaining to helping. Let me proceed further with a more striking claim:

(C2) This character trait which most adult human beings possess, does not correspond to any of the words or concepts which ordinary people have for traits associated with helping.

We have a bunch of different words which we use in ordinary life to label the helpfulness of another person. But the trait I am interested in is *not* accurately described by *any* of them. It does not fit the concepts expressed by such ordinary positive trait terms such as "kind," "compassionate," or "caring." Nor does it fit the concepts expressed by negative terms either such as "callous," "selfish," or "cold-hearted."

So the striking claim I want to make is that there is a trait of character which influences helping in significant ways, and which most people possess. Yet at the same time it has not been recognized in ordinary thought and discourse.[6]

Why doesn't the trait in (C1) fall under these concepts? As will become clearer in section seven of this chapter, the trait has both morally positive

---

[6] The idea that there are character traits for which we do not have ordinary words and concepts to describe them, is not a new one. Indeed, Aristotle long ago made this point often in his discussion of virtues as mean states. For instance he writes that, "in feelings of fear and confidence the mean is bravery. The excessively fearless person is nameless (and in fact many cases are nameless), while the one who is excessively confident is rash" (1985: 1107b). I return to this topic again in *Character and Moral Psychology*, chapter eight.

elements and morally negative elements that prevent it from being accurately classified using a simple virtue or vice label. On the one hand, it consists of some mental state dispositions which seem as if they would belong in a virtue like compassion, such as dispositions to empathetically help others for altruistic reasons. On the other hand, it consists of some mental state dispositions which seem as if they would belong to a vice like selfishness, such as dispositions to not help others if so doing would perpetuate a negative mood. Hence I claim (and will argue in section seven) that because of this mixture of mental state dispositions the trait does not meet the requirements in the minimal threshold for being *either* a virtue *or* a vice.

Thus if ordinary terms do not describe it, I will need to come up with my own label for this trait. Let me call it—in a rather boring fashion—a "Mixed Helping Trait," with the capital letters meant to remind the reader that this is an expression I have invented which does not map onto any ordinary concepts. The "Mixed" refers to the fact that this trait is neither a virtue nor a vice. The "Helping" refers to the part of our lives to which this trait pertains.[7]

It is important to be clear about the sense in which this trait is "mixed." The claim is *not* that this trait is a virtue in some situations or contexts, and a vice in others. Rather the claim is that this trait is *not a virtue in any situations or contexts*. Nor is it a vice in any situations or contexts. Nor is it entirely morally good or bad in any situations or contexts. Instead a Mixed Helping Trait is neither a virtue nor a vice, neither entirely good nor bad in *every* situation or context in which a person possesses it.

My next claim is that:

(C3) When a person has a Mixed Helping Trait, it can serve in a wide variety of different situations as a causal intermediary between relevant stimuli on the one hand, and helping-relevant thoughts and behavior on the other. Whether it is activated or not will depend on whether any of the specific mental state dispositions that it consists of (such as (a) through (f) above) are activated.

With this claim I want to highlight explicitly that a Mixed Helping Trait plays a causal role in leading to actual behavior, and does so in virtue of the specific mental state dispositions which make it up. In addition, this trait is not intended to be a narrowly local one; rather it can be causally activated when a variety of different helping opportunities and situations arise. This point will be developed more below when I discuss cross-situational consistency.

So to summarize, what a Mixed Helping Trait *actually is*, what it *consists of*, is a set of specific dispositions to form beliefs and desires that pertain to helping. These are not the same beliefs and desires which a virtue like compassion consists in. Nor are they the beliefs and desires that a vice like

---

[7] In earlier work, I used the label "global helping trait." See my 2009a, 2009b, 2010a, 2010b, 2011a.

selfishness consists in. Rather, they are beliefs and desires, some of which are morally admirable, but some of which are not. Because of the particular moral features of these mental states, a Mixed Helping Trait itself does not qualify as either a moral virtue or a moral vice.

In much of the rest of this chapter, I focus less on what these Traits *are*, and more on how they tend to *function*. In the process, I hope it will become clearer from their functioning why I think they are best described as "mixed."

Here is a claim about how this Trait functions with respect to causing behavior:

> (C4) A person with a Mixed Helping Trait will typically exhibit behavior from one situation to the next which can seem fragmented to observers.[8]

To illustrate this, let me make use of the helpful tool of a profile.

As it will be used here, a *profile* is a set of scores for the same kind of behavior exhibited by a person(s) in different situations.[9] Such scores can be plotted graphically as in Figure 7.1, which scores Smith's action of being helpful in four different situations.

The x-axis lists the situations, and I will operationalize them using psychologically salient features for the person in question (in this case Smith), features such as watching my favorite TV show, getting into an argument, taking a break, and so forth.[10] The y-axis is the scale used to measure helpfulness. In general it could be a binary scale of whether Smith was helpful *in any*

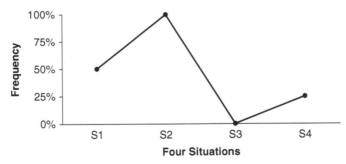

Fig. 7.1. Smith's helping profile (frequency).

<hr />

[8] Naturally it is assumed that other things are being held equal. I omit this clause from (C4) and the remaining claims in order to make them less cumbersome. Also, the "observers" here are best understood as psychologists who are carefully observing the person's patterns of behavior over time, although there is no reason to restrict the class of observers in (C4) just to psychologists.

[9] I have been helped by the discussion of profiles in Furr 2009. More precisely, as Furr notes the above characterization applies to only one kind of profile among many that could be used in psychology (2009: 197).

[10] For the terminology of "psychologically salient features," see chapter one, section four.

way or not in these situations. It could be a conditional probability scale for helpful behavior which ranges from 0.0 to 1.0. It could be a Likert scale from 1 to 5 or 1 to 7 of the degree to which Smith *self-reported* that he would expect to be helpful in these various situations. It could be a scale measuring how *deep or thorough* his helping was if he did help in that situation. But here I have let the y-axis represent the *frequency* of helping actions over a given period of time, such as a year. Thus Smith might have encountered situation S1 twenty times during the year, and exhibited helping behavior on ten occasions, giving him a frequency of 50 percent for that year and situation. But in S3, which he encountered thirty times, he was never helpful, and so his frequency is 0 percent. Ideally, of course, one would need to make sure that there are a sufficient number of instances of each situation, so that Smith's being helpful in 1 out of 2 occasions of a situation does not get plotted alongside 20 or 30 occasions of another situation.[11]

Smith's profile is highly fragmented—he seems to be very helpful in some situations, and not helpful at all in others, all in the course of a given period of time. It is not as if his character has changed significantly—both because the time period is too short for typical character change to occur, but also because these situations are interspersed with each other since S1 can precede S2 which can precede S1 again which can precede an occurrence of S3 and so forth. Finally, remember that Smith is supposed to be representative of you and I, or at least most of us.

But there is an obvious sense in which Smith's profile in Figure 7.1 as well as the claim in (C4) are completely unsurprising. For suppose that S3 is a situation such as eating breakfast by yourself—then naturally helping would be expected to be low there. Suppose S2 involves a baby drowning in a shallow pond when you are the only one around to help—then it is natural to suppose that Smith would help every time he encounters that situation.[12] So let me revise (C4) to make it clearer why it is a significant claim:

(C4*) A person with a Mixed Helping Trait will typically exhibit behavior from one *helping-relevant* situation to the next which can seem to be fragmented to observers.

Now consider Smith's profile only with respect to helping-relevant situations, that is, situations where a helping opportunity is available to him, and so not (normally) when he is eating breakfast alone or going to the bathroom.[13]

---

[11] For relevant discussion, see Johnson 1999: 448 and Furr 2009: 197.

[12] Obviously I need to take some imaginative license here, since few of us would ever encounter a drowning baby once in our lives, much less several times in one year. The same imaginative license should be taken with the other examples of situations used throughout this chapter. Remember that profiles are only being used in this chapter as a visual aide to help illustrate and explain the central claims, not as reports of actual data.

[13] Here I am focusing on immediate helping opportunities. In a sense, I have a chance to help someone every waking moment of the day, for instance by calling in a donation to charity, but

But again this profile might not be very surprising either. Suppose S3 is a situation which would require a tremendous act of self-sacrifice—say, running over burning coals or donating all of one's disposable income—in order to help a person with only a moderate need. Then it would not be surprising at all to find Smith exhibiting a frequency of 0 percent for situations of that kind. Most of us would be just like Smith too.

The intended claim, though, is not (C4) or (C4*) but rather this:

> (C4!) A person with a Mixed Helping Trait will typically exhibit behavior from one helping-relevant situation to the next which can seem to be fragmented to observers. Furthermore, each of the helping tasks is only *moderately demanding* for the person to perform.

Let S2 continue to be a baby drowning in a pond—that is still a moderately demanding helping situation since all Smith would have to do is reach into the pond and pull the child out. But now let S3 be a situation of being with a stranger and hearing someone cry out in pain in a neighboring room,[14] or picking up dropped computer-punched cards,[15] or signing up to volunteer for desk work with the American Cancer Society.[16] Smith, if he is like most of us, will exhibit a very low helping frequency—perhaps not 0 percent, but nothing like 50 percent or higher either.

This, I think we would say, is very surprising—how can he on the one hand rescue the drowning child so readily, and yet typically not even call out to the person in pain in the next room, or pick up dropped cards? More generally, one of the functional roles of character traits is to serve as the basis for making predictions about future behavior. If observers determine that Jones is highly compassionate based on his behavior in multiple situations, then they should be able to reasonably predict what he is likely to do in a new helping-relevant one. But here, even if we observed Smith exhibiting a high frequency of helping in some situations, we do not seem to have any idea what he will do when a different moderate helping opportunity arises. For now, his behavior seems to be unintelligible, although in section three it will hopefully become clearer how to make sense of it.

This takes me to the following claim:

> (C5) A person with a Mixed Helping Trait will often *not* exhibit helping behavior even in some moderately demanding situations relevant to helping.

---

that would count here as a remote helping opportunity. In a more developed account I would need to tell a psychological story about both immediate and remote helping behavior.

[14] Latané and Rodin 1969.
[15] Konečni 1972.
[16] Weyant 1978.

I illustrated this claim with a helping profile, but recall the actual study by Regan from the preface. There 17 out of 20 control participants in a mall did not bother to notify a shopper that candy was falling out of her bag, even though they all noticed what was happening and could have said something about it very easily and with a minimal interruption to their plans.[17]

Note that I have only focused on the relationship between a Mixed Helping Trait and the *actual frequency* of helping. But there are other respects in which a character trait has an impact. For instance, here is a claim, not about actual helping, but about how people *report* that they *would* be willing to help someone if they happened to be in various situations when a helping opportunity arises:

(C6) A person with a Mixed Helping Trait will typically report a degree of willingness to help others in various helping-relevant situations that can seem to be fragmented to observers, even though the helping tasks are moderately demanding for the person to perform.

Smith's profile could still have various situations on the x-axis, but the y-axis would now have a scale which measures the degree to which he reports that he would help in these situations. For instance, Smith might be asked to rank, on a scale of 1 to 7, the degree to which he thinks he would be willing to help pick up dropped papers, rescue the drowning baby, and so forth.[18] Here in Figure 7.2 is how his profile might turn out, for four arbitrarily chosen new situations.[19]

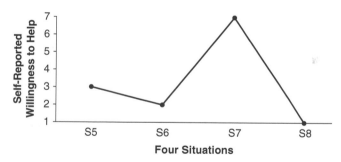

Fig. 7.2. Smith's helping profile (willingness).

---

[17] Regan et al. 1972. As Besser-Jones remarks more generally about psychology experiments on moral behavior, "One thing we can be certain of is that the large majority of people fail to do what is right in the experiments in question" (2008: 325).

[18] For a helping profile very much along these lines which uses real data, see van Mechelen 2009: 185.

[19] Here I am concerned with honest self-reporting, i.e. with Smith ranking the degree to which he *really does* think he would be willing to do these things if he were being honest with himself. Of course, much actual reporting of this kind would be distorted by impression management, i.e. by trying to make oneself look like a more helpful person than one really is or would be.

Alternatively, instead of examining how willing Smith reports that he *would* be to help in these four situations, a profile could be created for how helpful he reports himself to *have been* after the fact in these situations.

Lastly, nothing has been said about the *level* of helpfulness, that is, not just whether the person helps or not, but the *depth* or *thoroughness* of the helping. There is a difference between superficial helping and genuine, careful helping—a dramatic example would be giving directions to the hospital to someone who has a broken arm and then continuing on one's way, versus staying with the person and making sure he is able to actually arrive there safely. In a more mundane case, someone might do the bare minimum needed to help clean up the kitchen after dinner, versus also taking on the task of scrubbing the oven or wiping the counter. Here too I claim that:

(C7) When a person with a Mixed Helping Trait does exhibit helping behavior in moderately demanding situations relevant to helping, then typically the level of that helping from one such situation to the next can seem fragmented to observers.

In this case, Smith's profile might look at his average level of helpfulness over time in each of the different situations in which he helped someone else. This level of helpfulness could be measured by, for instance, Smith's self-reporting after the fact, or by the ratings of degree of helpfulness carried out by friends, family members, or other observers. Using a scale from 1 to 7 with 7 being thoroughly helpful, there can be different, seemingly inconsistent ways in which Smith's profile might turn out from one situation to the next. So this is yet another respect in which I am making the seemingly paradoxical claim that, while Smith is supposed to have a character trait which plays a robust causal role in leading to helping, nevertheless that behavior looks to be fragmented in a variety of respects.

Let me end this section by noting that so far I have focused on Smith's helping with respect to four arbitrarily chosen situations. But during the course of a month or a year, Smith will encounter *hundreds* of different situations, and it is worth considering what patterns might emerge when this much larger range is used. Figure 7.3, for instance, is one possibility for several dozen situations.

Again in a sense this is not surprising. As I have noted, many situations such as eating breakfast alone may not serve as helping opportunities. Hence we should expect to see a number of data points at 0 percent. But the surprising claim is that even when the situations during the year are restricted to just those involving moderate helping-relevant circumstances, Smith's profile might still be extremely messy as in Figure 7.3. In other words, Smith exhibits a great deal of within-person variability in his helping across these situations, even though the circumstances are all of the same moderately demanding type.

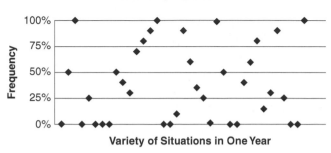

Fig. 7.3. Smith's helping profile for many situations (frequency).

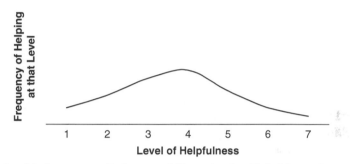

Fig. 7.4. Smith's frequency of helping at different levels of helpfulness during a year.

Or instead switch from frequency of helping to the question of how often Smith exhibited different levels of helpfulness, that is, how often he was deeply or thoroughly helpful as measured by self-reports, peer-reports, or neutral observer reports. Over the course of a year, Smith's distribution might look like Figure 7.4. While there might be a concentration around 4 on the 7-point scale of degree of helpfulness, note that Smith still exhibits the entire range in his behavior over the course of the year. How helpful he is during any given hour of this year, will not be very useful in predicting how helpful he is during any other given hour.[20]

In this section, I have said that most people have a character trait of an unfamiliar kind, called a Mixed Helping Trait, which causally mediates between relevant stimuli and helping behavior, and yet does not always end up leading to such behavior in either actual or hypothetical situations, even when helping would be fairly simple and straightforward. Nor does it exhibit patterns of helping which appear, at first glance, to be obviously consistent, predictable, or even intelligible.

---

[20] For similar claims as a result of studying non-moral behavior, see Fleeson 2001.

7.2 ENHANCING AND INHIBITING
MIXED HELPING TRAITS

It turns out that there are ways of reliably improving the frequency with which people with these Traits generally help, even if ordinarily they would not often help otherwise in these situations. In other words:

> (C8) There are certain *enhancers* for a person's Mixed Helping Trait which can influence the Trait in such a way that there is an increase in motivation to help when in moderately demanding situations relevant to helping, as compared to the level of motivation to help in these situations apart from the influence of the enhancer. Furthermore, these enhancers can give rise to egoistic, altruistic, or moralistic kinds of motives to help (and perhaps even some additional kinds).[21]

This idea should come as no surprise at this point. For instance, a person who is experiencing moral guilt would be expected to help more frequently when certain helping opportunities present themselves. Why? According to the guilt-relief model, it is precisely so as to no longer feel guilty. Diagrammatically, the role of enhancers can be represented as follows:

Appropriate enhancer is activated
(such as guilt over a perceived wrongdoing)
↓

Relevant motive is formed (such as a motive to
relieve my guilt)
+
Beliefs about opportunities to help in my circumstances
↓

Activation of a Mixed Helping Trait
(in this case, activation of the underlying beliefs about which forms of
helping are conducive to relieving my guilt and which are not, combined with
desires to help or to not help depending upon whether such
helping would be conducive)
↓

Increased motivation to help
(in this case, so long as I am still feeling guilty)
↓

Increased helping behavior
(in this case, so long as I am still feeling guilty)

where the arrows are intended to symbolize causal influence.

---

[21] In earlier papers, I used the label "triggers" instead. See my 2009a, 2009b, 2010a, 2010b, and 2011a.

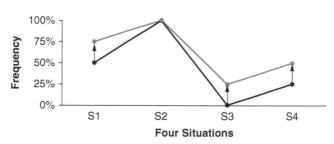

Fig. 7.5. Smith's helping frequency in control and guilt enhancement conditions.

I can also illustrate the effect of an enhancer like guilt using a helping profile. For instance, Figure 7.5 takes the original profile for Smith and then compares it to the helping frequencies he might exhibit for the same situations if (i) he were also experiencing guilt, if (ii) he thought these helping tasks were conducive to alleviating guilt, and if (iii) everything else were held equal.[22] Are there any other enhancers for helping besides guilt? At the start of chapter six I listed a number of them, and also categorized them under the heading of giving rise to egoistic, altruistic, and moralistic motivation.

Not surprisingly, there are ways in which a Mixed Helping Trait can work to also *decrease* the frequency with which a person who possesses it normally helps:

(C9) There are certain *inhibitors* for a person's Mixed Helping Trait which can influence the Trait in such a way that there is an increase in motivation to not help when in moderately demanding situations relevant to helping,

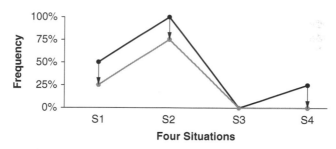

Fig. 7.6. Smith's helping frequency in control and embarrassment inhibiting conditions.

---

[22] Of course it is artificial to suppose that the helping frequencies would increase to the *same* extent in these different situations. Again, profiles in this chapter are used purely for illustration.

as compared to the level of motivation to not help in these situations apart from the influence of the inhibitor.

For instance, the role of anticipated embarrassment can be represented as follows:

Appropriate inhibitor is activated
(such as a belief about a potentially embarrassing situation)

↓

Relevant motive is formed (such as a motive to avoid
feeling embarrassed)

+

Beliefs about reasonable opportunities for me to help in
this situation

↓

Activation of a Mixed Helping Trait
(in this case, activation of the beliefs and desire
pertaining to not helping in this situation so as to not
embarrass myself)

↓

Increased motivation to not help
(in this case, so long as I am still motivated to
avoid feeling embarrassment)

↓

Absent or decreased helping behavior
(in this case, so long as I am still motivated to
avoid feeling embarrassment)

Similarly, in Figure 7.6 I can use the original profile for Smith and compare it to the helping frequencies he might exhibit for the same situations if he thought they were potentially embarrassing. In addition to anticipated embarrassment, a number of inhibitors were listed in chapter six.

The effects of enhancers and inhibitors are not just limited to the frequency of helping which is being exhibited by those with Mixed Helping Traits. There can also be effects on self-reported willingness to help, depth of helping, and thoroughness of helping. To take just one example, Figure 7.7 shows what might happen to Smith's profile from Figure 7.2 of self-reported willingness to help on a 1 to 7 scale for four situations.

Thus in this section, I have developed the picture of Mixed Helping Traits further by noting certain select stimuli for these traits which, when present, can serve to either enhance or inhibit motivation to help and, thereby, helping behavior itself.

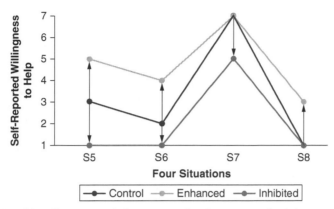

Fig. 7.7. Smith's willingness to help in control, enhancing, and inhibiting conditions.

7.3 CONSISTENCY

Given that Mixed Helping Traits lead to seemingly fragmented helping that can also be enhanced or inhibited, it might initially seem as if they will demonstrate little consistency either across time or across situations. But in fact, another surprising feature of these traits is that they are remarkably consistent in a variety of ways, provided care is taken as to how "consistency" is understood.

Start with the time dimension. One form of stability mentioned in chapter one is:

> *Single-situation trait stability*: A person regularly manifests behavior which is in accordance with the trait in question, over several instances of the same trait-relevant situation. So, for instance, if Jones is deeply compassionate, he might donate to the Salvation Army representative every time he goes to the grocery store this month.

A Mixed Helping Trait certainly can exhibit this. Smith might not run across burning coals to help someone with a small problem on Wednesday, and he is likely to not do so either the following week. But if, for instance, he has empathy for a person's hardship on two separate occasions, and helping that person is only moderately demanding and would (he thinks) be effective in alleviating the hardship, then other things being equal he is likely to help on both occasions. Or if instead he does not feel empathy at all for this person, and furthermore believes that trying to help could be embarrassing, then he might fail to help on both occasions, which is also in accordance with having a Mixed Helping Trait.

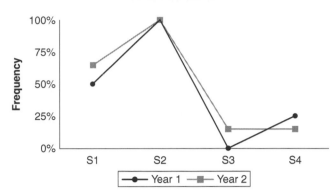

Fig. 7.8. Smith's partial helping profile over two years (frequency).

So the frequency of Smith's helping behavior in one situation during a given month or year, is expected to be significantly correlated with the frequency of that behavior in the same situation during the next month or year. Another way to illustrate this point is to return to the notion of a profile. Here in Figure 7.8, for instance, is Smith's profile for actual helping behavior over four situations and during two non-overlapping periods of time. In this case, Smith's profile exhibits significant stability over time, which can be measured rigorously by psychologists in terms of similarity in profile shape and assessed using a Pearson correlation.[23]

Yet another way to approach single-situation stability is by comparing the average *level* of helpfulness actually exhibited by Smith in one situation during one period of time, with the average level of helpfulness that he exhibited in the same situation during the next period of time, say a week or a month. In other words, observers could examine how stable Smith's level of helpfulness is in the same situations over extended periods of time. Figure 7.9 is an example, where each data point represents a different situation. In this figure, while Smith exhibits a great deal of variation *across* situations in his level of helpfulness, how helpful he acts in the *same* situations is highly similar in these two weeks.[24]

I should also mention the other kind of stability that was distinguished in chapter one:

Aggregate trait stability: A person regularly manifests similar levels of aggregate behavior which is in accordance with the trait in question, over different periods of time. So, for instance, while Jones might have helped in different ways during two different time periods, his average level of compassionate behavior across all these helping situations might still be very similar.

---

[23] See Cronbach and Gleser 1953, Shoda 1999b: 366, and Furr 2009: 198.
[24] In this figure I have been helped by Fleeson 2001: 1018.

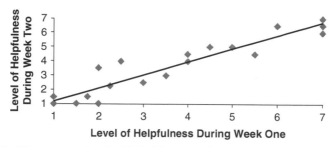

Fig. 7.9. Smith's average level of helpfulness in the same twenty situations during two weeks.

Here the focus would not be on how stable a person's trait behavior is in the *same* situation, but rather on how stable his *overall level* of trait behavior is from one time period to the next. So Smith might encounter dozens of helping-relevant situations in one month, and dozens more in the next, some of which are not at all similar to each other. If he has a Mixed Helping Trait, then he should manifest an average level of helpfulness in one month (say, 4.5 on a scale of 1 to 7) that is robustly correlated with his average level in the second month (say, a 4 or a 5—other things equal, of course, so as to exclude such factors as a serious mental breakdown in the interim). So too the average for the first month of the year would be expected to be strongly correlated with the average for the first month of the next year. Same for the average level for one entire year as compared to the average level for the previous year, and so forth.

Thus there are several respects in which Mixed Helping Traits are expected to be stable. Yet to claim that there is a stable trait associated with helping is not likely to surprise many psychologists or philosophers who work on traits. It is largely uncontroversial in the relevant literature that there are stable traits in *some* sense of "stable," even according to those scholars who are among the most skeptical of traditional trait views in both fields.[25] Where the real attention has focused is on the issue of consistency *across situations*.

---

[25] As Shoda et al. note, "the phenomenon of temporal stability is widely accepted" (Shoda et al. 1993: 1024). Even Mischel wrote in 1968 that, "Considerable stability over time has been demonstrated" (36). In psychology see, e.g. Mischel 1968: 36, 135, 281–98, 1973: 253, 1984: 362, 1999b: 43, 2004: 6–8, 2009: 285, Bem and Allen 1974: 508, Hogan et al. 1977: 258, Epstein 1979: 1122, Mischel and Peake 1982: 732, 734–7, 749, Zuroff 1986: 998, Wright and Mischel 1987: 1161–2, Ross and Nisbett 1991: 101, Shoda et al. 1993: 1023–4, 1994: 675–85, Mischel and Shoda 1995: 253, 1998: 242–5, 2008: 208, 219, 224, 229, Kunda 1999: 443–4, 499, Shoda 1999a: 160, 1999b: 365–6, Shoda and LeeTiernan 2002: 249–56, Mischel et al. 2002: 52, Penner et al. 2005: 374–5, Fleeson and Noftle 2009: 151, and Roberts 2009: 140. In philosophy see Doris 1998: 507–8, 2002: 23–5, 64–6, Goldie 2004: 68, Upton 2009a: 55, and Russell 2009: 247.

There are several clear senses in which a Mixed Helping Trait does *not* lead to cross-situationally consistent behavior. With claim (C4) I said that a person with such a trait will act in a highly inconsistent manner, but that many situations during a day or week will have nothing to do directly with helping. So this form of inconsistency is undeniable, but also less interesting.

Similarly with claim (C4*). A person with a Mixed Helping Trait might be very helpful in one kind of helping-relevant situation and unhelpful in another, which is also a form of inconsistency but one that is not surprising if the latter situation involves a great sacrifice just to help someone with a minor ailment.

Now consider (C4!). Even when the focus is just on helping-relevant situations, and even when they are limited to moderate tasks, it is still the case that helping due to a Mixed Helping Trait appears highly inconsistent. For instance, I think most of us would agree that Smith's original profile in Figure 7.1 does not resemble what we would expect from a character trait that leads to consistent behavior across all relevant situations. So the tentative conclusion is that Mixed Helping Traits typically lead to stable but cross-situationally inconsistent helping behavior.

But this conclusion is premature. For we can examine whether someone like Smith acts consistently based upon the features of situations which are *psychologically relevant to Smith*. What is relevant to Smith is a function of *his own interpretations* of that situation and what beliefs and desires he has that are activated by its particular features. For one person, features A and C of a situation might be highly relevant, whereas for another person, only features B and D are, even though the situation includes all four of these features. It just so happens that these two individuals care only about certain features and not others.[26]

To apply this to helping, consider a case where two situations seem alike with respect to their standard nominal features, and so they generate the expectation in observers that Smith will act consistently in both of them. But suppose they also diverge in some important way given what is psychologically relevant to Smith. For example, let S1 be a situation where Smith is approached to make change for a dollar in a shopping mall and there are neutral fragrances in the air, while in S2 Smith is similarly approached in the same mall but there is also a pleasant aroma coming from Cinnabon or Mrs. Field's Cookies. On a surface inspection, these look like almost identical situations (with morally irrelevant differences), and the helping task is moderate in both of them. So it is natural to expect something like the profile illustrated in

---

[26] For further discussion of the distinction been nominal and psychologically relevant features of situations, see chapter one, section four and the references cited therein.

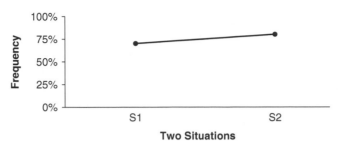

Fig. 7.10. Smith's expected partial helping profile for a shopping mall (frequency).

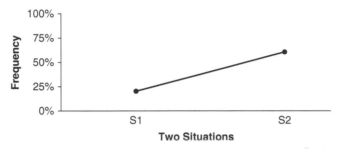

Fig. 7.11. Smith's actual partial helping profile for a shopping mall (frequency).

Figure 7.10 for Smith. In other words, whatever frequency he helps at in S1, would likely be roughly the same as he also helps at in S2.

But instead it could very well turn out that Smith's profile is more like Figure 7.11. For recall Robert Baron's study with precisely this setup that was discussed in chapter three. He found that roughly 19 percent of participants helped in the control condition versus roughly 57 percent who helped in the pleasant fragrance condition.[27]

It appears that Smith is highly fragmented and inconsistent in his helping in nearly identical situations. But if he has a Mixed Helping Trait, then such a profile makes perfect sense. While the two situations are very similar in a number of respects (same location, same helping task, etc.), they have different psychologically salient features for Smith—S2 involves pleasant fragrances

---

[27] Baron 1997. I am not assuming that these percentages correspond directly to how frequently *any particular individual* would help in multiple iterations of these two situations. Instead my only point is that an individual's helping frequency could be significantly different in these situations despite how similar they might seem to each other. Figure 7.11 assumes that the results in Baron's study hold true for the same person in both situations in the same way as they do in the actual experiment involving two non-overlapping groups of people. I explore this assumption in section four of the next chapter.

which put Smith in a good mood, thereby functioning as an enhancer for helping for reasons already examined in chapter three. Thus it seems that the mental states which constitute a Mixed Helping Trait can respond to different features of these two very similar situations, and so subsequently bring about importantly different thoughts and actions.

Now consider two helping opportunities which seem remarkably *different*— say, where S1 is signing up to donate blood and S2 is doing the dishes at home after dinner. On a given day, it might be expected that many people will help in one but not both of these situations. In other words, perhaps it is expected that most people's profiles will look like Figure 7.11. But in Smith's case, on this particular day he ends up doing both of these helping tasks. Again this might be surprising, just looking at the nominal features of these situations and wondering what they have in common. A simple explanation would be that he just has a general desire to help (period), and then these two opportunities came along. But this explanation may not work for Smith, since suppose that on *other* days his profile *does* indeed look like Figure 7.11, and he does not usually bother with the dishes.

Instead, what explains this consistency across nominally different situations could be a matter of Smith feeling very guilty about something he did at work or being in a bad mood, and then (subconsciously) thinking that these situations have features which could provide him with an opportunity to relieve his guilt or bad mood at a low cost to himself. Hence these two different helping acts can be done on behalf of the same underlying goal (again, perhaps unbeknownst to him). By looking to the mental states which make up a Mixed Helping Trait and to the psychologically salient features of these situations, there is a good explanation available for this momentary cross-situational consistency.

More generally, the mental states which make up a Mixed Helping Trait can render different nominal situations psychologically similar in a person's mind by picking up on what seem to her to be their similar features. This is the case, even *despite* the variability in helping that the person exhibits in other nominal situations, as the earlier profiles have illustrated. To adopt a phrase from Yuichi Shoda and Scott LeeTiernan, the person is exhibiting a *consistent pattern of variability* in helping across different situations, or what they call "higher-order consistency."[28] This consistency is explained by the particular mental states in a Mixed Helping Trait which are responding appropriately to the various features of each new helping-relevant situation that pertain to them.

So on the one hand, based upon observations of what they are doing, it seems that most people exhibit a high degree of within-person variability

---

[28] Shoda and LeeTiernan 2002: 266. See also Smith et al. 2009.

in helping from one situation to the next and from one hour to the next. The expectation is that these within-person behavioral correlations will turn out to be discouragingly low, just as behavioral correlations associated with a variety of personality traits have often failed to cross the 0.30 threshold during the past several decades of psychological research.[29]

But now suppose I am right in thinking that most people also have a Mixed Helping Trait which, I claim, gives rise to stable and cross-situationally consistent helping over time. Surprisingly, this variability noted above is not an embarrassment for the existence of such traits. It does not have to be due to measurement error or environmental noise or randomness or any other factors that need to be discounted, say by aggregating over multiple situations in order to arrive at a person's average level of helpfulness.[30] Instead the variability in helping can be understood as a product of the person encountering different helping opportunities, and having a multitude of mental state dispositions which, subtly and often below the level of conscious awareness, can coherently *adjust* her willingness to help, actual helping, and depth of helping to the situational features as she perceives them. If observers do not appreciate those mental state dispositions, then this person can seem to exhibit deeply fragmented behavior that is evidence of a failure or lack of character. But once these dispositions are recognized and better understood, the person's patterns of helping become intelligible as a product of *both* situational features and character traits working together. This is perhaps the central thesis of my entire framework for thinking about our moral character, and will be elaborated on several more times in the rest of this book as well as in *Character and Moral Psychology*.

These observations lead to two more claims:

(C10) A person with a Mixed Helping Trait will often show momentary or extended cross-situational *inconsistency* in his helping in moderately demanding situations relevant to helping, when those situations are compared based solely upon their nominal features.

(C11) A person with a Mixed Helping Trait will often show momentary or extended cross-situational *consistency* in his helping in moderately demanding situations relevant to helping, when those situations are compared based upon the features which are psychologically salient to him.

---

[29] This last point is examined at length in *Character and Moral Psychology*, chapter four.

[30] Hence I do not follow Seymour Epstein, who claims that, "Single items of behavior, no matter how carefully measured, like single items in a test, normally have too high a component of error of measurement to permit demonstration of high degrees of stability" (1979: 1121). Instead my view here closely aligns with how advocates of the CAPS model treat within-person variability and aggregation. For more see *Character and Moral Psychology*, chapter five, section two.

Again, what counts as "salient" for a person will be a function in large part of the various mental state dispositions—such as dispositions to form beliefs and desires concerned with alleviating guilt—which make up that person's Mixed Helping Trait.

To summarize, then, the issue of consistency is complicated, and can be assessed along a number of dimensions. According to the proposal of this chapter, Mixed Helping Traits can lead to helping which is consistent over time and also across situations so long as those situations are understood in a way that takes the person's own psychological perspective into account.

7.4 DIFFERENCES BETWEEN PEOPLE

Mixed Helping Traits are made up of a cluster of mental states pertaining to helping, they lead to helping behavior which is both consistent and inconsistent in various ways, they can be significantly enhanced and inhibited, and they are not a familiar part of our conceptual repertoire. I said from the very beginning that most people have such traits. And now I am in a position to add one more wrinkle—they also come in degrees.

Like familiar virtues and vices, it is a mistake to think that a person must either lack a Mixed Helping Trait, or have it in its entirety or completely. Rather, two people can both have a Mixed Helping Trait, but exhibit significantly different patterns of helping behavior in the same nominal situations. To use a common expression in the psychology literature, they each have different behavioral *signatures*.[31] This difference in degree can be illustrated by comparing the profiles for two people, Smith and Robinson, across three situations.[32] Figure 7.12 is one such profile.

Smith and Robinson differ in their respective frequency of helping, but they share the same rank order of situations. For both of them, S3 has features which have a more significant impact on their Mixed Helping Traits than S1 does, even though from their profiles we can see that they do not seem to have these traits to the same extent. In other words, by their lights these situations have increased excitatory strength.

Figure 7.13 is another way their profiles might have turned out for the same three situations. In this profile, the two people do not share the same rank

[31] See, e.g. Shoda et al. 1994: 675–8, Mischel and Shoda 1995: 249, 251, 255, 258, 1998: 242, 245, 2008: 208, 224, 228, 233, Shoda and Mischel 1996: 419, Mischel 1999a: 459, 1999b: 44, 2004: 8, 10–11, 16, 2009: 285, Shoda 1999a: 160, 1999b: 366, Cervone and Shoda 1999: 21, Caprara and Cervone 2000: 80, Shoda and LeeTiernan 2002: 245, 264, Mischel et al. 2002: 51, Fournier et al. 2008, 2009, Andersen and Thorpe 2009: 163, Smith et al. 2009, and van Mechelen 2009.

[32] For these next few profiles, I have been helped by van Mechelen 2009. For discussion of multiple person behavioral profiles, see Furr 2009: 201–3.

Fig. 7.12. Two helping profiles for three situations.

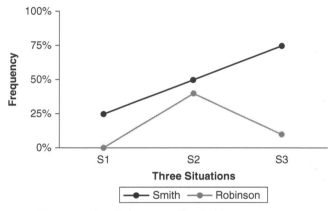

Fig. 7.13. Two helping profiles for three situations.

ordering of *situations*, but there is a consistent rank order of the *persons*—Smith exhibits a higher frequency of helping in all three situations. This suggests, on the face of it, that he has a Mixed Helping Trait to a greater degree than does Robinson.

Of course, observers should be careful in drawing such an inference given the role of enhancers and inhibitors. For this difference in their profiles could be due to Smith experiencing an enhancer while Robinson was not (or Robinson experiencing an inhibitor while Smith was not) during the period when their helping was measured. In that case, Figure 7.13 could still be consistent with their possessing a Mixed Helping Trait to roughly the *same* degree.

Fig. 7.14. Two helping profiles for three situations.

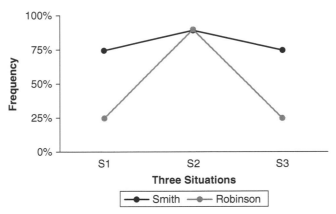

Fig. 7.15. Two helping profiles for three situations.

The same caution applies to a profile like Figure 7.14. It is tempting to infer similarity of degree of trait possession, but that could be a mistake if one of the profiles is shifted up or down due to an enhancer or an inhibitor. Furthermore, even without these variables, it could just be that the three situations chosen for the profile do not helpfully explore whether there are differences in the degree of their Mixed Helping Traits.[33] To see this point, consider a new profile, Figure 7.15.

---

[33] As van Mechelen writes more generally, "two persons may display very similar behavioral signatures . . . whereas their signatures may result from quite different cognitive-affective processes or mechanisms" (2009: 186).

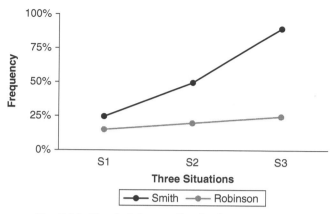

Fig. 7.16. Two helping profiles for three situations.

Just examining S2 might lead people to think that Smith and Robinson have the trait to the same degree. But this could be a situation such as rescuing a drowning baby from a shallow pond, in which everyone with even a modest Mixed Helping Trait would likely help, other things being equal.[34] It is S1 and S3 which can really serve to illustrate the difference in degree.

Finally, consider a profile like Figure 7.16. Here the differences between Smith and Robinson are pronounced. In the same situations, Smith is consistently more helpful over time than Robinson. But Smith also seems to exhibit more *situational discrimination* than Robinson; S3 tends to motivate him much more often to be helpful than does S1, whereas there is no noticeable difference between these situations for Robinson.

Despite the differences in the degree to which multiple people might possess Mixed Helping Traits, if they are possessed at all they should still exhibit stability and cross-situational consistency relative to their particular mental state dispositions. This might not manifest itself in obvious ways in the short term. For instance, if someone's level of helpfulness during one hour is compared with the same person's level of helpfulness during the next hour, then there may be little correlation between the two. As already noted in section one, there is a high degree of within-person variability when it comes to the different dimensions of helping. Looking now at multiple people instead of just one, the same variability can be illustrated for twenty people using the following (again, only fictional) diagram in Figure 7.17.

---

[34] These are what psychologists call "strong" situations, as opposed to "weak" situations in which there is typically more diversity in people's responses (Leising and Müller-Plath 2009: 221, Fleeson and Noftle 2009: 151. For doubts see Hogan 2009: 249 and Krueger 2009: 130). The standard examples of such situations are, respectively, funerals and bars.

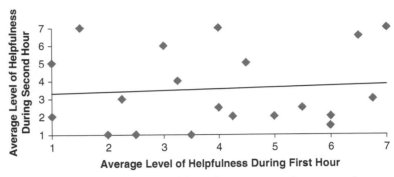

Fig. 7.17. Average level of helpfulness for twenty people over two hours.

In this chart, one person exhibits a low level of helpfulness in the first hour (say, 0.5), but then in the next hour can be at the very high end (say, 7). This could be because, perhaps, in the second hour he is now in a good mood or empathizing with someone's distress. In contrast, another person is a 7 in both the first hour and the second. So there is a great deal of variability both for each individual from one hour to the next, and between these individuals during the two hours. Finally, when looking at all twenty people in this figure, there is almost no statistical correlation between their levels of helpfulness during the first and second hours.

On the other hand, take these same twenty people who have Mixed Helping Traits, and gather many reports of their helpfulness over an extended period of time (weeks, months, or years). Then compute the average level of their helpfulness in a randomly selected half of all their reports and compare it with the average level of helpfulness in the other half of the reports in order to assess split-half reliability. Something like Figure 7.18 is likely to emerge.

Note that again no two people are identical in this figure, with some demonstrating considerably higher average levels of helpfulness than others. But the crucial point for my purposes is that all twenty people nevertheless show a remarkable degree of consistency over time in what their own average levels turns out to be—what they are like in half of these reports strongly predicts what they are like in the other half.[35]

---

[35] Hence they exhibit what I have called Aggregate Trait Stability. In this figure, I have been helped by Fleeson 2004: 86.

The same point illustrated above in Figure 7.18 about stabilities in average tendencies for multiple individuals can be made in a slightly different way by focusing, not on how each of these people acts on average over a *variety* of helping situations, but on how each acts in the *same* situation over an extended period of time (here the issue is not Aggregate but Single-Situation Trait Stability). In other words, observers can examine how helpful Smith and Robinson are when asked to hold the door during one year, compared with how helpful they are when asked to do the very same thing in the next year. Similar to Figure 7.18, the expectation is that for each of

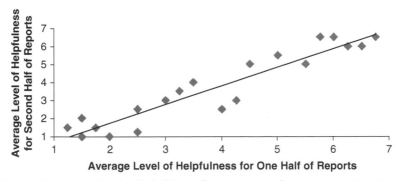

Fig. 7.18. Average level of helpfulness for twenty people over many situations.

When thinking about average levels, it is easy to forget about the individual variation in helpfulness too. For any two people who might have very similar average levels of helpfulness, each of their behavioral signatures or patterns of helpfulness can still vary widely from particular situation to situation in such a way as to appear highly fragmented. This is a familiar point from section one. But it can also be the case that, *when compared to each other*, their behavioral signatures are also very different, *even though* their average level of helpfulness is roughly the same. Averages can obscure more specific individual differences in responses to particular situations, and can make two people seem the same in their specific behavioral patterns when they really are not.[36]

If Mixed Helping Traits can come in degrees, then what explains why one person might have such a trait to a greater degree than another? Here I look to the mental state dispositions. Smith and Robinson might have the exact same dispositions making up their Mixed Helping Traits, but still have differences in the strength of their desires or the confidence of their beliefs. That would naturally explain a profile such as Figure 7.15. Alternatively, another way to account for differences in how their Traits function is in terms of different specific mental state dispositions which make up the Trait. For instance, Robinson might not have thought very carefully about the rewards for helping in different situations. Hence in Figure 7.16 he does not show any variation in

these individuals with Mixed Helping Traits, their average level of helpfulness in a helping-relevant situation in one year (whatever that might be) strongly predicts their average level of helpfulness in the same situation the next year. At the same time, what this average level turns out to be might differ significantly from one person to the next.

[36] For related discussion of these issues, see Shoda and LeeTiernan 2002: 242, 267. Concerns about aggregation omitting important data about individual differences will be raised again in *Character and Moral Psychology*, chapter five.

his profile for situations S2 and S3, whereas Smith is more aware of the reward differences across all three situations.[37]

The important conclusion to draw from this section is that:

(C12)   The possession of a Mixed Helping Trait comes in degrees of more or less, and two people can both have a Mixed Helping Trait and still exhibit significant differences in their patterns of helping in the same nominal situations, while two other people might exhibit similar patterns of helping in some of the same nominal situations and actually possess a Mixed Helping Trait to different degrees.

This naturally leads to the question of the scope of such traits.

7.5 LEVELS OF MIXED HELPING TRAITS

Recall from chapter one that character traits exist at different levels of generality. Someone might be an honest person, and so has a trait at a very high level of generality that pertains to all situations relevant to truth-telling. But someone else might only be honest in a more specific respect, such as when at home (but not at parties or at the office), or with those she trusts (but not otherwise). These two ways of narrowing down the trait of honesty can be importantly different—the first ties the more local trait to a nominal feature of the situation (e.g. whether the person is at home or not),[38] whereas the second ties the trait to a psychologically relevant feature (e.g. who she thinks is trustworthy).

Thus far I have been presenting Mixed Helping Traits at a very high level of generality—as traits which are relevant to helping across *many* situations and periods of time. This is due to the way Mixed Helping Traits are grounded— they have in their causal bases a diverse array of mental state dispositions, including dispositions to form beliefs and desires (broadly understood) which pertain to empathy, guilt, anger, good moods, bad moods, embarrassment, anticipated embarrassment, and so forth.

But certain people might have some of these dispositions and not others. For instance, a person might not be capable of feeling empathy for the distress of others, while still wanting to alleviate feelings of guilt. This naturally suggests that Mixed Helping Traits can be formulated at different degrees of generality. Of the two approaches for understanding more local character

---

[37] Other factors can explain differences in the degree that two people might possess a Mixed Helping Trait. The two given here are only offered as natural candidates.

[38] Being at home can be and often is a psychologically relevant feature for most people too— the only point here is that whether it is or not for this person was not determined to be the case before classifying her as being honest when at home.

traits—by using nominal features of situations or by using psychologically relevant features—I naturally want to adopt the latter.

So consider the possibility of a Mixed Helping Guilt Trait, Empathy Trait, Mood Trait, and so forth. And there is no reason to stop there. Recall I said there are two desires pertaining to guilt relief—a desire to help so long as helping will contribute to alleviating my guilty feelings, and a desire to not help so long as helping will perpetuate or worsen my guilty feelings. So it is at least conceivable that there could be a Mixed Positive Helping Guilt Trait and a Mixed Negative Helping Guilt Trait. Figure 7.19 is a rough diagram of how such a framework might look.

Of course once these more local traits are mentioned, there is a natural tendency to want to either deny or at least ignore the existence of the more global ones. So maybe I have made a mistake by starting at the top level of generality and working down, rather than focusing only on the most narrowly construed Mixed Helping Traits.

But I am not yet convinced that I have made a mistake. First of all, there is no reason to deny the existence of more global traits. Character traits, recall, are not mysterious entities—they consist of certain clusters of interrelated mental state dispositions. So there is no reason why the mental states which make up the two guilt traits cannot serve as a Helping Guilt Trait in most people, and why in turn many people cannot also have the mental states which underlie a Helping Empathy Trait, Mood Trait, and so on, which together give rise to a Mixed Helping Trait.[39]

As far as the practicality of global traits is concerned, it is true that more local traits have a significant edge in terms of prediction. If a person has a Helping Guilt Trait but not a Helping Empathy Trait, then predictions based on attributing a Mixed Helping Trait in general to him will not turn out to be

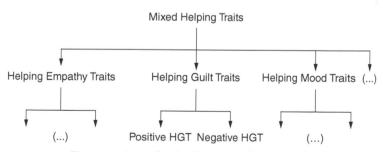

Fig. 7.19. Some levels of Mixed Helping Traits.

---

[39] For a similar point about honesty, see Kamtekar 2004: 469. See also the helpful related discussion in Buss 1989: 1384–5 and Adams 2006: 125–7.

as accurate as those which are formulated at this narrower level. Nevertheless, three things can still be said for the practicality of more global traits. First, there will often be cases in which a person does not just have a single local trait but several local traits whose mental state dispositions give rise to a more global one. So predictions based on the more global one will be just as accurate as those using the more cumbersome local trait framework. Secondly, in cases where a person does not have all the local traits which make up a Mixed Helping Trait, it does not follow that predictions using such a trait attribution have no predictive value—they can still be highly accurate in a number of situations, and certainly are much more valuable than not postulating any Mixed Helping Trait whatsoever in the first place. This leads to the final point, which is that most people simply do not have the time during their busy days to assess whether other people have certain local traits and not others, and so given our cognitive limitations and the demands that we are already under, making use of more global traits like a Mixed Helping Trait can be highly useful in our daily lives.[40]

Let me end this section by saying a bit more about Mixed Helping Traits and prediction. Since they are character traits with behavioral implications, one of the roles Mixed Helping Traits will play is to shape predictions about what a person with such a trait would likely do in the relevant situations. More precisely, as dispositional states, Mixed Helping Traits ground the truth of conditionals concerning the person, certain helping-relevant situations, and helping behavior. The goal is to then formulate these conditionals so that they can offer fairly precise, testable empirical predictions for that behavior. Of course, it is a mistake to expect too much from such predictions—for instance, they will not be very accurate in specifying what a person *is* going to do in a given situation, but rather (other things being equal) they can help predict what he is *likely* to do in some situations, and even better, what he is *more likely* to do in those situations as compared to someone else who does not possess the trait or has it to a lesser degree. To use examples of ordinary traits, a person who is said to be an *adulterer* or *lascivious* does not attempt to have sexual relations with every relevant person when alone together. Someone who is *compassionate* does not always make a donation whenever approached for money, nor does someone who is *dishonest* always tell a lie in all social occasions. Rather, such people are more likely to perform these actions both on a given occasion and over the course of many relevant opportunities, than is someone who is sexually temperate, or selfish, or honest.

So returning to Mixed Helping Traits, here is one predictive conditional concerning moral guilt that we already saw in chapter two:

---

[40] I return to this last point in *Character and Moral Psychology*, chapter seven.

(a) Other things being equal, if a person with a Mixed Helping Trait is experiencing guilt as a result of something he thinks he has done wrong, and:

    (i) is presented with a moderately demanding opportunity to help

    (ii) takes himself to be able to help

    (iii) takes the benefits of helping in terms of guilt relief to outweigh the costs associated with helping

    (iv) does not take there to be any more effective means available for relieving the guilt

that person will probably attempt to help so long as the background conditions are otherwise appropriate to allow for the functioning of the Mixed Helping Trait.[41]

Note that (a) is not predicting that the person definitely *will* help, just that there is a significant likelihood that she will. Over time, she would be expected to exhibit a high frequency of such helping in repetitions of these same conditions.[42]

On the other hand, I would also predict that:

(b) Other things being equal, if a person with a Mixed Helping Trait:

    (i) is presented with a moderately demanding helping opportunity

    (ii) takes himself to be able to perform the helping task

but there is no enhancer activated, then that person will sometimes not attempt to perform certain helping tasks even if the background conditions are otherwise appropriate to allow for the functioning of the Mixed Helping Trait.[43]

Recall that in the Regan study only 15 percent of controls notified the shopper about her bag.[44]

Stepping back, the main conclusion that can be drawn from this section concerning levels of generality and prediction is the following:

---

[41] It would be difficult to specify these background conditions rigorously, but they would include (at a general level) the absence of relevant mental or physical impairments such as severe depression or a sudden heart attack. For some of the challenges associated with developing an account of background conditions relevant to character traits, see Upton 2009a: chapter two.

[42] As John Doris notes, "sporadic failures of trait-relevant behavior probably shouldn't be taken to disconfirm attributions" (2002: 19). Similarly according to Stuart Hampshire, "To attribute a disposition to someone is never to preclude that he may on some occasion act, or have acted, in some way contrary to his general tendency or disposition . . . It is typical of human character that it allows of lapses, and that people sometimes behave in a way which is not in accordance with their character" (1953: 7). See also Allport 1931: 371, Goldie 2004: 15, Upton 2005: 137, Adams 2006: 123–4, and Doris 2010: 139.

[43] If no enhancer is present and an *inhibitor* is present, then it is even less likely that the person will attempt to perform the helping task.

[44] Regan et al. 1972: 44.

(C13) Mixed Helping Traits exist at different levels of generality, and while more local specifications of Mixed Helping Traits have increased predictive value, predictions can be formulated which are accurate in many situations using Mixed Helping Traits.

Of course, people would only make predictions using Mixed Helping Traits if they believed that these traits exist in the first place. Back in the first section of this chapter, I said that we do not recognize these traits in everyday thought. Some of the implications of this failure of recognition are worth noting.

7.6 UNDERSTANDING ONE'S OWN MIXED HELPING TRAITS

Even though according to my view people do not think of Mixed Helping Traits themselves in their ordinary lives, these traits can still be manifesting themselves in all kinds of ways which *are* perfectly familiar. For instance, one of the enhancers of a Mixed Helping Trait is activated moral norms, and we know what it feels like to deliberate about whether and how to help someone, to consciously arrive at a moral judgment, and to then implement that judgment in action. Some of the mental state dispositions which a Mixed Helping Trait consists of—such as desires concerned with helping when doing so will contribute towards complying with the relevant moral norms—can be responsible for carrying this process out.[45] Similarly, I might imagine what a friend in distress is experiencing, come to empathize with his situation, and then help him as a result of being in this empathetic state of mind.[46] Such a process is also perfectly familiar from ordinary life.

But Mixed Helping Traits function in other ways too. One common way involves a kind of automatic functioning whereby the trait leads to helping or a failure to help for reasons that are below the person's conscious awareness. For instance, he might not help when given a chance to address an obvious and simple need, and when pressed he cites certain plausible sounding reasons for why he supposedly chose not to do so. But, it turns out, these "reasons" do not correspond to what actually motivated him (subconsciously), and instead serve just as post-hoc confabulations or rationalizations. This is not because the person is lying about what really was motivating him—like the rest of us, he sometimes is simply not aware of the psychological forces that are at work in his mind.[47]

---

[45] As we saw in chapter four, these desires are a bit more complicated than stated here.
[46] See chapter five.
[47] For dual process theories of automatic and controlled psychological processing, see Chaiken and Trope 1999. Discussion of what counts as "automatic" in the psychology literature is

An example from Part II which illustrates this phenomenon is Latané and Rodin's "Lady in Distress" group effect study in which a woman is heard crying out in pain in the next room.[48] Recall that when a single participant was placed in the room with a stranger who did nothing in response to the cries, only 7 percent of participants did anything helpful themselves.[49] But what is relevant here is that, when asked afterwards about why they did not help, participants were quick to come up with all kinds of reasons. Noticeably absent was the inhibiting effect of the stranger, which was in fact the real reason.[50]

In a more recent study, ninety-nine students were divided into two groups and individually assigned to complete a packet of various unrelated tasks, some of which pertained to helping. It turned out that willingness to donate to Habitat for Humanity was 22 percent for one group and 6 percent for the second group, and the average level of interest in volunteering (on a 1–7 scale) was 4.21 for the former group and 3.29 for the latter.[51] The only difference between the two groups? The first had participants fill out the packet in a room sprayed with Windex. No participants during post-experiment questioning reported the scent of the room as having an influence on their willingness to helping.[52] But clearly it did at least for some of them.

I claim that Mixed Helping Traits can function in a variety of different ways including:

---

vast and confusing. John Bargh has helpfully identified the following features of processing that are typically related to automaticity in this literature—such processing is said to be unaware, relatively effortless, unintentional, autonomous, and involuntary (1989: 3–5, see also his 1994). Bargh then argues (persuasively in my view) that these features are not all necessary for a process to be automatic, and often do not all jointly occur together. Rather they together serve to represent an extreme form of automaticity on one end of a broad continuum, with highly controlled processing on the opposite end of the spectrum.

When it comes to Mixed Helping Traits, my main focus is on the awareness feature, along with the autonomy feature in the sense that processes with this feature, "will run by themselves to completion, without the need of conscious attentional monitoring" (Bargh 1989: 5). Bargh also distinguishes between preconscious, postconscious, and goal-dependent automaticity (10). The variety that is most relevant to Mixed Helping Traits is the last one where, "automatized memory structures guide attention, make behavioral decisions, and direct action within the situation with a minimum of attentional control necessary" (24). However, all three varieties are relevant to some extent.

For related discussion of automaticity and character, see Appiah 2008: 42–5 and especially Snow 2010: chapter two.

[48] Latané and Darley 1970: 58. For the original study, see Latané and Rodin 1969.

[49] Latané and Rodin 1969: 193–5 and Latané and Darley 1970: 60–3.

[50] See Latané and Darley 1970 and Staub 1974: 321. For general observations, see Sober and Wilson 1998: 255.

[51] Liljenquist et al. 2010: 382.

[52] Liljenquist et al. 2010. For a study of donating behavior using moral and non-moral adjective primes, see Aquino and Freeman 2009: 387.

(a) primarily at a conscious level, as part of ordinary moral thought and decision-making. Standard cases of careful moral deliberation and judgment can serve as examples.[53]

(b) primarily at a subconscious level, where they lead to the formation of mental states and to the eventual performance of actions which are not influenced in the way the person consciously assumes them to be. At the same time he does not seem surprised by his behavior and does not raise any objections to it. Hence the reasons why the person *actually* performs the actions, are not the same as the reasons why he *thinks* he is doing them. Furthermore, if he were made aware of the mental states actually giving rise to these actions, he would endorse those states.[54] This could be true in the Windex study—perhaps some (although likely not all) of the participants who signed up to donate money would endorse the role of whatever beliefs and desires were being influenced by the smell of Windex.

(c) primarily at a subconscious level, where they lead to the formation of mental states and to the eventual performance of actions which are not influenced in the way the person consciously assumes them to be. At the same time she does not seem surprised by her behavior and does not raise any objections to it. Hence the reasons why the person actually performs the actions, are not the same as the reasons why she thinks she is doing them. However, if she were made aware of the mental states behind the particular actions, she would *not* endorse them. Some participants in the Latané and Rodin group effect study might be like this—they may not object to their lack of helping, instead trying to offer reasons for why they did not help which had nothing to do with the inhibiting effect of the stranger. But if they knew the motives that really were at work and were responsible for their failure, such as embarrassment avoidance, it is likely that at least some participants would not endorse them and would express disappointment with themselves for being motivated in that way.

(d) primarily at a subconscious level, where they lead to the formation of mental states and to the eventual performance of actions which are not influenced in the way the person consciously assumes them to be. But in this case the behavior confuses the person who performs it, leaving her wondering why she finds herself acting in this way, and

---

[53] These are cases where our conscious deliberation is in fact what is causally responsible for the behavior, rather than one or more subconscious forces primarily doing the causal work. For such cases with respect to helping, see chapter four, section two.

[54] For relevant discussion, see Snow 2010: 51.

perhaps leading her to express disappointment with herself for her behavior.[55]

One conclusion to draw from these observations is that ordinarily people who have Mixed Helping Traits will have only a limited understanding of their own helpfulness in many cases. They might think that they are really helpful people, but not in fact be helpful in certain situations, say while feeling guilt when the helping task does not offer guilt relief. This mistaken view of themselves does not have to be malicious or self-deceptive, but just can be a matter of their failing to understand how their minds work and what actually motivates them. In other words, they might not be aware of the automatic functioning of desires aimed at, for instance, relieving guilt, eliminating negative mood, and avoiding embarrassment, blame, or empathy.

On the other hand, they might think that they are *not* very helpful people, and in their conscious deliberation this could even be true. But in their automatic functioning at the subconscious level, they could be causally influenced to consistently perform all kinds of helpful acts, perhaps even to their own surprise. Again, this could be the result of unappreciated dispositions concerned, for instance, with activated moral norms, elevation, positive mood maintenance, and so forth.[56]

The same claims hold, I submit, not just for ourselves but also with respect to the limited understanding we have of other people's helping tendencies. Unless we are in tune with the nature of Mixed Helping Traits and their various enhancers and inhibitors, we can end up being surprised to find strangers or even friends and family members not helping in certain contexts. This surprise has manifested itself in various famous and dramatic ways, such as the Kitty Genovese murder in 1964 or the standard Milgram experiment (1974) where it was mistakenly expected that the majority of participants would stop administering painful shocks well before the lethal XXX level.[57] But it also might manifest itself in everyday contexts, say when someone else

[55] A nice illustration of this with respect to harmful as opposed to helpful behavior is the state of mind of some participants in the standard Milgram experiment. Milgram's work will be discussed in chapter nine, section four.

The above four ways in which Mixed Helping Traits can function are not intended to be exhaustive. For instance, they can also function in some cases primarily at the subconscious level, but be subject to what Pollard calls "intervention control" in which conscious processing can intervene and redirect or simply stop the particular subconscious processes at work. See Pollard 2003: 415–516 and Snow 2010: chapter two, 72.

[56] For helpful discussion of automaticity, character, and activated goals, see Snow 2010: chapter two. For more general discussion of recent work on automaticity and goals, see Bargh and Ferguson 2000 and Bargh et al. 2001.

[57] Technically the Milgram experiments involve a failure to refrain from harming someone rather than a failure to help someone, and hence will be discussed in chapter nine on aggression and harming. But I mention them here since they are the most famous illustration of these claims in the psychology literature.

surprises us by helping when we would have least expected it, or (unfortunately) the opposite.[58]

Thus in this section I have explored the following claim:

(C14) Mixed Helping Traits do not only function at the conscious level, and can often automatically cause behavior for motivating reasons which are unknown to the person acting at the time and which may even conflict with what he thinks is a morally appropriate way to be motivated and to act. Because of this capacity for automatic functioning which at times operates without the person's conscious understanding, many people with Mixed Helping Traits do not have an accurate view of the extent to which they are or are not helpful people.

7.7 EVALUATING MIXED HELPING TRAITS

This chapter has avoided ethical claims as much as possible by trying to focus at the descriptive level on character traits that most people have (so I say). But recall that one of the functional roles of character traits is to serve as a basis for the normative assessment of a person. So what should be made of these Mixed Helping Traits?

My central claim here will be that Mixed Helping Traits do not belong among the virtues, and in particular are importantly distinct from the virtue of compassion.[59] In the language of psychology, these are *categorically different traits*, and not simply one trait that comes in various degrees. Finding support for this claim will be much easier given the discussion in Part II of the requirements that a character trait must satisfy in order to count as compassion. Here I will revisit four of these requirements, while also adding two new ones. With these requirements in hand, they can be used to assess whether Mixed Helping Traits qualify as compassionate traits.

But first let me say a bit more about how I regard these requirements in general. The various requirements for different virtues and vices which are outlined in this book and summarized in the Appendix are to be understood in most instances as (what I believe are) *commonsense platitudes* which reflect our ordinary moral thinking. In a few cases, however, these requirements are instead derived specifically from the Aristotelian tradition of thinking about virtue and vice. So, for instance, five of the requirements discussed in this section are intended to reflect commonplace assumptions about compassion, while the sixth is taken directly from Aristotle. Naturally there will be some

---

[58] The issues raised in this paragraph are considered in much more detail in *Character and Moral Psychology*, chapter seven.

[59] Or "benevolence" or "kindness" which I will treat as interchangeable with "compassion."

overlap as well, where a commonsense platitude can also be found in the Aristotelian tradition.[60]

With that said, in this book I do not normatively evaluate character traits using alternative ways of thinking about virtue and vice as developed by, for instance, Kantians or trait-consequentialists.[61] Nevertheless, their proposals can be easily adapted to this discussion, and in fact I am confident that similar conclusions about the lack of both widespread virtue and vice (where these notions are to be understood by their respective normative theories) would emerge.[62] Indeed, I would even claim something stronger—*if* similar conclusions do not emerge, then that is a sign that the account of virtue and vice in question is *seriously flawed*.

Back then to some of the requirements for compassion. The first one was introduced in chapter two:

(a) A person who is compassionate, when acting in character, will typically attempt to help when in moderately demanding situations relevant to helping.[63]

Note that this is *not* saying that helping behavior is all there is to being compassionate—underlying motivation is also crucial. But a person who does not help at all when moderately demanding helping opportunities present themselves, seems to be falling short of being compassionate.

How do Mixed Helping Traits fare in this regard? In section one, I made the following claim:

(C5) A person with a Mixed Helping Trait, when acting in character, will often *not* help even in some moderately demanding situations relevant to helping.[64]

This claim seems to stand in direct opposition to what the behavior of a compassionate person is expected to be like.

Things are a bit more complicated, though. For one natural response is that a compassionate person is not expected to help in *every* helping-relevant

---

[60] In footnotes, I refer to a few places where a philosopher working on virtue in the Aristotelian tradition has discussed one of these requirements.

[61] For the former, see for instance Baxley 2010. For the latter, see for instance Adams 1976, 2006: 53–60. In what follows, I do include references to Robert Adams' theory of virtue (2006), even though it is explicitly non-Aristotelian. But in the respects that concern me in this section, these differences from Aristotelian approaches do not end up mattering. Where I part ways with Adams is his conclusion that, "there are real moral virtues that are not extremely rare and that play a part in a wide variety of human lives" (2006: 119).

[62] To take just one example, John Rawls at one point claims that virtues are, "strong and normally effective desires to act on the basic principles of right" (1971: 436). But given that understanding, precisely the same conclusion about the virtue of compassion will still follow, namely that most people do not in fact have that virtue.

[63] For this and all other requirements on virtues and vices in this book, I assume that other things are held equal.

[64] In light of the subsequent discussion of enhancers, I should add the clause "apart from the presence of an enhancer."

situation, even those that are moderately demanding. This would be impossible practically and extremely demanding.[65] Hence the failure to help in some of these moderate helping-relevant situations is not evidence by itself, on this line of reasoning, that a person is not compassionate.[66] Furthermore, compassion also comes in degrees, and just because someone with a Mixed Helping Trait does not have compassion to a full or complete degree, it does not follow that a Mixed Helping Trait is not a form of *moderate or weak* compassion.

Both of these claims are correct, in my opinion. But they overlook the crucial point here, which is that the standard being used for normatively evaluating a Mixed Helping Trait is whether the trait will lead to helping in contexts where the need for help is *obvious*, and the effort involved in helping is very *minimal*. In other words, I can re-write the first requirement for being a compassionate person as follows:

(a*) A person who is compassionate, when acting in character, will typically attempt to help when, at the very least, the need for help is obvious and the effort involved in helping is very minimal.[67]

---

[65] Another way to put this point is that for many helping tasks, there are only imperfect obligations which apply to them, obligations which do not require that a person help on every relevant occasion. See Adams 2006: 124, 145–8.

As John Doris writes in describing Aristotle's view, "the virtue of magnificence does not entail giving a gift of equal value on every occasion but consistently giving gifts of a value proper to each occasion where a gift is appropriate. To attribute a virtue is not to say that a person can be counted on to reliably do the same thing but that they can be counted on to reliably do whatever is appropriate to that virtue" (2002: 176). Similar Rachana Kamtekar notes that, "Even our lay understanding of character doesn't ordinarily lead us to expect that someone whom we may legitimately call helpful will display actions of the helpful type on every occasion, and so we wouldn't conclude from one failure to help that a person lacks the character trait of helpfulness" (2004: 475). For relevant discussion, see also Brandt 1970: 35, Blasi 1980: 25–6, Butler 1988: 237, Kupperman 1991: 59, Sreenivasan 2002: 60, 2008: 608, Vranas 2005: 18–19, Adams 2006: 123–4, Sosa 2009: 281, and Lukes 2009: 294.

[66] As Gopal Sreenivasan argues, it is consistent with the possession of compassion that a person have certain "blindspots" which signal an incomplete form of the virtue, but do not automatically preclude the possession of the virtue (2008: 609). See also Hursthouse 1999: 149–50 and Upton 2009a: 8–9. As Doris rightly notes, though, a lot depends on the nature of the particular helping opportunity—my possession of the trait of compassion can be justifiably doubted to some extent if, other things being equal, I coldly ignore a drowning baby in a shallow pond (Doris 2010: 139).

[67] Following Sreenivasan's terminology (see previous footnote), if a person does not attempt to help in *these* cases, then he has certain "blackspots" or, "holes in a reliable behavioural disposition . . . that are themselves sufficient to disqualify traits containing them from the status of 'virtue'" (2008: 609). Hence I agree with Doris when he writes that, "failures to behave compassionately when doing so is appropriate and not unduly costly are evidence against attributing the trait" (2002: 29; see also 84, 2010: 139). See also Brandt 1970: 36, McDowell 1979: 142, Hursthouse 1999: 149–50, Goldie 2004: 14, and Russell 2009: 324. The above is straightforwardly compatible with Kamtekar's claim that, "We should not (and I think do not) expect even a very helpful person to stop to help a person in distress if she thinks that doing so will interfere with her doing something else she considers to be very important; we should only expect that the very helpful person will stop often, and more often than the not-so-helpful person." (2004: 475).

This requirement illustrates the idea expressed in chapter one that there is a *minimal threshold*, or a set of necessary conditions which a character trait has to satisfy, before it can count as a particular virtue. Once the trait makes it over that threshold, then it can count as that virtue at least to a weak degree. In the case of compassion, I claim that one of these necessary conditions is (a*); if a person has a character trait relevant to helping, but it does not even lead him to reliably help in *these* kinds of situations, then whatever else might be said about that trait, it has not qualified yet as the virtue of compassion, even to a weak degree.

Mixed Helping Traits, in my opinion, do not meet this standard in (a*). For in hundreds of actual studies, it has been found that many control participants do not help even in highly conducive circumstances, although they might have helped if they were experiencing guilt, a positive mood, or some other enhancer.[68] Often these studies involved precisely the kinds of obvious and incredibly easy helping tasks—notifying someone of a torn shopping bag, stopping to pick up a few dropped papers or computer cards, checking on someone in another room who is screaming in pain—which even a weakly compassionate person should perform. Also, as the last example indicates, often the need in question was not minor either. To take another example, Ervin Staub (1974) ran a study which found that only 15 out of 60 participants approached a person who had fallen, either because of a bad knee or because of chest pains. In particular *not one participant* approached when a man across the street "collapsed after grabbing his chest over his heart . . . [he] attempted to struggle to his feet, could not, and after three attempts remained sitting on the ground."[69] Furthermore recordings "made during the experiment showed that a number of subjects . . . looked at the confederate and immediately turned their head, never looking back again."[70]

Let me turn to a second requirement for compassion which was also introduced earlier:

(b) A compassionate person's trait of compassion will not be dependent on the presence of certain enhancers (such as moderate guilt, embarrassment, or good mood, or even more morally admirable ones such as empathy) in

---

[68] Here I am relying on an assumption to be explicitly mentioned in the next chapter, namely that these control participants, if they had instead been the participants in the experimental condition, would have shown the same trends of enhanced helping.

[69] Staub 1974: 303–4. As Staub writes, "This is a surprising and to some extent an upsetting finding, since there is extreme need for help in the case of a heart problem, and the consequences could possibly be fatal for the distressed person if he does not get assistance" (304–5). However, in another variation when the collapsed person was in the participant's path on the same side of the road as opposed to the opposite side (thereby making it difficult for them to escape), helping rates went significantly up (306).

[70] Staub 1974: 307. Even in the difficult to escape variant, "A number of the subjects who did not help the victim in their path got off the sidewalk and circled around him—a couple of them even crossed over to the other side of the street" (Staub 1974).

leading him to perform helpful actions, such that if these enhancers were not present, then his frequency of helping would significantly decrease in the same nominal situations.[71]

Thus (b) is, I claim, another one of the necessary conditions in compassion's minimal threshold. It says that it is natural to expect compassionate people to reliably help in standard cases *regardless of whether*, for instance, they are in a good mood or not.[72] To have one's frequency of helping in the same moderately demanding situations fluctuate with how guilty or upbeat one is, is a sign that the person is not compassionate to begin with.[73] Yet that is precisely how Mixed Helping Traits operate. So this is a second respect in which these traits fail to qualify as compassionate.

While at it, I might as well mention the corresponding claim about inhibitors as well:

(c) A compassionate person's trait of compassion will not be dependent on the absence of certain inhibitors (such as anticipated moderate embarrassment or blame, or moderately bad moods) in leading him to perform helpful actions, such that if these inhibitors were not present, then his frequency of helping would significantly increase in the same nominal situations.

Compassionate people are expected to reliably help regardless of whether they are in a moderately bad mood or fear embarrassing themselves. But I also claimed that Mixed Helping Traits are highly sensitive to such inhibitors. So this is a third respect in which they fail to qualify.

Fourth is a familiar requirement, not about how a compassionate person would behave, but about what *motivates* her to help:

(d) A compassionate person's trait of compassion will typically lead to helping which is done at least primarily for motivating reasons that are morally

---

[71] As John McDowell writes, "It would disqualify an action from counting as a manifestation of kindness if its agent needed some extraneous incentive to compliance with the requirement— say, the rewards of a good reputation" (1979: 143). See also Webber 2006a: 654, Adams 2006: 137, and Upton 2009a: 13, 2009b: 179. But for an opposing claim, see Adams 2006: 145.

As noted in chapter five, section four, this formulation of (b) above does not quite work with respect to the specific case of an admirable enhancer like empathy, but there I provided a revised version which is more plausible.

[72] The same kind of thought is captured by Irwin when he writes that, "A genuinely kind person is preferable to someone who simply does the kind action in order to look good, because the kind person will keep on doing the kind action in cases where other people benefit just as much but the kindness will not be as conspicuous to others" (1996: 47).

[73] This is not in any way intended to downplay the positive contributions that guilt, for instance, can make. Audiences where I have presented these ideas often interpret me as suggesting that feeling guilt is somehow incompatible with being a virtuous person or is somehow a morally problematic state of mind. But that is *not* my claim here at all. I agree that sometimes guilty feelings can be highly valuable and can spur on moral improvement. My only point here is that a compassionate person would be expected to reliably help (at least in the cases of obvious need and minimal sacrifice) *even if* she is not feeling moral guilt about some past action.

admirable and deserving of moral praise, and not primarily for motivating reasons which are either morally problematic or morally neutral.[74]

When making a donation to charity, for instance, a compassionate person would not donate primarily to look good in the eyes of society, or to be rewarded by God, or to eliminate some underlying guilt, or to maintain a good mood, and so forth. In those cases, we might morally approve of the fact that the donation was made rather than not, but the person deserves no moral praise for these kinds of motives, and his action would have no moral worth to the extent that it is caused by them. It is primarily self-serving, rather than showing an ultimate concern for the needs of the people served by the charity. Indeed in chapter two I strengthened this requirement so that:

(d*) The virtue of compassion gives rise to compassionate motivation to help another person, and that motivation is *altruistic* motivation to help. Indeed, it is the fact that it is altruistic which grounds the moral praiseworthiness of this motivation.[75]

It should be clear how Mixed Helping Traits fare in this regard as well. Given that many of the mental state dispositions which underlie the Trait give rise to egoistic, or at the very least not altruistic, motives I conclude that:

(~d) A person's Mixed Helping Trait will often *not* lead to helping which is primarily done for the same kind of motives caused by the trait of compassion.

Here then is a fourth respect in which the two traits diverge.

Staying with the topic of motivation, consider another feature of compassion that has not been discussed in earlier chapters:

[74] For such a claim about the virtues in general, see, e.g. Brandt 1970: 30, 33–4, 1988: 64, Foot 1972: 164–5, 1978: 166, Aristotle 1985: 1105a28–5b10, Trianosky 1990: 95, Watson 1990: 459, Audi 1991: 160, 162, Zagzebski 1996: 137, 249, Irwin 1996: 44, 47, 54, Hursthouse 1999: 11–12, 100, chapter six, Swanton 2003: 1, 19, 26–8, Goldie 2004: 14–15, 36–7, Webber 2006b: 206, Taylor 2006: 12, Adams 2006: 14, 23–4, 35, 121, 124, 127, 130–8, Appiah 2008: 35, 45, 47, Russell 2009: 69, 134, 184–6, 191, 324, 375, Badhwar 2009: 274–5, Snow 2010: 53–5, 92, 94, 117, and Annas 2011: 27, 66–8. For instance, on Robert Adams's view, "A virtuous person, a morally good person, will of course be for good things and against bad things—and not in just any way, but excellently" (2006: 14).

[75] See, e.g. Foot 1972: 165, 1978: 170, 172, Brandt 1988: 69, Trianosky 1990: 101–2, Watson 1990: 459, Adams 2006: 76, 133, Russell 2009: 324, and Snow 2010: 92. As Foot writes, "Of course he must want not the reputation of charity, nor even a gratifying role helping others, but, quite simply, their good. If this is what he does care about, then he will be attached to the end proper to the virtue of charity." (1972: 165). Indeed as noted in chapter two, Robert Adams claims that, "we think not caring for the good of other people, for its own sake, is morally *bad*—in extreme cases, even wicked. If it is a settled motivational pattern, it is a *vice*." (2006: 76, emphasis his).

Note that this claim about altruistic motivation need not apply to other virtues besides compassion. As Adams notes, "caring appropriately for one's own good, and more broadly for the values in one's own life, has also had a place in classical conceptions of virtue, and rightly so." (2006: 20).

(e) A compassionate person, when acting in character, would *not* help or refrain
    from helping in moderately demanding situations relevant to helping, as a
    result of the significant causal influence of subconscious motives which he
    would not endorse (if he knew about them).[76]

This condition can be seen as a corollary of (d), but stating it explicitly serves
to emphasize that while a compassionate person's helping can arise from
subconscious motives (that by itself seems unproblematic), those motives
had better not conflict with what he consciously thinks *qua* compassionate
person. And yet in section six, I claimed that Mixed Helping Traits can lead to
precisely this result. For instance, suppose that I do not help in an emergency
situation when I am with an unresponsive bystander. Later I might read some
psychology and learn that this was because of the influence of a subconscious
fear of embarrassment on my part. I could experience a great deal of regret,
disappointment, or shame for having been influenced by this fear, especially if
I consciously try to be a compassionate person.

Finally, according to a long tradition of thought about the virtues (at least
in Western philosophy), the possession of any given virtue requires the
prior possession of *practical wisdom*.[77] There are different accounts of practical wisdom, and I do not intend to survey them here or develop my own
proposal. Rather I only want to present what I take to be two commonly
held and largely uncontroversial theses about how practical wisdom is supposed to function:

[76] For relevant discussion of virtue and the endorsement of subconscious motives, see Snow
2010: 51, 60. See also Russell 2009: 329.

The above is a version of the traditional Aristotelian distinction between acting from
virtue and acting continently as a result of motives which reason opposes. The compassionate
person, in other words, acts from a harmonious relationship between her conscious beliefs
and motives, including presumably subconscious motives as well. As Anne Margaret Baxley
notes, "on a widely held view about human goodness that would seem . . . to capture our
commonsense understanding of morality, there is something deficient or lacking in the divided
or conflicted person" (2010: 40). For related discussion of virtue and incontinence, see Aristotle
1985: 1145a15–52a35 (especially 1150a20, 1150b30, 1151b35–2a4), McDowell 1979: 145–6,
Irwin 1996: 49–50, Hursthouse 1999: chapter four, Webber 2006b: 207, Annas 2007: 517,
2011: 67–8, 75, Taylor 2006: 5–6, and Baxley 2010: 40–1.

There do seem to be some exceptional cases of continent action where, if a person struggles
against but ultimately overcomes certain serious obstacles, then that can be a sign of her virtue
too (see, e.g. Foot 1978: 171–2, Upton 2009a: 8–11, 2009b: 177–9, Hursthouse 1999: 95–8, Baxley
2010: 43–5, and Annas 2011: 77–8). But these cases are not at issue in the above. They do,
however, serve to make clear that I am not committing myself to the claim that commonsense
moral thinking accepts *all* aspects of the traditional Aristotelian framework in this area. For more
general criticism of the Aristotelian framework, see Adams 2006: 155–6. See also Goldie 2004:
70–5.

[77] The most famous articulation of this proposal can be found in Aristotle 1985. For an
excellent recent discussion, see Russell 2009.

(W1) A person with practical wisdom is able to reliably *identify* the good reasons for acting in a given set of circumstances, as well as how strong they are for and against various courses of action.[78]

Suppose such a person were to come across an injured child who needs to be taken to the hospital. The person with practical wisdom would in this case be able to recognize that the child's injury and pain are excellent reasons for going to the hospital, and that the promise to meet a friend for lunch, even though it is *a* reason for not helping the child, is seriously outweighed in this case by the stronger reasons to help the child. Of course, such a person need not think explicitly in terms of "reasons" or consciously and reflectively weigh these competing reasons. That would be an overly intellectual conception of practical wisdom. Rather, this recognition can be largely automatic and implicit, and still satisfy (W1).[79]

Now consider a second thesis about practical wisdom:

(W2) A person with practical wisdom is disposed so as to be reliably *motivated* to act in a way that is appropriately responsive to the good reasons there are to act in a given set of circumstances.[80]

So in addition, the person in our example would not merely recognize the correct considerations favoring helping the child in this situation, but would also have those *normative reasons* be reflected as *motivating reasons* for her to act, although again this can be a relatively automatic process not requiring conscious deliberation.[81] Hence she would be motivated by the child's injury and pain to go to the hospital, and motivated to a greater degree than she is motivated to keep the lunch date. Claims (i) and (ii) are not unique to any one ethical theory or approach in philosophy; instead they strike me as platitudes about practical wisdom which any theory should accept.

[78] Hence Aristotle: "Intelligence is a state grasping the truth, involving reason, concerned with action about what is good or bad for a human being" (1140b5). See also 1142b28, 1143a9, Foot 1978: 167–8, Brandt 1988: 79, Irwin 1996: 53, Hursthouse 1999: 13, Kamtekar 2004: 480–2, Adams 2006: 10, and Russell 2009: x. Russell also adds to this the role of practical wisdom in, "the specification of the very *content* of virtuous ends (e.g. what would in fact be, in these circumstances, a generous act)" (2009: x, emphasis his; see also 30, 79–81, 101, 329). This addition only strengthens the conclusion I will arrive at in what follows.

[79] Thanks to an anonymous referee for asking me to clarify this.

[80] Ernest Sosa expresses a similar point when he writes that "One manifests practical wisdom in any given situation to the degree that one's motivational structure reflects the relevant rational structure in that situation" (2009: 282). See also Russell 2009: 111 and Badhwar 2009: 269.

[81] Normative reasons are what in fact are good reasons for us to act. Motivating reasons are the considerations which motivate us to act, and may or may not be good normative reasons. For instance, someone might be motivated by a desire to torture someone purely for amusement, where the amusement derived from torturing might be a motivating reason for him but is certainly not a normative reason. For more on this distinction, see Smith 1994: chapter four and Dancy 2000: chapter one, as well as my 2008a.

But if so, then I can develop a sixth and final argument concerning the normative status of Mixed Helping Traits as follows:

(i) The virtue of compassion requires practical wisdom.[82]

(ii) Part of what practical wisdom involves is being disposed to be reliably motivated to act in a way that is appropriately responsive to the good reasons there are to act in a given set of circumstances. (W2)

(iii) A person with a Mixed Helping Trait, when acting in character, is not reliably motivated in this way. Such a person often gives too much weight to considerations which should have less or even no weight (such as relieving his own guilt), and often gives too little weight to considerations which should have more weight (such as the needs of other people).[83]

(iv) Therefore, having a Mixed Helping Trait does not require practical wisdom, understood as a reliable disposition along the lines of (W1) and (W2).

(v) Therefore, given (i) and (iv), a Mixed Helping Trait is distinct from the virtue of compassion.

Less formally, I have already clarified in this section how a person with a Mixed Helping Trait will often be motivated by considerations which have little if any moral value, instead of being moved primarily by what someone in need requires or by what would be good for that person for her own sake. This is not how a person with practical wisdom would be motivated.

Similar points could be made about the virtue of compassion without having to invoke what, for some philosophers, is a controversial claim in (i) about its relationship to practical wisdom. I have noted that Mixed Helping Traits do exhibit cross-situational consistency relative to the mental state dispositions which constitute them. Some of those dispositions have to do with embarrassment, mood states, guilt, blame, and the like. But consistency relative to *those* mental state dispositions is not the form of consistency across situations which is expected of compassion. There should primarily be consistency relative to what are the *actual normative considerations* that are related to helping; in other words, such dispositions should be appropriately reasons-responsive. As Peter Goldie claims, "We value traits, calling them virtues, because they are dispositions reliably to recognize what is of value or

---

[82] For the claim that all virtues require practical wisdom, see Aristotle 1985: 1107a2, 1144b15–16 and related discussion in Zagzebski 1996: 211–31, Irwin 1996: 53, Hursthouse 1999: 13, Kamtekar 2004: 485, Taylor 2006: 2, Snow 2010: 53–4, 116, and especially Russell 2009.

[83] Here and throughout this discussion of practical wisdom I have been helped by Sosa 2009: 280–3. Note that I am claiming *both* an over-sensitivity to morally irrelevant factors, and an under-sensitivity to morally relevant factors. Even if the former could be reconciled with practical wisdom in some way, it is hard to see how both of these claims could be. Thanks to Anne Baril for discussion here.

disvalue in the world, and reliably to respond appropriately in thought, feeling and action."[84] Whether a person who can help is in a moderately bad mood which helping can alleviate, for instance, is not a consideration which should typically be relevant to whether he helps someone, and yet there are various situations in which it seems to be highly relevant without adequate moral justification.

These then are six important ways in which I believe Mixed Helping Traits do not meet the minimal threshold for compassion. One response is to concede that I am right as far as compassion is concerned, and note that this does not show that such traits could not qualify as some *other* virtue instead.[85] Perhaps they count as a different traditional virtue, such as kindness, or perhaps they count as one of the virtues for which humans have yet to come up with a name.

These are possibilities worth considering, but they do not strike me as promising. Recall again that a person with a Mixed Helping Trait might often not help with a simple task, such as notifying someone of a torn shopping bag. And even when he does help, he might do so primarily as a result of feeling guilty or embarrassed, thereby making helping dependent on morally suspect motives like a desire to help so as to overcome one's guilt, rather than being motivated primarily by what would benefit the other person. So while I cannot definitively rule out the possibilities mentioned in the previous paragraph, these features of Mixed Helping Traits do not strike me as charac-teristics that could be had by *any* virtue, nor do they meet the standards for virtue that most philosophers have offered going back all the way to Plato and Aristotle.

At the same time, this discussion should not be taken to imply that therefore a Mixed Helping Trait is a *vice* such as cold-heartedness, callousness, indiffer-ence, or selfishness. I have said comparatively little about vices in the book so far, and I could develop requirements for, say, selfishness that invert the same requirements outlined earlier for compassion. But I hope that the work in prior chapters makes this unnecessary. Someone with a Mixed Helping Trait will still help stably over time, and in a cross-situationally consistent manner

---

[84] Goldie 2004: 42. Similarly John McDowell notes that "A kind person has a reliable sensitivity to a certain sort of requirement which situations impose on behaviour" (1979: 142). Again as Philippa Foot writes, "Those who possess these virtues [such as compassion] possess them in so far as they recognize certain considerations as powerful, and in many circumstances compelling, reasons for acting. They recognize the reasons, and act on them" (2001: 12). And according to Daniel Russell, "a virtue, like generosity, is to be individuated by the reasons there are to act generously, and . . . having the virtue of generosity is (among other things) to be characteristically responsive to those 'reasons there are' by making them the 'reasons for which' one acts" (2009: 186). For similar remarks, see McDowell 1979: 143–6, Williams 1985: 10, Butler 1988: 220–4, Zagzebski 1996: 134, Hursthouse 1999: 129, Foot 2001: 12–13, Doris 2002: 84, Swanton 2003: 1, 19, Goldie 2004: 43–7, Adams 2006: 10, Appiah 2008: 45, Upton 2009a: 4, 2009b: 177, and Russell 2009: 29, 101, 173, 179–80, 183–6, 324, 329, 375.

[85] I am grateful to Brian Robinson for raising this concern.

in many contexts. That helping will be influenced by enhancers such as activated moral norms, elevation, and empathy that would not be expected to play a significant psychological role in someone who is selfish or otherwise vicious. Furthermore, given the pluralistic theory of motivation, a person with a Mixed Helping Trait can sometimes be expected to help for moralistic rather than only egoistic reasons. Indeed, if Batson's empathy-altruism hypothesis is correct, then that person is also disposed to reliably help when in an empathetic state of mind, and to do so for genuinely *caring and altruistic* reasons, even at some sacrifice to her own concerns. A vicious person would not be like that.[86]

The temptation to conclude that, if it is not a virtue, then a Mixed Helping Trait must be a vice, likely arises from the mistaken assumption that these are the only two forms that moral character traits can take. But as I said at the end of chapter one, this assumption is false—many moral character traits can be *neither* virtues nor vices. Hence I arrive at the main conclusion of this section:

(C15) A Mixed Helping Trait is a moral character trait, but it is neither a moral virtue nor a moral vice.

Let me represent this diagrammatically in Figure 7.20.

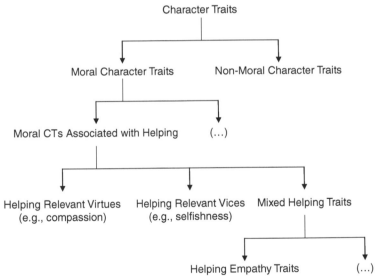

Fig. 7.20. A partial taxonomy of character traits.[87]

---

[86] For relevant discussion aimed against the claim that there is widespread possession of a vice pertaining to helping, see Vranas 2005: 12–16. In chapter nine I consider psychological research on aggressive behavior, and argue there in some detail that most of us do not have the vice of cruelty. I do the same thing in chapter ten with respect to the vice of dishonesty. So for readers who find the above dismissal of the hypothesis of widespread vice to be too quick, the points I make in those chapters carry over straightforwardly to this discussion as well.

[87] These are 'moral' character traits in the sense that distinguishes them from epistemic, prudential, aesthetic, and other character traits. They are not 'moral' in the sense of only referring to the moral virtues. The moral vices and my Mixed Traits fall under this heading as well.

Given (C15) and given my very first claim in this chapter about the extent to which people have Mixed Helping Traits, I want to maintain that:

> (C16) Most people have a Mixed Helping Trait at some level of generality and to some degree, and not the virtue of compassion.

I also maintain that the evidence from psychological studies on helping provides good reason to *reject* the claim that:

> (C17) Most people have the virtue of compassion to some degree, and not a Mixed Helping Trait.

But rejecting this claim does not amount to rejecting the existence of any compassionate people. Indeed, on my reading the experimental literature is compatible with the idea that:

> (C18) A few people have the virtue of compassion to some degree, and not a Mixed Helping Trait.

It is also compatible with:

> (C19) A few people have the vice of selfishness to some degree, and not a Mixed Helping Trait.

So Mixed Helping Traits are not supposed to be part of the explanation for *all* instances of helping, just for most of them. Indeed, it may even be the case that:

> (C20) Some people do not have Mixed Helping Traits, compassion, or selfishness when it comes to what gives rise to their helping behavior.

I have in mind especially infants and young children, who may not have character traits in the first place, or if they do, these traits may not exhibit the patterns that would be expected from any of the above. This claim might also be true of psychopaths and those with various mental handicaps or illnesses, although a detailed look at the empirical literature would be needed here too.

The main point for now, though, is that when it comes to most of us, the part of our moral character which pertains to helping is not only extremely complex at the psychological level, but ethically it also has a number of different positive and negative elements which together preclude it from counting as either a moral virtue or a moral vice.

7.8 CONCLUSION

In this chapter, I have made a number of important observations about something I call a Mixed Helping Trait. At the same time, I have not come close to exhaustively outlining its nature and functioning. In particular, while

I indicated *some* of the mental state dispositions that make up this trait, I have not offered anything like a complete inventory of all these dispositions (not that I could do so even if I tried!).

Rather than focus on providing such an inventory, I have instead devoted most of my attention to the various ways in which a Mixed Helping Trait functions—how it can lead to patterns of helping behavior which seem fragmented, how it can be enhanced or inhibited, how it is stable and cross-situationally consistent in certain respects, how it comes in degrees and exists at different levels of generality, how it can be used to make reasonably accurate predictions, how it can function at the level of conscious awareness or below it, and how it is neither a moral virtue nor a vice. I suggest that these are the kinds of observations which are important to make initially when trying to understand a trait of character that has not been recognized by ordinary thought. Once convinced of its existence we can then go about filling in the details about what the trait's remaining dispositional components are.[88]

All of this is by way of saying that while in my view Mixed Helping Traits give us a new and promising approach to understanding moral character and helping, it is an approach that is complicated and messy. As, I think, we should expect any story about our actual moral character to be.

---

[88] Here I am following the same broad procedure for studying personality outlined by Shoda et al. 1994: 686.

8

Generalizing the Account

After the sustained focus on Mixed Helping Traits in chapter seven, I do not want to lose sight of the larger purpose that this discussion was meant to serve in the book. While it is important to get a clearer picture of character and helping, I also want to use that picture as a template from which to generalize to *other* moral character traits that might exist alongside Mixed Helping Traits. In other words, I want to suggest that a parallel framework for thinking about most people's character traits in other areas *besides* helping—truth-telling, not harming others, showing thanks, keeping promises, and so forth—is also promising.

But before I do so, in section one I need to address a challenge to my proposal that comes from a rival psychological model of character and helping. Then in section two, I sketch some of the aspects of the account of Mixed Helping Traits which can be carried over to thinking about our character traits in general. In section three, I examine a few important studies of non-moral traits which, if they had arrived at similar results for moral traits, would have supported the general framework that I am advancing here. Section four briefly reviews an important set of studies on specifically moral behavior which found results very much in line with my approach. Finally, section five develops some general principles for the experimental study of moral character which should seem plausible in light of Parts II and III. At the same time, these principles also serve to illustrate some of the limitations of the existing studies in this area and constrain what I can say about the empirical adequacy of my framework.

8.1 STEPPING BACK AND COMPARING MODELS

Before generalizing the picture of Mixed Helping Traits to other moral domains, I want to step back from the details of the past few chapters and try to tie together a number of different ideas. This will also serve to set the stage for introducing a competing model which purports to do a better job of fitting the empirical evidence.

Let me start with my familiar friend—the virtue of compassion—and consider the diagram in Figure 8.1. There compassion is understood as first and foremost a disposition that a person can come to develop, and so is sensitive to relevant stimuli and, other things being equal, gives rise to relevant outputs. Furthermore, it consists of certain underlying mental state dispositions. These cannot be just any dispositions to believe and desire; rather they are dispositions which satisfy all the necessary conditions in what I called the minimal threshold for a trait to be the virtue of compassion. For instance, the dispositional desires are typically altruistic ones, and these mental states will not fail to motivate helping even if that counts to some moderate degree against what the person thinks is in her self-interest. So once she learns relevant information about the situation, the specific belief and desire dispositions can respond accordingly, giving rise to altruistic motivation to help.

Contrast this picture with Figure 8.2. There the initial setup is much the same—the person comes across a situation where someone appears to be in distress, and believes that there are things he can do to help relieve the distress. But in my story, it is an open question whether he is going to then be motivated to relieve that distress. If he feels empathy for the person, then he might be, which in turn can activate the part of the Mixed Helping Trait that has to do with altruistic desires to help. Or if instead he sees the person in distress and is feeling guilty, then he could be motivated to find ways to alleviate the guilt, which could activate the part of the Mixed Helping Trait that has to do with helping and guilt-relief. Similarly if he reflects on what the morally right thing to do is, that can stimulate a desire to do the right thing,

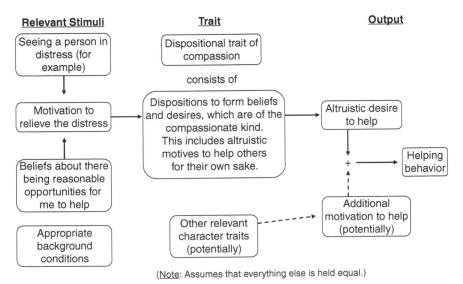

Fig. 8.1. Modeling the functioning of the virtue of compassion.

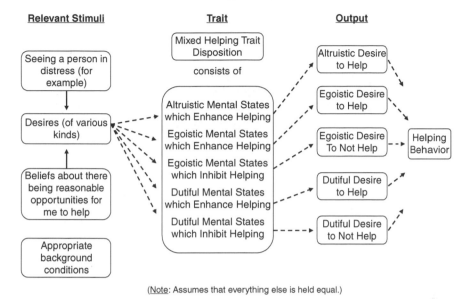

Fig. 8.2. Modeling the functioning of a Mixed Helping Trait.

and activate the relevant dutiful mental states that enhance helping. But of course there are ways inhibitors might be at work which instead trigger desires to not help.

As mentioned in the previous chapter, the virtue of compassion and a Mixed Helping Trait are categorically different traits, rather than one trait which comes in varying degrees. We have seen various ways in which these traits function in opposing ways from each other, which thereby serves to clarify how they are different. But ultimately their difference is deeper—they simply consist of different mental state dispositions, different dispositions to form beliefs and desires broadly understood. Many of the mental state dispositions which make up a Mixed Helping Trait are simply precluded on normative grounds from playing a constitutive role in the virtue of compassion. And it is because of these differences in their makeup, that the two kinds of traits function so differently.

Hopefully these figures serve as useful guides to my framework for thinking about the moral character traits with respect to helping that most of us possess. Whenever I present the idea of Mixed Helping Traits, I am almost inevitably asked about a third model.[1] On my approach, most people have a number of what might be called "conditional desires," such as a desire to help another person so long as helping will serve to alleviate my guilt. The only case

---

[1] David Wong and an anonymous journal referee especially encouraged me to address this view. See also Sabini and Silver 2005: 560 n. 56.

in which I have suggested we do not have such conditional desires is with empathy, where we seem to desire to help another person, period.

According to the third model, which I will call the Simple Desire (SD) model, we do *not* in fact have an array of conditional desires, but just one central desire when it comes to helping—the (*de dicto*) desire to help other people as such. So when I see my friend in need of help, this can activate my desire to help other people, which in turn can cause the formation of a desire to help my friend. The story is as simple as that.

Furthermore, the view maintains that inhibited helping can be explained, not by appealing to conditional desires like a desire to not help if so doing would worsen my feelings of guilt, but rather simply to cases in which the desire to not feel any guiltier is stronger than the desire to help, and so outweighs it. Similarly in other cases a desire to not embarrass myself in front of others can outweigh a desire to help someone in need, say in the "Lady in Distress" group effect experiment. In the language of the philosophical literature on dispositions, other desires can *mask* the activity of the disposition to desire to help.[2] In doing so, the desire is still present, but it is not strong enough to lead to action in those cases. It can still make its presence known, though, in the form of inner conflict and behavioral signs of struggle and tension.

The advocate of the SD model can go on and argue further that not only do most people have this general desire to help others, but that the desire enables them to count as having the virtue of compassion to some degree. Note, though, that this is an optional further step. One could hold the SD model and still accept my claim that most people are not virtuous in this area. For instance, one could argue that even though this desire is present in most people, it so happens that it is not held strongly enough, or it is too fragile and easily outweighed by other desires, to qualify those people as compassionate. After all, there are morally appropriate masks for dispositions and morally inappropriate ones too. Being asleep can be a perfectly fine mask for the virtue of compassion, but being in a bad mood typically is not. Since in earlier chapters I have already extensively discussed the virtue of compassion and the extent to which I believe most people actually possess it today, let me leave aside this further addition to the view and just stick with the SD model as initially presented.[3]

---

[2] For something like this proposal, see Sabini and Silver 2005: 560 n. 56 and perhaps Adams 2006: 154. For recent discussion of masking and dispositions, see Manley and Wasserman 2008. The use of the language of "masking" is not intended to correspond exactly to how that terminology is used in the metaphysics of dispositions literature, where it can refer to cases where the disposition is not manifested at all. In the above, while the desire to help may not be manifested *in behavior*, according to the SD model it is still being activated and has some motivational upshot but is outweighed.

[3] For relevant discussion of the compatibility of the SD model with the virtues of compassion and kindness, see Butler 1988: 233–5. I do, however, return to the idea of a simple desire to help

The SD model clearly has the advantage of being extremely simple and elegant. It only needs to postulate one desire to try to explain what motivates vast quantities of helping behavior in a variety of different circumstances. Furthermore, the model's story about inhibited helping is intuitive and easy to understand. And I have no reason to doubt that some people might have a general desire like this. But do most of us? Here, I fear, the psychological reality is not as simple as the SD model makes it sound.

In order to comparatively assess the two models, I want to derive a few predictions from them and then briefly test each prediction using the available empirical data. Here is one set of predictions:

SD Model: If most of us have a desire to help other people, then control participants in studies of helping should do so at fairly high levels, other things being equal, at least when given simple and obvious opportunities to help.

MHT Model: If most of us have a Mixed Helping Trait, then there is no expectation that control participants will help at fairly high levels when given simple and obvious opportunities to help, other things being equal. In some situations they might, and in others they might not.

Here the experimental evidence clearly favors my MHT model. In hundreds of studies, only some of which were reviewed in earlier chapters, the majority of control participants do not perform even the simplest of helping tasks. This also tells against a *combined* model where most people are said to have *both* a general desire to help along with conditional desires to help and not help based on the presence of variables like guilt and mood.

The advocate of the SD model could respond by arguing that, for various reasons, the desire to help was still present and activated in these control participants, but was being masked. Now this strikes me as an intelligible response. But the burden is on the advocate of the SD model to motivate this response. Why should we think that the majority of the control participants were conflicted, rather than think that a desire to help was simply not present in the first place? Furthermore, the advocate of the SD model needs to avoid the danger of making it unfalsifiable if most cases of lack of helping are going to be explained away by claiming that the desire to help was active but masked.[4]

Most important of all, there is rarely any evidence recorded in the published studies of psychological conflict among control participants in these simple

being the basis for widespread compassion in *Character and Moral Psychology*, chapter eight, section four when discussing the idea of "competing virtues." There the thought is that perhaps results of studies which found an absence of virtuous behavior can be explained by one virtue, such as compassion, being masked by another virtue, such as trust or cooperativeness. As I do with the SD model, I formulate empirical predictions that would be generated by this proposal, and argue that they do not sit well with the existing evidence.

[4] For a related discussion and similar conclusion to mine, see Snow 2010: 95–6.

helping studies (whether the conflict is self-reported by the participants themselves or observed in their behavior by experimenters), although to be fair the studies were not typically interested in this issue in the first place. Recall, for instance, that in the Konečni study of guilt in which controls had the opportunity to help pick up dropped computer cards, only 16 percent did so and, "the control subjects tended to make a fairly large and unnecessary semicircle around the pile of cards, and hardly ever commented on what had happened."[5] Similarly in the Isen and Levin dime phone booth experiment where (ignoring the replication difficulties for a moment) only 1 out of 25 helped pick up dropped papers, "[i]n numerous instances . . . nonhelping subjects literally trampled the fallen papers."[6]

So the SD model does not seem to fare well when the above prediction is put to the test. Just for good measure, here is another prediction:

> *SD Model*: If most of us have a desire to help other people, then even when feelings of guilt or positive mood or embarrassment subside, participants in studies of helping should still continue to help at fairly high levels in moderate helping relevant situations, other things being equal.

> *MHT Model*: If most of us have a Mixed Helping Trait, then when feelings of guilt or positive mood or embarrassment subside, participants in studies of helping are not expected to continue to help at fairly high levels in moderate helping-relevant situations, other things being equal. In some situations they might, and in others they might not.

While there are fewer studies to draw on here, the ones I am familiar with seem to point in the direction of the second prediction. For instance, recall the Zhong and Liljenquist (2006) study from chapter two where participants remembered one of their unethical actions, did or did not use an antiseptic wipe to cleanse their hands, and were then given an opportunity to be an unpaid volunteer for a desperate graduate student in another study. Seventy-four percent of guilt-induced controls volunteered to help, whereas only 41 percent did who used the wipes, which was theorized to cleanse at least some of their guilt.[7] Helping dropped off significantly even with such a minor

---

[5] Konečni 1972: 32.

[6] Doris 2002: 31. One noticeable exception from chapter six has to do with the group effect literature, where participants who did not help often seemed to experience motivational tension between, for instance, fear of embarrassment and some kind of motivation to help, with the latter being outweighed by the former. As an illustration of this tension, Latané and Darley observed about their epileptic seizure experiment that, "Many of these subjects [who did not help] showed signs of nervousness: they often had trembling hands and wreathing palms. If anything, they seemed more emotionally aroused than did the subjects who reported the emergency" (1970: 100). As Ross and Nisbett write, this cognitive dissonance in group settings is, "characteristically resolved in favor of the group's view, often not by simple compromise, but by wholesale adoption of the group's view and suppression of one's own doubts" (1991: 46).

[7] Zhong and Liljenquist 2006: 1452.

manipulation in the study. And more effective means of cleansing guilt would likely have reduced the percentage to an even greater extent.

In this section I briefly summarized my approach to character and helping, as well as two other competing models. Of course, much more needs to be done in testing the predictions generated by these models, and it would be far too premature to rule out any of them. For now, however, it seems to me that my Mixed Helping Trait model has the upper hand. So let me see take the approach one step further by applying it to other moral domains besides helping.

8.2 GENERALIZING BEYOND MIXED HELPING TRAITS

Chapter seven highlighted twenty different claims about Mixed Helping Traits. Now clearly it would be tedious to revisit all of them here, and it should be straightforward how they can be restated to apply to other domains besides helping. So in this section I want to just hit a few highlights of what the generalized account looks like.

Let me begin with the existence of character traits:

(G1) Most people possess a number of different moral character traits with their own corresponding mental state dispositions. These traits will each typically cause trait-relevant behavior from one trait-relevant situation to the next that can seem fragmented to observers, even though the trait-relevant task is moderately demanding for the person to perform or refrain from performing.[8]

As before, the underlying mental state dispositions do not include any individually unique or idiosyncratic dispositions, but rather the generic dispositions common to all individuals who possess that particular trait.[9]

So the idea is that most people possess a trait pertaining, for instance, to forgiving others, which consists of various mental state dispositions that are relevant to forgiving and yet which, from the outside, seems to give rise to fragmented behavior. In some situations the person is frequently forgiving and in others he is not, but these are all situations which are relevant to forgiveness

---

[8] Again I will assume here and in all the claims which follow in this section that other things are being held equal.

[9] As Mischel notes about our mental lives in general, "[t]o the degree that idiosyncratic social learning histories characterize each person's life, idiosyncratic (rather than culturally shared) stimulus equivalences and hence idiosyncratic behavior patterns may be expected" (1973: 259). This certainly seems right and should be kept in mind when trying to experimentally determine the mental state dispositions of a particular individual. They will not be exhausted just by the generic or widely held dispositions to form certain beliefs or desires.

Fig. 8.3. Smith's profile (frequency).

and are only moderately demanding. Hence for each of these character traits, there might be a situation-behavior profile like Figure 8.3.

Is this profile really so surprising given what we see in our ordinary lives? Many of the people we know sometimes forgive and sometimes hold a grudge, or sometimes tell the truth and sometimes lie, or sometimes are polite and sometime rude. They seem to act in various opposing or inconsistent ways, morally speaking, throughout a day, week, or year. Their behavior is, as I prefer to say, decidedly mixed.[10]

What may seem more surprising is this:

> (G2) The moral character traits which most adult human beings possess do not correspond to any of the words or concepts which ordinary people have for traits.

In one sense this almost seems unbelievable. How can it be that we have developed hundreds of character concepts, and yet none of them does a good job in applying to how people actually are? How, in other words, could we have done such a bad job in our ordinary thinking and not developed concepts to capture such important traits?[11]

Yet in another sense this might not be so surprising at all. Most of our character concepts pertain to moral heroes or moral villains, and it is rare to find someone who is truly honest, courageous, and compassionate, or on the flip side, dishonest, cowardly, and selfish. These moral concepts can still serve a number of helpful purposes—emulation, guidance, instruction, education, and so forth—even if they are not in fact accurately reflecting how most people actually are.

Instead, most people we come across in life, read about in history, or see on television seem to exhibit some complex mixture of good and bad characteristics. We seem to display plenty of virtuous actions in some moments and

---

[10] For a similar profile and overall approach, see Shoda and LeeTiernan 2002: 242. I will discuss their work in section four of this chapter.

[11] I discuss these questions in more detail in *Character and Moral Psychology*, chapter seven.

plenty of vicious ones in others that collectively defy easy categorization or labeling. We tend to be, not "good" or "bad" or "virtuous" or "vicious" people in general, but simply ordinary people struggling with our moral flaws while trying to exhibit moral strengths.[12]

So for each domain of the moral where the character traits in (G1) exist, I claim that we need to invent new terminology—such as "Mixed Helping Traits"—in order to usefully label them. For my purposes, to make it clear that I am talking about these unfamiliar traits rather than traits like courage or greed, in what follows I will refer to them as "Mixed Character Traits" or "Mixed Traits" with capital letters, with the reminder that I am only focusing on the moral as opposed to the non-moral ones.

From here the presentation of the rest of the framework proceeds straight-forwardly. For instance, I claim that:

(G3) There are certain stimuli for each of a person's Mixed Traits which can function as *enhancers* or as *inhibitors* of that Mixed Trait in a given instance. They influence the trait in such a way that there is an increase or decrease in motivation to exhibit relevant behavior in moderately demanding relevant situations, as compared to the level of motivation to act in these situations apart from the influence of the enhancer or inhibitor.

It is natural to expect a fair amount of overlap between the various Mixed Traits as to what enhances and inhibits them. For instance, prior to examining the empirical literature, I would imagine that anticipated embarrassment might inhibit truth-telling in certain situations, as it does helping behavior.[13]

Furthermore, these traits are both stable through time and cross-situation-ally consistent in important senses that have already been outlined with Mixed Helping Traits. In particular:

(G4) A person with a Mixed Trait will often exhibit relevant behavior that is (momentarily and in an extended sense) cross-situationally consistent in moderately demanding Mixed Trait-relevant situations, when those situations are compared based upon the features which are psychologically relevant to the person in question.

What grounds this cross-situational consistency will be the specific mental state dispositions unique to each Mixed Trait. So if, speaking hypothetically, one such disposition underlying a Mixed Forgiving Trait is to desire to forgive

---

[12] As Mischel and Mischel write, "It is tempting but misleading to categorize people into the cross-situationally moral versus the broadly immoral. A world of good guys versus bad guys—as in the Western films in which the cowboys' white or black hats permit easy identification of the virtuous and the villainous—is seductive" (1976: 209). Similarly, Joel Kupperman claims that, "any individual is likely to have drives and habits of mind that in some contexts can manifest themselves in virtuous behavior, and in other contexts in behavior that fails to be virtuous" (2009: 248).

[13] In chapter ten, I suggest that there is indeed empirical support for this hypothesis.

only so long as doing so will alleviate my sense of feeling wronged, then that can help make sense of patterns of forgiving (and not forgiving) across situations which otherwise seem disconnected based upon their nominal features.

More generally, I claim we should expect to find that people with Mixed Character Traits adjust their morally relevant behavior, often implicitly and automatically, to the different features of the situations in which they find themselves, as a result of those situations causing different mental state dispositions to be activated in the respective Mixed Traits.[14] As Walter Mischel notes, "people behave in ways that are consistent with the meanings that particular situations have for them . . . there is no theoretical reason to expect the person to behave similarly in relation to different psychological situations unless they are functionally equivalent in meaning."[15] So the moral behavioral patterns of many people need not be deeply fragmented after all or show a lack of character, but rather can be intelligible products of both situations and Mixed Traits interacting together.[16]

Furthermore, while any one Mixed Trait is sensitive to a variety of different situational factors over time, it also differs from another kind of Mixed Trait in its sensitivity to specific situational factors. For instance, the fact that someone is asking me to break a promise is a situational factor that might obviously pertain to certain Mixed Traits more so than others. So if observers knew what Mixed Traits a person possesses and what the features are of a situation he is about to encounter, then they could develop predictions about which one of

[14] This is not to deny that people (and their character traits) also play an active role in determining which situations to enter into in the first place, and what to do when in those situations in order to modify them. The causal forces of the person and the situation work in both directions. For related discussion, see Snyder and Gangestad 1982 and Ross and Nisbett 1991: 163–8. This point is developed in more detail in *Character and Moral Psychology*, chapter four.

[15] Mischel 2007: 266. Paul Wachtel also notes that "the postulation of consistency of personality need not be incompatible with the view that people may be acutely sensitive to changes in the stimulus situation. For consistency need not be the result of a static structure that moves from situation to situation and pays no need to stimuli" (1973: 330). Similarly Orom and Cervone write that "identifying cross-situational consistency is a fairly simple matter once one attends to the potentially idiosyncratic sets of social contexts that are psychologically significant to the individual" (2009: 239). See also Bem and Allen 1974: 509–11.

[16] As Yuichi Shoda and Scott LeeTiernan remark, "When the situation changes, so do the behaviors, but the relationship between the situations and behaviors may be stable and may express an individual's distinctive cognitive, behavioral, and affective response characteristics" (2002: 244). Similarly as William Fleeson notes about within-person variability, it "may be the result of flexible and responsive discrimination among situations and of planful action, suggesting that an important aspect of personality may be how individuals react to context and how they carry out sequences of action. In these cases, personality units that capture such contingencies of behavior would be needed to explain the variability within a person in behavior" (2007: 828).

these Mixed Traits would likely be impacted the most based on the mental state dispositions which make up each of them.

Of course these Mixed Character Traits need not be held to the same degree from one person to the next. Two people might exhibit different behavioral signatures and different amounts of within-person variability in their relevant behavior even though they both have exactly the same Mixed Traits to different degrees. Because of these individual differences, certain situational features can be expected to have more of an impact on one of them than on the other.

Similarly, I claim that:

> (G5) Mixed Traits exist at different levels of generality, and while narrower specifications of Mixed Traits will have increased predictive value, we can often formulate predictions which are accurate in many situations using more general Mixed Traits.

At the broadest level, there is a Mixed Character Trait for each of the moral domains (helping, truth-telling, promise-keeping, etc.), and it consists of a vast array of mental state dispositions. From there, the scope of these Traits can be narrowed down as done in the previous chapter, with the recommended strategy being to focus on the psychologically relevant features of the situation as assessed by the person in question. This can result in several levels of more specific Traits. And regardless of the level at which these Traits exist in a given person, they need not actually function in only one specific way. While Mixed Traits would certainly relate in various respects to our conscious deliberation about moral issues, they also often function subconsciously without the person entirely knowing what is leading him to act in a morally relevant way.

Finally, it should be no surprise that I claim these Mixed Traits are not virtues, and for the same reasons that a Mixed Helping Trait is not a trait of compassion. Mixed Traits will sometimes not lead to morally appropriate behavior even in obvious and easy cases. Their functioning will be dependent on the presence or absence of certain enhancers and inhibitors in such a way that is incompatible with being virtuous. Such Mixed Traits will often lead to actions which are not performed for morally praiseworthy reasons, and at times for motivating reasons which the person in question would not even endorse if he were aware of them. Finally, they will display failures of practical wisdom. Hence:

> (G6) A Mixed Trait is a moral character trait, but it is neither a moral virtue nor a moral vice.

So it follows from this and (G1) that:

(G7) Most people have a variety of Mixed Traits as part of their character at some level of generality and to some degree, and not a variety of virtues.[17]

But of course this is compatible with it also being the case that:

(G8) A few people have one or more virtues to some degree, rather than the corresponding Mixed Trait(s).

(G9) A few people have one or more vices to some degree, rather than the corresponding Mixed Trait(s).

And it is also compatible with:

(G10) Some people do not have Mixed Traits, virtues, or vices when it comes to what causes their morally relevant behavior.

Again such people might include infants, psychopaths, and those suffering from various severe mental handicaps which do more than just block the activation of these character traits but actually undermine or prevent them from obtaining.[18]

When I began chapter two, I raised a series of questions about character traits. Now I am in a position to answer them, provided that the framework which has been outlined is largely correct:

(i) Do most people actually have character traits which pertain to moral thought and action?

Yes.

(ii) If most people have such traits, what do they consist in and how do they tend to function?

They consist in a number of dispositions to form particular beliefs and desires, and these traits tend to function in a way that can appear to be deeply fragmented and inconsistent.

(iii) If most people have such traits, what tends to enhance and inhibit their operation?

Whatever it is that will trigger one or more of the motivational dispositions which partially make up the trait. For a Mixed Helping Trait, this includes feeling empathy, guilt, embarrassment, anger, positive mood, negative mood, and so forth.

---

[17] Nafsika Athanassoulis wonders whether, "Perhaps people, on the whole, possess less flattering character traits than is usually assumed, few people possess strong and fixed dispositions to behave appropriately in the face of difficulty or temptation, and most people are in a state of moral development where they are likely to succumb to temptations... None of the above conclusions though, threaten the idea that there are such things as character traits." (2000: 220–1). This seems exactly right.

[18] For evidence that Aristotle held a view according to which some people do not possess any firm and stable character traits at all, see Kristjánsson 2008: 70.

(iv) If most people have such traits, how consistent are they in leading to relevant behavior both over time and across situations?

They are highly consistent both over time and across situations, provided different forms of consistency are carefully distinguished.

(v) If most people have such traits, are they moral virtues or are they moral vices?

Neither, in a number of respects.

Let me turn to some recent work in psychology which seems to be consistent with this overall picture of character.

8.3 SOME STUDIES OF NON-MORAL TRAITS

I think it is worth briefly mentioning a few prominent studies in the past thirty years which have generated data relevant to *non-moral* traits. I do this for two main reasons. First, if it is plausible to assume that both moral and non-moral traits are likely to function in similar ways at the psychological level (albeit using different underlying mental state dispositions), then experimental results on non-moral traits could provide useful insights for thinking about the moral ones. In particular, here I will examine a few important studies of non-moral traits which, if they had arrived at similar results for moral traits, could be used to support the framework from section two. Secondly, I can also use this opportunity to highlight some of the different experimental strategies that have been used to study non-moral traits in order to outline, in section five, how I think it would be best to go about empirically studying the specifically moral ones. So not only the results of these studies, but also their specific methodologies, will be worth briefly examining in what follows.[19]

Lord 1982. In "Predicting Behavioral Consistency from an Individual's Perception of Situational Similarities," Charles Lord investigated eight methods for assessing similarity between situations in order to determine how well they would do in predicting cross-situationally consistent behavior relevant to the trait of conscientiousness. Students first filled out various questionnaires, and then those who consented were rated for their conscientious behavior in six

---

[19] Of course there are far too many important studies than can be summarized here. One noticeable omission in particular are the studies by Walter Mischel, Yuichi Shoda, and Jack Wright of children at a summer camp treatment facility. This work is discussed in *Character and Moral Psychology*, chapter five in the context of assessing the CAPS model.

Also relevant to claims made by the Mixed Trait framework is a recent study by Sherman et al. 2010 which found a strong relationship between situation similarity and behavioral consistency across four situations. See also Vansteelandt and Van Mechelen 1998 on if-then predictions about what a person is likely to do in various circumstances.

situations at three undisclosed times during the academic quarter. The behavior in question had to do with the student's dorm closet and desk, personal appearance, pages of course reading done, promptness in returning forms, quality of lecture notes, and schedule of activities during 126 one-hour time periods. All of these appear to be primarily non-moral behaviors.

Four of the methods were nomothetic approaches, that is, they used criteria for what makes two situations similar which were supplied by students other than the participant in question. It turned out that there were no significant behavioral differences between situations that were rated as similar versus those rated as dissimilar using any of these four methods.

The other four approaches were idiographic, and used criteria for similarity which were based on information supplied by the participant in question.[20] Here, three of the four approaches did map on to behavioral differences. For instance, one approach drew on the goals that the participant had, and so assumed that whether a goal would be satisfied can become a criterion for how to act from one situation to the next. But what counts as a goal for a given person is not factored into nomothetic approaches—"only the idiographic version permits one to discern this."[21]

For my purposes, I do not need to get into all the details of Lord's study. I need only note that, for one trait, he found a positive relationship between (i) conscientious behavior that was cross-situationally consistent, and (ii) various measures of what features of a situation are salient to the individual in question. This should be a familiar point from earlier discussions of the importance of paying attention to what are the psychologically salient features of situations for a person when determining whether he is behaving consistently or not.

Funder and Colvin 1991. In their "Explorations in Behavioral Consistency: Properties of Persons, Situations, and Behaviors," David Funder and C. Randall Colvin conducted a longitudinal study in which 140 students were rated by independent observers and by two people who knew the student well. There were three situations involved—(1) an unstructured interaction between the student and a member of the opposite sex, (2) another unstructured interaction a few weeks later with a different member of the opposite sex, and (3) a forced debate on capital punishment for five minutes with the same

---

[20] This is one among many ways of distinguishing "nomothetic" and "idiographic," terms which have become notorious in the psychology literature for their many characterizations. For the above understanding of the terms, see, e.g. Hogan et al. 1977: 258 and Russell 2009: 263. Another slightly different approach, which will not be used here, is to define the nomothetic as universal and the idiographic as individual (see, e.g. Mischel 1968: 188, 190, 2007: 271, Bem and Allen 1974: 509, Bem and Funder 1978: 499, Tellegen 1991: 28, and Johnson 1997: 86). On yet another approach, the idiographic pertains to the unique organization of traits within individuals (Mischel and Peake 1982: 745) or of behaviors within a person (Furr 2009: 203). For a careful discussion of the terms, see Lamiell 1997.

[21] Lord 1982: 1083.

person immediately after the situation 2 interaction. Close acquaintances of the student rated the person (not the specific behaviors) using 100 statements about his or her personality in general, modified from the California Q-sort. For the independent raters, the specific behaviors were coded in such a way that they could be statistically assessed using a 62-item Q-sort deck. So instead of having to rate a student in situation 1 as being cheerful (a general personality rating), for instance, the item was written as "behaves in a cheerful manner."[22]

The results were impressive. For situations 1 and 2, the ratings by the independent raters showed that 45 of 62 correlations between behavioral items were significant at the $p < 0.05$ level, with the highest ("speaks in a loud voice") at 0.70. Similarly, 41 correlations were significant between situations 2 and 3, and 30 were significant between situations 1 and 3. At the same time, the students did seem to change their behavior across the situations in psychologically meaningful ways. For example, the mean level between situations 1 and 2 on "talks at rather than with partner" and "shows physical signs of tension or anxiety" decreased from 3.98 to 3.51 and from 5.19 to 4.66, respectively on a 9-point scale. This is natural to expect from people the second time they participate in an unstructured interaction as part of the same overall study. In the reverse direction, "exhibits social skills" increased from 5.94 to 6.46.[23]

These results, if they also obtained for specifically moral behavior, would be in line with my Mixed Trait framework. Note that the items used to rate behaviors are (intentionally) written so as to get at the psychological meaning that the situation has for the student (i.e. "appears to be relaxed and comfortable," "shows lack of interest in the interaction," etc.), rather than focusing on whether the student performed a specific task. This fits nicely with grounding traits in mental state dispositions, and then understanding cross-situational consistency in terms of whether these dispositions are activated by various situations or not. For instance, it is natural to suppose that dispositions to form anxious thoughts are more likely to be activated in an initial encounter with a stranger, but then less so the second time around in a similar environment. So a decrease in the mean level of observed "signs of tension or anxiety" makes perfect sense when we think about these situations from the student's own point of view. Thus it is no surprise to find that, "These correlations are much greater than the highest consistency correlations reported in some of the most widely cited studies in the personality literature... What people manifest consistently across situations, the present results imply, may not be so much specific behaviors but *underlying psychological dispositions that can be expressed behaviorally in numerous ways.*"[24]

Another interesting similarity can be derived from their correlation findings between the specific laboratory behaviors and the broad personality

---

[22] Funder and Colvin 1991: 776.   [23] Funder and Colvin 1991: 783.
[24] Funder and Colvin 1991: 777, emphasis mine.

judgments that were made about the students. When comparing the ratings of the specific behavior from the three situations with the general judgments about personality supplied by the two people who knew each student well, Funder and Colvin found that many of the correlations were low, with the highest one ("regards self as physically attractive" as the personality item) at 0.41, and only 8 out of 41 above 0.30. Some interesting ones, such as "is calm," "generally fearful," and "basically nervous" were not significantly correlated with behavior at all.[25] Again this should not be surprising on my approach. I have said that moral character traits will lead to behavior which can seem highly fragmented, even to those who know a person well. Such behavior may not be easily categorized using simple labels and concepts. Perhaps the same is true for non-moral traits as well.

Fleeson 2001. In his paper, "Toward a Structure- and Process-Integrated View of Personality: Traits as Density Distributions of States," William Fleeson used the experience-sampling method to generate self-reported longitudinal data on personality traits. More precisely, the first study of three in the paper had participants describe their actions and feelings five times per day for thirteen days at three-hour intervals using a hand-held Palm Pilot device. Of the possible 65 reports per participant, the mean generated was 49.6 (76 percent), and the Palm Pilot secretly recorded the actual date and time of report completion to guard against participants completing a bunch of reports at once.[26] The crucial part of each report for my purposes is that participants had to rate, from 1 to 7, how descriptive a given adjective was of their behavior during the previous hour. So, for instance, at noon they had to rate, "During the previous hour, how well does 'talkative' describe you?" There were four adjectives for each of the Big Five personality traits as follows:[27]

Extraversion	Agreeableness	Conscientiousness
Talkative	Cooperative	Organized
Energetic	Trustful	Undependable
Assertive	Rude	Hardworking
Adventurous	Warm	Responsible

Emotional Stability		Intellect
Perturbable		Intelligent
Insecure		Philosophical
Optimistic		Inquisitive
Vulnerable		Creative

---

[25] Funder and Colvin 1991: 788.
[26] Fleeson 2001: 1014.
[27] Fleeson 2001: 1015. The Big Five traits are discussed at length in *Character and Moral Psychology*, chapter six.

The results Fleeson generated were interesting. On the one hand, people exhibited a great deal of within-person variation for all Big Five traits. In other words, "one individual's behavior varies from hour to hour over a two-week period close to the maximum extreme possible, almost as much as affect varies from hour to hour and at least as much as individuals differ from each other. Such variability is near the high end of expected possibilities."[28] Correlations between two single reports for each individual and each Big Five trait ranged between 0.28 (conscientiousness) and 0.54 (intellect).[29]

On the other hand, when each participant's reports for a given trait were randomly divided in half, means for each half were calculated, and correlations were determined between the means, then the results suggested tremendous within-person consistency. The lowest correlation was 0.87 for conscientiousness, and the highest was 0.94 for agreeableness and intellect.[30] As Fleeson notes, these are among the highest correlations ever recorded in personality psychology.[31] Figure 8.4 provides a helpful visual illustration for both sets of results.[32] Finally, also worth mentioning is that time of day and the number of other people who were reported as being present with the participant were also found to be statistically significant situational cues for the trait of extraversion.[33]

In a recent paper, Fleeson and Patrick Gallagher (2009) summarized fifteen longitudinal studies which employed roughly the same methodology as outlined above, where each used standard personality surveys and experience-sampling devices which recorded self-reports of Big Five states several times a day over multiple days. The results were in line with the above. On the one hand, individuals tended to exhibit a great deal of variability with respect to these traits from one time period to the next, and for the "majority of the time, participants reported acting at a different level than their typical levels."[34] On the other hand, correlations were strong between how participants assessed themselves for a given trait on a personality survey, and the overall average level of their distribution of reported trait behavior during several days of normal living. In their meta-analysis, for instance, correlations of 0.50 for agreeableness and 0.49 for emotional stability were found between how agreeable or stable people reported themselves to be in a survey, and how

---

[28] Fleeson 2001: 1016.   [29] Fleeson 2001: 1017.
[30] Fleeson 2001: 1017.   [31] Fleeson 2004: 86.   [32] Fleeson 2001: 1018.
[33] Fleeson 2001: 1019. In his 2007, Fleeson describes how he used the same experience-sampling approach to record self-report ratings on trait adjectives (pertaining to extraversion, agreeableness, and conscientiousness in Study 1), but he also asked participants to report on eleven situation characteristics. Among the results from Study 1 was that for every one point increase in the friendliness of the people the participant was interacting with, there was a 0.67 of a point increase in average state extraversion (2007: 838–40).
[34] Fleeson and Gallagher 2009: 1105.

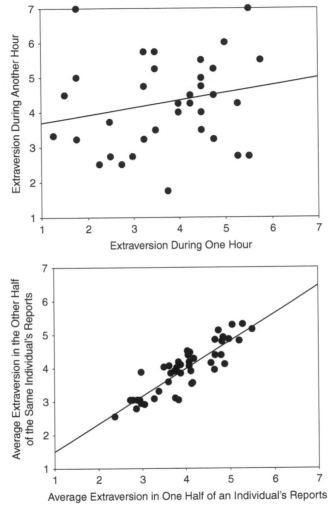

Fig. 8.4. Fleeson 2001. Reprinted with permission.

their behavior on average tended to actually be (or at least, as they reported it to be using the experience-sampling devices).[35]

These results with respect to non-moral traits show a number of similarities to my framework for understanding our moral character. For one thing, they support the thought that there is high within-person variability from one moment to the next in the extent to which a given person acts in a trait appropriate way. Hence the person's trait-relevant behavior can appear

---

[35] Fleeson and Gallagher 2009: 1108.

fragmented to observers, and can be hard to predict in specific instances. Yet at the same time, there is a striking level of stability as well, once we aggregate the reports and look at the mean level of trait behavior over time.[36] This suggests a psychological structure underlying the single trait-relevant behaviors which, if understood better, could help make sense of the patterns of behavior which are exhibited. This structure is not fixed for each individual, but appears to come in degrees which lead to individual differences in mean levels. Finally, this psychological structure appears to be remarkably sensitive to situational variables—in the original Fleeson study, the time of day and the number of people present were both shown to be tied to self-reported extraversion states. All of these results mirror claims I have made about Mixed Traits.

Most of the trait adjectives that Fleeson studied do not have any obvious connection to moral character. But it is worth thinking about what his method might and also might not be able to tell us about the possession of specifically moral traits. Before proceeding, though, I want to be clear that my concern is only with the *application* of his method to the moral domain— which has not yet been done extensively—rather than with the actual studies he in fact carried out.[37]

In Fleeson's 2001 study, recall that participants rated their behavior in the previous hour. Suppose that a question they were given had instead been, "During the previous hour, how well does 'helpful' describe you?" Now consider the following complications:

---

[36] These results bear important similarities to Seymour Epstein's well-known 1979 studies. Study 1 used self-report data of pleasant and unpleasant experiences from twenty-eight students as recorded daily for one month on special forms. A 90-item adjective checklist for emotions and a 66-item one for response and action tendencies were used. Some of the broad pleasant emotion scales that were determined by factor analysis included happy, kindly, calm, adequate, unified, and energetic, while the pleasant response scales included pleasure seeking, nurturance, exuberance, stimulus seeking, problem-solving, affiliation, and achievement. Between-subject reliability coefficients were low when one day was correlated with the next. But when the mean of all odd days was correlated with the mean of all even days, the numbers went way up. For instance, with pleasant emotions, they had a coefficient of roughly 0.36 from day 1 to day 2 averaged over all the scales, but 0.88 for all odd versus even days. When they switched to within-subject reliability, the mean for all participants ranged from 0.60 for unpleasant behavior to 0.90 for pleasant impulses and also for pleasant behavior. Hence, "It may be concluded that within-subject reliability coefficients provide evidence for a relatively high degree of stability of the organization of variables within most individuals when the data are derived from sufficient observations but provide no such evidence when the data are derived from single observations" (Epstein 1979: 1110). Interestingly, and again in line with chapter seven, there was significant variability in individual differences, with some participants showing a great deal of stability, and a few showing almost none (Epstein 1979: 1110).

Epstein did not just stop with self-report data. Study 2 used reports by others, Study 3 used direct measures of objective behavior, and Study 4 examined the relationship between personality inventories and objective behavior. All found dramatic increases in reliability as data from additional days was incorporated.

[37] The concerns raised below might turn out to also raise problems for the study of non-moral traits using Fleeson's approach, but again that is not my concern in this chapter.

   (i) We do not know how many helping-relevant situations the person encountered during the previous hour.

  (ii) We do not know how many of these situations he *accurately* recognized as being helping-relevant versus how many he failed to recognize as helping-relevant.

 (iii) We do not know how many of these situations he thought (whether accurately or not) were helping-relevant.

 (iv) We do not know which of those situations he helped in and which he did not.[38]

  (v) We do not know, of the situations in which he helped, the degree to which he was helpful in those particular situations.

 (vi) We do not know his motivation for helping or not helping in any of those situations.

 (vii) We do not know whether he in fact was helpful in general during the past hour, as opposed to only *thinking* that he was helpful.

(viii) We do not know to what extent, if any, he is either consciously or subconsciously misreporting or even distorting his helpfulness.[39]

So it appears true that in the case of a moral trait like helpfulness, this method could tell us interesting and important information, but I think it would mainly be about the following—the degree to which a person, if he is telling the truth as he sees it, *thinks* of his general behavior during a given period as being helpful. That is a different matter from the degree to which his behavior in the various situations during that given period of time was *in fact* helpful, and if it was, for what reasons.[40]

Wu and Clark 2003. In "Relations between Personality Traits and Self-Reports of Daily Behavior," Kevin Wu and Lee Clark followed much the same general methodology as Fleeson did. They first administered a questionnaire to 197 undergraduates with eighteen items assessing aggression, seventeen items for exhibitionism, and twenty for impulsivity. This was followed by a behavior record containing fifty-five items about what happened during that day.

---

[38] As Fleeson himself notes, "Adjective ratings sacrifice specificity in that a given rating on an adjective—for instance, a 5 on assertiveness—could correspond to any number of actions" (2001: 1025). See also Fleeson 2007: 826 and Fleeson and Gallagher 2009: 1110–11.

[39] As Kupperman writes about self-report data in general on character, "the questionnaire method cannot distinguish among (1) what someone's character genuinely is, (2) what someone is pretending his or her character is, and the intermediate case of (3) what someone thinks incorrectly his or her character is. The only way of distinguishing among these is . . . to put subjects under pressure or to present temptations, and then surreptitiously to observe how they actually behave" (1991: 161). See also Winter et al. 1998: 235.

[40] For one assessment of the strengths and weaknesses of using trait adjective self-report data, see Fleeson and Gallagher 2009: 1110–11.

Participants then had to fill out the same record once again each evening for the next fourteen days.[41]

Focusing just on the first two traits (there were complications which arose with impulsivity that can be ignored here), Wu and Clark found that on the one hand behavioral scores showed a great deal of variation from person to person, with aggregated scores for aggression ranging from 0 to 8.77 (out of 18) with a mean of 2.08, and for exhibitionism ranging from 0.93 to 15.69 (out of 17) with a mean of 4.87.[42]

On the other hand, there were remarkable correlations between the results of the general personality measures and the behavioral measures. The total score on one personality measure of aggression, for instance, correlated at 0.48 with the behavioral measures of aggression, but only 0.12 with exhibitionism, thereby illustrating some discrimination ability. Similarly, one of the personality measures for exhibitionism correlated 0.55 with self-reported behavioral exhibitionism, but only 0.32 with behavioral aggression.[43] And when it came to specific behaviors, the correlations were just as robust—0.47 for trait aggression and "hitting someone in anger," 0.44 for "got into an argument," and 0.42 for "lost my temper," while the correlation was 0.46 for trait exhibitionism and "drew attention to myself," 0.50 for "enjoyed being the topic of conversation," and 0.44 for "showed off in the company of others."[44]

Wu and Clark claimed that, "these findings demonstrate that psychometrically robust personality traits have identifiable behavioral correlates at the level of daily behaviors."[45] This is broadly in line with what I think we should expect in the moral case. If we have a good measure of a moral character trait, then if that trait is found to be possessed by a person to a high degree, it should show robust correlations with certain trait-relevant behaviors throughout the day when the person is in the appropriate situations.

One important difference from the Fleeson approach is that Wu and Clark had participants rate their behavior, not using trait adjectives such as "talkative" or "rude," but rather using simple yes/no questions concerning whether they had performed a given behavior during that day—hit someone in anger, got into an argument, lost their temper, and so forth. Thus this approach does attempt to distinguish between various specific behaviors that the person exhibited during that time period, rather than just asking in a broad way how "rude" he thinks he was. So it would not fall prey to some of the worries raised above if it were instead used to assess moral character traits.

Nevertheless, there are important limitations with how much could be learned about someone's moral character if this approach were to be adopted.

---

[41] Wu and Clark 2003: 237.
[42] Wu and Clark 2003: 241.   [43] Wu and Clark 2003: 243.
[44] Wu and Clark 2003: 245.   [45] Wu and Clark 2003: 247.

Using the familiar example of helping, it would still be true that given these kinds of daily behavior reports:

(i) We do not know how many helping-relevant situations the person in fact encountered during the day (some of which he may not have recognized).

(ii) We do not know how many of these situations he *thought* were helping-relevant (given the practical limitations of how many questions about different situations one can ask participants to answer on a daily basis).

(iii) We do not know, of the situations in which he helped, the degree to which he was helpful in those particular situations.

(iv) We do not know his motivation for helping or not helping in any of those situations.

(v) We do not know to what extent, if any, he is either consciously or subconsciously misreporting his helpfulness.

Again, this is not meant to be a criticism of Wu and Clark's research. Their concern was not with moral character traits.

Fournier, Moskowitz, and Zuroff 2008. In their "Integrating Dispositions, Signatures, and the Interpersonal Domain," Marc Fournier and his colleagues provided support for a picture of non-moral traits and behavior that bears some striking similarities to my claims about the moral ones.[46] They were interested in studying both participants' dispositions, which they defined as the "mean level of behavior," and participants' signatures, which are "the patterning of behavior around that mean level."[47] In order to do so, they employed profiles of the kind used in chapter seven, and took the shape of those profiles to correspond to the person's distinctive signature.

One hundred and twenty-one individuals from the community provided usable data in the form of an initial questionnaire and then were supposed to complete a form over the next twenty days after each social interaction with another person that lasted for at least five minutes.[48] The forms measured *behavior* relevant to four traits using twelve items per traits—dominance included items like, "I expressed an opinion," submissiveness included, "I did not state my own views," agreeableness included, "I expressed reassurance," and quarrelsomeness included, "I made a sarcastic comment."[49] *Situations*, on the other hand, were assessed using the "interpersonal grid," where participants placed an "x" on a grid with "dominant" on the top, "submissive" on the bottom, "quarrelsome" on the left, and "agreeable" on the right.[50] The idea is to rate the other person that the participant was interacting with using these measures.

---

[46] Fournier et al. 2008. See also their 2009 for additional discussion.
[47] Fournier et al. 2008: 532.   [48] Fournier et al. 2008: 534–5.
[49] Fournier et al. 2008: 535.   [50] Fournier et al. 2008: 535.

Note that *the other person as perceived by the participant*, becomes the situation, and so the point is *not* to assess how dominant, submissive, quarrelsome, and agreeable the participant sees himself to have been in this situation.

A number of interesting findings emerged. One is that participants' self-reported behavior varied based upon the situation, that is, the perceived characteristics of the interaction partner. Here is a helpful figure (Figure 8.5) illustrating this (AD = agreeable-dominant, AS = agreeable-submissive, QS = quarrelsome-submissive, and QD = quarrelsome-dominant).[51]

As they remark, "individuals reported higher levels of submissiveness when they saw the other as dominant and higher levels of dominance when they saw the other as submissive . . . individuals reported higher levels of quarrelsomeness when they saw the other as cold and quarrelsome and higher levels of agreeableness when they saw the other as warm and agreeable."[52] In other words, participants naturally adjusted their behavior depending on what they considered to be the salient characteristics of their interaction partner.[53]

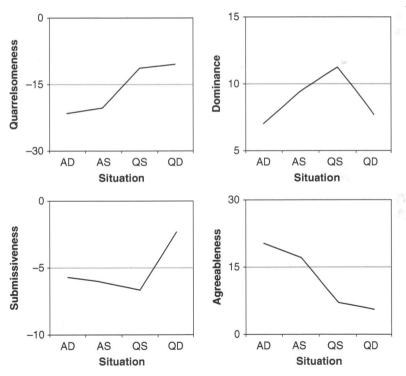

Fig. 8.5. Fournier, Moskowitz, and Zuroff 2008. Reprinted with permission.

---

[51] Fournier et al. 2008: 537.   [52] Fournier et al. 2008: 536.
[53] A more technical set of findings had to do with calculating data for each participant's own idiographic patterns of behavior by removing nomothetic influences. Fournier and his colleagues

Perhaps most interesting of all were the stability results. A participant's submissiveness ratings for all his interactions with another person, for instance, were separated into the four types of situations (AD, AS, QS, QD). These rating scores were them randomly divided in half for that individual, so that one profile is created using one half of the data, and another profile is created using the remaining half. Figure 8.6 provides a helpful visual illustration of this idea.

How similar were the *average* ratings of dominant, agreeable, submissive, and quarrelsome behavior between the two profiles for each of the participants in the study? As with Fleeson 2001, these correlations were strikingly high, ranging from 0.76 for dominance to 0.83 for quarrelsomeness.[54] So these four behavioral dispositions were remarkably stable in their mean levels.

Fournier and his colleagues also assessed the stability of the behavioral *signatures*, or the patterns around the mean level. In other words, how similar were the *shapes* of the two profiles in the same randomly divided data? A highly stable profile in this sense would look like Figure 8.6, where positive numbers reflect a level of submissiveness that is above the mean for all the participants, and negative scores reflect a level of submissiveness that is below the mean.[55]

It turned out that overall stability in profile shape was not as high as this figure would suggest, but correlations did range from 0.24 for dominance to 0.52 for quarrelsomeness.[56] So in a seemingly paradoxical way, but also a way that is not surprising from chapter seven, it turned out that an individual's own variability from situation to situation is itself something that is often a stable part of his personality, at least in these areas.[57]

So people responded in a highly variable manner to their interaction partner in different situations. But this variability makes sense given how they viewed the situation. And furthermore, this variability itself is relatively stable over time. This leads to what I think is the most important conclusion

---

wanted to determine what better explains why individuals act differently from each other with respect to these kinds of behavior—is it that they are in different situations (within-person variability), or is it that there are individual differences from one person to the next in their trait levels (between-person variability)? Using the language of profiles, if there is little within-subject variation, then all variance between profiles is a function of individual differences in mean levels, i.e. differences in the degrees the traits are held between participants. If, on the other hand, there is little between-subject variation (and so little difference in mean levels), then the variance can be attributed to difference in the patterns of within-person behavior, i.e. to the individuals' own unique behavioral signatures. The results were in the middle—there was as much within-person variation in behavior as there was between-person variation (538). A person's profile mean and profile signature are *both* important and distinctive features of that individual.

[54] Fournier et al. 2008: 539. Here and throughout the review of this study, I have omitted details about how the results were calculated in order to simplify the presentation.

[55] Fournier et al. 2008: 540.

[56] Fournier et al. 2008: 540.

[57] See also Fournier et al. 2009 for additional discussion.

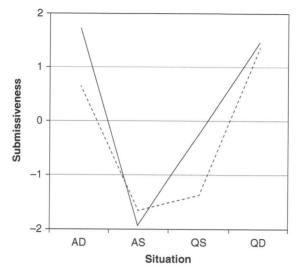

Fig. 8.6. Fournier, Moskowitz, and Zuroff 2008. Reprinted with Permission.

of their paper that "one underlying system of interrelated structures and processes is capable of producing both trait-like consistencies *and* signature patterns of variability."[58] In the moral case, this is exactly how I have understood a Mixed Helping Trait, and indeed all the Mixed Traits more generally.

Despite these promising results, it should be noted that if this approach were to be extended to the study of moral character traits, many of the same concerns that were raised above would apply. For instance, their measure of behavior relied on simple self-report questionnaires, thereby potentially omitting much morally relevant information. But as I have stressed throughout, in none of these studies is this intended as a criticism of the researchers' original work.

The upshot of this section is that these studies, and many others beside them, support a variety of important claims about non-moral traits which are similar to the claims I have made about moral traits earlier in this book, including the importance of the individual's perspective when understanding behavior, the high within-person variability in trait-relevant behavior across situations, the unreliability of predicting how someone will behave from one specific situation to another without insight into that individual's perspective, and the stability (in more than one way) of trait-relevant behavior over time. Yet since they only focus on non-moral traits, these studies do not *directly* support my view about moral character. Furthermore, I have tried to highlight various concerns with trying to adapt some of their techniques

---

[58] Fournier et al. 2008: 542, emphasis theirs.

to the study of moral character. So at this point, I need to say more about how moral character should in fact be studied experimentally, and I will do just that in section five. But before I do, let me briefly summarize one set of studies which *does* bear on my claims about moral character in important ways.

8.4 A STRIKING SET OF STUDIES RELATED TO HELPING

In what I take to be a highly important paper, "What Remains Invariant? Finding Order within a Person's Thoughts, Feelings, and Behaviors across Situations," Yuichi Shoda and Scott LeeTiernan focused on the distinction between nominal and psychologically relevant features of situations, and attempted to test the claim that there is significant stability over time and consistency across situations in the variability of behavior that each person exhibits.

Their procedure involved participants spending an hour listening to audio clips involving sixty different versions of the same general scenario, each version being a discrete "situation." One commonly used scenario, for instance, featured a person who forgot his or her wallet and asked to borrow a dollar to make photocopies.[59] The variations had to do with such features as tone of voice, facial expression, level of confidence, attractiveness, sincerity, quality of clothes, and so forth. The idea was that, "By holding the scenario constant but varying the stimulus . . . this study seeks to find those psychological features of situations that make up important ways in which social situations differ as a function of the individuals who are in them."[60]

In their first study, Shoda and LeeTiernan wanted to test for stability over time, so they had participants respond to the same sixty situations in different sequences on two occasions separated by one–two weeks. They were told to imagine that they were approached in the library copy center by another student whom they had seen around in one of their classes. Participants reported their likelihood of loaning the dollar on a 9-point Likert scale. Note that this is a morally evaluable action, and one that pertains to helping.

For the seven participants, each of their behavioral signatures was highly varied, using almost the entire range of the scale.[61] This is exactly what my view would expect. At the same time, it would also expect their signatures to be stable over the time interval. And indeed, the mean correlation for the seven

[59] Shoda and LeeTiernan 2002: 248.
[60] Shoda and LeeTiernan 2002: 249.
[61] Shoda and LeeTiernan 2002: 250.

participants was 0.62. Furthermore, noting that this stability could be due just to all of the seven participants behaving very similarly to each other in the same situations, Shoda and LeeTiernan also calculated the stability in the *unique* way that each participant responded.[62] It turned out that there were significant individual differences in behavioral signatures from one person to the next, as my view would predict, and also that even the unique response signatures were correlated at 0.55.[63]

These findings were not just limited to the one task of loaning a dollar. Other actions included borrowing class notes, picking up a book from the bookstore, and saving a seat in a movie theater. Similarly high stability correlations were found.

From there, Shoda and LeeTiernan turned to cross-situational consistency and attempted to identify psychological features of situations which could explain the patterns of variability across the sixty situations. If they are able to do so, then they could not only (at least partially) explain those patterns, but also be able to point to features which could predict the likelihood of future helping in such a scenario. If, on the other hand, they just stuck with the nominal features of situations then such predictions might be highly inaccurate. As they note, "if we observe that a given participant was reliably reluctant to loan a dollar to John but reliably more willing to do so to David, would we expect the same participant to be more willing to agree to the same request from a third person, Michael, than to a request from Paul? Because David and John are nominal situations, we are unable to generalize to the situations with Michael or Paul."[64]

In order to get at these psychologically relevant features, the participants, after completing the procedure the second time around, also were asked to list as many of the sixty situations which they thought had some influence on their responses. Shoda and LeeTiernan identified seventeen such features in the dollar scenario, including the sincerity, attractiveness, and eloquence of the other person.

My view would predict that, for a given person who is disposed to care about another's sincerity, for instance, his likelihood of helping in the sixty situations would fluctuate directly with his perception of the sincerity of each of these people (other things being equal). And this is exactly what Shoda and LeeTiernan found. For instance, Figure 8.7 is the profile of participant 33 in an additional study involving the dollar scenario.[65]

---

[62] They did this by subtracting the group's average response in a particular situation from that particular individual's response (Shoda and LeeTiernan 2002: 250).

[63] Shoda and LeeTiernan 2002: 252.

[64] Shoda and LeeTiernan 2002: 257.

[65] Shoda and LeeTiernan 2002: 259.

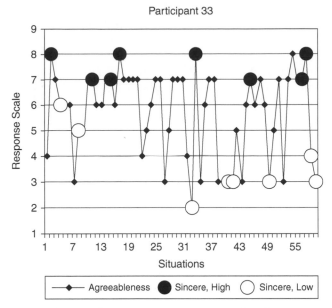

Fig. 8.7. Shoda and LeeTiernan 2002. Reprinted with Permission.

The black circles are situations where the other person was independently rated as highly sincere, whereas the white circles are for situations where the other person was independently rated as low in sincerity.[66] So for participant 33, the sincerity of the other person seemed to be a very psychologically relevant feature.

But the same was not true of all the participants. For instance, participant 38's profile did not seem to correspond at all to perceived sincerity, and so that particular feature did not seem to be psychologically relevant for this individual whereas it was for participant 33. Instead, as Figure 8.8 shows, another feature played a much more salient role for participant 38, namely how well dressed the other person was.[67]

So as I have suggested previously, individuals seem to vary in what features of their situations they take to be psychologically relevant. At the same time, within a given individual there is a great deal of consistency to their variability in behavior, something that can be recognized once it is learned what that particular person cares about.

[66] Unfortunately these are independent rating of these situational features, not the participant's own rating of the sincerity of each of the sixty people. Shoda and LeeTiernan are assuming that there will be reasonable overlap in these assessments, but it would have been nice to test this more directly.

[67] Shoda and LeeTiernan 2002: 261.

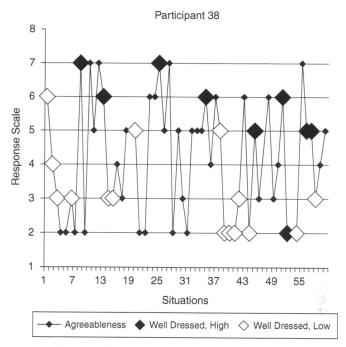

Fig. 8.8. Shoda and LeeTiernan 2002. Reprinted with Permission.

This consistency can also lead to predictability. Shoda and LeeTiernan could easily test predictability by simply taking the sixty situations, and using the first thirty to predict responses in the second thirty given what weights each individual was assigning to the seventeen different psychological features in the dollar scenario. For the seven participants in the original study, the median correlation across them was 0.53.[68]

Stepping back, the results that Shoda and LeeTiernan report both concern a morally relevant task (loaning a dollar), and are in line with what would be expected by my approach to moral character traits. They found a high degree of within-person variability in behavior, stability over time in patterns of behavior, consistency across situations relative to psychologically salient features, and diversity from one person to another in what is psychologically relevant.

At the same time, there are some clear limitations to their results. The first and most obvious one is that they did not study actual moral behavior, but rather the self-reported likelihood of performing this task. There could be a large divergence between the two. Secondly, the features of situations which were said to be of importance to participants, were also culled from self-report

[68] Shoda and LeeTiernan 2002: 262.

data. But this omits the ways in which features of situations could be having their effects at the subconscious level. Finally, one might wonder whether their results would generalize if a given participant were presented, not just with one scenario, but rather with multiple significantly different scenarios over a longer period of time.

Nevertheless, despite these concerns, this work by Shoda and Lee Tiernan comes the closest of all the experimental research that I am familiar with in supporting the various aspects of my approach to moral character traits.

8.5 THE STUDY OF MORAL CHARACTER TRAITS

Given the methodological points that have been made in this chapter, I think we are in a good position to arrive at some basic principles for how to go about studying the existence and nature of moral traits. These principles are important because they suggest the kind of research that I think we really need going forward in the future in order to advance the empirical study of character traits. They are also important because they serve to constrain my level of optimism about the evidence there is for my view at the present time.

Here is one such principle:

> (P1) It is better to study each individual's trait-relevant behavior rather than aggregating or averaging behavioral data from *multiple* individuals.[69]

The reason for this is simple—since two people can fail to have the same moral trait, or even if they do have it, can fail to have it to the same degree, then by drawing conclusions about the traits of the group, this can wash out important individual differences. For example, when studies of personality traits in the 1960s and 1970s found correlations between personality measures and relevant behaviors which rarely crossed Walter Mischel's famous "predictability ceiling" of 0.30, those correlations were usually for the *population* of participants as a whole, not for individual participants and their own behaviors over time. Similarly, in Hartshorne and May's famous 1928 study of honesty in school children, the average correlation between any pair of measures of honesty was 0.23, but this was for all the children studied as a whole, rather than any given individual. Hence some of these individuals might have been highly consistent in their trait-relevant behavior.[70]

---

[69] Here and with the other principles in this section, it is assumed that other things are held equal. I have omitted this qualification from the above to make the principles less cumbersome.

[70] I return to these issues at greater length in *Character and Moral Psychology*, chapter four when evaluating the situationist position in psychology.

Given (P1) and the focus on each individual's behavior, another important principle is that:

(P2) It is better to conduct longitudinal studies of an individual's trait-relevant behavior rather than "single-shot" experiments testing one behavior in one situation.

When someone helps in a study, for instance, the experimenters will not be able to know from that one instance whether this behavior was an aberration for that person, or instead sometime arising from a stable and predictable character trait.[71] Similarly, when someone does not help, that failure could still be consistent with the possession of a moral trait such as compassion (if the person had the trait to a weak degree, say, or if it were a demanding helping task), or with the possession of a Mixed Helping Trait. What we need, I want to suggest, is to examine *patterns* of behavior, not isolated behaviors.[72]

The next principle makes a claim about the best way to examine such patterns:

(P3) Morally relevant behavior should be observed in natural environments rather than lab environments, and both should be preferred to self-report studies.

Such a principle is an instance of an obvious platitude about behavioral studies in psychology in general, but it is worth emphasizing its specific importance when it comes to moral character. As noted in section three, there is a great deal of important moral information that self-report data can omit, not to mention the dangers of conscious or subconscious distortion.[73]

Furthermore, when it comes to conducting natural and lab environment studies:

---

[71] For rare exceptions, see Brandt 1970: 26, 34. As Brandt writes, "we also infer traits on the basis of behavior in a single situation, when this can be explained only by the presence of a strong motive presumably of a relatively permanent kind" (34). See also Sabini and Silver 2005: 544 and Badhwar 2009: 263 for related discussion.

[72] Compare Hampshire 1953: 6, Epstein 1979: 1102, Small et al. 1983: 2–3, Kenrick and Funder 1988: 31, Buss 1989: 1380, Kupperman 1991: 162–3, Winter et al. 1998: 239, Athanassoulis 2000: 219, Sreenivasan 2002: 52–3, 2008: 605–6, 609–11, Webber 2006b: 209, Kristjánsson 2008: 76, Krueger 2009: 134–5, Upton 2009a: 18, Fleeson and Gallagher 2009: 1099, and Funder 2009: 125.

[73] As Epstein remarks, "we will not consider investigations relying on self-report inventories, as such studies can simply demonstrate that people's beliefs about their behavior are consistent, which is a far cry from demonstrating that the behavior itself is consistent" (1979: 1100). For additional reasons to avoid self-report and favor natural environment studies, see Allport 1937: 313, Mischel 1973: 261, 278, 2009: 284–5, Small et al. 1983: 2–3, Funder 1995: 662, Batson et al. 1997a: 1337, Winter et al. 1998: 235, Doris 2002: 26–7, Batson 2008: 54, 2011: 22–3, 55–6, 108, and Vazire and Doris 2009: 274. For the merits of lab environments, see Buss 1989: 1380–1.

(P4) Attempt to observe how multiple participants behave when in many of the *same* types of nominal situations over time, and not just how they each behave in various different types of nominal situations over time.

That way studies can explore individual trait differences that become manifest when some participants act differently than others while the situations are held fixed. For instance, if a group of participants all have the trait of honesty, the extent to which each of them possesses the trait can be explored by studying how they behave in the same nominal situation involving, say, a particular temptation to tell an unjustified lie. Although it is possible that all the participants in question will have the same character trait to the exact same degree, this is highly unlikely to turn out to be the case, and so such differences can emerge in different behaviors and thereby provide useful insights into how people differ in their characters.[74]

In addition, studies should focus on those situations which meet the following requirement:

(P5) The situations used to study moral character traits should be clearly relevant to the trait in question, and, as far as possible, should not involve any considerations which could prevent the operation of that trait or activate other traits which would be more relevant in the circumstances.

So for the trait of compassion, for instance, a clearly relevant situation might be helping a person who seems to be in a moderate degree of distress when there is no one else around to help. But if the participants might have some reason for thinking that by doing so they would miss an appointment that, reasonably, could be construed as more important, then their lack of helping does not provide any clear evidence that they are not compassionate.[75]

Longitudinal studies of the moral behavior of participants in natural environments—while the most promising studies in my opinion—might not in fact be feasible or even ethical to conduct in certain circumstances. So if instead self-report data is the only kind that can be acquired, then based on (P2) it should be longitudinal self-report data, recorded perhaps with the assistance of report sheets[76] or electronic devices.[77] In addition:

(P6) If gathering longitudinal self-report data, then have the items concern behavioral questions that do not involve ordinary trait-terms.

---

[74] See also Ross and Nisbett 1991: 149, Harman 1999: 317, and Doris 2002: 19.
[75] For helpful discussion, see Sreenivasan 2002: 58–62 and Russell 2009: 270. See also Kenrick and Funder 1988: 31 and Funder 1995: 658.
[76] See Wu and Clark 2003 and Fournier et al. 2008.
[77] See Fleeson 2001 and Fleeson and Gallagher 2009.

As discussed in section three, questions about how "honest," "compassionate," or "greedy" a person was in the last hour, for instance, might tell us something about the degree to which the person, if he is telling the truth, *thinks* of his general behavior this way. But it tells us less about whether he actually behaved in those ways, and even less about whether he was that kind of person. Furthermore, the additional complication of moral character traits which do not have any conceptual representation in our ordinary thinking, such as Mixed Traits, also calls into question the wisdom of gathering self-report data involving ordinary words for moral traits.[78]

Regardless of what kind they are, longitudinal studies should not only just examine participant's behavior. Moral character traits also involve patterns of motivation as well as (at least attempted) behavior. Hence:

(P7) Studies should attempt to assess the motivation behind an individual's behavior as well as the behavior itself.

A person might, for instance, exhibit a pattern of being helpful in a variety of different situations, but be motivated to do so for social rewards or negative emotion relief.[79]

How could psychologists implement a principle like (P7)? Daniel Batson's work on the empathy-altruism hypothesis, which was reviewed in chapter five, provides an important illustration. Two motivational hypotheses could be formulated which generate conflicting predictions about how people would likely behave in certain morally relevant situations if those were their primary motives. Then studies can be run which actually put subjects in those situations, so that psychologists can see which prediction ends up being supported based on the resulting behavior. For instance, if one hypothesis appeals to a certain kind of egoistic motive and the other to an altruistic motive, then the experimental situation could be one in which participants are told that the particular egoistic benefit will not be available, and then are observed to see if they still do the morally appropriate action to the same extent as controls or not.[80]

Once we turn to examining the psychological processes behind behavior, it seems that longitudinal studies should not be limited just to motivating states of mind, but should also examine other relevant beliefs and desires. In other words:

---

[78] On the other hand, the recommended method in (P6) faces the challenge of having to identify which specific behaviors do and do not count as expressions of a given moral trait. Providing an exhaustive list of such behaviors can seem to be an overwhelming task, although paradigm instances can be readily arrived at, as I have done with compassion. Similar paradigm actions naturally come to mind with most if not all of the moral trait concepts which are familiar from ordinary thought, and I will mention examples with respect to honesty and non-malevolence in Part Four. For relevant discussion, see Fleeson and Gallagher 2009: 1099, 1112.

[79] For a similar claim to (P7), see Webber 2006b: 212.

[80] For helpful discussion of how to study motivation, see Batson 2011: 74, 90.

(P8) Studies of moral character should attempt to discern, not just how an
     individual does or would behave in various ways, but also what stable
     clusters of interrelated psychological states she has which give rise to her
     moral behavior.

Such an idiographic approach is committed to the important idea that behavior (over time and across situations) is a function of what matters or is salient
to the individual in question, and what matters to an individual is itself
determined by her dispositions to form beliefs and desires whose contents
function as goals, policies, norms, commitments, values, plans, and the like.
As Lee Ross and Richard Nisbett put the point, "the key to a more powerful
conception of individual differences is to be found in the enduring motivational concerns and cognitive schemes that guide attention, interpretation,
and the formulation of goals and plans."[81]

Do we actually have studies of *moral* (as opposed to non-moral) character
traits that follow these eight principles? Very few exist to my knowledge.
Indeed, there are almost no longitudinal studies in the first place of moral
character, regardless of whether they involve self-report data, laboratory
environments, or natural environments.[82]

This absence is not surprising. Longitudinal studies naturally take time
to conduct and are often expensive. This does not sit well with professional
pressures to generate publications rapidly so as to further career advancement
and to secure and renew grant funding. Not to mention that it can be complicated to track adults and their behavior over extended periods of time.
Furthermore, since most people tend to act in superficially moral ways
when in public, in order to really probe a participant's motives or behavior
in important moral situations, deception, social pressure, and manipulation
may be needed, which raise a host of ethical concerns. And while it is true that
the best data would be from natural environments where the participants do

---

[81] Ross and Nisbett 1991: 20. For similar remarks, see Bem and Allen 1974: 508–12, Mischel
1973: 259–61, 263, 2004: 15, 2009: 284, Tellegen 1991: 19, Shoda et al. 1993: 1024–5, 1029, 1994:
685, Mischel and Shoda 1995: 248, 1998: 247–8, Shoda and Mischel 1996: 421–2, Shoda 1999a:
163, Mischel et al. 2002: 51, Sreenivasan 2002: 58, 63, 65, Kamtekar 2004: 476–7, 485, and
especially Shoda et al. 1994: 675–6.
[82] Similar claims are made by Carlson 1971: 206, Epstein 1979: 1102, Kupperman 1991:
162–3, Doris 2002: 38, Kamtekar 2004: 466 n. 30, Sabini and Silver 2005: 541 n. 21, and Funder
2009: 125. Two notable exceptions are studies by Walter Mischel and colleagues using students at
Carleton College (Mischel and Peake 1982) and children at a summer camp (Shoda et al. 1993,
1994). This work is discussed in the context of evaluating Mischel's CAPS model in *Character
and Moral Psychology*, chapter five. Another exception on a much smaller scale can be found in
Small et al. 1983. They observed dominance and prosocial behavior during a camping trip on
three separate occasions, and found extremely high temporal stability coefficients and cross-
situational consistency correlations. Unfortunately, as they note about their approach, "the data
tell us little about the instability or stability of behavior within any one given individual" (13,
emphasis removed).

not even know that they are part of an experiment, secretly observing people without their consent can also be highly problematic.[83]

What then is there to work with instead? As we have seen in Part II, the majority of studies on moral behavior in the past fifty years have been studies of one, or at best, two to three single behaviors. The Regan et al. study from the preface is a nice illustration. In the experimental group, an individual attempted to take a picture, was told that she had broken the camera, and then had an opportunity to notify a shopper about a tear in her bag. Recall that these participants who were presumably experiencing guilt helped at a much higher rate as a group than did the control participants (55 percent versus 15 percent).[84]

By itself, this study gives us almost no positive information about character. We do not know how stable a control participant's failure to help would have been over time, nor how stable a guilty participant's helping would have been when she experienced guilt again. We do not know anything about how the people involved would act in other situations besides these very specific ones. Nor do we know anything about why, in the control case, three people still did help, and why, in the *guilt* case, nine people still did not help.[85]

As far as much of the existing psychology literature is concerned, if this kind of study is representative of what has been done in examining moral character traits, then it is tempting to just give up on trying to advance different models of moral character at the present time.[86] For while I may have outlined an interesting theory about what our character *might* be like, there would be nothing approaching adequate experimental evidence from which to draw in determining what it is reasonable to think our character *is* indeed like.

However, I think this pessimism is unwarranted. For I think that studies like Regan's, while they are a far cry from the kind of studies we really need in this area, can still serve at least two important functions. First, *negatively* they can give us some reason to think that certain people do *not* possess a given character trait.[87] For instance, in the previous chapter I said that:

---

[83] For some of these same claims, see Carlson 1971: 214, Kupperman 1991: 160–1, Doris 2002: 38, Webber 2006b: 209, and Funder 2008: 570, 2009: 125.

[84] Regan et al. 1972.

[85] Regan et al. 1972: 44.

[86] As Funder notes, "Studies that test hypotheses about how one individual difference variable interacts with experimental manipulation of one situational variable to affect one behavioral outcome can be interesting, valuable, and for the most part represent the current state of the art. But we need a map of the broader terrain" (2009: 125). See also Athanassoulis 2000: 219–20.

[87] As John Doris writes, "The burden of proof lies with someone attributing friendliness in the face of repeated failures to act friendly, while someone asserting the opposite view occupies an enviable rhetorical position" (2002: 16). Similarly Robert Adams claims that, "straightforwardly behavioral tests can in principle give strong evidence of the absence of some virtues" (2006: 121). See also Badhwar 2009: 263, 265 and Doris 2010: 141.

(1) A person who is compassionate, when acting in character, will typically attempt to help when, at the very least, the need for help is obvious and the effort involved in helping is very minimal.

The Regan study involves an opportunity to help which falls under this description, thereby providing some evidence about the moral character of the control participants who did not help.[88] A similar principle could be formulated for the vice of cruelty as well, as we will see in the next chapter:

(2) A cruel person, when acting in character, will reliably attempt to harm others when in situations where opportunities to harm present themselves, at least when those opportunities are not thought to involve significant inconvenience to him and he believes he will not get punished or otherwise negatively affected by others for doing so.

Thus the fact that a person enjoys playing with his cat in the privacy of his home, counts as a bit of (defeasible) evidence that he does not have the vice pertaining to harming others.

Clearly criteria like (1) and (2) could be formulated for other virtues and vices as well, and many such criteria are developed in this book and summarized in the Appendix. So by providing data which is relevant to these various criteria, experiments in the psychology literature can be used to help draw conclusions with some degree of evidential support about whether certain people do or do not have these character traits.

But second and more positively, while *any one* of these studies of moral behavior might have limited usefulness when it comes to developing an account of our actual moral character, *cumulatively* the hundreds of relevant studies in psychology journals can tell a different story. To return to helping, suppose it turns out that in dozens of other studies besides Regan's, most control participants typically fail to perform other routine helping tasks, whereas most participants who are made to feel guilty typically help at higher rates. Then by examining the cumulative data closely, I think we can start to draw conclusions about the underlying psychological mechanisms that exist in most people's minds with respect to guilt and helping. This is in fact precisely what psychologists do when, as we saw in chapter two, they construct different models of guilt and helping.

With a better understanding of these mechanisms on hand, we can then formulate testable predictions about what behavioral trends should likely be found in novel situations. So, for instance, I might predict what would happen with controls versus those participants who are made to feel guilty and are then given a chance to volunteer to clean up a beach after an oil spill. If these

---

[88] Note that the claim is intentionally modest and the evidence is certainly defeasible. No claim is being made that any one study which fails to find virtuous behavior will be decisive by itself in arriving at a conclusion about the participants' lack of the relevant virtue.

guilty participants volunteer at a higher rate than controls, then there would be further support for postulating an underlying psychological association between guilt and motivation to help.

This in fact is the main form of argumentation I have used in Parts II and III of the book—draw on a host of studies, rather than only one single-shot study, to infer the existence of widely held psychological processes underlying morally relevant behavior. Then claim that our character traits would be constituted by such processes. Finally evaluate these processes from a moral perspective using widely held criteria for having the relevant virtue.[89]

In order to carry out this strategy, I have had to assume the following:

(3) *The assumption*. What patterns emerge with the experimental group of participants in one study, would have also emerged to a similar degree if the participants in the control group had instead been in the experimental group. Similarly, what patterns emerge with the control group of participants in one study, would have also emerged to a similar degree if the participants in the experimental group had instead been in the control group. The same is true across studies. So, what patterns emerge for the control group in study 2, would have also emerged to a similar degree if a control group from study 1 that is similar in relevant respects had instead been the control group in study 2.

This way of stating the idea is rather abstract, but the idea itself is simple enough. Return to the familiar standby of Regan's study. Twenty participants were controls and twenty were in the guilt condition. A pattern emerged of low helping in the first group and much higher helping in the second. So the study suggests that guilt can lead many people to help more than they would otherwise. But note that this would be a more forceful conclusion if the twenty participants were the *same people* who came across both situations on different occasions. Then the experimenters could see how they behaved both with the guilt manipulation and without it.

As is almost always the case with these experiments, however, the two groups did not overlap.[90] Hence we do not know for sure what these very same people would have done if they had also been in the other group. Rather, it is simply *assumed* in accordance with (3) above that, if they had been in the other group, then they would have tended to behave roughly how that group in fact did.

In the same way, when I compare studies on similar topics and try to draw a conclusion about moral character from their combined results, I also

---

[89] This discussion here more carefully develops similar themes from chapter two, section three, where I clarified the way in which I am using the experimental data in my reasoning about the extent to which people tend to possess the virtue of compassion.

[90] As Funder writes, "The classic studies of social psychology placed subjects into evocative situations (e.g. Milgram's obedience experiment, the Zimbardo prison study), but almost never, if ever, placed the same participant into *more than one* situation so that consistent patterns of behavior and associated traits could be detected" (2009: 125 n. 5, emphasis his).

assume that (3) is true, as there is no overlap at all between the participants in any of the groups used in the studies. So I assume that what holds true about the control participants in a given study, would have held true if instead the participants from other experimental groups had instead been used as controls, and similarly if these controls had been used in the experimental groups.[91]

I am not the only one who accepts the assumption. Psychologists do too. In other words, they are assuming that people in general are typically put together in a way that significantly overlaps with how these few participants in a given study are. Otherwise, they would not have any basis upon which to draw psychological conclusions about anyone *other than* those participants involved in the study in the first place, which needless to say would severely restrict the scope, relevance, and importance of their work.[92] So let me end this section by explicitly drawing attention to the assumption's importance as (I think) an uncontroversial background commitment in this book.

8.6 CONCLUSION

After considering a competing Simple Desire model, I have taken my picture of Mixed Helping Traits from the previous chapter and generalized it to make claims about the Mixed Traits had by most people in other areas of their moral lives. From there I surveyed some of the most important recent studies of both non-moral and moral traits and behavior. Finally I developed what I take to be central guiding principles for how to approach the experimental study of moral character.

Now it is time to see if psychological research in other moral domains besides helping supports my approach.

---

[91] Other things being equal, of course. If the experimental group was chosen because of the severe intellectual or emotional handicaps of its members as compared to members of the control group, for instance, then if they had been the controls there might have been significantly different results.

[92] Indeed the Assumption is related to the standard procedure in conducting psychological research of randomly *selecting* the participants and randomly *assigning* them to control and experimental conditions. Thanks to Mike Furr for related discussion here. See also Carlson 1971: 208 and Batson 2011: 91.

Part IV

Extending the Framework

9

Aggression and Harming Others

Most of the book so far has focused on our moral character with respect to helping other people. But in the previous chapter, I claimed that the framework I am proposing generalizes to other moral domains as well. Here in Part IV I try to make good on this claim, at least in a preliminary way—in this chapter I examine some of the ways in which we are capable of harming others, while the next chapter focuses on lying.

In the psychology literature, research on harming others is framed in terms of the study of "aggression." This term is applied to a number of different things, including aggressive behavior, aggressive motives, and the trait of aggression. In this chapter, I will use the term to apply only to aggressive behavior, and so talk of "aggression" should be assumed to be restricted in this way.

Furthermore, in order to engage with the research literature I will use a widely accepted characterization of aggressive behavior as "any behavior directed toward another individual that is carried out with the proximate (immediate) intent to cause harm . . . the perpetrator must believe that the behavior will harm the target and that the target is motivated to avoid the behavior."[1] Several elements of this proposal deserve a brief mention. First, because of the condition on intending to harm, any behavior which accidentally does harm to another person would not count as aggressive behavior, such as if I have a heart attack while driving which leads to a serious

---

[1] Bushman and Anderson 2001: 274 and Anderson and Bushman 2002: 28. Similarly, Bettencourt et al. write that aggression, "is defined as any behavior intended to harm another individual who is motivated to avoid being harmed" (2006: 752). And for Baron and Richardson, "Aggression is any form of behavior directed toward the goal of harming or injuring another living being who is motivated to avoid such treatment" (1994: 7). See also Krahé 2001: 10–11 and Geen 2001: 3.

I will restrict the focus just to aggressive actions as opposed to non-actions. On some characterizations, not helping a person in certain cases counts as aggressive behavior (Krahé 2001: 10), but I have already discussed failures to help in previous chapters and will not revisit them here. Furthermore, the objects of aggression in the characterization above are other human beings, but I see no reason to restrict the scope of aggressive behavior to living things as opposed to, say, my car that I am trying to repair and kick out of frustration.

wreck.[2] I will understand this "intention" very loosely as equivalent to what I called the broad sense of "desire" (as opposed to belief) in chapter one.[3] Furthermore, this part of the characterization is also important since it excludes cases of benevolent harming done by, say, a doctor or a dentist who intends to help rather than harm.[4] Finally, the last clause about the other person wanting to avoid the harm is used to address cases such as masochism. Since these harmful actions are actually desired, they do not count as "aggressive" if they are performed against willing masochists.[5] As usual, I am not putting this characterization of aggressive behavior forward as a strict analysis of our ordinary folk concept, but rather as a rough account that captures at least most of the cases which interest me.

It has long been standard in the research literature to distinguish between two kinds or types of aggression—reactive and proactive.[6] The first involves harmful behaviors done "in the heat of the moment" or "in hot blood," as a result of impulsive reactions such as feelings of anger or frustration. Someone who is verbally insulted to his face and then reacts by throwing a punch is exhibiting reactive aggression. Proactive aggression, on the other hand, is harmful behavior which is said to be done planfully and in a premeditated way, "in cold blood." This behavior does not respond to an immediate provocation but deliberatively uses a harmful action to achieve an end such as making money or eliminating a competitor or enemy. A general who is

---

[2] Baron and Richardson 1994: 9, Krahé 2001: 10, Geen 2001: 2, and Anderson and Bushman 2002: 29.

[3] It would be far too restrictive if a characterization of aggression required the formation of an intention in the narrow sense often used by philosophers of a planful attitude that is not reducible to states of ordinary belief or desire (for this narrow sense, see Bratman 1987). Surely there can be cases of aggressive behavior which arises from simple wants, wishes, and emotions, rather than intentions in this narrow sense. Hence Robinson and Wilkowski state this part of their characterization of aggression in terms of a "desire to hurt or punish" rather than an intention (2010: 2).

[4] Baron and Richardson 1994: 9.

[5] Baron and Richardson 1994: 11. Bushman and Anderson 2001: 274, Krahé 2001: 11, Geen 2001: 2-3, and Anderson and Bushman 2002: 29. Another case that is relevant here is suicide, which would not count as an act of aggression because of this clause.

[6] For this terminology, see, e.g. Dodge and Coie 1987: 1147, Geen 2001: 5, Bettencourt et al. 2006: 753-4, Wilkowski and Robinson 2010: 11-12, and Robinson and Wilkowski 2010: 2. At various times in the history of psychology a more common set of terms for this distinction has been "hostile" versus "instrumental" aggression, but I find these labels misleading since there is no sense in which instrumental aggression cannot be just as "hostile" as hostile aggression. Furthermore, as noted in the next footnote, hostile aggression can be instrumental as well. For this terminology, see Dodge and Coie 1987: 1147, Baron and Richardson 1994: 11-13, Bushman and Anderson 2001: 274, Krahé 2001: 11, and Anderson and Bushman 2002: 29.

Miller and Eisenberg distinguish between "instrumental" and "retaliatory" aggression (1988: 325). Geen uses "affective" and "instrumental" (2001: 4).

ordering his troops to begin a carefully orchestrated offensive is being pro-actively aggressive.[7]

For many years studies in psychology examined reactive and proactive aggression separately. But I think we should be suspicious that there is anything like a sharp division between the two, rather than a continuum of more or less. On the one extreme is a psychopath who plans a harmful action for months in a completely cool and calm manner, solely for the sake of some personal gain. At the other extreme is a person who is insulted and spontaneously lashes out in a blinding rage. Most cases of aggression fall somewhere in-between, with elements of reaction, deliberation, and emotion behind them. For instance, a teenager might be insulted or threatened by a bully, but does not respond immediately and instead takes some time to craft his revenge. This "proactive" form of aggression can still be driven by resent-ment or anger towards the bully, and is a response to an act of provocation.[8]

I focus in sections one and two of this chapter on psychological research that examines aggressive behavior more on the reactive end of the continuum, whereas in section three I shift to the proactive side. But it is important to keep in mind that much of this research has implications for the study of aggression in general, rather than just one kind of aggression. Section four continues the discussion of proactive aggression with a look at certain versions of the Milgram experiment as well as some other closely related experiments on obedience. No book on moral character, after all, especially one that draws so heavily on psychological work as this one does, can avoid discussing Milgram's

---

[7] For a helpful review of these claims, see Bushman and Anderson 2001 and Anderson and Bushman 2002: 29. On some ways of making the distinction, reactive aggression is said to (primarily) involve an intention to cause harm, whereas proactive aggression does not (e.g. Baron and Richardson 1994: 12, Krahé 2001: 11). But this strikes me as problematic for two reasons. First of all, aggression itself is standardly characterized in terms of an intention to harm, as noted in the text. So this cannot then be used to distinguish between different kinds of aggression. Secondly, even in cases of more deliberative, premeditated aggression, the action is caused by an immediate intention or (broadly speaking) desire to harm another person.

In response, it might be claimed that I have misrepresented the proposal. The claim is that what distinguishes reactive aggression is an *ultimate* goal of causing harm to others, whereas for proactive aggression this is only an immediate goal which is a means to some other ultimate goal such as making money or gaining power. But this proposal will not work either. As will be clearer in section two, reactive aggression also involves instrumental motivation to harm others in order to, say, get revenge or protect one's self-esteem.

I have a similar concern with characterizations of proactive aggression as distinctive in that it involves instrumental motivation or an instrumental goal (e.g. Dodge and Coie 1987: 1147, Miller and Eisenberg 1988: 325, Baron and Richardson 1994: 12, Geen 2001: 4–5, Bettencourt et al. 2006: 754, Wilkowski and Robinson 2010: 12, and Robinson and Wilkowski 2010: 2). Reactive aggression also involves instrumental motivation and the pursuit of goals. For related discussion, See also Bushman and Anderson 2001: 275 and Anderson and Bushman 2002: 29.

[8] For additional reasons to reject a sharp distinction between reactive and proactive aggres-sion, see Geen 2001: 5, Bettencourt et al. 2006: 754, and especially Bushman and Anderson 2001. For an opposing view, see Baron and Richardson 1994: 11–13.

research.[9] Finally, the chapter ends by relating the previous sections to my view of Mixed Traits (section five), and by evaluating how virtuous and vicious most of us appear to be in this area (section six).

In addition to shifting the focus away from helping behavior, this chapter also serves to counterbalance the focus in previous chapters on whether most people have a particular *virtue*. When it comes to aggression, in my opinion it is fairly obvious that most people are not virtuous in this area of their lives. In fact, what is far more challenging to show is that they are not *vicious*. So in contrast to the preceding chapters, most of the ethical discussion here will be aimed at showing, not only that most of us are not virtuous when it comes to aggression, but that we are not vicious either.

9.1 REACTIVE AGGRESSION AND BEHAVIOR

Bryan Stow was a 42-year-old paramedic leaving a baseball game at Dodger Stadium in March of 2011. In the parking lot he was attacked by one or more Dodger fans whose identities remain unclear as I write this chapter. They beat Bryan terribly, knocking out an eye and disabling his tongue, leaving him with paralysis and barely alive in a coma. What was his offense? While the details are not known at this point, one explanation seems to be that he was simply a fan of the rival San Francisco Giants.

This looks to be a case of reactive aggression. Likely his attackers did not plan out their actions ahead of time, but rather attacked "in the heat of the moment." Nor is it a rare occurrence in human history. I could spend the rest of this chapter documenting well-known examples of aggressive behavior which seems to be largely impulsive, immediate, and impassioned. We can all come up with stories from our own lives I am sure.

But my interest here is not in these specific incidents, but rather in trying to more carefully determine how most of us are disposed to be in this area of our lives. For that, I turn to carefully controlled experiments which manipulate one or more variables and see what impact they have on the aggressive behavior of a group of participants.[10] Fortunately there is a long-standing research tradition on reactive aggression in the psychology literature which can help. This tradition has operationalized such behavior in a number of

---

[9] In a longer discussion, I would also take up Zimbardo's prison study (Haney et al. 1973), but have omitted it here due to limitations of space.

[10] For helpful discussion of whether these experiments are useful for understanding aggressive behavior that is not done in a controlled lab environment (or as psychologists would say, whether these experiments have external validity), see Anderson and Bushman 1997 and Bushman and Anderson 1998.

ways, with the leading approach being the use of a machine to deliver (simulated) electric shocks to others.[11]

In this section I will only briefly mention a few studies where one or both of the following variables were manipulated: provocation and temperature. These variables have an effect which is representative of many other variables studied in the literature, and collectively they suggest that most people are disposed such that, given the right stimuli, they will be influenced to behave in a harmful way towards others.

Provocation. What does "reactive" aggression react to? The most obvious answer is some form of provocation by another person, such as an insult, demeaning comment, offensive gesture, or the like. Many studies have been run which compare the aggressive behavior of controls with that of participants who have been provoked in some way in a laboratory context.

For instance, one of the leading researchers on aggression, Leonard Berkowitz, told participants that they would take part in a study of physiological reactions to stress caused by electric shocks.[12] A participant and a confederate (who was introduced as a psychology student doing his own research) had to first complete a task (for the participant this was to come up with ideas to help better the record sales and image of a singer), and then they were separated in different rooms and hooked up to the shock machine. The confederate next evaluated the participant's performance on the task. In the control condition this resulted in one shock for the participant, whereas in the provoked condition it resulted in seven shocks.[13] Then it was the participant's turn to evaluate the confederate's work. Not surprisingly, the earlier provocation made a big difference:[14]

	Control	Provoked
Average number of shocks	3.07	4.67
Average duration of shocks (in thousandths of a minute)	24.47	34.80

But that is not all. In an interesting variation, Berkowitz also had another group of participants use the shock machine while a 12-guage shotgun and a 0.38 caliber revolver were on the same table as the machine. The cover story said that these were being used by the psychology student in his own lab research. In this group the results become even more dramatic:[15]

---

[11] This is the so-called Buss aggression machine paradigm (Buss 1961).
[12] Berkowitz and LePage 1967.
[13] Berkowitz and LePage 1967: 204.
[14] Berkowitz and LePage 1967: 205–6.
[15] Berkowitz and LePage 1967: 205–6.

	Control	Provoked
Average number of shocks	2.60	6.07
Average duration of shocks (in thousandths of a minute)	17.93	46.93

So the mere presence of an aggression cue in the situation, even though it had nothing to do with the task at hand, contributed to even higher rates of mean aggressive behavior.[16]

Russell Geen and David Stonner (1973) had a similar experimental design involving electric shocks, although this time the participant was to state his opinion on twelve controversial topics and the confederate would shock him each time he disagreed with the opinion. In the control condition, only two mild shocks were given for the twelve topics. In the provocation condition, two mild and eight moderate shocks were delivered.[17] Next, Geen and Stonner showed all participants a clip from the prize-fighting film *Champion*.[18] Some were told that the main character Dunne was out to get vengeance on the other fighter. Control participants were not told anything. Then, instead of reversing roles, Geen and Stonner had the participants administer a learning exam to the confederate where wrong answers could receive a shock ranging from 1 to 10 in intensity. Here were the results:[19]

	Control	Vengeance
Average shock intensity no provocation	4.72	4.14
Provocation	5.34	6.88

In other words, the average participant, having been provoked in the first place and after watching a fighting film, delivered more intense shocks as punishment to the provoker. But when also primed to think in terms of vengeance, even though the film had nothing to do with the confederate or his ability to learn, participants became much more severe in their aggression.[20]

Finally, let me mention one more study which I find truly disturbing. Robert Baron (1974) had participants complete a task and then be evaluated by a confederate. In the control condition, they received a positive evaluation of

---

[16] Part of what explains this effect is said to be a series of activations of other thoughts related to guns, i.e. thoughts associated with shooting, killing, death, etc. See, e.g. Berkowitz 1965, 1990 and Krahé 2001: 68. For more recent reviews of the literature on this so-called "weapons effect," see Carlson et al. 1990 and Baron and Richardson 1994: 188–90.

[17] Geen and Stonner 1973: 147.

[18] Following an earlier experimental setup by Berkowitz 1965.

[19] Geen and Stonner 1973: 147.

[20] For a review of various studies using short clips of movie depictions of violence, see Baron and Richardson 1994: 186–7, 190–3.

their work and were given one light flash (which is a very mild response). In the provocation condition, the evaluation was negative and was followed by nine electric shocks. Then the next part of the study had the participant in a position to give shocks between levels 1 and 10 in intensity to the confederate each time a red light on the machine went off. So there was no incentive to increase the shocks to, perhaps, help the confederate learn better. Rather, it was made perfectly clear that any level of shock was fine as far as the experiment was concerned. Furthermore, participants got to feel what shocks at levels 4 and 5 were like ahead of time, and they were "generally found to be moderately noxious by subjects."[21]

Here's one last wrinkle—some participants also were given a pain meter which (allegedly) reported the confederate's feelings of pain and was labeled "mild," "moderate," "strong," and "very strong."[22] These are some of the results:[23]

	No pain meter	Pain meter
Average shock intensity no provocation	5.05	4.10
Provocation	3.84	4.07

Note that there was a significant drop in the level of shock for controls when a pain meter was used. But, and here is the disturbing part, for provoked participants, *their level of shocking went up when they got to see the amount of pain they were causing.*

This same pattern showed up again for the duration of the shocks—with the provoked participants, their average shock duration was 0.51 of a second without the pain meter but increased to 0.68 with the pain meter.[24] And that is not the end of it. Baron also had another version of the study where a second confederate would go before the participant and carry out the shocks in a very aggressive way but without using a pain meter. Then it was the participant's turn, having just seen what the first person already did. Would observing the behavior of the model make a big difference? It sure did! For provoked participants without the pain meter, their average shock intensity was 4.97 and the average duration was 0.71 of a second. But now with the pain meter, it goes way up—to 6.18 in intensity and 1.01 seconds in duration![25] So the model's behavior seemed to prompt them to be even more harmful to the confederate than they would have been, and when they knew how much harm they were causing that only made things worse.

Temperature. A specific provocation by another person clearly can make a significant difference to our reactive aggression—I doubt we needed to consult empirical studies to accept this general point. Less obvious, perhaps, is the

[21] Baron 1974: 120. [22] Baron 1974: 120. [23] Baron 1974: 120.
[24] Baron 1974: 121. [25] Baron 1974: 120–1.

effect that other background features of a situation can have on aggressive behavior. In fact, we have already seen an example of such an effect with the presence of the two weapons in the Berkowitz study. And to take one other example, consider temperature.

It is a widely held cultural assumption that hotter temperatures will precipitate more harmful behavior. But the research literature on the so-called "heat hypothesis" suggests that the story is more complicated. For instance, Baron (1972) also ran another study in which participants were evaluated by a confederate as having done well or badly on a task and given either 1 or 9 shocks accordingly. They then had to administer a learning task to the confederate, and deliver shocks of their choosing, ranging in intensity from 1 to 10 as punishment. The twist now was that some participants carried out the study in rooms kept at roughly 74–75 degrees, while for the others the rooms were 91–95 degrees.[26] As expected, the provoked participants on average shocked more intensely and for a longer duration than the controls did. But, surprisingly, both of these figures were significantly *lower* for all participants in the hot rooms as compared to the cool ones.[27]

Baron found a similar trend in other variations of this setup.[28] His hypothesis is that such hot temperatures generate negative affect (because of how uncomfortable the person is feeling), and relieving the negative affect becomes more important than aggressing against the provoker if there is an opportunity to do so.[29] By giving less intense shocks, possible criticism is avoided (both from the confederate and experimenter), additional negative feelings are not formed (i.e. guilt, shame, etc.), and escape can happen faster.[30] In a test of this hypothesis, participants were given some cool lemonade before the opportunity to shock the confederate (as a means of reducing their negative affect), and it seems that, as a result, their levels of shock intensity and duration in the hot condition did not go down as significantly.[31]

---

[26] Baron 1972: 185.   [27] Baron 1972: 186.

[28] See Baron and Bell 1975, 1976.

[29] This became known as the "negative affect model" or "negative affect escape theory." As Baron and Bell write, "there is evidence that subjects in the hot-angry group found these conditions so unpleasant that they lost interest in everything but obtaining release from the study as quickly as possible" (1975: 830). However, if there is not an opportunity to relieve the negative affect, such as by escaping from a hot room, then the negative affect could serve to increase rather than decrease aggressive behavior. For relevant discussion, see Anderson 1987, Geen 2001: 32–5, and Anderson and Bushman 2002: 38–9. For recent defenses of the theory, see Bell 1992 and Baron and Richardson 1994: 170–7.

[30] Baron 1972: 187 and Baron and Bell 1975: 830, 1976: 246.

[31] Baron and Bell 1976: 252. There is much more to be said about the relationship between temperature and aggression. For instance, it is not clear whether Baron's results would carry over to natural environments where there may not be similar opportunities to escape as there are in his experimental setup.

In fact, there is a quite contentious debate ongoing in the psychology literature between those who argue for a positive linear relationship between temperature and aggressive behavior in natural environments (e.g. Anderson 1987, Bushman et al. 2005), and those who argue that the relationship is curvilinear (e.g. Cohn and Rotton 1997, 2005). Fortunately the outcome of this

The upshot of this brief look at the empirical literature is that various environmental variables seem to be able to reliably influence many people's level of reactive aggression. Some of these stimuli might be obvious ones, such as a direct insult or an inappropriate level of shock.[32] In other studies involving clear provocations, participants were also found to give more intense blasts of noise[33] or worse evaluations of an experimenter[34] or of a job candidate.[35] On the other hand, other stimuli might be much more subtle in their impact, such as the temperature of the room, watching a movie depicting a violent act, the presence of weapons nearby, or, in other studies, slides of weapons, the background noise level, playing violent video games, unpleasant odors, crowding, ions in the air, and ozone levels.[36] But regardless of whether the stimuli are obvious or not, most of us seem to have dispositions which are remarkably sensitive to various environmental variables and which can motivate us to harm others at least to some extent, depending on how we (implicitly and explicitly) interpret what is happening in those situations.[37]

9.2 REACTIVE AGGRESSION AND MOTIVATION

What psychological states mediate the relationship between these environmental factors and reactive aggression? In particular, what are the motivating states which can influence such behavior? One way to get at least some insight into these motives is to examine what enhances and inhibits aggression. In this section I will mention three of each briefly before looking at one enhancer in a bit more detail. But it will turn out that I cannot get very far here, as unlike in the case of helping, there seems to be little empirical work designed to test competing theories of motivation for aggressive behavior.

---

debate does not affect what follows. For an introduction to the research on heat and aggression, see Baron and Richardson 1994: 167–77, Krahé 2001: 80–5, and Geen 2001: 32–5.

[32] For references and a list of commonly used forms of provocation designed to generate aggression, see Krahé 2001: chapter one and Bettencourt et al. 2006: 752–3. See also Anderson and Bushman 2002: 37.

[33] Bushman and Baumeister 1998.

[34] Berkowitz 1965.

[35] Caprara 1987: 11.

[36] For the slides of weapons, see Caprara 1987: 9. For noise level, see Baron and Richardson 1994: 177–9 and Geen 2001: 36–7. For violent video games, see Giumetti and Markey 2007. For the remaining environmental factors listed, see Anderson 1987: 1161, Baron and Richardson 1994: 167–85, and Krahé 2001: 86–7. See also Carver et al. 1983, Baron and Richardson 1994: 167, and Anderson and Bushman 2002: 37–8.

[37] Clearly if a violent action is interpreted as part of a drama performance, then that might not activate dispositions associated with reactive aggression. But if the same violent action is interpreted in a different context as motivated by an intention to harm the person, then that is a different story. For more on interpretation and aggression, see Dodge and Coie 1987: 1146–7, Baron and Richardson 1994: 144–5, and Geen 2001: 27–30, 46–59.

Anger. When participants were told by the confederate that they have done poorly on their task and then are given eight or nine electric shocks, what effect will this have on them? Naturally, they will likely experience anger.[38] Provocation, in other words, can often enhance aggression by first enhancing feelings of anger.[39] Anger in turn can have an impact on aggression in a variety of different ways.[40] But my main interest is motivational. What is the nature of the motivation to harm which can be caused by feelings of anger towards another person who has insulted me?

Here is a natural answer, and one which is common in the research literature—states of anger can activate a desire to harm the offender in order to retaliate for his offense, or to get even with him, or to get revenge.[41] Note that these are not anger-relief desires—the object of the desires is not the person's own state of anger. Nor do they even seem to be egoistic desires, as I have understood that notion in chapter two. And they certainly are not altruistic desires. Rather, they seem to be moralistic desires, in the sense that they are concerned with what is fair and just. If I am electrically shocked an excessive amount, then when I get the chance to reciprocate I want to make sure to shock back at a high rate too—that's only fair and exactly what the other person deserves, regardless of whether it makes me feel any better about myself or is a loving or kind thing to do.

Unfortunately, though, so far as I know there is little research which explores this proposal. And I am only claiming that this is *one* kind of motive that anger can activate, not that it is the only motive behind anger-enhanced aggression.[42]

---

[38] This is state anger, as opposed to trait anger. But individuals who are higher in their trait anger will also be increasingly likely to form states of anger in the face of provocation. See, e.g. Eisenberg 2000: 683 and Wilkowski and Robinson 2010: 11.

[39] See, e.g. Berkowitz 1965, Buss 1966, Berkowitz and LePage 1967, Baron 1972, 1974, Geen and Stonner 1973, Baron and Bell 1975, 1976, Bettencourt et al. 2006: 755, Wilkowski and Robinson 2010: 11, and Denson et al. 2011.

[40] For five different effects, see Anderson and Bushman 2002: 44–5. For more on anger and aggression in general, see Eisenberg 2000: 683–4, Bandura et al. 2001: 127, 132, Robinson and Wilkowski 2010, and Wilkowski and Robinson 2010.

[41] See, e.g. Berkowitz 1965: 359, Geen and Stonner 1973: 150, Caprara and Pastorelli 1989: 125, Bushman and Anderson 2001: 275, 278, Geen 2001: 27, 42, Anderson and Bushman 2002: 41, Bettencourt et al. 2006: 754, Wilkowski and Robinson 2010: 26, and Wilkowski et al. 2010: 830–1.

[42] For instance, on Giumetti and Markey's model (2007), anger moderates the aggressive impact of violent video games, but with such games there is often not a clear provocation of the player nor it is clear why the player would be out for revenge. Wilkowski and Robinson (2010) also mention a goal of, "forcefully removing obstacles to goal attainment" (26). Anger might also lead to action aimed at upholding important religious, social, ethical, or communal norms and standards (Geen 2001: 44).

Frustration. Frustration has been linked to aggression by psychologists for many years.[43] This can be frustration caused by another person or thing serving as an obstacle to achieving something I desire. Or it can be frustration at myself for not being able to accomplish something that I desire to do. There need not be a particular provocation like an insult which first gives rise to frustration; rather frustration often arises simply because of some perceived impediment which is in the way of realizing my goal. I get frustrated easily, for instance, when I have to wait on the phone to speak to a customer service representative. Often I give up and say some hurtful things about the company.[44]

What is the best motivational story here? Perhaps it is a desire to harm in order to vent or give expression to my frustration. Or to harm in order to alleviate my feelings of frustration. Or to harm when doing so would help remove the source of frustration.[45] Or perhaps some other story instead, or combination of these stories. Not enough research has been done to say.

Shame. In chapters two and three I already noted some features of shame, in particular that it involves a negative evaluation of one's entire self and feelings of exposure, withdrawal, degradation, and helplessness. This might not seem like the kind of state that would enhance aggression. But both theoretical arguments and empirical research suggest otherwise. Because the self has been, in a loose sense, damaged or wounded, it can react defensively with anger and aggression, blaming others for what has happened.[46] Research has found links between shame and externalizing blame on the one hand, and between externalizing blame and aggression on the other.[47] This suggests the work of a

---

[43] Closely related psychological phenomena such as irritation, agitation, and annoyance are also enhancers for aggressive behavior. See, e.g. Caprara 1987, Caprara and Pastorelli 1989, Baron and Richardson 1994: 212–14, Geen 2001: 22, and Bettencourt et al. 2006: 755, 757.

In earlier research on reactive aggression, there was much more interest in the variable of frustration, and some even advocated a frustration-aggression hypothesis according to which, "frustration produces a condition of readiness or instigation to aggress, and that aggression is always preceded by some form of frustration" (Geen 2001: 22; see also Baron and Richardson 1994: 21). But over time, it has become apparent that frustration is not necessary for many cases of aggression (Baron and Richardson 1994: 22–3, Baumeister et al. 1996: 10, Krahé 2001: 35, and Geen 2001: 22). Furthermore, some studies have not found support for the sufficiency condition either in certain cases (Buss 1966, Baron and Richardson 1994: 21–2, and Geen 2001: 27). For related discussion and recent evidence which still does favor the idea that frustration gives rise to aggression at least in some cases, see Caprara 1987, Caprara and Pastorelli 1989: 124, Baron and Richardson 1994: 21–6, 128–40, Krahé 2001: 34–6, Geen 2001: 21–7, and Anderson and Bushman 2002: 37.

[44] In many cases, it may be that frustration gives rise to anger, and so it is really anger which is the driving motivation behind subsequent aggression. But not all cases of aggression initiated by frustration need to be mediated by anger.

[45] Buss 1966: 154.

[46] Here I have been helped by Stuewig et al. 2010: 92.

[47] For references, see Stuewig et al. 2010: 92. The relationship between externalized blame and aggression will be discussed in some detail in the remaining sections of this chapter.

desire to harm others in order to avoid the threat of being blamed myself, but at this point such a proposal is largely speculative.[48]

Guilt. On the flip side, one of the *inhibitors* for aggression is guilt. If I feel guilty about how I behaved towards a person, then I can be motivated to apologize and seek forgiveness from that person, rather than wanting to harm her. I also tend to take responsibility for my own actions rather than deflecting blame onto others.[49] Guilt has also been linked to perspective-taking and empathy, which as noted below inhibit aggression too.[50] But does a person want to not harm others when feeling guilt so as to atone for a particular wrong? Or to relieve the feeling of guilt? Or for the sake of one of the other goals relating to guilt that was considered in chapter two? Again, I can find little evidence which bears on these specific models.[51]

Negative affect. As illustrated in the previous section, there are certain cases in which negative affect can inhibit aggression by making relief of those feelings more important than getting revenge or satisfying whatever other goal might lead to aggressive behavior. Hence high temperatures can generate negative affect, and even though a person might be angry at an earlier provocation, to him escaping from the situation becomes a greater priority in order to get some relief from the discomfort.[52]

Empathy. Perhaps the most obvious candidate for an inhibitor of aggression is empathy. By taking the perspective of another who might be harmed by my actions, and experiencing something similar to what that person is experiencing, I can become less motivated to harm her and/or increasingly motivated to not harm her. While the empirical literature is not entirely clear here,

---

[48] For more on shame and aggression, see Baron and Richardson 1994: 222–3, Tangney 1995: 120–9, 1998: 7, Lindsay-Hartz et al. 1995: 296, Baumeister et al. 1996: 10, Eisenberg 2000: 669, Geen 2001: 71, Tangney et al. 2007a: 351–2, 2007b: 27, Hosser et al. 2008: 139, and especially Stuewig et al. 2010.

[49] For more on guilt and aggression, see Caprara and Pastorelli 1989: 126, 133, Baumeister et al. 1996: 10, Eisenberg 2000: 667–71, and especially Stuewig et al. 2010. In a longitudinal study of six German prisons and 1,243 inmates, Daniela Hosser and her colleagues (2008) examined the relationship between guilt and shame on the one hand, and criminal convictions after release from prison on the other. They found that twenty-four months after being released, 54.1 percent of inmates who felt guilt, but no shame, during imprisonment had no new convictions, compared to 39.7 percent of those who felt shame but no guilt (146).

[50] See, e.g. Baumeister et al. 1994: 254–5, Tangney 1995: 129–33, Lindsay-Hartz et al. 1995: 296, Eisenberg 2000: 668, Manion 2002: 81, Tangney et al. 2007a: 350, 2007b: 26–7, and Stuewig et al. 2010.

[51] For how guilt might also serve as an enhancer for aggression in some cases, see Caprara and Pastorelli 1989: 126, 133.

[52] Baron 1972: 187 and Baron and Bell 1975: 830, 1976: 246. In other cases, though, negative affect might serve as an enhancer rather than an inhibitor for aggression. See, e.g. Baron and Bell 1976: 254, Anderson 1987: 1161–2, and Anderson and Bushman 2002: 38–9.

For other environmental variables and their relationship to negative affect and aggression, see Anderson 1987: 1161. In this context, I am using "negative affect" narrowly to refer to a passing state of negative mood, as I did in chapter six. Hence negative affect is distinct from frustration and from anger.

the emerging picture is that empathy is indeed negatively correlated with aggression.[53]

In what way might empathy affect aggressive behavior? In particular, do feelings of empathy in cases of potentially harmful actions typically lead to personal distress for the empathizer, and so inhibit aggression via *egoistic* motives to not feel this distress? Or do feelings of empathy in these cases typically lead to *altruistic* concern for the well-being of the other person, thereby supporting an empathy-altruism hypothesis for avoiding harm as opposed to actively helping others? Can we experience these different kinds of motives in different situations (or even the same ones)?[54] Again, not enough research has been done.

Self-Esteem. As should be clear from the above, while a number of psychological enhancers and inhibitors for aggression have been identified, the exact contribution they make to motivation to harm or not harm another person remains murky at best. This is not the case with the enhancer of self-esteem, at least if a recent proposal is on target.[55] Here the motivational story has been worked out in detail. Furthermore, according to this proposal self-esteem plays a role in explaining why in many cases people, among other things, murder, assault, rape, commit domestic abuse, act violently in gangs, and serve as agents of terrorism, oppression, and genocide.[56] So let me say a bit more here about this enhancer.

I follow Roy Baumeister in understanding self-esteem as a "favorable global evaluation of oneself."[57] A person high in self-esteem, then, has a very positive evaluation of herself. That may not necessarily be a mistake on her part or a sign of pride or arrogance. In some cases, the positive evaluation is entirely appropriate and warranted. In other cases, of course, it is not.

Now the long-standing view both in our culture and in the research literature, is that there is a positive correlation between aggression and *low*

---

[53] See, e.g. Baumeister et al. 1996: 10, Eisenberg 2000: 674, Stuewig et al. 2010: 93, 100, Baron-Cohen 2011, Batson 2011: 165–8, and especially Miller and Eisenberg 1988. As they write, "individuals who vicariously experience the negative reactions of others that occur because of their own aggressive behavior may be less inclined to continue their aggression or to aggress in future interactions" (1988: 324).

[54] For more on these options, see Miller and Eisenberg 1988: 326, 340.

[55] Baumeister et al. 1996. See also Caprara and Pastorelli 1989: 132, Baron and Richardson 1994: 12, Bushman and Baumeister 1998, Baumeister et al. 2000, Bushman and Anderson 2001: 275–6, 278, Geen 2001: 44, 71–2, Anderson and Bushman 2002: 35, and Baumeister and Vohs 2004: 91–3. For a theoretical perspective that is amenable to this empirical work, see Taylor 2006: chapter five.

[56] Although Baumeister is quick to note that "many aggressive acts may have little or no relation to self-esteem. Moreover, when self-appraisals are involved, they may be only one of several factors, and so we are not asserting that other causes become irrelevant or secondary" (Baumeister et al. 1996: 6).

[57] Baumeister et al. 1996: 5.

self-esteem. But this view has been challenged in recent years, and an emerging perspective is instead that *high* self-esteem, rather than low, is what often contributes to harmful behavior.[58]

This is too simple of a way of stating the proposal. High self-esteem by itself is not likely to lead to aggression—why would it? Rather, the proposed cause is high self-esteem *combined with* a threat to that positive view of oneself.[59] Claiming that someone is a "loser" or a "retard" or a "cheater" can clash with the person's own self-image and put pressure on him to revise it downward.

Here he has reached what Baumeister calls a "choice point."[60] On the one hand, he can accept this new way of thinking about himself, rather than resist it. Perhaps, he comes to think, he really is a loser. This lowers his self-esteem and leads to withdrawal feelings such as sadness and disappointment.[61] Increased aggression is not likely going to result; if anything, lower self-esteem has functioned as an *inhibitor* of aggression and an enhancer of withdrawal.

But this is only one of the options. And there is good empirical reason to think that many of us will not want to go down that road. We seem to either want to enhance our view of ourselves, or at the very least to resist making revisions to that view.[62] As Baumeister writes, "people are reluctant to change toward more unflattering views of themselves. The avoidance of loss of esteem is thus the clearest and presumably strongest pattern of self-concept motivation. Decreases in self-esteem are aversive for nearly everyone."[63]

Hence there appears to be powerful motivation to not lower self-esteem, and to avoid the feelings of sadness, disappointment, and the like which would result if one does. But how does aggression fit into this picture? Even if the person has taken the option of preserving his positive evaluation in the face of the threat, the threat itself still remains. So by acting aggressively, "the person may accomplish several things, including punishing the evaluator for the bad feedback, impugning the other's right to criticize, and discouraging that person (and others) from expressing similar evaluations in the future."[64]

---

[58] For criticism of the low self-esteem hypothesis, see Bushman and Baumeister 1998, Baumeister et al. 2000, and especially the very thorough discussion in Baumeister et al. 1996, upon which much of what follows will draw. For a recent opposing study, see Donnellan et al. 2005.

[59] Baumeister et al. 1996: 8, 26. For further development of this proposal, including qualifications about when threats to high self-esteem do and do not foster aggression, see Bushman and Baumeister 1998: 227–8, Baumeister et al. 2000: 27, and Baumeister and Vohs 2004: 92–3.

[60] Baumeister et al. 1996: 10.

[61] These are mentioned in Baumeister et al. 1996: 11.

[62] Baumeister et al. 1996: 8.

[63] Baumeister et al. 1996: 8.

[64] Baumeister et al. 1996: 11. Baumeister and his colleagues discuss the way in which aggression can also be important for purposes of symbolic dominance and self-affirmation (11). But they are careful to note that, "in many circles, ego threats are common whereas violence is rare, and so one must conclude that violence is only one among many possible responses to ego threats" (29).

The upshot is a detailed account of one way in which provocation can lead to aggressive behavior. It also provides some clarity about the various motives which mediate that process. Of particular interest to me is the role of the following:

> Beliefs and desires concerned with harming others in order to maintain a positive opinion of myself.

Now of course these beliefs and desires need not have this precise propositional content. Rather, the claim is that most people have dispositions to form mental states which, *as a matter of fact*, serve to function psychologically in this way.

A vast quantity of data has been cited in support of this self-esteem-aggression model, and I will not review it here.[65] Instead let me end this section by returning to one of the studies from earlier and seeing how the model might account for that data. Recall that in Berkowitz's study, participants in the provocation condition were shocked seven times by the confederate as a way of evaluating their ideas. Now following the reasoning of the self-esteem model, these participants could have simply accepted the evaluation as fair and come to think of themselves as not very competent in this area. Perhaps some of them did come to think this—we only have data for the average behavior of the group. But it seems clear that some of the participants instead showed signs of elevated aggression in the form of increased and longer electric shocks that were subsequently delivered to the confederate. One story could be, then, that for these participants they refused to accept the negative evaluation of the confederate and instead wanted to punish him and perhaps discourage him from issuing future evaluations.

Now to be clear, I am not claiming that this study *supports* the self-esteem-aggression model, only that it can be plausibly interpreted in terms of that model. Alternatively, it could be that the participants wanted to harm the confederate simply to get even with him for the earlier shocks, a motivational story that was suggested earlier in relation to anger.[66] Much further work is needed to determine how comparatively important these and other forms of motivation to harm really are in our minds.

In this section, I have highlighted many of the enhancers and inhibitors for reactive aggression that have received attention in the research literature. How exactly they function at the psychological level, however, often remains to be seen.

---

[65] See in particular Baumeister et al. 1996. In a longer discussion, it would be important to compare the importance for aggression of maintaining positive *self*-esteem with maintaining positive *social*-esteem or social-image (Baron and Richardson 1994: 146–7).

[66] Baumeister et al. 1996 appeal to anger at one stage in their model (10, 27), but there it plays a more complex role than fostering revengeful desires.

9.3 PROACTIVE AGGRESSION

To this point I have been focusing on what the research literature has to say about reactive aggression. By comparison, far less work has been done on trying to better understand proactive aggression,[67] which involves harmful actions that are more calculated and less immediate reactions to some specific earlier incident of provocation. Bank robberies and political assassinations are two fairly straightforward examples of such actions. Naturally when it comes to many actions like these, it is easy to see why doing controlled laboratory experiments becomes such a challenge! Again, though, the same reminder is in place that the difference between reactive and proactive aggression is merely a difference in degree. Because of this, some of the proposals for understanding reactive aggression, such as the self-esteem-aggression model, may shed some helpful light here too.

But in this section I do not want to revisit the previous proposals; instead I want to touch on two important variables which are closely related to proactive aggression—displacement of responsibility and dehumanization. Let me set the stage for introducing them.

It is a striking fact that acts of proactive aggression have been widespread throughout history, and yet at the same time most people have also considered them to be, at least in general terms, morally wrong. Indeed it is not just that these actions are taken to be wrong in the sense that they are regarded as socially prohibited. Rather, the striking fact is that proactive aggression is so widespread, despite the fact that these acts are, again in general terms, considered to be morally wrong *by the person's own moral principles*. How is it, for instance, that most people genuinely believe that premeditated murder, assault, rape, domestic abuse, stealing, and the like are morally wrong,[68] and yet hundreds of thousands of these incidents happen every day?

Not only are such actions thought to be morally wrong, but there are also significant external costs associated with them. An act of aggression can lead, for instance, to jail time, financial hardship, the breakup of the family, and the loss of friendships. Furthermore, people typically do not get away with them, at least in more serious cases.

On top of the opposing moral beliefs and the high external costs, there are in addition very serious *internal* costs for acting aggressively too. Because these moral principles against harming others have become personal and internalized, they are bound up with the person's own conception of himself as a moral person. Violation of them can lead to self-censure,

---

[67] For similar observations, see Jaffe and Yinon 1979: 183, Bandura et al. 1996: 372, and Geen 2001: xi.

[68] At least in most cases—I ignore cases where, for instance, stealing might be considered permissible to feed one's starving family.

self-condemnation, and self-contempt,[69] and more specifically to moral guilt and shame, a loss of self-esteem, and an increase in anxiety.[70] People generally know this ahead of time, and so would be motivated to not harm others in order to avoid these psychological costs. So together all of these ways of moderating aggressive tendencies serve to make the actual widespread extent of proactive aggression look quite puzzling.

Various proposals have been made in the psychology literature to account for this phenomenon of "moral disengagement"[71] whereby there are "many social and psychological maneuvers by which moral self-sanctions can be disengaged from inhumane conduct."[72] For instance, one contributing factor to disengagement is moral justification, where we justify to ourselves how, for instance, although stealing might be wrong in general, this *particular* act of taking someone's property without her consent does not really count as stealing, or if it does, then it is morally permissible in this situation.[73] Similarly, another contributing factor to moral disengagement is ignoring or distorting the negative consequences of actions. If we minimize the pain and suffering that a potentially harmful action might cause, and just focus on the benefits, then that can make us much more comfortable with doing it.[74]

My goal here is not to survey all the various factors which are claimed to contribute to moral disengagement.[75] Instead I want to focus on just two factors, namely displacement of responsibility and dehumanization. Each plays a central role in many different kinds of aggressive behavior, and either one or both of them has been important in most of the famous cases of proactive aggression throughout history. Furthermore, they will offer helpful insights into the extent to which most of us are virtuous or vicious people in this area of our lives. In the remainder of this section I say something separately about each of them, and will also consider displacement of responsibility again in the next section when discussing the Milgram experiments.

---

[69] Bandura et al. 1975: 254–5, 1996: 364, 371 and Bandura 1990: 161, 164, 190, 1999: 194.

[70] For similar claims, see Bandura et al. 1996: 368, 371.

[71] The leading contributor in psychology to developing an account of moral disengagement has been Albert Bandura. See in particular his 1990, 1999 and Bandura et al. 1975, 1996, 2001. For discussion of his account in the philosophy literature, see Snow 2009.

[72] Bandura 1999: 194. Note that moral disengagement arises in cases having to do with (not) helping others, as well as in cases of harming people. So in this chapter I am only looking at the relationship of moral disengagement to one area of moral life.

[73] For relevant discussion, see Bandura et al. 1975: 254, 1996: 365, 2001: 126, Diener et al. 1975, Diener 1977: 149, Bandura 1990: 163–7, 1999: 194–5, and Anderson and Bushman 2002: 44.

[74] On the other hand, "when people can see and hear the suffering they cause, vicariously aroused distress and self-censure serve as self-restraining influences" (Bandura 1990: 177). For relevant discussion, see Bandura et al. 1975: 255, 1996: 365–6, 2001: 126 and Bandura 1990: 176–80, 1999: 199.

[75] See, e.g. Bandura 1990: 162.

Displacement. Displacement of responsibility concerns the way in which I think about myself as the cause of a harmful action. On one end of the continuum, I can see myself as being solely responsible for the harm. On the other end, I can claim that I am not responsible at all, perhaps because I was directly ordered by a superior to pull the trigger.[76]

Steven Prentice-Dunn and Ronald Rogers (1980) ran a shock study which nicely illustrates the difference that displacement can make. In one condition, participants were treated anonymously by the experimenter, told that they would not meet the recipient of the shocks, and assured that the experimenter assumed complete responsibility for any harm done. The other condition involved the opposite treatment of participants. Both groups were told to shock when a signal light went off. They could choose the intensity level from 1 to 10, and it was made clear that the different levels had equal effects as far as their task was concerned and so a higher level would only serve to increase pain for the person receiving the shock. Was there a difference in the results? On average the shock level in the responsibility condition was 4.3 and in the displaced responsibility condition it was 6.4.[77]

Many cases of harm involve, however, not the complete denial of responsibility but rather the partial *diffusion* of responsibility, a concept which was discussed in chapter six with the group effect studies. If, for instance, I am just one intermediary in a long command hierarchy which ends with a lowly underling pulling a trigger and shooting an innocent person, then I might take myself to have very little responsibility for the incident. The responsibility is spread over a number of people in the hierarchy, and I might claim to have only played a relatively minor role. Similarly, if I am a member of an execution squad, then I am just one of many people pulling a trigger, and it is likely that my bullet is not even the one that kills the person.[78]

It is important to be clear about what kind of responsibility is being displaced. It is not causal responsibility—under direct order from the superior I am still the one who causes the person to die by pulling the trigger. It is also not professional responsibility or the responsibility I have in carrying out my assigned task properly. Again, I am the one in charge of arranging the execution, getting the gun in good working order, disposing of the body, and so forth.[79] Rather, the responsibility that is being displaced is moral (and often, legal) responsibility. By claiming that my superior is the one who is

---

[76] For helpful discussions of displacement, see Bandura et al. 1975: 255, 1996: 365, 2001: 126, Diener et al. 1975, Diener 1977: 148–9, Jaffe and Yinon 1979, Bandura 1990: 173–6, 1999: 196–8, and Burger et al. 2011.

[77] Prentice-Dunn and Rogers 1980: 108.

[78] For additional examples and discussion, see Bandura 1990: 176, 1999: 198 and Bandura et al. 1996: 365. See also the results in Jaffe and Yinon 1979.

[79] For further discussion, see Bandura 1990: 175, 1999: 198. Also relevant is Milgram 1974: 143.

responsible for the death of the innocent while I was "just following orders" or "doing my job," I treat him as the proper object of the appropriate moral reactive attitudes—he is the one who should be blamed, found guilty, punished, criticized, condemned, and so on. The moral norm against killing an innocent person still applies in this case, but it applies to him and not me, since he was the one morally responsible for the action. Hence I can do what I was told without worrying about both the external costs—there will not be any punishment from my superior if I follow his orders—and the internal costs, since there is no blame or guilt to worry about if I go against my moral norm. With these costs diminished, and with there being significant costs if I disobey my superior, it is easy to see why many people in these kinds of situations would harm others.

So one thing the phenomenon of displacement of responsibility suggests is that most of us have desires concerned with not harming others when we would be the ones held personally accountable for doing so. But if we can avoid responsibility for the harm at least to some extent, then motivation to not harm diminishes.

Dehumanization. Unlike displacement of responsibility, the phenomenon of dehumanization concerns how I view the *object* of my harmful action. Implicitly it also involves seeing myself as superior in some way, but the main focus is on the status of the other person. As the name suggests, the other person is regarded as less than fully human and instead as more of an object or a primitive being. Such people are "savages," "impure," "diseased," or "three-fifths human." They are said to have severely diminished intellectual or emotional capacities, or behave in disgusting and revolting ways which make them lesser beings than the rest of us.[80]

If another person is seen as a human being with equal dignity and worth, then it is much harder to aggress against her. She is regarded as one of us, who can take pleasure and joy in the same kinds of things we can, and who would often react the same way we would if she were harmed. Moral norms are as applicable to her as they are to us. Empathy and guilt can come into play and inhibit aggression.[81]

But if she is dehumanized, these protections can go away. The moral norms against treating other humans in certain ways may no longer be thought to apply, and it is more difficult to experience empathy and anticipated guilt with respect to those who are considered significantly different from us as members of an out-group. Hence the internal costs for the person of going

---

[80] For helpful discussions of dehumanization, see Bandura et al. 1975: 255, 1996: 366, 2001: 126, Bandura 1990: 180–4, 1999: 200–3, Baron and Richardson 1994: 234–5, and Anderson and Bushman 2002: 44. For more extensive treatments of dehumanization aimed at a popular audience, see Glover 2001 and Smith 2011.

[81] See, e.g. Bandura 1990: 180, 1999: 200, 203 and Bandura et al. 1996: 368.

against his relevant moral norms are likely not going to be nearly as powerful in keeping him from aggressing.[82]

The important role of in-group versus out-group membership is powerfully illustrated by a recent neuroimaging study conducted by Lasana Harris and Susan Fiske (2006). They wanted to demonstrate in a scientifically rigorous way that in fact some groups are regarded as being less than fully human. So they examined activity in the medial prefrontal cortex (mPFC), an area of the brain associated with social interaction and treating others as humans, but which is not linked to interactions with objects. While in an fMRI machine, participants were shown pictures of, among others, the elderly, disabled, homeless, rich, Olympic athletes, and drug addicts, and for each picture they were asked to classify the emotion they were feeling as pity, envy, pride, or disgust. For the rich people, this tended to be envy, and the mPFC would light up. Similarly for the disabled and pity, or athletes and pride. But when it came to drug addicts and the homeless, the strongest correlation was with the emotion of disgust. Here no significant mPFC activity was discovered.[83] Activation was instead found in areas of the brain associated with objects, and in a second study, similar patterns of activation were found when participants were shown pictures of vomit and overflowing toilets.[84] The homeless and drug addicts were being regarded as members of out-groups, and as less than dignified human beings. No surprise, then, if it also turned out to be the case that there were fewer internal costs for such participants if they behaved aggressively towards members of these groups.

So one thing the phenomenon of dehumanization suggests is that most of us have desires concerned with not harming others when they are similar to us in important ways. But if the others are instead not considered to be members of groups that we care a lot about, then motivation to not harm them diminishes.[85]

Let me conclude by tying this discussion together using two influential experiments conducted by Albert Bandura and his colleagues (1975) which powerfully demonstrate the individual and joint contribution that displacement of responsibility and dehumanization can make to aggression. Once again the setup involved a shock machine. Participants were to deliver shocks (ranking in intensity from "mild" at level 1 to "painful" at level 10) as punishment for inadequate solutions by a group of (imaginary) people working on twenty-five bargaining problems. A red light would tell participants if the solution was inadequate. Responsibility was manipulated by having either

---

[82] Bandura 1999: 200.
[83] Harris and Fiske 2006: 850.
[84] Harris and Fiske 2006: 850.
[85] For a recent discussion of dehumanization which also addresses the Harris and Fiske study, see DeSteno and Valdesolo 2011: chapter five. As they write, "The tendency to dehumanize seems to be a fundamental part of our psychology." (146).

the participant be the only one to determine the level of shock (individual responsibility) or by having the level get averaged between his choice and that of two other participants in nearby cubicles (diffused responsibility).[86] Dehumanization was manipulated by the participants accidently hearing an exchange between the experimenter and his assistant in which the group of people coming up with the bargaining solutions was not labeled (neutral condition), labeled as "perceptive, understanding, and otherwise humanized" (humanized condition), or labeled as "an animalistic, rotten bunch" (dehumanized condition).[87]

Bandura provided the results in the form of charts, so the data reported below is just a rough estimate. But it is striking nonetheless. For individual responsibility, the mean level of shocks was roughly:[88]

Humanized   2
Neutral   4
Dehumanized   4.5

But for diffused responsibility, it was:[89]

Humanized   3
Neutral   4.25
Dehumanized   6.75

In other words, when responsibility could not be displaced, the average intensity of the shocks was lower independent of how the group was labeled.[90] Furthermore, regardless of level of responsibility, dehumanization resulted in the most severe shocks on average. But together, the results are the most striking of all. When there was personal responsibility in acting towards a humanized group, the average was 2 shocks; when responsibility was diffused towards a dehumanized "rotten bunch," the average was 6.75 shocks! As Bandura found when asking participants for their reactions afterwards, "When the [groups] were humanized, subjects strongly disapproved of physical punishment and rarely excused its use. By contrast, when performers were divested of humanness, subjects seldom condemned punitive techniques but often voiced self-absolving justifications."[91]

Bandura also looked at how the mean intensity of the shocks changed over the course of the trials. For instance, with the humanization variable, mean intensity started out as very similar (between 1.5 and 2) for all three conditions. With the humanized group, it only increased a small amount by the tenth trial (to 3). For the neutral condition, it increased from an average

---

[86] Bandura et al. 1975: 257.   [87] Bandura et al. 1975: 258.
[88] Bandura et al. 1975: 259.   [89] Bandura et al. 1975: 259.
[90] See also Bandura 1999: 198.
[91] Bandura et al. 1975: 262. See also Bandura 1999: 200.

of 2 to an average of 5 by the tenth trial. But for the dehumanized group, the average level went from 2 all the way to 7.[92] In other words, as time went on participants got increasingly punitive the less the group was considered human.

Using this last idea, Bandura ran another experiment where there were two different patterns of wrong answers. In the functional group, every wrong answer was followed by a correct one, which should suggest to the participant that the punishment was working and there was no need to increase the shock intensity. As predicted, the shock level stayed roughly the same throughout ten trials, and for the dehumanized group it never reached 5.[93] But for the dysfunctional group, where incorrect answers were grouped together so that punishment would seem less effective, "subjects suddenly escalated punitiveness toward dehumanized performers to near maximum intensities."[94]

In some ways, this result is even more disturbing than what Milgram found. In the standard Milgram paradigm, most participants would raise concerns and doubts long before they reached the maximum shock level, and it was only because of the continued orders of the experimenter that many of them even made it there. But in this experiment, there was no experimenter. As Bandura notes, "In studies of obedient aggression people are commanded to behave punitively. Here, participants escalated their punitiveness on their own."[95] I do not want to get ahead of myself, though. On to Milgram.

9.4 MILGRAM AND DISPLACEMENT OF RESPONSIBILITY

As Stanley Milgram writes in *Obedience to Authority*, "Of all moral principles, the one that comes closest to being universally accepted is this: one should not inflict suffering on a helpless person who is neither harmful nor threatening to oneself."[96] While we might come up with some exceptions to this principle, it certainly seems correct in the vast majority of cases. In particular, it seems to apply to the participants in his famous shock experiments.[97]

---

[92] Bandura et al. 1975: 260.
[93] Bandura et al. 1975: 264.
[94] Bandura et al. 1975: 266.
[95] Bandura et al. 1975: 268.
[96] Milgram 1974: 13.
[97] Milgram has said in more than one place that his studies do not pertain to the study of aggression. See, for instance, his 1974: 165–8, 188. But in these passages he has in mind a more

I assume that most readers are familiar with the basic Milgram paradigm.[98] At the simplest level, a participant is to serve as a teacher in charge of administering a test to a learner, who is actually a confederate. The learner is usually in another room, and in most variants of the study (there were eighteen reviewed in *Obedience to Authority*)[99] the learner can be heard by the teacher. For every wrong answer, the teacher is supposed to use a shock generator to deliver a shock of increasing magnitude, where the shock intensity starts at level 1 (labeled as 15 volts and a "slight shock") and goes to level 30 (labeled as 450 volts and "XXX"). Beforehand the teacher would receive a sample shock of 45 volts to improve the authenticity of the study. The learner would make sure to give roughly three wrong answers for every right one, hence putting the teacher in a position to have to potentially deliver more and more painful shocks to the learner over time.

Consider just this basic setup. If the teacher was told that he or she is entirely free to choose the level of shock to give for every wrong answer, then participants were remarkably gentle in their behavior. Their shock level maximum averaged only 5.50, and 38 out of 40 stopped the experiment when the learner strongly protested for the first time.[100]

Now make one modification. Suppose an experimenter is also present in the room wearing a technician's coat, and when the teacher hesitates or objects in some way, he says "Please continue." A series of four prods is used if necessary in the face of continued resistance by the teacher, with the last one being "You have no other choice, you *must* go on."[101] Only then if the teacher continues to object is the experiment over—unless the teacher turns the dial up all the way to level 30.

Now the results are (famously) different. In experiment 5 which employed this setup, 65 percent of participants inflicted apparently lethal 450-volt XXX shocks, and 80 percent gave shocks which were at least at the 270-volt level.[102] This despite the fact that at 270 volts the learner was heard making agonizing screams and demanding to be let out, with the pleas getting desperate and hysterical at higher levels. *And* if that were not enough, the teacher knew ahead of time that the learner had a slight heart condition, and at 150 volts the learner started demanding: "That's all. Get me out of here. I told you I had heart trouble. My heart's starting to bother me now."[103]

---

reactive notion of aggression, connected to "anger, vindictiveness, or hatred" (188), and his studies pertain instead to more proactive forms of aggression.

[98] In what follows I draw on Milgram 1974.
[99] Or 19 if one considers experiments 13 and 13a to be distinct.
[100] Milgram 1974: 61.
[101] Milgram 1974: 21, emphasis his.
[102] Milgram 1974: 60.
[103] Milgram 1974: 56. A replication of this setup was able to be done recently by Jerry Burger (2009), where use of the shock dial was stopped after the 150-volt level. This level, where the

What is it exactly about this setup that was able to take people who otherwise might have barely shocked a learner, and allow many of them to commit (apparent) manslaughter? What do *not* seem to matter significantly are factors such as the type of building used for the experiment (i.e. Yale University's psychology lab or a regular office building),[104] whether the participants are male or female,[105] or the particular country in which the research is conducted.[106] On the other hand, here are some things that *do* seem to matter to whether participants would shock all the way to level 30:

> *The proximity of the learner*: 65 percent were fully compliant when the learner could only be heard pounding on the wall, 62.5 percent when there was voice feedback as well, 40 percent when the learner was a few feet away in the same room, and 30 percent when at the 150-volt level the participant had to touch the learner and force his hand to come into contact with the shock apparatus (still, 30 percent!).[107]

> *Where the experimenter is*: If the experimenter left the room before the teacher started administering the test, and the prods were given over the phone, then full compliance was 20.5 percent.[108]

> *Who is giving the orders to continue*: If the experimenter is absent and another participant is the one who comes up with the shock system and demands that it be continued, then full compliance drops to 20 percent.[109] Similarly, if the experimenter is the one receiving the shocks and another participant demands that the procedure be continued despite the verbal protests from this learner, then 0 percent shocked all the way—in fact, everyone stopped when they heard the first protest.[110]

> *How authoritative the experimenter is*: If participants heard contradictory commands from two experimenters at the 150-volt level, then they all stopped at that point or one step afterwards.[111]

As Milgram notes, what these results suggest is that the crucial factor at work is the participants' willingness to defer to someone whom they regard as a legitimate authority figure.[112] If the person is not considered an *authority*

---

learner first verbally protests, has been found to be either a significant stopping point or a "point of no return" for most participants (Packer 2008, Burger 2009: 2, A. Miller 2009: 22). Burger found that 70 percent of participants continued after 150 volts, compared to 82.5 percent in Milgram's original experiment 5 (2009: 8).

[104] Milgram 1974: 61, 66–70.

[105] Milgram 1974: 61–3. For other relevant studies, see Doris 2002: 47 and Burger 2009.

[106] See, e.g. Brown 1986: 4 and Meeus and Raaijmakers 1986: 312.

[107] Milgram 1974: 35. See also Bandura 1999: 199 for the relation of this result to the distortion of consequences variable of moral disengagement.

[108] Milgram 1974: 60.

[109] Milgram 1974: 93–4, 96–7.

[110] Milgram 1974: 95, 99–105.

[111] Milgram 1974: 95, 105–7.

[112] Milgram 1974: 104, 138. More recent work has raised the possibility that perceived expertise is also a contributing factor (Burger 2009: 3).

figure, as when a participant is in charge, compliance drops. If the person is not considered *legitimate*, as when there are contradictory commands, compliance drops.[113]

So it appears that most people are disposed to form desires concerned with obeying those whom they think are legitimate authority figures.[114] In fact, the desires can become so strong or take on such a central psychological role that they lead to (what seems to be) the intentional killing of an innocent person.[115]

But at the same time, this authority figure is demanding that the participants go against what most of them believe is a clear moral prohibition against inflicting terrible pain on an innocent person in this way.[116] The participants should be (implicitly) aware of severe external costs here, such as possibly being arrested for manslaughter. They should be (implicitly) aware of severe internal costs here as well, in the form of anticipated guilt, loss of self-esteem, increased anxiety, and the like. Shouldn't these various costs, together with the moral prohibition, have been enough to stop them from going all the way to the XXX level?

What we have, then, is another instance of moral disengagement. It was clear that many of the participants were not able to *completely* disengage, but rather experienced internal struggle during the course of the experiment. For instance, Milgram remarks about experiment 1 (standard setup, but no verbal feedback from the learner and pounding on the walls at 300 volts followed by complete silence at 315 volts) that "After the maximum shocks had been delivered, and the experimenter called a halt to the proceedings, many obedient subjects heaved sighs of relief, mopped their brows, rubbed

---

In addition, in a recent paper using replication data from Burger 2009 of Milgram's experiment 5 up to the 150-volt level, Burger and his colleagues challenge the importance of obedience to orders from the experimenter, and argue that, "participants responded in exactly the opposite pattern that we would expect if they were following orders. That is, the more the experimenter's statement resembled an order, the less likely participants did what the experimenter wished" (Burger et al. 2011: 464). However, a lot hangs on how they are understanding "orders," and their treatment is impressionistic and, in my opinion, overly narrow. It will be interesting to follow future work in this area.

[113] Thus Penner et al. (1973) ran a variant of the standard setup, but with rats receiving actual (but mild) electric shocks. One condition of the study had a competent experimenter, while another condition used someone who acted incompetently. Disobedience of the experimenter was significantly higher in this second condition.

[114] For appropriate caution about whether the language of "obedience to authority" is the best choice for describing what happens in the standard Milgram experiment, see Helm and Morelli 1979: 338.

[115] As Mixon notes, "When we consider obedience in the experimental context one fact becomes evident: subjects accede to quite extraordinary requests; a casual examination of the experimental literature discloses the amazing range of compliant behavior in an experimental setting—from masturbation and sexual intercourse to starvation." (Mixon 1972: 155).

[116] Milgram 1974: 6, 41.

their fingers over their eyes, or nervously fumbled cigarettes. Some shook their heads, apparently in regret."[117]

So these participants may not have disengaged from their moral convictions completely, but many of them still did do so enough to perform over a dozen distinct acts of turning a dial which delivered electric shocks at a level which was clearly inhumane. Even granting that we are disposed to want to obey legitimate authorities, why wasn't such a desire regulated by the person's moral norms and all the internal and external costs which should have opposed it? What, in other words, could explain their disengagement?

Here I will not attempt to identify all the various psychological factors which might have played a role. Some commentators have pointed to the gradual stepwise nature of the procedure and the lack of a clear dividing line to use in stopping.[118] Other factors have been mentioned including a focus on narrow details,[119] not wanting to hurt the feelings of the experimenter,[120] or the pain of breaking a promise to the experimenter.[121]

Some complex, multi-faceted story is no doubt needed. But central to this story will surely be displacement of responsibility.[122] Indeed this was explicitly cited as a factor by some of the participants themselves.[123] For instance Jan Rensaleer, who ended his participation in experiment 2 (standard setup, including voice feedback through the wall) at the 255-volt level, was asked about who was responsible for the shocks, and answered, "I would

---

[117] Milgram 1974: 33. See also Milgram 1963: 375, 377, 1974: 42–3, 148, 153–64 and Miller 2004: 196. For variants of the standard Milgram setup that also found high levels of conflict in the participants, see Tilker 1970: 99, Larsen et al. 1972: 294, and Meeus and Raaijmakers 1986: 318–19.

[118] See, e.g. Milgram 1974: 149, Gilbert 1981, Ross and Nisbett 1991:56, Doris 2002: 50, Miller 2004: 197, Sabini and Silver 2005: 549, Adams 2006: 153, Packer 2008, Burger 2009: 3, and Burger et al. 2011.

[119] Milgram 1974: 7.

[120] Milgram 1974: 151, Sabini and Silver 2005: 559, and Adams 2006: 153–4.

[121] Milgram 1974: 7, 163–4. For still other factors, see Milgram 1974: 7–10, Badhwar 2009: 281–3, Burger 2009: 3, A. Miller 2009: 21, and Burger et al. 2011.

[122] As Milgram writes, "The disappearance of a sense of responsibility is the most far-reaching consequence of submission to authority" (1974: 8) and, "The act does not originate in his own motive system and thus is not checked by the inhibitory forces of his internal psychological system . . . The action . . . no longer reflects on his self-image and thus has no consequences for self-conception . . . . actions performed under command are, from the subject's viewpoint, virtually guiltless, however inhumane they may be" (146–7). For related discussion, see Milgram 1974: 7–8, 11, 85, 87, 120, 134, 145–7, 160–1, 176, 180, 187, 203–4, Baron and Richardson 1994: 157, Bandura 1999: 197, Miller 2004: 210, 217–21, 224–5, 230, Sabini and Silver 2005: 549 n. 37, Adams 2006: 150, Badhwar 2009: 285, Burger 2009: 4, and Burger et al. 2011.

[123] In Burger's (2009) replication of Milgram's experiment 5, 66.7 percent of participants who stopped before or at the 150-volt level had made comments indicating personal responsibility for harming the learner, whereas only 12.2 percent of those who continued past the 150-volt level did. See Burger et al. 2011: 463.

put it on myself entirely."[124] As Milgram notes, "he still feels responsible for administering any shocks beyond the victim's first protests. He is hard on himself and does not allow the structure of authority in which he is functioning to absolve him of any responsibility."[125]

Similarly, Fred Prozi in experiment 5 (standard setup) shocks all the way to the maximum level, but on more than one occasion asks about responsibility:

SUBJECT: I refuse to take the responsibility. He's in there hollering!

EXPERIMENTER: It's absolutely essential that you continue, Teacher.

SUBJECT: (indicating the unused questions): There's too many left here; I mean, geez, if he gets them wrong, there's too many of them left. I mean who's going to take the responsibility if anything happens to that gentleman?

EXPERIMENTER: I'm responsible for anything that happens to him. Continue, please.

SUBJECT: All right.

[later]

SUBJECT: You accept all responsibility?

EXPERIMENTER: The responsibility is mine. Correct. Please go on. (*Subject returns to his list, starts running through words as rapidly as he can read them, works through to 450 volts.*)[126]

For Prozi, he clearly put up a lot of verbal resistance along the way to 450 volts, and there is every reason to trust that this was a genuine expression of deep psychological tension on his part. Yet it seems that it was precisely his displacement of responsibility onto the experimenter that enabled just enough moral disengagement to occur for him to continue with the shocks.

The important role of responsibility has been explored in various follow-up studies to Milgram's which employ the same basic setup. For instance, Harvey Tilker (1970) introduced a variation where a confederate served as a teacher, and the participant was an observer (no experimenter was present during the shocking). In the instructions beforehand, participants in the *no responsibility* condition were told that the teacher had full responsibility for the study and the learner's well-being, in the *ambiguous* condition they were told they

---

[124] Milgram 1974: 51.

[125] Milgram 1974: 52. This case provides an important corrective to what Milgram says in a footnote: "Society promotes the ideology that an individual's actions stem from his character. This ideology has the pragmatic effect of stimulating people to act *as if* they alone controlled their behavior. This is, however, a seriously distorted view of the determinants of human action" (1974: 210 note 21, emphasis his). But it is not clear why Rensaleer's actions could not stem from his character, nor why those who are instead fully obedient are not also acting from their characters too, namely their dispositions to form obedient desires. Milgram might be right that we do not *fully* control our behavior, but there is no reason provided for thinking that we are not at least partially responsible (both causally and morally) for obedient actions which stem from these dispositions. For related criticism of Milgram here, see Helm and Morelli 1979: 339–42.

[126] Milgram 1974: 74–6, emphasis in original.

should resolve differences between themselves, and in the *total responsibility* condition the participant had full responsibility over the study and the well-being of the learner.[127] Once the test started, the confederate would use various scripts to resist any protests from the participant, that is, "Shut up! This is the way it is!"[128] It turned out that both the number of verbal protests and the percentage of participants who stopped the experiment increased significantly when they were made totally responsible.[129]

A study by Wesley Kilham and Leon Mann (1974) is even more helpful for illustrating the role of displaced responsibility. They had three conditions: (i) transmitter, where the participant was an intermediary between the experimenter and the confederate teacher, and announced whether the learner got an answer correct and what the shock level should be for a wrong answer, but deferred to the experimenter if the learner protested, (ii) executant, where the participant was the teacher and received orders from a confederate transmitter or the experimenter, and (iii) control, where the participant could be either the transmitter or the executant, but got to freely choose what shock level to use.[130] Here were the dramatic results:[131]

	Mean level of obedience	% who fully obeyed
Male transmitter	28.30	68
Male executant	23.00	40
Control	3.12	0

Again, when participants were told that they are free to choose for themselves what level of shock to use, they tended to stick with very mild ones. The mean level of obedience for the transmitters tells the opposite story. No one dropped out of the experiment until level 20 (beginning of "extreme intensity shock") and 28.30 was the average out of a possible 30![132]

---

[127] Tilker 1970: 97.

[128] Tilker 1970: 97.

[129] Tilker 1970: 98–9. This experiment has similarities to Milgram's experiment 13a, in which another participant took over the shocking and increased the shock levels at every wrong answer (1974: 97–8). Relevant also is a study by Penner et al. 1973, which found that participants had difficulty shifting responsibility onto the experimenter when the experimenter was incompetent, and so tended to retain responsibility themselves. Disobedience rates were significantly higher in this condition as compared to rates with a competent experimenter.

[130] Kilham and Mann 1974: 698.

[131] Kilham and Mann 1974: 699.

[132] In addition, "Surprisingly, none of the subjects attempted to form a coalition with the other teacher to defy the experimenter nor did they appeal to the other teacher for support" (Kilham and Mann 1974: 701).

Milgram's experiment 18 had a similar design to the Kilham and Mann study, and Milgram found that 37 of 40 participants functioning as intermediaries were involved until the end of the shock levels (1974: 121–2).

This last result serves to vividly illustrate the dangers of displacement of responsibility in an organization with intermediaries in the chain of command. Indeed, here a connection can be made to the other disengagement variable of dehumanization from the previous section. Before the object of dehumanization was described as a member of an out-group which triggers reactions of disgust. But it is worth noting that in the context of organizational structures with numerous intermediaries, dehumanization can happen to the intermediaries *themselves*.[133] They can think of themselves, in other words, not as fully responsible moral agents but rather as objects which function as parts in a larger machine. Adolf Eichmann himself claimed that, "In actual fact I was merely a little cog in the machinery that carried out the directives of the German Reich."[134] So just as causal responsibility for the proper functioning of a car is spread over many different parts, so too it can seem that moral responsibility for the proper functioning of an organization, military unit, or even laboratory experiment can seem to be spread over multiple individuals and rest very little on any one intermediary who is just "doing his job."[135]

There is much additional interesting research which pertains to the Milgram experiments, but at this point I want to step back from the psychology literature in order to start drawing some implications about moral character.

9.5 MIXED AGGRESSION TRAITS

It seems to me that the results reviewed in the previous sections fit very comfortably with the picture of character I developed in Part III of this book. I will not explore these results in nearly as much detail as I did with

---

[133] Milgram did note that dehumanization of the learners occurred, but it was *after* they had been shocked, perhaps as a means of justification for the harsh punishment (1974: 9–10, 160–1). As one participant said about the learner, "He was so stupid and stubborn he deserved to get shocked" (1974: 10).

[134] Quoted in Kilham and Mann 1974: 697. However, there is good reason to be suspicious about the truth of Eichmann's claim, and also to be very cautious more generally about using Milgram's results to provide a paradigm for understanding the Holocaust. For helpful discussion, see Miller 2004 and Haslam and Reicher 2007.

Still as a general phenomenon, "Perhaps it is one of the characteristic effects of the role that with the passage of time, individuals who act as transmitters often begin to respond as machines, dehumanizing themselves and others" (Kilham and Mann 1974: 701).

[135] For additional discussion, see Milgram 1974: xii, 11, 121–2 and Kilham and Mann 1974. Another point worth noting here is that as intermediaries, they are often shielded from seeing firsthand the consequences of the decisions which they assist in carrying out. This relates to the moral disengagement variable of distortion of an action's consequences, which was mentioned briefly in the previous section. For more on the relationship between distortion of consequences and serving as an intermediary, see Bandura 1990: 177–8, 190.

research on helping. But a few claims are worth making here. In doing so, I will combine the previous discussions of reactive and proactive aggression.

Research on aggression makes it clear to me that there is no plausible, simple dispositional story to tell about what gives rise to aggressive behavior in most people. When discussing helping, I considered a rival position to my own which I called the Simple Desire model. It claims that most of us have a disposition to want to help others which is causally responsible for such behavior in many cases. In the previous chapter I argued that such a position generates predictions which are not in line with the available empirical evidence, and so this view should not be preferred over my account of Mixed Helping Traits.

I think the corresponding Simple Aggression model looks even more implausible. According to this position, most people are disposed (to varying degrees) to want to hurt others in general.[136] To be fair to the view, this disposition may not actually lead to aggressive behavior very often, if various constraints on harming others are in place such as fear of punishment or a desire to not lose a positive self-image. However in certain circumstances the disposition can manifest itself in leading to aggressive behavior.

But on balance the studies reviewed in this chapter do not support this view. In particular, there were multiple studies in which control participants had ample opportunity to harm others without fear of punishment or blame, and yet did not do so. For instance with the simplest Milgram setup in which no experimenter was present, the maximum shock level averaged only 5.50 out of 30. Similarly we just saw above that controls who got to choose the shock level themselves as either transmitters or executants averaged only a shock level of 3.12.[137]

Not surprisingly, what I favor is a more complex account. On my view, most of us bring with us a variety of distinct dispositions pertaining to aggression. Which of these dispositions gets activated in a given situation, if any, depends on the nature of that situation as it is interpreted by the person (whether consciously or not), but it also depends on the nature of these dispositions

---

[136] This desire is meant to be understood as a *de dicto* desire—the content of the desire involves harming people as such, rather than harming Jones or Smith in particular.

[137] Kilham and Mann 1974: 699. For critical remarks directed at a position similar to the Simple Aggression model, see Milgram 1974: 72, 104, 165–8.

In response, the advocate of the model could argue that in these experimental situations, the disposition to want to harm others was still present, but for various reasons the experimental conditions did not allow for it to be expressed in aggressive behavior. For instance, it might have still been held in check by moral engagement and self-regulatory capacities.

This response is coherent, but it is also convenient. Any potentially disconfirming evidence can be explained away in this manner. What we need to find is some situation where the Simple Aggression model can be put to the test, and if it turns out that there is little evidence of motivation to harm, then that result should plausibly be taken as evidence against the view. I claim that the two studies above, among many others, do indeed provide such evidence.

themselves, what features they are sensitive to, and how they are interrelated. Given the earlier sections of this chapter, these dispositions include, but are certainly not limited to,[138] the following:

> Beliefs and desires concerned with harming the offender in order to retaliate for his offense, or to get even with him, or to get revenge.
>
> Beliefs and desires concerned with harming others in order to maintain a positive opinion of myself.
>
> Beliefs and desires concerned with harming others in order to obey instructions from a legitimate authority.[139]
>
> Beliefs and desires concerned with not harming others when they are similar to me in important ways.
>
> Beliefs and desires concerned with not harming others when I am thought to bear a significant degree of personal responsibility for the harm and would be blamed if I did.

Again, the claim is not that these beliefs and desires have precisely these propositional contents (say, with respect to "harming" or "personal responsibility"), but that they have contents which function in these particular ways.

This collection of beliefs and desires (and others besides them—again, this is just a selection of important ones) stands in stark contrast to the proposal made by the Simple Aggression model, which only posits one dispositional desire to harm others. It also stands in stark contrast to the mental states which make up a traditional moral virtue or moral vice pertaining to harming others. I will explain why in the next section. I think a cluster of such interrelated belief and desire dispositions can constitute a character trait, to be sure, but this trait is not one for which we have a concept in ordinary moral thought and discourse. Let me call it a "Mixed Aggression Trait"—"aggression" because of the area of our moral life to which it pertains, and "mixed" because it has some morally positive and some morally negative features which will be clarified in the next section.

With mental state dispositions such as the above, the expectation is that they will give rise to fragmented harming, even with respect to aggression-

---

[138] To be clear, I am not proposing anything remotely approaching a comprehensive model of the mental state dispositions which are primarily responsible for aggressive behavior. Rather my aim is to highlight *some* of the central dispositions that play a significant role in many actual cases of this behavior. In a longer discussion, I would want to relate the discussion here to some of the leading theories of aggressive behavior, such as Berkowitz's cognitive neoasssociation model (1993) and Anderson's general affective aggression model (Anderson and Bushman 2002).

[139] As Milgram himself wrote, "The person brings to the laboratory enduring dispositions toward authority and aggression." (1965: 274).

relevant situations where the moral wrongness of harming is obvious. For instance, in the Milgram setup where there is no experimenter present and the participant can choose the shock level, for most people they can be expected to only use mild shocks. In other Milgram setups, lethal shocks can be expected. Most of us have various dispositions that can lead to behavior spanning the gamut from extremely aggressive to extremely passive, based on our reactions to the specific features of a given situation. This is as powerful of an illustration of how fragmented moral behavior can be that I know of.

Clearly aggressive behavior can also be enhanced and inhibited. There seems to be strong empirical support for the psychological influence of at least the following variables (among many others, to be sure):[140]

> Enhancers:
>   Anger
>   Frustration
>   Shame
>   Threatened self-esteem
> Inhibitors:
>   Guilt
>   Empathy
>   Negative affect
>   Activated moral norms

Unfortunately, for several of these variables there has not been enough research done yet to get a clear picture of the psychological processes involved in enhancing or inhibiting aggression. Once this research is done, it can allow us to specify additional dispositional beliefs and desires (such as, *perhaps*, a desire to not harm others so as to avoid feeling guilty) which can be added to the makeup of a Mixed Aggression Trait.

Let me focus a bit more on the inhibitor of activated moral norms. Our moral principles and values are stored in memory, but they can be primed in different ways and lead to motivation to comply with them. As discussed earlier, most of us have moral norms prohibiting various kinds of harm to others, and their inhibiting effect in a given instance can be modeled as follows:[141]

---

[140] For instance, Caprara and Pastorelli briefly mention fear of punishment (1989: 126; See also Baron and Richardson 1994: 207, Krahé 2001: 35, and Geen 2001: 24) and resentment (133). Wilkowski et al. (2010) discuss forgiveness processes as inhibitors. Baumeister et al. mention envy as an enhancer in some cases (1996: 10).

[141] This figure closely parallels the model of activated moral norms and increased helping behavior from chapter four, section two.

Appropriate background conditions

↓

Activation of one or more moral norms relevant to the person's harming another

↓

Motive to comply with these norms

+

Potential beliefs about other actions available to the person besides harming

↓

Activation of the person's Mixed Aggression Trait
(Cost/benefit assessment and additional motives to support or avoid complying with
these moral norms depending on the assessment)

↓

Increased motivation to not harm

↓

Decreased harming behavior

This can be a case where, morally speaking, things go well. An opportunity to harm presents itself, say by turning up the dial on the shock machine another level after the learner has just screamed in pain, but the person's moral norms kick in and increase motivation to not harm.

The components of the Mixed Aggression Trait relevant to this process were not specified above, but they would include:

Beliefs concerned with the relationship between complying with the relevant moral norms against harming and various external benefits (e.g. punishment avoidance) and internal benefits (e.g. guilt avoidance).

Beliefs concerned with the relationship between complying with the relevant moral norms against harming and various external costs (e.g. lost income) and internal costs (e.g. continued frustration).

Beliefs concerned with the relationship between not complying with the relevant moral norms against harming and various external benefits (e.g. additional income) and internal benefits (e.g. relieved frustration).

Beliefs concerned with the relationship between not complying with the relevant moral norms against harming and various external costs (e.g. punishment) and internal costs (e.g. guilt).

Beliefs concerned with how to weigh these various costs and benefits.

Desires concerned with not harming others when doing so will contribute towards complying with the relevant moral norms against harming, provided the benefits of not harming are not (significantly) outweighed by the costs.

Desires concerned with harming others when the benefits of complying with the relevant moral norms against harming are (significantly) outweighed by the costs, while also desiring as much as possible to still appear to be moral both to others and to oneself.[142]

Now this is admittedly more detail than is warranted by the studies I have reviewed in this chapter, and so I advance it as a proposal for how to think going forward about the relationship between a person's moral norms against harming and her actual motivation and behavior.

An expanded version of this proposal would also have to say something about moral disengagement as well, and the two variables of dehumanization and displacement of responsibility can be nicely integrated into this discussion. The first would serve as one of the "appropriate background conditions" along with, for example, believing in certain moral norms against harming, one's degree of self-awareness of those norms at the time, and believing that one is able to do the harmful actions.[143] More specifically, if the homeless or if drug addicts are dehumanized and regarded as more like objects than human beings, then a person's moral norms against doing harm might not be activated in the first place because by his lights these norms do not apply.

With many cases of harm involving displacement of responsibility, it seems that a person's moral norms against harming *are* activated, leading to internal struggle and distress. But these norms provide inadequate motivation to refrain from harming. What is contributing to this struggle are the following:

> Beliefs and desires concerned with not harming others when I am thought to bear a significant degree of personal responsibility for the harm and would be blamed if I did.

In other words, most of us are motivated to not be blamed (by other human beings, by God, by our moral code, by ourselves, etc.) if we do something wrong. So one important internal cost that I am going to experience when I go against what an internalized moral harm norm says, is anticipated blame. But blame is a reactive attitude tied to personal responsibility. So if moral responsibility for the action can be partially displaced onto someone else, then I will not expect the same degree of anticipated blame, and suddenly an important enforcement mechanism for following this harm norm has weakened.

---

[142] This last idea was introduced in chapter four, section two.

[143] For self-awareness and aggression, see Diener 1977: 149 and the overview in Baron and Richardson 1994: 194–9, 236–7. In chapter four, section two, research was mentioned on the effect of mirrors in heightening self-awareness and thereby compliance with norms to help. A similar effect has been found with mirrors, heightened self-awareness, and decreased aggression (Diener 1977: 149). Self-awareness and the use of mirrors are also discussed in connection to cheating in *Character and Moral Psychology*, chapter three.

For self-efficacy and aggression, see Bushman and Anderson 2001: 277, Bandura et al. 2001, and Anderson and Bushman 2002: 36. Another relevant background condition is the person's level of self-regulation and self-control. See, e.g. Baron and Richardson 1994: 214–18, Eisenberg 2000: 685–8, Bandura et al. 2001, Krahé 2001: 58, Bettencourt et al. 2006: 753, Wilkowski et al. 2010, Wilkowski and Robinson 2010, and Denson et al. 2011.

Stepping back from this discussion of enhancers and inhibitors for harming others, let me very briefly mention a few other elements of my story about Mixed Traits. The mental state dispositions outlined in this section are expected to lead to stable behavior over time.[144] They can also lead to a kind of cross-situational consistency, indexed to the features of the various situations, such as the legitimacy of an authority figure or the humanity of the other person, which interact with these dispositions. When a person lashes out in anger in one situation but walks away from an insult in another, that can seem unintelligible and mysterious, but perhaps not if we first have some insight into what features mattered to him in each situation.

Individual differences will abound. Some people will put more importance on getting revenge than others. Some will care more about maintaining high self-esteem.[145] Some are more anger prone than others, or more easily frustrated, more empathetic, or more self-controlled. Lots of differences will be found with respect to whom we consider to be less than fully human. There has even been a recent flurry of work on individual differences in aggression that is relevant here.[146]

Nevertheless, despite these differences, there is enough commonality in the possession and strength of the dispositions making up a Mixed Aggression Trait to use them to ground some reliable predictions. For instance, predictions can be made about whether for most people it is the case that increased aggression will be shown when responsibility is completely displaced. Or about whether there will be decreased aggression when empathy is activated. Or about what would happen when contradictory orders to harm others are given by authority figures.[147]

And finally, much of the psychological processing discussed in this chapter does not function at the conscious level. Sometimes anger, for instance, leads to behavior that is hard to make sense of after the fact. Even proactive aggression can be influenced by guilt avoidance, or dehumanization, or displaced responsibility without our being aware of these factors at the moment.

[144] For overviews of the work on stability and aggressive behavior, see Baron and Richardson 1994: 121–3, 205–6, and Geen 2001: 67–9.

[145] For several individual differences relevant to self-esteem and aggression, see Baumeister et al. 1996: 9.

[146] See, e.g. Caprara 1987, Caprara and Pastorelli 1989, Bandura et al. 1996, Bushman and Baumeister 1998, Eisenberg 2000: 684–5, Krahé 2001: chapter three, Geen 2001: 67–75, Bandura et al. 2001: 127, Anderson and Bushman 2002: 35, Giumetti and Markey 2007, Robinson and Wilkowski 2010, Wilkowski et al. 2010, Wilkowski and Robinson 2010, and especially Bettencourt et al. 2006.

[147] Here, for instance, is a prediction in an old paper by Berkowitz: "If the presence of aggression-evoking cues gives rise to an activated aggressive response sequence, an inability to complete this sequence by inflicting sufficient injury on the aggression target will lead to feelings of tension and, possibly, to indirect expression of hostility" (1965: 365). For more recent results pertaining to predictions of aggressive behavior, see Vansteelandt and Van Mechelen 1998: 755–7.

One important piece of my story remains—the normative assessment of how most of us are doing in this area of our moral lives. Let me end this chapter with a discussion of virtue and vice.

9.6 NON-MALEVOLENCE AND CRUELTY

When it comes to the appropriate virtue concept with respect to harming others, I found it is a bit of a challenge at first to identify a good candidate. *Compassion, charity*, and *kindness* have to do with helping others rather than with (or in addition to) not harming them, at least in my mind.[148] The best choice, it seems to me, is *non-malevolence*, even if it is a cumbersome term.[149] I will understand non-malevolence as the moral virtue associated with being reliably disposed to not harm others when appropriate, and for the right reasons.

As I did with compassion, I could formulate a number of conditions in the minimal threshold for non-malevolence and compare them with the available data. But I will not bother to do that here. For I think it is clear that most of us do not meet the qualifications for this virtue, even to a minimal degree. We often do harmful things to others. That might be okay, morally speaking, if those harmful things are usually for some morally legitimate purpose (such as, say, a doctor or dentist causing pain during surgery). But consider most of the harmful things we do—lashing out verbally in anger, stealing a small item from a store, yelling at a spouse or child out of frustration, tearing down a colleague at work behind his back, and so on. These are rarely justified actions, morally speaking.[150]

---

[148] John Doris, on the other hand, uses "compassion" broadly to also encompass behavior that pertains to harming others (2002: 39). This is a common trend in the philosophical literature on character (see, e.g. Webber 2006a and Sreenivasan 2008, among many others). See also Russell 2009 with respect to benevolence (84) and minimal compassion (284).

[149] Christine Swanton, in a related context, mentions "non-maleficence," which could also be used here (2003: 31).

[150] Note as well that, in contrast to helping behavior, where only imperfect obligations exist in many cases, here typically there are perfect obligations against behaving aggressively in the relevant situations. See Adams 2006: 124, 148–9.

A striking example of a kind of commonplace, non-virtuous aggressive behavior is the phenomenon of *displaced aggression*, in which a provoked person behaves aggressively, not against the original source of the provocation, but against an innocent third party or against someone who has done something that is only a minor irritant or annoyance. For instance, William Pedersen and his colleagues (2000) had participants take an anagram test, and in the provocation condition they were insulted about their performance. Subsequently they answered trivia questions, and in the "trigger condition" the research assistant reading the questions did a poor job of doing so. Participants were given a chance to give feedback about the assistant as she applies for a job, and when both provoked and triggered, participants' aggression in the form of negative feedback about the assistant was much higher than any of the other three options

A more forceful way of making this point is with respect, not to what we actually do, but to what we are *disposed* to do. Unlike the participants in various studies mentioned in this chapter, most of us will never be in a situation where we have an opportunity to oversee the delivery of electric shocks to another person. But if the results do indeed generalize to most of us, then (other things being equal) it is also true that we *would* issue unnecessarily intense and punitive shocks when provoked in such cases.[151] We might even *increase* the level of the shocks if we had a pain meter telling us what effects they were having. And that is not all—for we might also use shocks of maximal intensity on members of a dehumanized group who are not performing well on a test that we are overseeing. Worst of all, we might willingly (albeit with some degree of internal conflict) *kill an innocent person* under pressure from a scientist or other seemingly legitimate authority figure. What makes a person virtuous is not simply a matter of what she does, but in the first instance it is a matter of what dispositions she has and what they dispose her to think and do. The above are not the dispositions of a virtuous person.[152]

(provoked-no trigger, not provoked-trigger, not provoked-no trigger) (917). In other words, these participants acted much more harshly towards this research assistant than her behavior warranted, as a result of the influence of another event (the outcome of the anagram test) that had nothing to do with her performance. More generally, displaced aggression, "reflects a level of aggression that incommensurably exceeds the level ordinarily warranted by the behavior of its target" (Pedersen et al. 2000: 913).

For more on displaced aggression, see Baron and Richardson 1994: 24–6, Pedersen et al. 2000, Marcus-Newhall et al. 2000, and Geen 2001: 37–9.

[151] Or, to use a different example, we *would* in certain conditions violently inflict harm on a non-responsive innocent person. In Diener et al. 1975, they varied displacement of responsibility, moral justification, and the behavior of a model, and observed how a participant would behave in a room with a non-responsive innocent person and various items such as rubber bands, rubber bricks, a plastic gun, and Styrofoam swords. In one condition, participants first watched a movie of a model being very aggressive with the innocent person, were told that the experimenter had full responsibility, and were told to role play military behavior. In another condition, the model was non-aggressive, the participants were told that they were responsible, and the task was described as just a game.

The results are amazing. Using the rating system devised by Diener, participants were found to be 38 times more aggressive in the first condition than the second (1975: 334). As they write, "To achieve a score of 463 (the average score for the highest condition), subjects could, for example, hit the other role player hard 65 times with the foam sword within a 2-minute period. The aggressive activity was often feverish in this condition, and in one case the session had to be prematurely terminated." (335).

Note that, in contrast to the standard Milgram setup, there was no authority figure influencing this outcome and the alternatives to aggressing (such as just playing with the objects) were obvious and readily available (335).

[152] As Bandura writes, "The overall findings from research on the different mechanisms of moral disengagement corroborate the historical chronicle of human atrocities: it requires conducive social conditions rather than monstrous people to produce heinous deeds. Given appropriate social conditions, decent, ordinary people can be led to do extraordinarily cruel things" (1990: 182). Milgram notes that "ordinary people, simply doing their jobs, and without any particular hostility on their part, can become agents in a terrible destructive process" (1974: 6) and again that "the kind of character produced in American democratic society, cannot be

Finally, throughout this book I have stressed the importance of the right kind of motivation to virtue. Here is no different. If most of us end up harming others often, but do so for altruistic or some other kind of morally admirable motives, that would be one thing. Similarly, if most of us refrain from harming because we care about what is good for others, or do not want to violate their dignity or rights, or are motivated by doing what morality requires, then those might be forms of motivation that are expected of someone who has a virtue like non-malevolence.

But, even granting that such forms of motivation for harming and refraining from harming are present in *some* cases, we have seen that they are not the only motives at work. Rather, threatened self-esteem has been found to play a significant psychological role, as we are willing in certain situations to harm others in order to maintain a positive view of ourselves. Similarly with the importance of desires to retaliate and get revenge. And again with desires concerned with not harming others in order to avoid being blamed for doing them harm, which were discussed in connection with displaced responsibility.

Many of the desires that have been mentioned in this chapter are egoistic desires. They can lead to very disturbing outcomes (as we have seen). And they are not what would be expected from a virtuous person, or at least not given how virtue concepts function for many of us and how the virtues have often been understood historically especially in the Aristotelian tradition.

To drive the point home that most of us do not possess the virtue of non-malevolence, let me present one more study, this time by Wim Meeus and Quinten Raaijmakers (1986). It is modeled after the Milgram setup, but is different enough that is provides a nice illustration of how the dangers associated with obedience to authority are not just limited to the specifics of Milgram's procedure. This time the confederate is taking a test, the participant is administering the test verbally from another room and records the answers, and the experimenter is with the participant. The participant knows that the test-taker is unemployed and that this test is very important as it must be passed for him to get a job. The participant is told that, during the course of the thirty-two-question test, he is to make certain negative and stressful remarks at set times.[153] These range from mild comments ("up to now, your test score is insufficient") to harsh ones ("if you continue like this, you will certainly fail the test," "according to the test, you are more suited for lower

counted on to insulate its citizens from brutality and inhumane treatment at the direction of malevolent authority" (189). Similarly Larsen notes at the end of his study using the basic Milgram setup that the, "sobering conclusion is that our homes and society evidently produce young people who are reluctant but nevertheless willing to act against their own conscience" (Larsen et al. 1972: 294–5). See also Helm and Morelli 1979: 330, Bandura 1999: 200, Miller 2004: 208, Webber 2006a: 656, Adams 2006: 148–9, Sreenivasan 2008: 606–7, Badhwar 2009: 263–4, and Merritt et al. 2010: 363–7.

[153] Meeus and Raaijmakers 1986: 314.

functions").[154] Participants could see a computer readout of the level of stress being experienced by the applicant, and also saw that as the test went on and the remarks were more stressful, the applicant's performance was getting worse. On top of all this, the participant knew that the applicant had been lied to ahead of time about the procedure, *and* for every stressful remark the applicant would protest in some way. At first these were mild protests, but by remark 10 the applicant "demanded that the subject stop making the remarks. He accused the experimenter of having given him false information about the nature of the experiment and withdrew his consent... After stress remarks 14 and 15, his response was one of despair."[155] Participants who raised objections were given the same four prods from the Milgram setup.

The results are hard to believe. Out of the 15 stress remarks, the median was 14.81 remarks. 91.7 percent of subjects used all 15 remarks on the applicant, and so they delivered remarks 14 and 15 *even after they had seen that the applicant had failed the test.*[156] So most participants were, in effect, willing to ruin an unemployed person's job prospects for the sake of complying with a seemingly legitimate authority.[157]

Enough, then, about whether most of us are virtuous in this area of our lives. Given this discussion, it might seem that the exact opposite is true, and that most of us are vicious when it comes to harming others. Here the vice often cited with respect to aggression is *cruelty*.[158]

Let me proceed more carefully at this point by identifying several claims in the minimum threshold of cruelty. These are claims which, in my view, reflect

---

[154] Meeus and Raaijmakers 1986: 323.

[155] Meeus and Raaijmakers 1986: 316.

[156] Meeus and Raaijmakers 1986: 317.

[157] Diffusion of responsibility seems to play an important role here too in explaining the results. In the post-experiment survey, participants on average claimed that 45 percent of the responsibility for the applicant's harm was due to the experimenter, 33 percent to the participant, and 22 percent to the applicant (Meeus and Raaijmakers 1986: 318). As Meeus and Raaijmakers write, "participants do not consider themselves primarily responsible... The subjects are extremely aloof towards the applicant. They hardly react to his protests, while their opposition to the experimenter is very slight. Both the subjects' statements and their behaviour indicate that they feel they are acting as the agent of the experimenter" (Meeus and Raaijmakers 1986: 319).

In a second study, Meeus and Raaijmakers found that when the experimenter was absent from the room or when two peers rebelled, compliance dropped significantly (36.4 percent and 15.8 percent respectively), as in the analogous versions of Milgram's experiments (Meeus and Raaijmakers 1986: 317).

[158] *Malevolence* could also be used here (Brandt 1988: 68). Gabriele Taylor (2006), following Aquinas, distinguishes cruelty from *brutality* (113–19). While there may be important conceptual differences between the two, the distinction does not affect what follows in the sense that there is no more reason to think that most of us have the vice of brutality as there is to think that most of us are cruel. The same point applies to Robert Adams's conception of *malice* as, "being against goods, and for evils, for their own sake, and not merely for the sake of other ends to which the evils may be means" (2006: 41; see also page 42). Similarly, this evidence does not support the widespread possession of *hatred* or *vindictiveness* or *ruthlessness* or *sadism*.

how that concept is ordinarily understood and are also consistent with how it has been conceived at various points in the philosophical tradition.

I will start with the behavior of a cruel person before turning to his motivation. A preliminary claim about that behavior might be stated like this:

> (1) A cruel person, when acting in character, will reliably attempt to harm others when in situations where opportunities to harm present themselves.

But this is clearly too flat-footed of a requirement. For instance, the person might regulate his aggression when the police are watching, or when the time and effort involved in harming others would be significant. Here is a better attempt:

> (1*) A cruel person, when acting in character, will reliably attempt to harm others when in situations where opportunities to harm present themselves, at least when those opportunities are not thought to involve significant inconvenience to him and he believes he will not get punished or otherwise be negatively affected by others for doing so.[159]

Suppose that at least something in the ballpark of this claim is correct. How does it match up with the evidence that has been reviewed in this chapter? Not well. As Anderson and Bushman note, "Most people do not commit extreme acts of violence even if they could do so with little chance of discovery or punishment . . . Self-image, self-standards, and sense of self-worth are used in normal self-regulation of behavior."[160]

Some of the studies reviewed in this chapter illustrate this point. While there were plenty of occasions where experimental participants did needlessly harmful things, there were other occasions where they barely aggressed at all. For instance, in the Meeus and Raaijmakers study just mentioned, there was a control condition in which participants were allowed to give as many stressful remarks as they liked. It turned out that no one gave all 15 remarks, and the median was only 6.75.[161] Similarly in the Kilham and Mann (1974) study, when participants were told that they were entirely free to choose the level of shock in the role of either the transmitter or the teacher, the mean shock level was only 3.12 (out of 30) and no one was fully obedient.[162] In the Tilker (1970) study, when the participants were mere observers but were told that they had complete responsibility for the well-being of the learner and could also both

---

[159] In this and the other requirements, I intend to exclude cases in which someone is trying to help others, but simply has been raised to have some distorted beliefs about what helping consists in, and so ends up harming them. This is not a feature of the psychological profile of a cruel person that I have in mind. Rather, a cruel person is aiming to harm others in certain ways and contexts, not help them.

[160] Anderson and Bushman 2002: 43.

[161] Meeus and Raaijmakers 1986: 317.

[162] Kilham and Mann 1974: 699.

see and hear the effects of the shocks on the learner, every single one of them interfered and tried to stop the experiment.[163] Bandura et al. (1975) found that participants who were made individually responsible for any harm done in giving electric shocks, averaged shocks of level 2 out of 10 towards the humanized group, and only increased to level 3 when responsibility was diffused.[164] In the Milgram experiment, when the participant was free to choose the shock level, the maximum level on average was just 5.50 out of 30.[165] And so on.[166]

More generally, when the various factors which foster moral disengagement are *not* present, proactive forms of aggression are rare. For instance, humanizing another person has a powerful effect on deterring aggression. As Bandura notes, "even under conditions that weaken self-deterrents, it is difficult for people to behave cruelly toward others when the potential victims are humanized or even personalized a bit."[167]

Let me shift away from the cruel person's behavior and probe his psychology a bit, starting with his moral beliefs. A cruel person is not expected to share the same moral beliefs with a non-malevolent person; rather he is going to find fewer aggressive actions to be morally forbidden than a virtuous person would. For instance, the two might differ in their view of stealing, or assault, or malicious gossiping in a number of cases.

At the very least, if they happen to share many of the same moral beliefs (which, again, I find doubtful), they would not share the same *commitment* to them. The virtuous person would have internalized those particular norms, integrating them into her ordinary psychological functioning (whether this functioning is conscious or not), and would have them serve as significant motivators for moral behavior. The cruel person, on the other hand, would not

---

[163] Tilker 1970: 99.

[164] Bandura et al. 1975: 259.

[165] Milgram 1974: 61. In fact, in the Milgram setup when the experimenter is absent (experiment 7), multiple participants, "specifically assured the experimenter that they were raising the shock level according to instruction, while, in reality, they repeatedly used the lowest shock on the board" (1974: 62). And in experiment 14, when the experimenter is the one receiving shocks and another participant is giving the instructions, "At the first protest of the shocked experimenter, every subject broke off, refusing to administer even a single shock beyond this point. There is no variation whatsoever in response. Furthermore, many subjects literally leapt to the aid of the experimenter, running into the other room to unstrap him. Subjects often expressed sympathy for the experimenter." (1974: 103). As Milgram notes, "if destructive impulses were really pressing for release, and the subject could justify his use of high shock levels in the cause of science, why did they not make the victim suffer?" (1974: 167; see also 165–8).

Also relevant is the finding by Arthur Miller that for 16 of Milgram's variations, 60 percent of participants disobeyed orders (A. Miller 2009: 23).

[166] See also the results in Larsen et al. 1972 and Prentice-Dunn and Rogers 1980.

[167] Bandura 1990: 182. For related discussion, see Bandura et al. 1975: 262, 267, 1996: 371 and Bandura 1990: 182–4, 1999: 202–3.

be expected to care significantly about these same norms, nor would they reliably motivate moral behavior on his part. Hence:

> (2) A cruel person will not have sincere moral beliefs about the moral wrongness of a wide variety of (what are considered to be) harmful actions, or if he does happen to have such beliefs, he will not care much about them and they will not play a significant motivational role in his psychology against harming others.[168]

Does this sound like an accurate description of the moral beliefs of most of us in this area of our lives? Does it sound like it reflects the research that was reviewed in earlier sections? In my opinion, the answer to these questions is—clearly not.

As a corollary of (2), I claim that:

> (2*) A cruel person is not such that his activated moral norms regularly serve as inhibitors of his aggressive behavior.

In other words, a cruel person is not expected to have a profile where the frequency of his aggressive actions decreases significantly whenever his moral beliefs are especially salient in his mind. Yet as already discussed, most of us seem to have moral commitments *against* various forms of aggression, commitments which when activated often impede such behavior (although not, by any means, preventing it in all cases).

This discussion gives rise to a third requirement on cruelty. As with the virtuous, the vicious have traditionally been thought to be single-minded in their pursuits. They do not experience significant internal conflict between, say, certain moral beliefs and their desires, and their actions which stem from their vicious character are not the product of weakness of will or internal strife. In other words:

> (3) A cruel person, when acting in character, will not first experience significant internal conflict about whether to act cruelly before in fact performing cruel actions as a result of his trait of cruelty.[169]

But recall Milgram's description of how participants in many variants of his standard setup experienced a great deal of psychological tension. In a famous passage, Milgram writes that, "I observed a mature and initially poised businessman enter the laboratory smiling and confident. Within twenty minutes he was reduced to a twitching, stuttering wreck, who was rapidly approaching

---

[168] Aristotle makes a similar claim about the intemperate person. See 1146b24, 1150a20, 1150b30, 1151a12. See also Smith 2008: 389–90.

[169] In traditional Aristotelian thinking, this would describe the incontinent person, not the vicious person. See, e.g. Aristotle 1985: 1145a15–1152a35 (especially 1150a20, 1150b30, 1151b35–1152a4), McDowell 1979: 145–6, Irwin 1996: 49–50, Hursthouse 1999: chapter four, Webber 2006b: 207, Annas 2007: 517, 2011: 67–8, 75, Taylor 2006: 5–6, and Baxley 2010: 40–1.

a point of nervous collapse."[170] Is this what we would expect from a cruel person? While this may be an extreme case, pronounced signs of conflict were, "characteristic rather than exceptional responses to the experiment."[171] Other studies also found participants aggressing but reporting elevated levels of distress.[172]

Here is a fourth and related condition. If a virtuous person does something virtuous, such as helping to pick up dropped papers, and in a way that seems to be an expression of her own character (rather than accidentally, or in a way that seems puzzling or alienating), then it is unlikely she would experience significant feelings of guilt for *that* action. Guilt would not be expected to result in this kind of case. Nor would she have acted that way because doing so would allow her to *avoid* feelings of guilt, even if this is just a partial but significant motive behind the action. Beliefs about anticipated guilt and desires to avoid such guilty feelings would also not be playing a large psychological role in a virtuous person, it seems to me.

In a parallel fashion, a vicious person who, for instance, enjoys hurting others would not be expected to feel guilty for doing so. He is doing what he wants to do, and given (2), he believes that these actions are morally okay (or at least he would not have internalized relevant moral beliefs against harming others that stand in his way). So there is a harmony between his beliefs and desires here. Similarly with respect to anticipated guilt, why would it occur to him to not harm someone in the future so as to avoid feeling guilty about doing so? Considerations about anticipated guilt as a reason to avoid harming others would not seem to be relevant to him.

Hence for the vice of cruelty, I claim that:

(4) A cruel person, when acting in character, will not regularly experience (significant) feelings of moral guilt when harming others, nor will his harming others be influenced in a significant way by avoiding anticipated guilt.[173]

But again, most of us are not like this (thankfully, I think we should say). Guilt is a significant inhibitor prior to performing aggressive actions, as mentioned in section two.[174] And guilt is often experienced after the performance of harmful actions too.

---

[170] Milgram 1963: 377. See also Miller 2004: 196, 215, 232. For discussion relevant to the possession of vice, see Webber 2006b: 199 and Krueger 2009: 130.

[171] Milgram 1963: 375.

[172] In the Meeus and Raaijmakers (1986) study, for instance, they found that participants, "intensely disliked making the stress remarks" (318).

[173] For Aristotle's similar claim about the intemperate person, see 1150a20, 1150b30.

[174] Milgram also considered guilt to be part of the explanation for diminished rates of obedience in his experiments 1 through 4 where the learner was placed successively closer to the participant (1974: 38–9).

Finally, the same remarks about guilt and the vice of cruelty apply to empathy as well:

> (5) A cruel person, when acting in character, will not regularly refrain from harming others as a result of feeling empathy for what they are thinking and feeling.[175]

This may be because a cruel person does not feel empathy for others in the first place. Or it may be because, while he experiences some degree of empathy on occasion, it ends up having no bearing on whether he harms someone or not. I do not need to decide between these options here. The point is only that for a cruel person, empathy is not expected to be a contributing factor to his refraining from harming others.

But for most of us, it is. Again, empathy serves as a significant inhibitor of harming.[176] To be fair, though, there is a complication here. As I noted in section two, there has not been enough work done to determine whether empathy typically inhibits altruistically by fostering other-regarding feelings for the person, or egoistically by fostering personal distress which can be reduced by not harming.[177] If it is the latter, then so long as a cruel person can feel empathy for another person *and* have that person's thoughts and feelings evoke personal distress in him, then he might not harm out of a motive like eliminating his distress. This motive and the resulting behavior need not conflict with what is expected of a vicious person, although his feeling empathy for the other person in the first place might be. So here I think we should await future research which can shed light on the psychological processes behind the effect of empathy on harming.

Stepping back from these various requirements, I want to stress certain parallels between the virtuous and the vicious person when it comes to aggression. Someone who is non-malevolent reliably refrains from harming others when it is morally inappropriate to do so. That person has moral norms which oppose such harming. He also has desires which are typically in harmony with those norms, so that when he does not harm another, this refraining is done from a mindset that is not conflicted. Furthermore, it is also not significantly motivated by considerations such as avoiding guilt.

Someone who is cruel, on the other hand, reliably harms others even when it is morally inappropriate to do so, provided that the harming is not overly costly in his eyes. That person does not have moral norms which oppose such harming, or if he does, he does not give them much if any weight. His desires

---

[175] Taylor 2006: 113, 119, 128–9.

[176] See section two. Milgram also noted this in relation to diminished rates of obedience in experiments 1 through 4 (1974: 36, 38).

[177] And perhaps for many people empathy inhibits in the first way in some cases and in the second way in other cases.

are in support of harming, and when he does these actions, it is not from a conflicted mindset. Whether he harms others will also not be significantly influenced by thoughts about avoiding guilt, nor by feelings of empathy for the suffering of another.

I claim that neither of these portraits best describes most actual people. Even despite how morally disturbing some of our dispositions are which can lead us to harm other people, there are a number of respects in which most of us are *not* cruel, vicious people. Of course, that is entirely compatible with a *few* people having a character which crosses over the minimum threshold for this vice, just as it is compatible with a few other people having a character that qualifies as virtuous in this area of their lives.

9.7 CONCLUSION

In this chapter, I have tried to show in a preliminary way that my model of Mixed Traits is not just limited to the domain of helping behavior but has broader applicability. The next chapter continues to support this claim by looking at lying motivation and behavior.

10

Lying

Helping and not harming other people might seem to be closely related areas of morality, and at the psychological level our thought processes in these areas appear to have many important similarities. In this chapter, I want to branch out a bit more and examine moral thought and behavior which pertains to the virtue of honesty. This virtue is notoriously broad in scope, encompassing everything from lying to cheating, promise-keeping, and stealing. In order to focus the discussion, I will only examine lying here, but in *Character and Moral Psychology* I also devote a chapter to a discussion of cheating.

In section one I first briefly mention how I will be understanding the term "lying" before reviewing some of the recent research on lying behavior. Section two turns from behavior to the motivation behind lying. By section three I begin to develop an account of what I will call Mixed Truthfulness Traits and outline some of their underlying mental state dispositions and functional properties. This should help make it clear by section four why such a character trait is neither a moral virtue like honesty nor a moral vice like dishonesty.

10.1 LYING BEHAVIOR

As I write this chapter, lying is once again dominating the news in the United States. Former US Representative Anthony Weiner has recently claimed that provocative pictures sent to six women via Facebook were the work of a hacker, and that he could not be sure that the pictures were really of him in his boxer shorts. Of course, the truth came out soon enough, leading to his eventual resignation. Clearly Weiner was lying to the public. He was making statements to the media which he knew were false—after all, he took and sent the pictures himself. Furthermore, he made those statements in order to deceive the public—he wanted them to continue to believe that he was a loyal husband who would not engage in such behavior.

This example highlights two commonly cited features of lying—first, the liar is said to be making statements which are false (by his own lights), and secondly he is doing so for the sake of deceiving others (or, perhaps, himself). As the *Oxford English Dictionary* (1989) puts it, a lie is, "a false statement made with the intent to deceive." These two features do seem to capture many cases of lying with which we are familiar, such as lying about an affair, about how good someone's cookies taste, or about how much one has accomplished on a resume. At the same time, they are not intended to serve as a strict analysis of the concept of lying.[1] Rather they only provide a rough characterization which is sufficient for my purposes.

In this section, I am interested in the empirical questions of how often people tend to lie, how serious those lies are, and towards whom they tend to be made. One way to go about answering these questions is to set up "single-shot" studies which measure lying behavior in a particular situation. For instance, Benjamin Newberry (1973) had participants take a word association test. In the experimental group, each participant met a confederate in the waiting room before the test who claimed to have already taken it and who tipped the participant off on the format and some of the answers. After the participant took the test, she was given a questionnaire in which was embedded the question, "Did you have any prior knowledge about this experiment?" While 100 percent of participants in the control group said they had no prior knowledge, 60 percent in the experimental group lied and gave the same answer.[2]

This result is striking—the majority of participants blatantly lied while taking part in research designed to advance scientific understanding. But note that it only pertains to one situation, and furthermore this is a situation which does not occur in ordinary life. Now I could proceed by examining other single-shot studies, and then try to draw inferences from all of them about lying behavior in general. This worked well in Part II for helping behavior, but the problem here is that comparatively speaking there are far fewer studies of lying behavior in laboratory or natural environments. So this strategy is not going to take me very far, at least at present.

Fortunately perhaps the leading psychologist working on lying, Bella DePaulo, has published a series of papers outlining a different approach to

---

[1] As an analysis, these two conditions are widely rejected in the philosophical literature on the definition of lying. For instance they seem to exclude bald-faced lies in which the liar does not have any hope of deceiving the target of the lie. Fortunately they do seem to capture *most* cases of lying, which is all I need here. For recent alternative approaches and relevant discussion, see Sorensen 2007, Fallis 2009, 2010, and Carson 2010: chapter one.

In addition, there is some question about whether lying requires believing something to be false, or merely not believing that it is true (see Carson 2010: 17–18, Fallis 2010: 1 n. 1). I adopt the former in what follows, but nothing hangs on this choice.

[2] Newberry 1973: 371.

measuring lying behavior.[3] She had two groups—one with undergraduate students and the other with members of the surrounding community—record all of their social interactions and their lies each day for a week. A "social interaction" was defined as lasting at least ten minutes (unless the participant told a lie, in which case that exchange would count as a social interaction even if it was shorter), and lying, "occurs any time you intentionally try to mislead someone."[4] This is consistent with how lying was understood earlier (although it does not emphasize that the liar has to believe that the statements being made are false). The forms given to participants asked them to record their responses to measures of, among other things, how intimate the interaction was, how much planning went into the lie, what their feelings were before, during, and after the lie, and how seriously they rate the lie. A number of steps were taken to try to ensure that the record-keeping was reliably maintained and was accurate. The results were fascinating.

DePaulo and her colleagues found two different trends depending on whether the lies in question were what they labeled "everyday" versus "serious." Everyday lies had a mean of 3.34 (out of 9) for the college group on the self-report measure of seriousness, and 3.08 for the community group.[5] Examples included: "Told her her muffins were the best ever," "Exaggerated how sorry I was to be late," and "Told customer it was her color." Note that seriousness here is not a reflection of the actual moral importance of these lies, but rather reflects how important the people who told them thought they were.

What did these two groups report about their actual lying behavior during one week? Here is some of the data:[6]

	College group (N = 77)	Community group (N = 70)
Average number of daily social interactions	6.6	5.8
Average number of daily lies	2	1
Lies per social interaction	0.3	0.2
Percent of people to whom at least one lie was told	38	30
Number who told zero lies	1	6

These numbers are striking—on average, members of each group ended up telling everyday lies to roughly a third of the people they interacted with during this week.

[3] See DePaulo et al. 1996, 2004, DePaulo and Bell 1996, Kashy and DePaulo 1996, DePaulo and Kashy 1998, and DePaulo 2004.
[4] DePaulo et al. 1996: 981, emphasis removed.
[5] DePaulo et al. 1996: 989.
[6] DePaulo 2004: 306. See also DePaulo et al. 1996: 984.

Now one obvious limitation of these results is that they are collected using self-reports. Clearly impression management and other distorting psychological biases could be influencing the participants. Even so, however, it is striking how high the lying statistics are *in spite of* these biases, which would be expected to lead to under—rather than over—reporting.

Another, more serious limitation is that these results are *group* averages, and so do not offer longitudinal data for each individual during the week. So it could be, for all these numbers say, that some people are lying a great deal and thereby skew the results while the majority lies very rarely.

Other data from the DePaulo studies is also worth mentioning. For instance, participants thought they were largely successful in their everyday lying (6.53 and 5.76 out of 9 for the college and community groups, respectively).[7] Very little planning tended to go into the lies (2.95 and 3.12), and participants did report feeling a moderate degree of distress:[8]

	College group (N = 77)	Community group (N = 70)
Distress before	3.56	4.09
Distress during	4.14	4.65
Distress after	4.03	4.54

Note that distress levels increased during the telling of the lie, and did not tend to diminish much on average afterwards. Finally once the week was over, participants in both groups reported that the majority of their everyday lies were not discovered (59.44 percent and 57.41 percent), and for most of their lies they would tell them again (72.75 percent and 82.10 percent).[9]

Recall that these were findings for *everyday* lies. What DePaulo and her colleagues call "serious lies," were reported much less frequently in their original self-report data set. In order to isolate these lies and study them in their own right, DePaulo ran a separate study with the same setup of a college and a community group. This time, however, the college students used a tape recorder to describe the most serious lie they had ever told, while the community participants did the same on a written form that was mailed to them, followed by both groups completing an extensive questionnaire.[10]

The mean seriousness of these lies was rated quite high, with 6.69 (out of 9) for the student group and 6.97 for the community group. Indeed, 47 percent of these lies were rated either an 8 or 9 by members of the community.[11] What were the lies about? Focusing on the community group, 23 percent concerned misdeeds such as lying on an application about being suspended for drugs, 22 percent concerned affairs, and 21 percent concerned money or a job.[12]

---

[7] DePaulo et al. 1996: 985.   [8] DePaulo et al. 1996: 989.
[9] DePaulo et al. 1996: 989.   [10] DePaulo et al. 2004: 150–1.
[11] DePaulo et al. 2004: 151.   [12] DePaulo 2004: 316–17.

Reported distress during the telling of the lie was much higher than for everyday lies (5.36 out of 9 for students, 5.05 for the community members).[13]

One way in which the difference between everyday and serious lies manifested itself in behavior, had to do with the object of those lies. Everyday lies tended to be told, not to people to whom participants felt that they were close, but rather to more distant others. For instance, DePaulo and Deborah Kashy (1998) found that for the community group, participants averaged less than one lie in every ten social interactions with their spouses and children.[14] Several factors could play a role in explaining this, such as the increased risk of detection for someone who knew the person well, or the higher value the person put on the relationship as opposed to what could be accomplished by telling a minor lie. On the other hand, serious lies were told more frequently on average to close relationship partners than to others—53 percent of the serious lies reported by the community group were to close partners, as were 72.7 percent in the student group.[15] It is not hard to see why—if the truth about an affair or other serious misdeed could damage the relationship, then the value of preserving the relationship can take on greater importance for many people than telling the truth.[16]

To summarize, the results reviewed here, if they generalize to the population at large, suggest that lying is a common fact of life for most people, with everyday lies a daily occurrence. Some lies are also thought to be more serious than others, are more distressful to tell, and are on average directed more towards close relationship partners rather than others.

10.2 LYING AND MOTIVATION

What leads us to tell these lies? What are the motives that best account for them? Perhaps there is only one basic motive for lying that can explain everything from lies about affairs to lies about how a friend's cookies taste. Or perhaps, as in the case of helping, a pluralistic theory of motivation is more promising. What does the data suggest?

It turns out that in her diary studies, DePaulo not only asked participants to record data about lying behavior, but she also had them briefly describe their motivating reasons for why the lie was told.[17] Since the results suggest the

---

[13] DePaulo et al. 2004: 159.

[14] DePaulo and Kashy 1998: 72. One striking anomaly to this trend was college students telling everyday lies to their mothers in one out of every *two* social interactions (DePaulo and Kashy 1998: 72). But perhaps that is not so surprising!

[15] DePaulo et al. 2004: 160.

[16] See DePaulo et al. 2004: 148–9 and DePaulo 2004: 317–18, 324–5.

[17] See also the brief review of different motives in Millar and Tesser 1988: 263–4.

same underlying psychological processes for both everyday and serious lies, I will focus on the data for the everyday ones. The self-reported reasons participants gave for their lies varied widely, but many of them can be grouped into two broad categories: self-oriented and other-oriented.[18]

Self-oriented reasons for lying encompass a number of distinct kinds of reasons themselves. For instance, some of these reasons have to do with material gain or the prevention of material loss.[19] Here is an actual example reported by DePaulo et al. 1996:

> "Lady on phone asked if a number was my current phone number. I said yes when it fact it isn't." Reason: "I want to make it hard for her to find me; they are after me for money."[20]

But it turns out that more widespread than these materialistic reasons for everyday lies are reasons having to do with impression management.[21] These could be reasons designed to inflate one's positive appearance. They could also include reasons having to do with protecting one's self-image from damage, for example, by avoiding appearing to others in an embarrassing or shameful light. Here is one such example:

> "I told her Ted and I still liked each other when really I don't know if he likes me at all." Reason: "Because I'm ashamed of the fact that he doesn't like me anymore."[22]

Still other kinds of self-oriented reasons for lying have been found, such as to avoid punishment or blame.[23]

Other-oriented reasons are common as well, and they closely parallel self-oriented reasons except that now the lie is done for the sake of another, rather than oneself. This could be in order to protect the other person from punishment, blame, embarrassment, shame, or material loss. Or the reason could have to do with promoting another's material gain or positive image. Here are two more actual self-reports:

> "Told her she looked well, voice sounded good when she looks less well than a few weeks ago." Reason: "Not to add worry as she undergoes chemotherapy treatments."

---

[18] See DePaulo et al. 1996: 983 and DePaulo 2004: 309–11. These categories are not intended by DePaulo to be exhaustive (1996: 983, note a, 2004: 157). For a more extensive set of categories, see DePaulo et al. 2004: 152.

[19] See also Rick and Loewenstein 2008: 645.

[20] DePaulo et al. 1996: 983.

[21] See DePaulo et al. 1996: 991, 2004: 148–9, 157 and DePaulo and Kashy 1998: 63. The opposite is true for serious lies (DePaulo et al. 2004: 157).

[22] DePaulo et al. 1996: 983.

[23] DePaulo et al. 1996: 983. See also DePaulo et al. 2004: 152. For power and achievement motives for lying, see Gillath et al. 2010.

"Lied about cost per square foot." Reason: "To make money for the company."[24]

Again, there seem to be just as many types of other-oriented reasons for lying as there are for self-oriented reasons.

Given these two broad categories, are the majority of the primary motivating reasons which participants cite for their lying self- or other-oriented? For everyday lies, DePaulo found that people more often have self-oriented reasons: 45 percent versus 26 percent of the lies for the college group, and 57 percent versus 24 percent of the lies for the community group.[25] When it comes to serious lies, one might expect the disparity to be even greater, given the subject matter of these lies that was mentioned in the previous section (affairs, misdeeds, money, jobs, etc.). This is indeed what DePaulo found: 94.4 percent self-oriented versus 5.6 percent other-oriented reasons in the community, and 85.9 percent versus 14.1 percent in the college group.[26]

Thus far other-oriented motivation for lying has been described in positive terms, as reasons which aim to either protect or promote what is thought to be good for another person. But there is another kind of "other-oriented" motivation which has a very different aim, namely hurtful motivation. Here is an example of a serious lie which can have such a hurtful motive:

"Her sister told her that her biological father was not the man who raised her."[27]

We can imagine cases where such a lie is told to protect rather than hurt her sister. But those are not the only possible cases.

It may be that all hurtful motivation is ultimately self-oriented. But that is not obvious, and here I think it is best to leave this question open. Using the categories for different types of motives that I tried to carefully develop in Part II, I propose to treat self-oriented motivation as egoistic, other-oriented motivation as altruistic, and hurtful motivation (at least provisionally) as neither egoistic nor altruistic. How often does this last category obtain? DePaulo found that of the list of serious lies that her two groups of participants reported, 4 percent of them were said to be done for a hurtful reason.[28]

I have just introduced the labels of "egoistic" and "altruistic" motives for lying. Does this research on lying therefore provide us with another reason for

[24] DePaulo et al. 1996: 983.
[25] DePaulo et al. 1996: 987. See her footnote to Table 5 for the reasons why these percentages do not equal 100.
[26] DePaulo et al. 2004: 157.
[27] DePaulo et al. 2004: 152. See also DePaulo et al. 1996: 983, note b.
[28] DePaulo et al. 2004: 163.

thinking that altruistic motivation really does exist, just as Batson's empathy-altruism hypothesis did for helping? Such a conclusion would be much too quick. This should be apparent already, as there are two important limitations to the DePaulo results.

First of all, as was the case with lying behavior, this data on lying motivation is self-report data. Trusting behavioral self-report data is one thing; trusting motivational self-report data is, in my opinion, another thing altogether. Not only could there be all kinds of biases in favor of making the reasons for lying look more altruistic than they really were, but even if a participant is accurately reporting what he *thinks* his primary reason was, that does not mean it was *in fact* his primary reason. A lie could seem to the person lying as if it was meant to protect someone else from harm, but unconsciously it could instead be motivated by, say, egoistic fear avoidance or self-rewards.[29]

But suppose I set aside this concern and trust the reasons that were given by participants in this research. Still, and this is the second limitation, these were only their *immediate* motives. As noted in chapter two, whether a motive is altruistic or not is a matter of the content of the *ultimate* motive behind the action. To see the difference this might make, consider one of the earlier examples:

"Lied about cost per square foot." Reason: "To make money for the company."

A natural suspicion is that this person ultimately cares about making money for the company so that its flourishing will in turn benefit him too, say in the form of job security or bonuses. So what started as an other-oriented reason could very well end up at bottom being egoistic.

This is not to take away from the work that DePaulo and her colleagues did, as their goal was not to investigate such questions about ultimate motivation. Rather, my only concern here is to note the limitations of the existing research on motivation for lying—nothing like Batson's careful behavioral studies designed to assess competing egoistic hypotheses have yet been carried out.

So the upshot as I see it is this. There is some initial evidence for a pluralistic theory of lying motivation, which holds that such motivation can be egoistic, altruistic, or hurtful, and in the next two sections of this chapter I will assume that such a theory is correct. At the same time, though, this assumption is only provisional, and much additional research is needed in this area.

[29] For related remarks, see Gordon and Miller 2000: 46–7.

10.3 LYING AND CHARACTER

Given the results presented in the previous two sections, I believe that a picture of character with respect to truth-telling can begin to emerge which is in line with my general account of Mixed Traits. I will not take the time to outline all the similarities here in detail, but instead will just focus on some central points before turning in section four to normative issues about whether most of us have the virtue of honesty.

If the pluralistic theory of motivation is accepted, then it appears that most of us have a wide array of different mental state dispositions any one of which, when appropriately activated, could lead to lying behavior. These dispositions include but are not limited to:

> Beliefs and desires concerned with lying in order to avoid personally feeling embarrassed.
> Beliefs and desires concerned with lying in order to avoid being shamed.
> Beliefs and desires concerned with lying in order to avoid certain material losses.
> Beliefs and desires concerned with lying in order to help another person avoid feeling embarrassed.
> Beliefs and desires concerned with lying in order to hurt another person in certain cases.

Now consider as well the dispositions which pertain, not to lying, but to telling the truth. These might be as simple as a disposition to desire to tell the truth (period), plus dispositions to form beliefs about what counts as the truth and what does not. Or a more complicated story might be needed, involving conditional desires to tell the truth if one can make a good impression, avoid financial losses, avoid embarrassment, and so forth. Let me leave these options open for my purposes in this chapter.

Take all of these mental state dispositions with respect to telling the truth and telling lies, and consider the character trait that they make up. As I will argue in the next section, it is not honesty. Nor is it dishonesty. Rather, it is a character trait for which our ordinary thought and language do not have a name. So I will call it a "Mixed Truthfulness Trait," which leads people who have the Trait to reliably tell the truth in some situations and to reliably lie in other situations.

In other words, people who possess these dispositions would be expected to exhibit truth-telling behavior that is highly *fragmented* from one situation to another. In certain situations, Smith might often tell the truth, but in others he

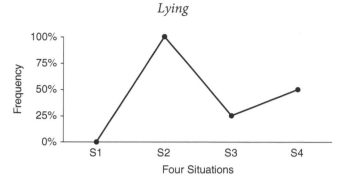

Fig. 10.1. Smith's lying profile (frequency).

might often lie. His profile for lying behavior in four situations might look like Figure 10.1. These situations have various features that activate different mental state dispositions in Smith's mind pertaining to truth-telling or lying. For instance, S2 might be a situation where a good friend asks for Smith's opinion about his (awful) cooking, whereas S1 is another situation involving giving directions to a lost driver.[30]

On this way of thinking, truth-telling and lying will be sensitive to various enhancers and inhibitors which activate specific mental state dispositions. Certain of these are obvious enough from the previous section:

Anticipated embarrassment
Anticipated shame
Anticipated material loss
Anticipated punishment
Anticipated blame

They can serve a dual role—as inhibitors for truth-telling, and as enhancers for lying. Thus in a particular situation, Smith might normally often tell the truth, but in this one instance if he is suddenly fearful that the truth might embarrass him, he could lie instead to avoid the embarrassment.

Indeed, it is plausible to think that something very much like this happened to Anthony Weiner. He knew the truth about the Facebook pictures, and recognized that if this truth came out it would result in enormous embarrassment for him (as well as shame, material losses, etc.). Thus this inhibitor on truth-telling might have worked in the following way in his mind:

---

[30] As Karen Millar and Abraham Tesser write, "people are not consistent in what they lie about, that is, a particular behavior may violate one role partner's expectations but not another's, nor do they consistently lie to the same person" (1988: 273).

Appropriate inhibitor is activated
(in this case a belief about a potentially embarrassing situation)

↓

Relevant motive is formed (in this case a motive to avoid
feeling embarrassed)
+
Beliefs about reasonable opportunities for me to not
tell the truth in this situation

↓

Activation of a Mixed Truthfulness Trait
(in this case, activation of the beliefs and desires pertaining to not
telling the truth in this situation so as to avoid embarrassing myself)

↓

Increased motivation to not tell the truth
(in this case, so long as I am still motivated to
avoid feeling embarrassment)

↓

Absent or decreased truth-telling behavior
(in this case, so long as I am still motivated to
avoid feeling embarrassment)

This psychological story about Weiner makes sense, even if it is only partial or incomplete. And note that such an outline of the inhibiting process for truth-telling closely parallels how inhibitors were said to work for helping behavior in chapter seven.

Given these various mental state dispositions, the resulting Mixed Truthfulness Trait is expected to function in ways which parallel what was said about Mixed Helping Traits. For instance, these dispositions should lead to stable behavior over time, as well as cross-situationally consistent behavior from one situation to the next where this is a matter of what is psychologically salient to the person in question. As a result, Smith's profile for lying might be stable over time as in Figure 10.2. Despite the high degree of within-person variability, such a profile indicates that this variability is itself stable. Furthermore, the changes in the frequency of his behavior in these four situations might be readily intelligible in light of which particular dispositions associated with lying and truth-telling happen to be activated.

Surely, though, not everyone possesses these mental state dispositions in exactly the same way. For instance, Kashy and DePaulo (1996) found that "Lies are [more likely] told by people who care deeply about what other people think of them. They are also told by people who are extraverted and

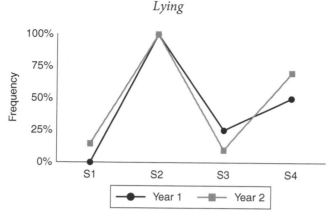

Fig. 10.2. Smith's lying profile over two years (frequency).

manipulative. Lies are less likely to be told by people who are responsible and who experience gratifying same-sex relationships."[31] Hence in the context of my framework, there is good reason to think that there are individual differences in the degree to which different people possess a Mixed Truthfulness Trait, in part as a function of broader features of their personality such as how manipulative they tend to be in general.

Such Mixed Traits are very broad, constituting a number of more specific clusters of dispositions. Yet there is no reason to deny the existence of more narrow traits—perhaps some people, for instance, are not disposed to hurt others with their lies.

These dispositions to form beliefs and desires pertaining to truth-telling and lying can also ground predictions. If I know about Smith's lying behavior with respect to how the neighbor's cookies taste (when he finds them really awful), then I can reasonably predict whether he will probably lie when asked by a friend to judge his latest (lousy) collection of artwork.

Finally, there is no reason to think that the work of these mental state dispositions will always be transparent to the person in question—motives for lying could be at work which Smith does not recognize. He may even be disappointed in himself if he knew about their existence.

Now clearly these claims above outstrip the evidence that I have reviewed in the first two sections. So once again I want to be cautious about the strength of the claims I am making here. In particular, I only want to suggest that my picture of Mixed Truthfulness Traits is compatible with the available psychological data, and that certain of my claims receive some initial support from that data.

---

[31] Kashy and DePaulo 1996: 1050. For a summary of their findings, see DePaulo 2004: 312. See also Gillath et al. 2010 on attachment security and honesty.

On the other hand, what does not seem to be supported is the widespread possession of the virtue of honesty.

10.4 LYING AND VIRTUE

As noted in the introduction to this chapter, the virtue of honesty is very broad in its scope, encompassing truth-telling behavior to be sure, but a whole lot more as well. With respect to truth-telling, the traditional virtue concept is *veracity*,[32] but I will stick with *honesty* because it is more familiar to ordinary thought. Furthermore, I am only concerned with whether there is widespread possession of the virtue of honesty with respect to truth-telling; nothing I say in this section is intended to bear on whether people are honest with respect to other matters such as cheating or stealing.[33]

A simple argument to show that most people are not honest could cite the behavioral evidence about how widespread everyday lies are, and use that data to argue that, since the virtue of honesty does not allow lying, most of us do not have such a trait. But clearly this is *too* simple of an argument—many ethicists have held that lying is morally permissible in certain cases, and hence can be compatible with being an honest person.[34] Indeed, perhaps sometimes telling a lie is even morally *obligatory*, such as in Kant's famous ax-murderer case where you can protect the life of an innocent person in your basement by lying to the ax-murderer who is searching the neighborhood for him.[35]

So instead of using this simple argument, I will proceed more carefully by taking the dispositions to form beliefs and desires pertaining to truth-telling and lying, together with the behavior that they give rise to, and comparing all of this with a few of the requirements needed in order to be honest. These requirements are part of the minimum threshold for instantiating this virtue. I will also note places where, as of now, the available empirical evidence is too limited or insufficient to draw conclusions with much data to support them.

Let me start with the behavioral evidence and the following requirement on the virtue of honesty:

---

[32] See, e.g. Baier 1990. Another candidate would be "truthfulness" (Adams 2006: 190).

[33] Thomas Carson distinguishes between honesty in a "negative sense" which involves, "a strong principled disinclination to tell lies or deceive others"), from honesty in a "positive" sense, which also involves this along with, "being candid, open, and willing to reveal information" (2010: 12, 63, chapter fourteen). He argues that only the first is a virtue in ordinary cases, whereas the second often is not a virtue (chapter fourteen). I agree, and so will focus only on this negative sense of honesty in this chapter. See also Adams 2006: 129, 190. Surprisingly, very little has been said in Western philosophy about the concept of honesty and the claim that honesty is a virtue, as Carson notes (257).

[34] For a thorough and careful discussion, see Carson 2010. See also Adams 2006: 129.

[35] Kant 1949.

(a) A person who is honest, when acting in character, will refrain from telling lies for self-oriented reasons about important moral matters when these lies are not morally justifiable.[36]

Straightforward examples of these lies include lying to a spouse about an extramarital affair or lying on one's resume in order to get a job.

Now the research by DePaulo and her colleagues on serious lies did not track such behavior longitudinally; rather they asked participants to mention the single most serious lie they have ever told. So we do not know how often serious lies were made by the participants in the student and community groups. Nevertheless, the results do provide some support for thinking that most of us do not satisfy (a). For instance, in the community group 22 percent of the serious lies had to do with affairs, and 21 percent had to do with money or jobs.[37] It is hard to imagine many of those lies being morally justifiable. Anthony Weiner's lies would belong in this discussion as well; could he do what he did and still have the virtue of honesty? Finally, most of us, I think it is fair to say, have committed at least one serious lie which would meet the description in (a) during the past year.

There is some initial evidence that many people would not consider someone who tells apparently unjustified lies about important moral matters to be trustworthy. For instance, Maureen O'Sullivan (2003) ran two studies involving recorded interviews of men, half of whom lied and half of whom told the truth about such issues as their opinion of the death penalty and whether they had stolen $50. Participants served as observers who rated the recordings using scales of, among other things, whether the man was telling the truth or lying, and how trustworthy a person he appeared to be. O'Sullivan's general finding was that "When they judged someone as lying, most observers also rated him as generally untrustworthy... Once a person has been labeled as a liar, a threshold seems to be crossed, so that his or her general trustworthiness is no longer assumed."[38]

Nevertheless, despite these various considerations, on normative grounds there may be some flexibility built into the virtue of honesty. Since the virtue can come in degrees, it could be argued that someone can be weakly honest and yet still tell such serious lies on occasion. So based on the behavioral evidence reviewed in section one, the conclusion that most people are not

---

[36] See, e.g. Aristotle 1985: 1127b3–7, Hursthouse 1999: 10, Adams 2006: 121, and Appiah 2008: 40.

[37] DePaulo 2004: 316. In general, 75 percent of serious lies among the community participants and 69 percent among the students were to cover for bad behavior (DePaulo et al. 2004: 156).

[38] O'Sullivan 2003: 1324. She also notes that, "Although more accurate observers can go in the other direction, that is, maintain the possibility that truthfulness in one situation does not necessarily generalize to trustworthiness in all situations, even they are unlikely to maintain open minds about the trustworthiness of liars" (O'Sullivan 2003: 1324).

honest may be too quick. I personally do not find this argument compelling, but I do not want to rest all of my case against the widespread possession of honesty on (a).

So here is another behavioral requirement:

> (b) A person who is honest, when acting in character, will regularly refrain from telling everyday lies for self-oriented reasons which are not morally justifiable.[39]

Examples of such lies are the more mundane ones we have already seen, such as exaggerating your accomplishments to a friend or inventing an excuse for a boss as to why you are fifteen minutes late to work.

Here DePaulo's data is more directly relevant, and suggests that many people tell these everyday lies on a daily basis. Furthermore, on average they do so without much thought, and while feeling only a moderate degree of distress. And as noted, for many of these everyday lies the participants said that they would tell them again. I suspect that our own personal experience is largely consistent with this data.

The tricky thing about (b) is that some of our self-oriented everyday lies may in fact be morally justifiable. Perhaps for the sake of a job which is the only source of income for my family, for instance, it is morally okay if I lie to my boss about why I am late, especially if being late might otherwise put me on thin ice. I am inclined to think that this would not be morally permissible, but others may disagree.

Clearly this is not the place to develop a principled account of when lies are morally justifiable.[40] But I think we can agree that, even if *some* everyday lies for self-oriented reasons are morally okay, many of the ones we actually tell are not. They may be overly manipulative, or lead the person to do something harmful to himself or others, or violate his autonomy, or significantly erode trust, or undermine healthy communication, or in some other way end up being morally objectionable.

Furthermore, there is research which suggests that what a person who lies might think is only an everyday or minor lie, could be viewed very differently by the target of the lie.[41] For instance, Anne Gordon and Arthur Miller (2000) had participants read a scenario where a person sees his or her serious partner, "leaving a restaurant with a former love interest after having stated that no such meeting would occur. The deception was furthered when this person did not acknowledge the meeting when given an opportunity to do so."[42] They

---

[39] As Aristotle says about a person who has the virtue of truthfulness, this is, "someone who is truthful both in what he says and in how he lives, when nothing about justice is at stake, simply because that is his state of character" (1127b1–2).

[40] For helpful discussion, see Carson 2010 and Fallis 2010: 17–19.

[41] See also DePaulo 2004: 319.

[42] Gordon and Miller 2000: 49.

asked participants to imagine themselves as the lie-teller, the lie-receiver, or a neutral observer and report what they were thinking in response to various measures on a questionnaire. It turned out that lie-tellers had the highest impression of themselves, were most likely to view their actions as justified, and were most likely to claim that their actions were misunderstood. In addition, many of the lie tellers used a variety of reasons for lying which tried to excuse themselves (i.e. the receiver of the lie was "overreacting") or to appeal to altruistic considerations such as protecting the other person from hurt feelings.[43] In sum, "Lie-tellers' accounts seemed to focus on minimizing the importance of the event, whereas lie-receivers' accounts seemed to focus on damage done to the relationship. Observers tended to describe the situation more evenhandedly than did lie tellers or lie receivers."[44] If these results generalize beyond this one experimental finding, then they support the claim that even when we might think an everyday lie is justified or not morally significant, we could often be mistaken.[45]

So unlike with (a), I think there already is good evidence to believe that these morally unjustified everyday lies are in fact commonplace and widespread. Surely someone who is even weakly honest would not regularly tell morally unjustified lies.

Here is a third requirement on honesty that should sound familiar:

(c) A person who is honest, when acting in character, will not allow his truth-telling and lying to be dependent, at least in many cases, on the presence of certain enhancers and inhibitors (such as fear of embarrassment, fear of shame, fear of punishment, and fear of financial loss), especially when important moral matters are at stake.[46]

Another way to put the point is that an honest person should tell the truth, when appropriate and excluding exceptional cases, regardless of whether doing so would be financially beneficial or lead to embarrassment for himself. If he does tell the truth, but often would not do so to avoid public embarrassment, then that is a good sign he is not an honest person.

The psychological evidence that we have is inconclusive here. On the one hand, the existing research gives us good reason to postulate dispositions to lie or not depending on whether embarrassment and the like would be involved. On the other hand, the studies did not track each individual discretely over time, and thereby did not see whether his or her lying behavior fluctuated with these fears. Ordinary experience leads me to think that it would, but we need

---

[43] Gordon and Miller 2000: 50

[44] Gordon and Miller 2000: 51.

[45] For ethical discussion of these issues, see Bok 1978.

[46] See, e.g. Upton 2005: 137. The above is an abbreviated formulation of the parallel claim about enhancers and inhibitors for helping from earlier chapters. A similarly more refined version could also be developed here.

the data to back that up. For now, then, it seems reasonable to claim only that preliminary evidence suggests that most people do not live up to (c).

Here is another familiar claim:

> (d) An honest person's trait of honesty will typically lead to truth-telling and lying behavior which is done at least primarily for motivating reasons that are morally admirable and deserving of moral praise, and not primarily for motivating reasons which are either morally problematic or morally neutral.[47]

Suppose that some lies are in fact morally justifiable. Suppose, in fact, that a particular person always and only tells either the truth or tells lies which are justifiable. Nothing else. Still, that certainly would not be enough to qualify the person as honest, at least on standard conceptions of the virtues. Motivation matters too.[48]

But the psychological research suggests that there is good reason to postulate some motives in this area which would not be morally admirable if they were the primary cause for behavior. Fear of embarrassment is one. A person who tells a morally justifiable lie, but does so primarily out of fear of embarrassment, is not satisfying the requirement in (d).

At the same time, the limitations of this research were noted earlier—it uses self-report data on motivation, and does not go beyond probing what the immediate rather than the ultimate motive is. Despite these limitations, I doubt that further research will undermine the existence and fairly extensive role of these less than admirable motives, and so again the balance of evidence in my opinion favors thinking that most people do not live up to (d).

Let me add just one more requirement (out of many others)[49] to this list. It may be the least controversial of them all:

> (e) A person who is honest, when acting in character, will refrain from telling lies for hurtful reasons which are not morally justifiable.

It is hard to see how a person could be honest to any extent and tell lies like *that*. And yet, it seems that most of us do precisely this. I think we can all come up with our own personal examples. But recall DePaulo found that in her participant group 4 percent of the *most* serious lies people told were ones with hurtful motivating reasons. Surely there were plenty of other, less serious

---

[47] See Foot 1972: 164–5, Audi 1991: 163, Hursthouse 1999: 11, 128, and Adams 2006: 121, 127.

[48] An anonymous referee pointed out to me that the role of morally admirable motivation may not be as central to the virtue of honesty as it is to the virtue of compassion. I am not sure about this, but regardless of whether it is central or not, it does seem to me that there has to be some motivational requirement on honesty. If a person always tells either the truth or justifiable lies, but in every case does so only as a form of impression management to look good in front of others, then it is hard to see how this complex disposition would qualify as a moral virtue.

[49] See Gordon and Miller 2000: 47, 51 for another respect in which most people are not honest with respect to truth-telling.

hurtful lies told during their lives that also could have been mentioned, although clearly more research is needed here.

At the end of the day, I personally doubt that we even need experimental evidence to convince us that most people are not honest. My ordinary experience in my personal life, my interactions with other people, and my observations of the news (i.e. politicians and celebrities) all seem to offer ample evidence against widespread honesty, and I have no reason to think that my experience is unique. If anything, the opposite can seem to be true, namely that most people today instead have the corresponding *vice* of dishonesty with respect to truth-telling (or what was traditionally called *mendacity*).[50] But I hold to a view of Mixed Truthfulness Traits. So I think that in general most people have some morally disadmirable *and* some morally admirable features of their characters when it comes to truth-telling and lying. Hence I need to address the widespread vice hypothesis as well.

Here is one consideration against that hypothesis. A vicious person, again on traditional conceptions, is someone whose vicious actions are caused by mental states that are in harmony rather than in conflict with each other. A conflict between, say, his moral judgments about what is right and actual motivation to act would signal incontinence, rather than vice. When it comes to dishonesty more specifically:

> (f) A person who is dishonest, when acting in character, will not experience distress during and after the telling of a lie, especially if they are everyday lies with little risk of being caught.

Whether this distress comes in the form of anxiety, guilt, shame, or the like, it would be in tension with the performance of the lie and so would not lead to the kind of wholehearted performance of the action that is typically expected of both the virtuous and the vicious when they act in character.[51]

But it was noted earlier that there is ample self-report data to suggest that many people *do* experience distress when they tell a lie, especially when these lies are deemed to be serious, but even for the everyday ones too. Recall that on average the college group showed a 3.56 rating (out of 9) on distress before their everyday lies, 4.14 during them, and 4.03 after.[52] For the serious lies, these numbers were much higher during the telling of the lie (5.36 out of 9 for students, 5.05 for the community members).[53]

---

[50] Baier 1990: 260.

[51] For related discussion with respect to lying, see Adler 1997: 441–2. For general discussion of the traditional Aristotelian framework of continence and incontinence, see Aristotle 1985: 1145a15–1152a35 (especially 1150a20, 1150b30, 1151b35–1152a4), McDowell 1979: 145–6, Irwin 1996: 49–50, Hursthouse 1999: chapter four, Webber 2006b: 207, Annas 2006: 517, 2011: 67–8, 75, Taylor 2006: 5–6, and Baxley 2010: 40–1.

[52] DePaulo et al. 1996: 989.

[53] DePaulo et al. 2004: 159.

These results should not be exaggerated, however. For one thing, the figures reflect group averages, rather than data on the distress levels of the particular individuals. A minority of highly distress prone individuals could be distorting the average. It could also be that higher levels of distress are being felt for only a few kinds of lies, and not for all of them.

Second and more importantly, though, the self-report scale used for measuring distress was very comfortable (1) to very uncomfortable (9). But it is not clear exactly what participants are supposed to be comfortable *about*. It is one thing to be uncomfortable about *telling a serious lie*. Evidence along these lines would support my argument. But it is another thing to be uncomfortable about *potentially getting caught lying*. A vicious person, it seems to me, could feel very comfortable about the mere telling of a serious lie, and at the same time feel very uncomfortable about the prospect of being discovered lying. If he knew for certain that he could get away with the lie, then his comfort level with telling the lie need not change but his anxiety over getting caught certainly would. So some caution is recommended about the empirical conclusions which can be drawn at the present time with respect to the requirement in (f).[54]

Here, though, is another requirement:

(g) A person who is dishonest, when acting in character, will not tell a lie primarily for an other-oriented reason which is morally justifiable and which is ultimately altruistic.

Suppose you have shared a deep personal secret with me. If that secret became public knowledge, it would cause you great psychological pain. Due to a series of events unrelated to me, it looks like the secret is going to be exposed. But at the last minute I lie on your behalf, thereby successfully diverting public attention and keeping the secret safe. Suppose, for the sake of discussion, that this lie is morally justified—perhaps the psychological harm that would have been done to you greatly outweighs the value of public knowledge of the secret. And suppose, again for the sake of discussion, that I told this lie ultimately for altruistic reasons, say because I care about you and what is good for you for its own sake. This kind of behavior does not seem to be the work of a vicious person, especially if it is not an isolated occurrence but happens on multiple occasions during my life.

Now the example is overly dramatic.[55] Yet there is the preliminary evidence reviewed in section two which suggests that we regularly tell other-oriented

[54] For a study specifically on guilt and lying, see Millar and Tesser 1988. They found that role partner's (e.g. a parent's or an employer's) expectations were important in contributing to the level of guilt a participant reported after lying (272).

[55] Here is one that is not. DePaulo and Kathy Bell (1996) ran an experiment where participants were brought to a room with several paintings, and told to pick their two favorites and their two least favorites. Afterwards, the participants were informed that they would be discussing the

lies for the immediate reason, not of benefitting ourselves, but of benefiting another person. Recall that 26 percent of the everyday lies for the college group and 24 percent for the community group were told for other-oriented reasons.[56] Furthermore, when it came to lying to others to whom they felt close, participants tended to more frequently tell other-oriented rather than self-oriented lies.[57] Even for the most serious lie of a person's life, 5.6 percent of such lies in the community and 14.1 percent in the college group were other-oriented.[58]

This all has to be taken with two grains of salt, as noted before. First, this is merely self-report data about the person's primary reason. Secondly, it does not probe down to what the ultimate reason was for lying. It could very well be that what initially seemed to be altruistic motives ended up being egoistic in some way. But that needs to be shown, and psychological egoism is by no means the default position in this discussion.

Hence in this section, I have tried to be cautious about what exactly can be concluded from the available psychological research about the extent to which there is widespread possession of either honesty or dishonesty. The overall balance of evidence suggests to me that there is no such widespread possession, and instead there is good reason to think that most people possess the mental state dispositions which make up what I call a Mixed Truthfulness Trait. Thus I tentatively claim that:

(C1) Most people have a Mixed Truthfulness Trait at some level of generality and to some degree, and not the virtue of honesty or the vice of dishonesty.

which is still compatible with saying that:

(C2) A few people have the virtue of honesty to some degree, and not a Mixed Truthfulness Trait.

---

paintings in the room with a female art student (who was typically a confederate). When the two met, the art student would claim to have done one of the paintings that, it turned out, was among the participant's favorites and one that was among the least favorites: "This is one that I did. What do you think of it?" (DePaulo 2004: 320). When it was one of the favorites, participants all said they liked it. Of course the interesting case is when the painting was one that the participant disliked. Here 16 percent flat out lied and said that they liked the painting. DePaulo and Bell also found, using some experimental methods not mentioned here, that many participants used misleading responses and engaged in what were considered to be subtle forms of lying. For more see DePaulo and Bell 1996 and DePaulo 2004: 319–23.

In general many participants were telling altruistic lies where the immediate reason was to protect the feelings of the art student. However, as before, it is not clear what the ultimate motivation was—it could be a genuine altruistic concern for what is good for the student, or an egoistic concern to, for instance, avoid getting into a conflict situation or avoid fostering dislike.

[56] DePaulo et al. 1996: 987.
[57] DePaulo and Kashy 1998: 71.
[58] DePaulo et al. 2004: 157.

10.5 CONCLUSION

Hopefully this chapter has gone some way towards showing that my model of Mixed Traits is not only applicable to helping and harming others. It also can be plausibly extended to lying as well. The same is true for other domains of moral thought and action, but those will have to be saved for another day.[59]

---

[59] See, for instance, *Character and Moral Psychology*, chapter three which is an extensive discussion of cheating behavior and cheating motivation within the context of the Mixed Trait framework.

Conclusion

Suppose it happened to be you walking in the shopping mall. You have just failed to take someone's picture, but it was through no fault of your own and you quickly forget about the incident. Now you come across a woman whose bag is leaking candy. Prior to reading this book, you would likely do nothing to help her, at least if the findings in Regan's study are representative of most of us. But if, instead, you had earlier been told that you had broken the expensive camera when trying to take a picture, then you probably would have alerted the woman about the candy.

Or suppose you were living in the 1960s and saw an advertisement for a study going on at Yale University's psychology department. You sign up, and on the day in question you are told to administer a test to a person in the next room. More specifically, you are to give increasingly severe electric shocks as punishment for wrong answers, while an authority figure watches over things and prompts you to continue if necessary. Again, if the Milgram findings are representative, then you would likely kill that innocent test-taker in a matter of minutes. But if instead the setup had been slightly different and there were two authority figures giving contradictory instructions, then you almost certainly would have stopped early on when the shocks were only mildly painful.

How would you make sense of your behavior? Would it show you that moral character is just an illusion? Or that deep down we are all really vicious people? Or that we have virtues like compassion, but they are just not activated very regularly? Or what?

As should be clear by now, my view is that experimental research by Regan, Milgram, and many other psychologists, points us in the direction of a new and unappreciated position about the empirical reality of moral character. On my Mixed Trait framework, character traits do indeed exist and are widely held. But they do not fall under the heading of either the traditional virtues or the traditional vices.

The focus of this book has been twofold: (i) to spell out the Mixed Trait view in some detail, and (ii) to review some of the empirical evidence which motivates and supports the view.

Of course there is much more that needs to be said. Hence to take the discussion further I have written a companion book to this one entitled *Character and Moral Psychology*. The main goals of that book are the following:

(a) Provide some additional discussion of the metaphysics of character dispositions and how they relate to dispositions to form beliefs and desires.

(b) Provide some additional support for the Mixed Trait framework by examining the literature in psychology on cheating motivation and behavior.

(c) Engage with the situationist approach in psychology and clarify where it is compatible and where it is incompatible with my framework.

(d) Engage with the "cognitive-affective personality system" or CAPS approach in psychology and clarify where it is compatible and where it is incompatible with my framework.

(e) Engage with the Big Five model in psychology and clarify where it is compatible and where it is incompatible with my framework.

(f) Apply my Mixed Trait Framework to certain issues in meta-ethics, and in particular develop a novel error theory about character judgments according to which most of the ones that we make on a daily basis are mistaken.

(g) Apply my Mixed Trait Framework to certain issues in normative ethical theory, and in particular engage with the situationist line of criticism advanced by Gilbert Harman and John Doris against Aristotelian versions of virtue ethics, before developing my own challenge to any position which takes the cultivation of the virtues seriously.

(h) Suggest in a preliminary way what some of the primary strategies might be for bridging the gap between our Mixed Traits and our possessing the traditional moral virtues.

I hope that together these two books will help us to understand our characters better and to appreciate the challenges and the possibilities of working towards becoming truly virtuous people.

Summary of Various Requirements for Different Virtues and Vices

(Note: The below are among the requirements in the minimal threshold for a given virtue or vice that a character trait must satisfy before it can qualify as that particular virtue or vice. It is assumed that other things are being held equal. The parenthetical reference is to the chapter where the respective requirement was first stated, but the numbering used here to the left of each requirement may not reflect the numbering in that chapter. Unless otherwise noted, the chapters are from this book and not *Character and Moral Psychology*.)

Some Requirements for the Traditional Virtue of Compassion (Chapters Two through Seven)

Behavior

(1) A person who is compassionate, when acting in character, will typically attempt to help when in moderately demanding situations relevant to helping (chapter two).

(1*) A person who is compassionate, when acting in character, will typically attempt to help when, at the very least, the need for help is obvious and the effort involved in helping is very minimal (chapter seven).

Enhancers and Inhibitors

(2) A compassionate person's trait of compassion will not be dependent on the presence of certain enhancers (such as moderate guilt, embarrassment, or good mood) in leading him to perform helpful actions, such that if these enhancers were not present, then his frequency of helping would significantly decrease in the same nominal situations (chapter two).

(3) A compassionate person's trait of compassion will not be dependent on the presence of even morally admirable enhancers (such as empathy) in leading him to perform helpful actions, if it is also the case that were these enhancers not present, then his frequency of helping would significantly decrease in the same nominal situations (chapter five).

(3*) A compassionate person's trait of compassion will not be dependent on the presence of even morally admirable enhancers (such as empathy) in leading him to perform helpful actions, if it is also the case that there are many occasions where these enhancers are not present and he does not help, even though it is true that *if* one of these enhancers were present, then his frequency of helping would significantly increase in the same nominal situations (chapter five).

(4) A compassionate person's trait of compassion will not be dependent on the absence of certain inhibitors (such as anticipated moderate embarrassment or blame, or moderately bad moods) in leading him to perform helpful actions, such that if these inhibitors were not present, then his frequency of helping would significantly increase in the same nominal situations (chapter six).

Motivation

(5) A compassionate person's trait of compassion will typically lead to helping which is done at least primarily for motivating reasons that are morally admirable and deserving of moral praise, and not primarily for motivating reasons which are either morally problematic or morally neutral (chapter two).

(5*) The virtue of compassion gives rise to compassionate motivation to help another person, and that motivation is *altruistic* motivation to help. Indeed, it is the fact that it is altruistic which grounds the moral praiseworthiness of this motivation (chapter two).

(6) A compassionate person, when acting in character, would *not* help or refrain from helping in moderately demanding situations relevant to helping, as a result of the significant causal influence of subconscious motives which he would not endorse (if he knew about them) (chapter seven).

(7) A compassionate person, when acting in character, does not regularly help from egoistic motives which are often powerful enough that, were they not present, he would not continue to reliably help, as his altruistic motives are not strong enough to motivate reliable helping by themselves (chapter two).

(8) A compassionate person, when acting in character, does not regularly help from egoistic motives which are often powerful enough that they would lead him to pursue another non-virtuous course of action besides helping, if that alternative is thought to be more conducive to the satisfaction of the egoistic motives (chapter two).

(9) A compassionate person, when acting in character, does not regularly refrain from helping from certain egoistic motives (such as the desire to avoid anticipated moderate embarrassment or blame, or the desire to relieve a moderately bad mood) which are often powerful enough that were they not present, she would reliably help in the same moderately demanding helping situations (chapter six).

(10) A compassionate person, when acting in character, does not regularly refrain from helping from certain egoistic motives (such as the desire to avoid anticipated moderate embarrassment or blame, or the desire to relieve a moderately bad mood) which are often powerful enough that they *also* lead her to pursue another non-virtuous course of action besides helping, if that alternative is thought to be more conducive to the satisfaction of those egoistic motives (chapter six).

Relation to Other Virtues

(11) The virtue of compassion requires practical wisdom (chapter seven).

Some Requirements for the Traditional Vice of Cruelty (Chapter Nine)

Behavior

(1) A cruel person, when acting in character, will reliably attempt to harm others when in situations where opportunities to harm present themselves.

(1*) A cruel person, when acting in character, will reliably attempt to harm others when in situations where opportunities to harm present themselves, at least when those opportunities are not thought to involve significant inconvenience to him and he believes he will not get punished or otherwise be negatively affected by others for doing so.

Enhancers and Inhibitors

(2) A cruel person will not have sincere moral beliefs about the moral wrongness of a wide variety of (what are considered to be) harmful actions, or if he does happen to have such beliefs, he will not care much about them and they will not play a significant motivational role in his psychology against harming others.

(2*) A cruel person is not such that his activated moral norms regularly serve as inhibitors of his aggressive behavior.

(3) A cruel person, when acting in character, will not regularly experience (significant) feelings of moral guilt when harming others, nor will his harming others be influenced in a significant way by avoiding anticipated guilt.

(4) A cruel person, when acting in character, will not regularly refrain from harming others as a result of feeling empathy for what they are thinking and feeling.

Moral Psychology

(5) A cruel person, when acting in character, will not first experience significant internal conflict about whether to act cruelly before in fact performing cruel actions as a result of his trait of cruelty.

Some Requirements for the Traditional Virtue of Honesty (Chapter Ten)

Behavior

(1) A person who is honest, when acting in character, will refrain from telling lies for self-oriented reasons about important moral matters when these lies are not morally justifiable.

(2) A person who is honest, when acting in character, will regularly refrain from telling everyday lies for self-oriented reasons which are not morally justifiable.

(3) A person who is honest, when acting in character, will refrain from telling lies for hurtful reasons which are not morally justifiable.

(4) A person who is honest, when acting in character, will regularly refrain from cheating in situations where he is a free and willing participant and the relevant rules are fair and appropriate, even if by cheating he is assured of acquiring some benefit for himself (*Character and Moral Psychology*, chapter three).

(5) A person who is honest will, when he cheats in ways that are clearly morally wrong, typically attempt to prevent the cheating from happening again and be disappointed in himself for cheating in the first place, rather than using self-deception or rationalization to avoid having to confront his cheating (*Character and Moral Psychology*, chapter three).

Enhancers and Inhibitors

(1) A person who is honest, when acting in character, will not allow his truth-telling and lying to be dependent, at least in many cases, on the presence of certain enhancers and inhibitors (such as fear of embarrassment, fear of shame, fear of punishment, and fear of financial loss), especially when important moral matters are at stake.

(2) A person who is honest, when acting in character, will not allow his honest behavior and cheating to be dependent, at least in many cases, on the presence of certain enhancers and inhibitors (such as anticipated punishment or anticipated embarrassment), especially when important moral matters are at stake (*Character and Moral Psychology*, chapter three).

(3) A person who is honest, when acting in character, will not exhibit cheating behavior which varies with whether her moral beliefs about the wrongness of cheating (when it is wrong) are salient (*Character and Moral Psychology*, chapter three).

Motivation

(4) An honest person's trait of honesty will typically lead to truth-telling and lying behavior which is done at least primarily for motivating reasons that are morally admirable and deserving of moral praise, and not primarily for motivating reasons which are either morally problematic or morally neutral.

(5) An honest person's trait of honesty will typically lead him to refrain from cheating primarily for motivating reasons that are morally admirable and deserving of moral praise, and not primarily for motivating reasons which are either morally problematic or morally neutral (*Character and Moral Psychology*, chapter three).

Some Requirements for the Traditional Vice of Dishonesty (Chapter Ten)

Behavior

(1) A dishonest person, when acting in character, would not genuinely commit himself to behaving honestly prior to a situation where (he thinks) he can cheat in a way that is completely undetectable, and do so for financial or other gain (*Character and Moral Psychology*, chapter three).

(2) A dishonest person, when acting in character, would try to maximize the benefits from cheating when he can cheat in a way that (he thinks) is completely undetectable and is beneficial overall to him (*Character and Moral Psychology*, chapter three).

Motivation

(3) A person who is dishonest, when acting in character, will not tell a lie primarily for an other-oriented reason which is morally justifiable and which is ultimately altruistic.

Moral Psychology

(4) A person who is dishonest, when acting in character, will not experience distress during and after the telling of a lie, especially if they are everyday lies with little risk of being caught.

(5) A dishonest person does not have moral beliefs to the effect that cheating is wrong in general, as well as wrong in most particular instances of what are widely considered to be acts of cheating. Or if he does happen to have such beliefs, he will not care much about them and they will not play a significant motivational role in his psychology (*Character and Moral Psychology*, chapter three).

(6) A dishonest person, when acting in character, might desire that *others* think he is honest, but he would not be strongly committed to thinking of *himself* as honest (*Character and Moral Psychology*, chapter three).

References

Adams, R. (1976). "Motive Utilitarianism." *The Journal of Philosophy* 73: 467–81.

——(2006). *A Theory of Virtue: Excellence in Being for the Good*. Oxford: Clarendon Press.

Adler, J. (1997). "Lying, Deceiving, or Falsely Implicating." *The Journal of Philosophy* 94: 435–52.

Alfano, M. (2011). "Explaining Away Intuitions about Traits: Why Virtue Ethics Seems Plausible (Even if it Isn't)." *Review of Philosophical Psychology* 2: 121–36.

Algoe, S. and J. Haidt. (2009). "Witnessing Excellence in Action: The 'Other-Praising' Emotions of Elevation, Gratitude, and Admiration." *The Journal of Positive Psychology* 4: 105–27.

Alloy, L. and L. Abramson. (1979). "Judgement of Contingency in Depressed and Nondepressed Students: Sadder but Wiser?" *Journal of Experimental Psychology: General* 108: 441–85.

Allport, G. (1931). "What is a Trait of Personality?" *Journal of Abnormal and Social Psychology* 25: 368–72.

——(1937). *Personality: A Psychological Interpretation*. New York: Holt, Rinehart, and Winston.

Alston, W. (1970). "Toward a Logical Geography of Personality: Traits and Deeper Lying Personality Characteristics," in *Mind, Science, and History*. Ed. H. Kiefer and M. Munitz. Albany: State University of New York Press, 59–92.

——(1975). "Traits, Consistency and Conceptual Alternatives for Personality Theory." *Journal for the Theory of Social Behaviour* 5: 17–48.

Amodio, D., P. Devine, and E. Harmon-Jones. (2007). "A Dynamic Model of Guilt: Implications for Motivation and Self-Regulation in the Context of Prejudice." *Psychological Science* 18: 524–30.

Andersen, S. and J. Thorpe. (2009). "An IF-THEN Theory of Personality: Significant Others and the Relational Self." *Journal of Research in Personality* 43: 163–70.

Anderson, C. (1987). "Temperature and Aggression: Effects on Quarterly, Yearly, and City Rates of Violent and Nonviolent Crime." *Journal of Personality and Social Psychology* 52: 1161–73.

Anderson, C. and B. Bushman. (1997). "External Validity of 'Trivial' Experiments: The Case of Laboratory Aggression." *Review of General Psychology* 1: 19–41.

————(2002). "Human Aggression." *Annual Review of Psychology* 53: 27–51.

Annas, J. (2007). "Virtue Ethics," in *The Oxford Handbook of Ethical Theory*. Ed. D. Copp. Oxford: Oxford University Press, 515–36.

——(2011). *Intelligent Virtue*. Oxford: Oxford University Press.

Appiah, K. (2008). *Experiments in Ethics*. Cambridge, MA: Harvard University Press.

Apsler, R. (1975). "Effects of Embarrassment on Behavior Toward Others." *Journal of Personality and Social Psychology* 32: 145–53.

Aquino, K. and D. Freeman. (2009). "Moral Identity in Business Situations: A Social-Cognitive Framework for Understanding Moral Functioning," in *Personality,*

Identity, and Character: Explorations in Moral Psychology. Cambridge: Cambridge University Press, 375–95.

——B. McFerran, and M. Laven. (2011). "Moral Identity and the Experience of Moral Elevation in Response to Acts of Uncommon Goodness." *Journal of Personality and Social Psychology* 100: 703–18.

——and A. Reed. (2002). "The Self-Importance of Moral Identity." *Journal of Personality and Social Psychology* 83: 1423–40.

Aristotle. (1985). *Nicomachean Ethics.* Trans. T. Irwin. Indianapolis: Hackett.

Athanassoulis, N. (2000). "A Response to Harman: Virtue Ethics and Character Traits." *Proceedings of the Aristotelian Society* 100: 215–21.

Audi, R. (1991). "Responsible Action and Virtuous Character." *Ethics* 101. Reprinted in *Moral Knowledge and Ethical Character.* New York: Oxford University Press, 1997, 157–73.

Babcock, M. and J. Sabini. (1990). "On Differentiating Embarrassment from Shame." *European Journal of Social Psychology* 20: 151–69.

Badhwar, N. (2009). "The Milgram Experiments, Learned Helplessness, and Character Traits." *The Journal of Ethics* 13: 257–89.

Baier, A. (1990). "Why Honesty is a Hard Virtue," in *Identity, Character, and Morality: Essays in Moral Philosophy.* Ed. O. Flanagan and A. Rorty. Cambridge, MA: MIT Press, 259–82.

Bandura, A. (1990). "Mechanisms of Moral Disengagement," in *Origins of Terrorism: Psychologies, Ideologies, States of Mind.* Ed. W. Reich. Cambridge: Cambridge University Press, 161–91.

——(1999). "Moral Disengagement in the Perpetration of Inhumanities." *Personality and Social Psychology Review* 3: 193–209.

——C. Barbaranelli, G. Caprara et al. (1996). "Mechanisms of Moral Disengagement in the Exercise of Moral Agency." *Journal of Personality and Social Psychology* 71: 364–74.

——G. Caprara, C. Barbaranelli et al. (2001). "Sociocognitive Self-Regulatory Mechanisms Governing Transgressive Behavior." *Journal of Personality and Social Psychology* 80: 125–35.

——B. Underwood, and M. Fromson. (1975). "Disinhibition of Aggression through Diffusion of Responsibility and Dehumanization of Victims." *Journal of Research in Personality* 9: 253–69.

Barden, R., J. Garber, S. Duncan et al. (1981). "Cumulative Effects of Induced Affective States in Children: Accentuation, Inoculation, and Remediation." *Journal of Personality and Social Psychology* 40: 750–60.

Bargh, J. (1989). "Conditional Automaticity: Varieties of Automatic Influence in Social Perception and Cognition," in *Unintended Thought.* Ed. J. Uleman and J. Bargh. New York: The Guilford Press, 3–51.

——(1994). "The Four Horsemen of Automaticity: Awareness, Intention, Efficiency, and Control in Social Cognition," in *Handbook in Social Cognition,* i. Ed. R. Wyer and T. Srull, 2nd edn. Hillsdale: Erlbaum, 1–40.

——and M. Ferguson. (2000). "Beyond Behaviorism: On the Automaticity of Higher Mental Processes." *Psychological Bulletin* 126: 925–45.

Bargh, J., P. Gollwitzer, A. Lee-Chai et al. (2001). "The Automated Will: Nonconscious Activation and Pursuit of Behavioral Goals." *Journal of Personality and Social Psychology* 81: 1014–27.

Barnett, M. (1987). "Empathy and Related Responses to Children," in N. Eisenberg and J. Strayer. *Empathy and its Development*. Cambridge: Cambridge University Press, 146–62.

Baron, R. (1972). "Aggression as a Function of Ambient Temperature and Prior Anger Arousal." *Journal of Personality and Social Psychology* 21: 183–9.

—— (1974). "Aggression as a Function of Victim's Pain Cues, Level of Prior Anger Arousal, and Exposure to an Aggressive Model." *Journal of Personality and Social Psychology* 29: 117–24.

—— (1997). "The Sweet Smell of . . . Helping: Effects of Pleasant Ambient Fragrance on Prosocial Behavior in Shopping Malls." *Personality and Social Psychology Bulletin* 23: 498–503.

—— and P. Bell. (1975). "Aggression and Heat: Mediating Effects of Prior Provocation and Exposure to an Aggressive Model." *Journal of Personality and Social Psychology* 31: 825–32.

—— —— (1976). "Aggression and Heat: The Influence of Ambient Temperature, Negative Affect, and a Cooling Drink on Physical Aggression." *Journal of Personality and Social Psychology* 33: 245–55.

—— and D. Richardson. (1994). *Human Aggression*, 2nd edn. New York: Plenum Press.

—— and J. Thomley. (1994). "A Whiff of Reality: Positive Affect as a Potential Mediator of the Effects of Pleasant Fragrances on Task Performance and Helping." *Environment and Behavior* 26: 766–84.

Baron-Cohen, S. (2011). *The Science of Evil: On Empathy and the Origins of Cruelty*. New York: Basic Books.

Barrett, K. (1995). "A Functionalist Approach to Shame and Guilt," in *Self-Conscious Emotions: The Psychology of Shame, Guilt, Embarrassment, and Pride*. Ed. J. Tangney and K. Fischer. New York: The Guilford Press, 25–63.

Basil, D., N. Ridgway, and M. Basil. (2006). "Guilt Appeals: The Mediating Effect of Responsibility." *Psychology & Marketing* 23: 1035–54.

Batson, C. (1987). "Prosocial Motivation: Is it Ever Truly Altruistic?" in *Advances in Experimental Social Psychology*, xx. Ed. L. Berkowitz. San Diego: Academic Press, 65–122.

—— (1991). *The Altruism Question: Toward a Social-Psychological Answer*. Hillsdale: Erlbaum.

—— (2000). "Unto Others: A Service . . . and a Disservice." *Journal of Consciousness Studies* 7: 207–10.

—— (2002). "Addressing the Altruism Question Experimentally," in *Altruism & Altruistic Love: Science, Philosophy, & Religion in Dialogue*. Ed. S. Post, L. Underwood, J. Schloss et al. Oxford: Oxford University Press, 89–105.

—— (2008). "Moral Masquerades: Experimental Exploration of the Nature of Moral Motivation." *Phenomenology and the Cognitive Sciences* 7: 51–66.

—— (2009). "These Things Called Empathy: Eight Related but Distinct Phenomena," in *The Social Neuroscience of Empathy*. Eds. J. Decety and W. Ickes. Cambridge, MA: MIT Press, 3–15.

—— (2011). *Altruism in Humans*. New York: Oxford University Press.

—— J. Batson, C. Griffitt et al. (1989). "Negative-State Relief and the Empathy-Altruism Hypothesis." *Journal of Personality and Social Psychology* 56: 922–33.

—— —— J. Slingsby et al. (1991). "Empathic Joy and the Empathy-Altruism Hypothesis." *Journal of Personality and Social Psychology* 61: 413–26.

—— —— R. Todd et al. (1995b). "Empathy and the Collective Good: Caring for One of the Others in a Social Dilemma." *Journal of Personality and Social Psychology* 68: 619–31.

—— M. Bolen, J. Cross et al. (1986). "Where is the Altruism in the Altruistic Personality?" *Journal of Personality and Social Psychology* 50: 212–20.

—— J. Chang, R. Orr et al. (2002b). "Empathy, Attitudes, and Action: Can Feeling for a Member of a Stigmatized Group Motivate One to Help the Group?" *Personality and Social Psychology Bulletin* 28: 1656–66.

—— J. Coke, F. Chard et al. (1979). "Generality of the 'Glow of Goodwill': Effects of Mood on Helping and Information Acquisition." *Social Psychology Quarterly* 42: 176–9.

—— B. Duncan, P. Ackerman et al. (1981). "Is Empathic Emotion a Source of Altruistic Motivation?" *Journal of Personality and Social Psychology* 40: 290–302.

—— J. Fultz, and P. Schoenrade. (1987). "Adults' Emotional Reactions to the Distress of Others," in N. Eisenberg and J. Strayer. *Empathy and its Development*. Cambridge: Cambridge University Press, 163–84.

—— J. Dyck, J. Brandt et al. (1988). "Five Studies Testing Two New Egoistic Alternatives to the Empathy-Altruism Hypothesis." *Journal of Personality and Social Psychology* 55: 52–77.

—— S. Early, and G. Salvarani. (1997b). "Perspective Taking: Imagining How Another Feels versus Imagining How You Would Feel." *Personality and Social Psychology Bulletin* 23: 751–8.

—— T. Klein, L. Highberger et al. (1995a). "Immorality from Empathy-Induced Altruism: When Compassion and Justice Conflict." *Journal of Personality and Social Psychology* 68: 1042–54.

—— D. Kobrynowicz, J. Dinnerstein et al. (1997a). "In a Very Different Voice: Unmasking Moral Hypocrisy." *Journal of Personality and Social Psychology* 72: 1335–48.

—— K. Sager, E. Garst et al. (1997c). "Is Empathy-Induced Helping due to Self-Other Merging?" *Journal of Personality and Social Psychology* 73: 495–509.

—— D. Lishner, A. Carpenter et al. (2003b). "'. . . As You Would Have Them Do Unto You': Does Imagining Yourself in the Other's Place Stimulate Moral Action?" *Personality and Social Psychology Bulletin* 29: 1190–201.

—— K. O'Quin, J. Fultz et al. (1983). "Influence of Self-Reported Distress and Empathy on Egoistic versus Altruistic Motivation to Help." *Journal of Personality and Social Psychology* 45: 706–18.

Batson, C., M. Polycarpou, E. Harmon-Jones et al. (1997d). "Empathy and Attitudes: Can Feeling for a Member of a Stigmatized Group Improve Feelings toward the Group?" *Journal of Personality and Social Psychology* 72: 105–18.

——and E. Thompson. (2001). "Why Don't Moral People Act Morally? Motivational Considerations." *Current Directions in Psychological Science* 10: 54–7.

——— and H. Chen. (2002a). "Moral Hypocrisy: Addressing Some Alternatives." *Journal of Personality and Social Psychology* 83: 330–9.

——— G. Seuferling et al. (1999). "Moral Hypocrisy: Appearing Moral to Oneself without Being So." *Journal of Personality and Social Psychology* 77: 525–37.

——P. van Lange, N. Ahmad et al. (2003a). "Altruism and Helping Behavior," in *The Sage Handbook of Social Psychology*. Ed. M. Hogg and J. Cooper. London: Sage Publications, 279–95.

——and J. Weeks. (1996). "Mood Effects of Unsuccessful Helping: Another Test of the Empathy-Altruism Hypothesis." *Personality and Social Psychology Bulletin* 22: 148–57.

Baumeister, R., B. Bushman, and W. Campbell. (2000). "Self-Esteem, Narcissism, and Aggression: Does Violence Result from Low Self-Esteem or from Threatened Egotism." *Current Directions in Psychological Science* 9: 26–9.

——E. Masicampo, and C. DeWall. (2009). "Prosocial Benefits of Feeling Free: Disbelief in Free Will Increases Aggression and Reduces Helpfulness." *Personality and Social Psychology Bulletin* 35: 260–8.

——L. Smart, and J. Boden. (1996). "Relation of Threatened Egotism to Violence and Aggression: The Dark Side of High Self-Esteem." *Psychological Review* 103: 5–33.

——A. Stillwell, and T. Heatherton. (1994). "Guilt: An Interpersonal Approach." *Psychological Bulletin* 115: 243–67.

——and K. Vohs. (2004). "Four Roots of Evil," in *The Social Psychology of Good and Evil*. Ed. A. Miller. New York: The Guilford Press, 85–101.

Baxley, A. (2010). *Kant's Theory of Virtue: The Value of Autocracy*. Cambridge: Cambridge University Press.

Bell, P. (1992). "In Defense of the Negative Affect Escape Model of Heat and Aggression." *Psychological Bulletin* 111: 342–6.

Bem, D. and A. Allen. (1974). "On Predicting Some of the People Some of the Time: The Search for Cross-Situational Consistencies in Behavior." *Psychological Review* 81: 506–20.

——and D. Funder. (1978). "Predicting More of the People More of the Time: Assessing the Personality of Situations." *Psychological Review* 85: 485–501.

Benson, P. (1978). "Social Feedback, Self-Esteem State, and Prosocial Behavior." *Representative Research in Social Psychology* 9: 43–56.

Berg, B. (1978). "Helping Behavior on the Gridiron: It Helps if You're Winning." *Psychological Reports* 42: 531–4.

Berkowitz, L. (1965). "Some Aspects of Observed Aggression." *Journal of Personality and Social Psychology* 2: 359–69.

——(1990). "On the Formation and Regulation of Anger and Aggression: A Cognitive-Neoassociationistic Analysis." *American Psychologist* 45: 494–503.

——(1993). *Aggression: Its Causes, Consequences, and Control*. Philadelphia: Temple University Press.

——and A. LePage. (1967). "Weapons as Aggression-Eliciting Stimuli." *Journal of Personality and Social Psychology* 7: 202–7.

Besser-Jones, L. (2008). "Social Psychology, Moral Character, and Moral Fallibility." *Philosophy and Phenomenological Research* 76: 310–32.

Bettencourt, B., A. Talley, A. Benjamin et al. (2006). "Personality and Aggressive Behavior Under Provoking and Neutral Conditions: A Meta-Analytic Review." *Psychological Bulletin* 132: 751–77.

Blasi, A. (1980). "Bridging Moral Cognition and Moral Action: A Critical Review of the Literature." *Psychological Bulletin* 88: 1–45.

——(2005). "Moral Character: A Psychological Approach," in *Character Psychology and Character Education.* Ed. D. Lapsley and F. Power. Notre Dame: University of Notre Dame Press, 67–100.

——(2009). "The Moral Functioning of Mature Adults and the Possibility of Fair Moral Reasoning," in *Personality, Identity, and Character: Explorations in Moral Psychology.* Cambridge: Cambridge University Press, 396–440.

Blevins, G. and T. Murphy. (1974). "Feeling Good and Helping: Further Phone Booth Findings." *Psychological Reports* 34: 326.

Bok, S. (1978). *Lying: Moral Choice in Public and Private Life.* New York: Random House.

Brandt, R. (1970). "Traits of Character: A Conceptual Analysis." *American Philosophical Quarterly* 7: 23–37.

——(1988). "The Structure of Virtue." *Midwest Studies in Philosophy* 13: 64–82.

Bratman, M. (1987). *Intention, Plans, and Practical Reason.* Cambridge: Harvard University Press.

Brown, R. (1986). *Social Psychology: The Second Edition.* New York: Macmillan.

Burger, J. (2009). "Replicating Milgram: Would People Still Obey Today?" *American Psychologist* 64: 1–11.

——Z. Girgis, and C. Manning. (2011). "In Their Own Words: Explaining Obedience to Authority through an Examination of Participants' Comments." *Social Psychological and Personality Science* 2: 460–6.

Bushman, B. and C. Anderson. (1998). "Methodology in the Study of Aggression: Integrating Experimental and Nonexperimental Findings," in *Human Aggression: Theories, Research, and Implications for Social Policy.* Ed. R. Geen and E. Donnerstein. San Diego: Academic Press, 23–48.

————(2001). "Is It Time to Pull the Plug on the Hostile versus Instrumental Aggression Dichotomy?" *Psychological Review* 108: 273–9.

——and R. Baumeister. (1998). "Threatened Egotism, Narcissism, Self-Esteem, and Direct and Displaced Aggression: Does Self-Love or Self-Hate Lead to Violence?" *Journal of Personality and Social Psychology* 75: 219–29.

——M. Wang, and C. Anderson. (2005). "Is the Curve Relating Temperature to Aggression Linear or Curvilinear? Assaults and Temperature in Minneapolis Reexamined." *Journal of Personality and Social Psychology* 89: 62–6.

Buss, A. (1961). *The Psychology of Aggression.* New York: Wiley.

——(1966). "Instrumentality of Aggression, Feedback, and Frustration as Determinants of Physical Aggression." *Journal of Personality and Social Psychology* 3: 153–62.

——(1989). "Personality as Traits." *American Psychologist* 44: 1378–88.

Butler, D. (1988). "Character Traits in Explanation." *Philosophy and Phenomenological Research* 49: 215–38.

Bybee, J. and Z. Quiles. (1998). "Guilt and Mental Health," in *Guilt and Children*. Ed. J. Bybee. San Diego: Academic Press, 269–91.

Cacioppo, J., R. Petty, and M. Losch. (1986). "Attributions of Responsibility for Helping and Doing Harm: Evidence for Confusion of Responsibility." *Journal of Personality and Social Psychology* 50: 100–5.

Cann, A. and J. Blackwelder. (1984). "Compliance and Mood: A Field Investigation of the Impact of Embarrassment." *The Journal of Psychology* 117: 221–6.

Caprara, G. (1987). "The Disposition-Situation Debate and Research on Aggression." *European Journal of Personality* 1: 1–16.

——C. Barbaranelli, C. Pastorelli et al. (2001). "Facing Guilt: Role of Negative Affectivity, Need for Reparation, and Fear of Punishment in Leading to Prosocial Behaviour and Aggression." *European Journal of Personality* 15: 219–37.

——and D. Cervone. (2000). *Personality: Determinants, Dynamics, and Potentials*. Cambridge: Cambridge University Press.

——and C. Pastorelli. (1989). "Toward a Reorientation of Research on Aggression." *European Journal of Personality* 3: 121–38.

Carlsmith, J. M. and A. Gross. (1969). "Some Effects of Guilt on Compliance." *Journal of Personality and Social Psychology* 11: 232–9.

Carlson, M., V. Charlin, and N. Miller. (1988). "Positive Mood and Helping Behavior: A Test of Six Hypotheses." *Journal of Personality and Social Psychology* 55: 211–29.

——A. Marcus-Newhall, and N. Miller. (1990). "Effects of Situational Aggression Cues: A Quantitative Review." *Journal of Personality and Social Psychology* 58: 622–33.

——and N. Miller. (1987). "Explanation of the Relationship between Negative Mood and Helping." *Psychological Bulletin* 102: 91–108.

Carlson, R. (1971). "Where Is the Person in Personality Research?" *Psychological Bulletin* 75: 203–19.

Carson, T. (2010). *Lying and Deception: Theory and Practice*. Oxford: Oxford University Press.

Carver, C., R. Ganellen, W. Froming et al. (1983). "Modeling: An Analysis in Terms of Category Accessibility." *Journal of Experimental Social Psychology* 19: 403–21.

Cervone, D. (1999). "Bottom-Up Explanation in Personality Psychology: The Case of Cross-Situational Coherence," in *The Coherence of Personality: Social-Cognitive Bases of Consistency, Variability, and Organization*. Ed. D. Cervone and Y. Shoda. New York: The Guilford Press, 303–41.

——and Y. Shoda. (1999). "Social-Cognitive Theories and the Coherence of Personality," in *The Coherence of Personality: Social-Cognitive Bases of Consistency, Variability, and Organization*. Ed. D. Cervone and Y. Shoda. New York: The Guilford Press, 3–33.

Chaiken, S. and Y. Trope (eds.) (1999). *Dual Process Theories in Social Psychology*. New York: Guilford Press.

Chekroun, P. and M. Brauer. (2002). "The Bystander Effect and Social Control Behavior: The Effect of the Presence of Others on People's Reactions to Norm Violations." *European Journal of Social Psychology* 32: 853–67.

Cialdini, R., D. Baumann, and D. Kenrick. (1981). "Insights from Sadness: A Three-Step Model of the Development of Altruism as Hedonism." *Developmental Review* 1: 207–23.

——S. Brown, B. Lewis et al. (1997). "Reinterpreting the Empathy-Altruism Relationship: When One into One Equals Oneness." *Journal of Personality and Social Psychology* 73: 481–94.

——B. Darby, and J. Vincent. (1973). "Transgression and Altruism: A Case for Hedonism." *Journal of Experimental Social Psychology* 9: 502–16.

——and J. Fultz. (1990). "Interpreting the Negative Mood-Helping Literature via 'Mega' Analysis: A Contrary View." *Psychological Bulletin* 107: 210–4.

——and D. Kenrick. (1976). "Altruism as Hedonism: A Social Development Perspective on the Relationship of Negative Mood State and Helping." *Journal of Personality and Social Psychology* 34: 907–14.

—— —— and D. Baumann. (1982). "Effects of Mood on Prosocial Behavior in Children and Adults," in *The Development of Prosocial Behavior*. Ed. N. Eisenberg-Berg. New York: Academic Press. 339–59.

——M. Schaller, D. Houlihan et al. (1987). "Empathy-Based Helping: Is It Selflessly or Selfishly Motivated?" *Journal of Personality and Social Psychology* 52: 749–58.

Clark, R. and L. Word. (1972). "Why Don't Bystanders Help? Because of Ambiguity?" *Journal of Personality and Social Psychology* 24: 392–400.

—— —— (1974). "Where is the Apathetic Bystander? Situational Characteristics of the Emergency." *Journal of Personality and Social Psychology* 29: 279–87.

Cohn, E. and J. Rotton. (1997). "Assault as a Function of Time and Temperature: A Moderator-Variable Time-Series Analysis." *Journal of Personality and Social Psychology* 72: 1322–34.

—— —— (2005). "The Curve Is Still Out There: A Reply to Bushman, Wang, and Anderson's (2005) 'Is the Curve Relating Temperature to Aggression Linear or Curvilinear?" *Journal of Personality and Social Psychology* 89: 67–70.

Coke, J., C. Batson, and K. McDavis. (1978). "Empathic Mediation of Helping: A Two-Stage Model." *Journal of Personality and Social Psychology* 36: 752–66.

Coplan, A. (2011). "Will the Real Empathy Please Stand Up? A Case for a Narrow Conceptualization." *The Southern Journal of Philosophy Spindel Volume* 49: 40–65.

Cronbach, L. and G. Gleser. (1953). "Assessing Similarity between Profiles." *Psychological Bulletin* 50: 456–73.

Cunningham, M. (1979). "Weather, Mood, and Helping Behavior: The Sunshine Samaritan." *Journal of Personality and Social Psychology* 37: 1947–56.

——D. Shaffer, A. Barbee et al. (1990). "Separate Processes in the Relation of Elation and Depression to Altruism: Social and Personal Concerns." *Journal of Experimental Social Psychology* 26: 13–33.

——J. Steinberg, and R. Grev. (1980). "Wanting to and Having to Help: Separate Motivations for Positive Mood and Guilt-Induced Helping." *Journal of Personality and Social Psychology* 38: 181–92.

Dancy, J. (2000). *Practical Reality*. Oxford: Oxford University Press.

Darley, J. and B. Latané. (1968). "Bystander Intervention in Emergencies: Diffusion of Responsibility." *Journal of Personality and Social Psychology* 8: 377–83.

Darley, J. and B. Latané. (1970). "Norms and Normative Behavior: Field Studies of Social Interdependence," in *Altruism and Helping Behavior: Social Psychological Studies of Some Antecedents and Consequences*. Ed. J. Macaulay and L. Berkowitz. New York: Academic Press, 83–101.

——L. Lewis, and A. Teger. (1973). "Do Groups Always Inhibit Individuals' Responses to Potential Emergencies?" *Journal of Personality and Social Psychology* 26: 395–9.

Darlington, R. and C. Macker. (1966). "Displacement of Guilt-Produced Altruistic Behavior." *Journal of Personality and Social Psychology* 4: 442–3.

Darwall, S. (1998). "Empathy, Sympathy, Care." *Philosophical Studies* 89: 261–82.

——(2011). "Being With." *The Southern Journal of Philosophy Spindel Volume* 49: 4–24.

Davis, M. (1994). *Empathy: A Social Psychological Approach*. Boulder: Westview Press.

Dawes, R., A. van de Kragt, and J. Orbell. (1990). "Cooperate for the Benefit of Us—Not Me, or My Conscience," in *Beyond Self-Interest*. Ed. J. J. Mansbridge. Chicago: University of Chicago Press, 97–110.

Day, A., S. Casey, and A. Gerace. (2010). "Interventions to Improve Empathy Awareness in Sexual and Violent Offenders: Conceptual, Empirical, and Clinical Issues." *Aggression and Violent Behavior* 15: 201–8.

Denson, T., M. Capper, M. Oaten et al. (2011). "Self-Control Training Decreases Aggression in Response to Provocation in Aggressive Individuals." *Journal of Research in Personality* 45: 252–6.

Dent, N. J. H. (1975). "Virtues and Actions." *The Philosophical Quarterly* 25: 318–35.

DePaul, M. (1999). "Character Traits, Virtues, and Vices: Are There None?" *Proceedings of the World Congress of Philosophy*. Philosophy Documentation Center. 1: 141–57.

DePaul, M. and L. Zagzebski. (2003). *Intellectual Virtue: Perspectives from Ethics and Epistemology*. Oxford: Clarendon Press.

DePaulo, B. (2004). "The Many Faces of Lies," in *The Social Psychology of Good and Evil*. Ed. A. Miller. New York: The Guilford Press, 303–26.

——M. Ansfield, S. Kirkendol et al. (2004). "Serious Lies." *Basic and Applied Social Psychology* 26: 147–67.

——and K. Bell. (1996). "Truth and Investment: Lies Are Told to Those Who Care." *Journal of Personality and Social Psychology* 71: 703–16.

——and D. Kashy. (1998). "Everyday Lies in Close and Casual Relationships." *Journal of Personality and Social Psychology* 74: 63–79.

————S. Kirkendol et al. (1996). "Lying in Everyday Life." *Journal of Personality and Social Psychology* 70: 979–95.

DeSteno, D. and P. Valdesolo. (2011). *Out of Character: Surprising Truths about the Liar, Cheat, Sinner (and Saint) Lurking in All of Us*. New York: Crown Publishing.

Diener, E. (1977). "Deindividuation: Causes and Consequences." *Social Behavior and Personality* 5: 143–55.

——J. Dineen, and K. Endresen. (1975). "Effects of Altered Responsibility, Cognitive Set, and Modeling on Physical Aggression and Deindividuation." *Journal of Personality and Social Psychology* 31: 328–37.

Dodge, K. and J. Coie. (1987). "Social Information Processing Factors in Reactive and Proactive Aggression in Children's Peer Groups." *Journal of Personality and Social Psychology* 53: 1146–58.

Donnellan, M., K. Trzesniewski, R. Robins et al. (2005). "Low Self-Esteem Is Related to Aggression, Antisocial Behavior, and Delinquency." *Psychological Science* 16: 328–35.

Donnerstein, E., M. Donnerstein, and G. Munger. (1975). "Helping Behavior as a Function of Pictorially Induced Moods." *Journal of Social Psychology* 97: 221–5.

Doris, J. (1998). "Persons, Situations, and Virtue Ethics." *Noûs* 32: 504–30.

——(2002). *Lack of Character: Personality and Moral Behavior.* Cambridge: Cambridge University Press.

——(2010). "Heated Agreement: *Lack of Character* as *Being for the Good.*" *Philosophical Studies* 148: 135–46.

Dovido, J., J. Allen, and D. Schroeder. (1990). "Specificity of Empathy-Induced Helping: Evidence of Altruistic Motivation." *Journal of Personality and Social Psychology* 59: 249–60.

——and L. Penner. (2001). "Helping and Altruism," in *Blackwell Handbook of Social Psychology: Interpersonal Processes.* Ed. G. Fletcher and M. Clark. Oxford: Blackwell, 162–95.

Driver, J. (2001). *Uneasy Virtue.* Cambridge: Cambridge University Press.

Eaton, N., S. South, and R. Krueger. (2009). "The Cognitive-Affective Processing System (CAPS) Approach to Personality and the Concept of Personality Disorder: Integrating Clinical and Social-Cognitive Research." *Journal of Research in Personality* 43: 208–17.

Eklund, M. (2011). "What Are Thick Concepts?" *Canadian Journal of Philosophy* 41: 25–49.

Edelmann, R. (1987). *The Psychology of Embarrassment.* Chichester: Wiley.

——(1990). "Embarrassment and Blushing: A Component-Process Model, Some Initial Descriptive and Cross-Cultural Data," in *Shyness and Embarrassment: Perspectives from Social Psychology.* Ed. W. Crozier. Cambridge: Cambridge University Press, 205–29.

——J. Childs, S. Harvey et al. (1984). "The Effect of Embarrassment on Helping." *The Journal of Social Psychology* 124: 253–4.

Eisenberg, N. (2000). "Emotion, Regulation, and Moral Development." *Annual Review of Psychology* 51: 665–97.

——and P. Miller. (1987a). "Empathy, Sympathy, and Altruism: Empirical and Conceptual Links," in N. Eisenberg and J. Strayer. *Empathy and its Development.* Cambridge: Cambridge University Press, 292–316.

————(1987b). "The Relation of Empathy to Prosocial and Related Behaviors." *Psychological Bulletin* 101: 91–119.

——and J. Strayer. (1987a). *Empathy and its Development.* Cambridge: Cambridge University Press.

————(1987b). "Critical Issues in the Study of Empathy," in N. Eisenberg and J. Strayer. *Empathy and its Development.* Cambridge: Cambridge University Press, 3–13.

Ellis, H. and T. Ashbrook. (1988). "Resource Allocation Model of the Effects of Depressed Mood State on Memory," in *Affect, Cognition, and Social Behavior*. Ed. J. Fiedler and J. Forgas. Göttingen: Hogrefe.

Epstein, S. (1979). "The Stability of Behavior: I. On Predicting Most of the People Much of the Time." *Journal of Personality and Social Psychology* 37: 1097–126.

Erkut, S., D. Jaquette, and E. Staub. (1981). "Moral Judgment-Situation Interactions as a Basis for Predicting Prosocial Behavior." *Journal of Personality* 49: 1–14.

Estrada-Hollenbeck, M. and T. Heatherton. (1998). "Avoiding and Alleviating Guilt through Prosocial Behavior," in *Guilt and Children*. Ed. J. Bybee. San Diego: Academic Press, 215–31.

Fallis, D. (2009). "What is Lying?" *The Journal of Philosophy* 106: 29–56.

——(2010). "Lying and Deception." *Philosophers' Imprint* 10: 1–22.

Fernandez-Dols, J., P. Aguilar, S. Campo et al. (2010). "Hypocrites or Maligned Cooperative Participants? Experimenter Induced Normative Conflict in Zero-Sum Situations." *Journal of Experimental Social Psychology* 46: 525–30.

Fischer, P., T. Greitemeyer, F. Pollozek et al. (2006). "The Unresponsive Bystander: Are Bystanders More Responsive in Dangerous Emergencies?" *European Journal of Social Psychology* 36: 267–78.

Flanagan, O. (1991). *Varieties of Moral Personality*. Cambridge, MA: Harvard University Press.

——(2009). "Moral Science? Still Metaphysical after All These Years," in *Personality, Identity, and Character: Explorations in Moral Psychology*. Ed. D. Narvaez and D. Lapsley. Cambridge: Cambridge University Press, 52–78.

Fleeson, W. (2001). "Toward a Structure-and Process-Integrated View of Personality: Traits as Density Distributions of States." *Journal of Personality and Social Psychology* 80: 1011–27.

——(2004). "Moving Personality beyond the Person-Situation Debate: The Challenge and the Opportunity of Within-Person Variability." *Current Directions in Psychological Science* 13: 83–7.

——(2007). "Situation-Based Contingencies Underlying Trait-Content Manifestation in Behavior." *Journal of Personality* 75: 825–61.

——and P. Gallagher. (2009). "The Implications of Big Five Standing for the Distribution of Trait Manifestation in Behavior: Fifteen Experience-Sampling Studies and a Meta-Analysis." *Journal of Personality and Social Psychology* 98: 1097–114.

——and E. Noftle. (2008a). "Where Does Personality Have its Influence? A Supermatrix of Consistency Concepts." *Journal of Personality* 76: 1355–85.

————(2008b). "The End of the Person-Situation Debate: An Emerging Synthesis in the Answer to the Consistency Question." *Social and Personality Psychology Compass* 2: 1667–84.

————(2009). "In Favor of the Synthetic Resolution to the Person-Situation Debate." *Journal of Research in Personality* 43: 150–4.

Foot, P. (1972). "Morality as a System of Hypothetical Imperatives." *The Philosophical Review* 81. Reprinted in *Virtues and Vices and Other Essays in Moral Philosophy*. Oxford: Clarendon Press, 2002, 157–73.

——(1978). "Virtues and Vices," in *Virtues and Vices and Other Essays in Moral Philosophy*. Oxford: Blackwell. Reprinted in *Virtue Ethics*. Ed. R. Crisp and M. Slote. Oxford: Oxford University Press, 163–177.

——(2001). *Natural Goodness*. Oxford: Clarendon Press.

Forest, D., M. Clark, J. Mills, et al. (1979). "Helping as a Function of Feeling State and Nature of the Helping Behavior." *Motivation and Emotion* 3: 161–9.

Forgas, J. (1995). "Mood and Judgment: The Affect Infusion Model (AIM)." *Psychological Bulletin* 117: 39–66.

Foss, R. and N. Crenshaw. (1978). "Risk of Embarrassment and Helping." *Social Behavior and Personality* 6: 243–5.

Fournier, M., D. Moskowitz, and D. Zuroff. (2008). "Integrating Dispositions, Signatures, and the Interpersonal Domain." *Journal of Personality and Social Psychology* 94: 531–45.

——————(2009). "The Interpersonal Signature." *Journal of Research in Personality* 43: 155–62.

Freedman, J., S. Wallington, and E. Bless. (1967). "Compliance without Pressure: The Effect of Guilt." *Journal of Personality and Social Psychology* 7: 117–24.

Freeman, D., K. Aquino, and B. McFerran. (2009). "Overcoming Beneficiary Race as an Impediment to Charitable Donations: Social Dominance Orientation, the Experience of Moral Elevation, and Donation Behavior." *Personality and Social Psychology Bulletin* 35: 72–84.

Funder, D. (1994). "Explaining Traits." *Psychological Inquiry* 5: 125–7.

——(1995). "On the Accuracy of Personality Judgment: A Realistic Approach." *Psychological Review* 102: 652–70.

——(2008). "Persons, Situations, and Person-Situation Interactions," in *Handbook of Personality: Theory and Research*, 3rd edn. Ed. O. John, R. Robins, and L. Pervin. New York: The Guilford Press, 568–80.

——(2009). "Persons, Behaviors, and Situations: An Agenda for Personality Psychology in the Postwar Era." *Journal of Research in Personality* 43: 120–6.

——and C. Colvin. (1991). "Explorations in Behavioral Consistency: Properties of Persons, Situations, and Behaviors." *Journal of Personality and Social Psychology* 60: 773–94.

Furr, R. (2009). "Profile Analysis in Person-Situation Integration." *Journal of Research in Personality* 43: 196–207.

Garcia, S., K. Weaver, G. Moskowitz et al. (2002). "Crowded Minds: The Implicit Bystander Effect." *Journal of Personality and Social Psychology* 83: 843–53.

Geen, R. (2001). *Human Aggression*, 2nd edn. Buckingham: Open University Press.

——and D. Stonner. (1973). "Context Effects in Observed Violence." *Journal of Personality and Social Psychology* 25: 145–50.

Gert, B. (2011). "The Definition of Morality." *Stanford Encyclopedia of Philosophy*, [online] <http://plato.stanford.edu/entries/morality-definition/> accessed 20 July 2012.

Gilbert, S. (1981). "Another Look at the Milgram Obedience Studies: The Role of a Graduated Series of Shocks." *Personality and Social Psychology Bulletin* 7: 690–5.

Gillath, O., A. Sesko, P. Shaver et al. (2010). "Attachment, Authenticity, and Honesty: Dispositional and Experimentally Induced Security Can Reduce Self- and Other-Deception." *Journal of Personality and Social Psychology* 98: 841–55.

Giumetti, G. and P. Markey. (2007). "Violent Video Games and Anger as Predictors of Aggression." *Journal of Research in Personality* 41: 1234–43.

Glover, J. (2001). *Humanity: A Moral History of the Twentieth Century*. New Haven: Yale University Press.

Goffman, E. (1959). *The Presentation of Self in Everyday Life*. Garden City: Doubleday.

Goldie, P. (2004). *On Personality*. London: Routledge.

Gonzales, M., J. Pederson, D. Manning et al. (1990). "Pardon my Gaffe: Effects of Sex, Status, and Consequence Severity on Accounts." *Journal of Personality and Social Psychology* 58: 610–21.

Gordon, A. and A. Miller. (2000). "Perspective Differences in the Construal of Lies: Is Deception in the Eye of the Beholder?" *Personality and Social Psychology Bulletin* 26: 46–55.

Gottlieb, J. and C. Carver. (1980). "Anticipation of Future Interaction and the Bystander Effect." *Journal of Experimental Social Psychology* 16: 253–60.

Greene, J. and J. Haidt. (2002). "How (and Where) Does Moral Judgment Work?" *Trends in Cognitive Sciences* 6: 517–23.

Grusec, J. and E. Redler. (1980). "Attribution, Reinforcement, and Altruism: A Developmental Analysis." *Developmental Psychology* 16: 525–34.

Haidt, J. (2000). "The Positive Emotion of Elevation." *Prevention and Treatment* 3: 1–5.

—— (2001). "The Emotional Dog and its Rational Tail: A Social Intuitionist Approach to Moral Judgment." *Psychological Review* 108: 814–34.

—— (2003a). "Elevation and the Positive Psychology of Morality," in *Flourishing: Positive Psychology and the Life Well-Lived*. Ed. C. Keyes and J. Haidt. Washington: American Psychological Association, 275–89.

—— (2003b). "The Emotional Dog Does Learn New Tricks: A Reply to Pizarro and Bloom (2003)." *Psychological Review* 110: 197–8.

—— and F. Bjorklund. (2008a). "Social Intuitionists Answer Six Questions about Moral Psychology," in *Moral Psychology, ii: The Cognitive Science of Morality: Intuition and Diversity*. Ed. W. Sinnott-Armstrong. Cambridge, MA: MIT Press, 191–217.

—— —— (2008b). "Social Intuitionists Reason, in Conversation," in *Moral Psychology, ii: The Cognitive Science of Morality: Intuition and Diversity*. Ed. W. Sinnott-Armstrong. Cambridge, MA: MIT Press, 241–54.

—— and C. Joseph. (2004). "Intuitive Ethics: How Innately Prepared Intuitions Generate Culturally Variable Virtues." *Daedalus* 133: 55–66.

Hampshire, S. (1953). "Dispositions." *Analysis* 14: 5–11.

Haney, C., C. Banks, and P. Zimbardo. (1973). "A Study of Prisoners and Guards in a Simulated Prison," in *Readings about the Social Animal*, 3rd edn. Ed. E. Aronson. San Francisco: Freeman, 52–67.

Harada, J. (1983). "The Effects of Positive and Negative Experiences on Helping Behavior." *Japanese Psychological Research* 25: 47–51.

Harman, G. (1999). "Moral Philosophy Meets Social Psychology: Virtue Ethics and the Fundamental Attribution Error." *Proceedings of the Aristotelian Society* 99: 315–31.

—— (2000). "The Nonexistence of Character Traits." *Proceedings of the Aristotelian Society* 100: 223–6.

—— (2003). "No Character or Personality." *Business Ethics Quarterly* 13: 87–94.

Harré, R. (1990). "Embarrassment: A Conceptual Analysis," in *Shyness and Embarrassment: Perspectives from Social Psychology*. Ed. W. Crozier. Cambridge: Cambridge University Press, 181–204.

Harris, L. and S. Fiske. (2006). "Dehumanizing the Lowest of the Low: Neuroimaging Responses to Extreme Out-Groups." *Psychological Science* 17: 847–53.

Harris, M., S. Benson, and C. Hall. (1975). "The Effects of Confession on Altruism." *The Journal of Social Psychology* 96: 187–92.

—— and G. Samerotte. (1976). "The Effects of Actual and Attempted Theft, Need, and a Previous Favor on Altruism." *The Journal of Social Psychology* 99: 193–202.

Helm, C. and M. Morelli. (1979). "Stanley Milgram and the Obedience Experiment: Authority, Legitimacy, and Human Action." *Political Theory* 7: 321–45.

Hogan, R. (1996). "A Socioanalytic Perspective on the Five-Factor Model," in *The Five-Factor Model of Personality: Theoretical Perspectives*. Ed. J. Wiggins. New York: The Guilford Press, 163–79.

—— (2009). "Much Ado about Nothing: The Person-Situation Debate." *Journal of Research in Personality* 43: 249.

—— C. DeSoto, and C. Solano. (1977). "Traits, Tests, and Personality Research." *American Psychologist* 32: 255–64.

Hosser, D., M. Windzio, and W. Greve. (2008). "Guilt and Shame as Predictors of Recidivism: A Longitudinal Study with Young Prisoners." *Criminal Justice and Behavior* 35: 138–52.

Humberstone, I. L. (1992). "Direction of Fit." *Mind* 101: 59–83.

Hurka, T. (2006). "Virtuous Act, Virtuous Dispositions." *Analysis* 66: 69–76.

Hursthouse, R. (1999). *On Virtue Ethics*. Oxford: Oxford University Press.

Irwin, T. H. (1996). "The Virtues: Theory and Common Sense in Greek Philosophy," in *How Should One Live? Essays on the Virtues*. Ed. R. Crisp. Oxford: Clarendon Press, 37–55.

Isen, A. (1987). "Positive Affect, Cognitive Processes, and Social Behavior," in *Advances in Experimental Social Psychology*. Ed. L. Berkowitz. San Diego: Academic Press. 203–54.

—— (1999). "Positive Affect," in *Handbook of Cognition and Emotion*. Ed. T. Dalgleish and M. Power. Chichester: Wiley. 521–39.

—— and P. Levin. (1972). "Effect of Feeling Good on Helping: Cookies and Kindness." *Journal of Personality and Social Psychology* 21: 384–8.

—— and B. Means. (1983). "The Influence of Positive Affect on Decision-Making Strategy." *Social Cognition* 2: 18–31.

—— T. Shalker, M. Clark et al. (1978). "Affect, Accessibility of Material in Memory, and Behavior: A Cognitive Loop?" *Journal of Personality and Social Psychology* 36: 1–12.

—— and S. Simmonds. (1978). "The Effect of Feeling Good on a Helping Task that Is Incompatible with Good Mood." *Social Psychology* 41: 346–9.

Jacobson, D. (2008). "Does Social Intuitionism Flatter Morality or Challenge It?" in *Moral Psychology, ii: The Cognitive Science of Morality: Intuition and Diversity.* Ed. W. Sinnott-Armstrong. Cambridge, MA: MIT Press, 219–32.

Jaffe, Y. and Y. Yinon. (1979). "Retaliatory Aggression in Individuals and Groups." *European Journal of Social Psychology* 9: 177–86.

Johnson, J. (1997). "Units of Analysis for the Description and Explanation of Personality," in *Handbook of Personality Psychology.* Ed. R. Hogan, J. Johnson, and S. Briggs. San Diego: Academic Press, 73–93.

—— (1999). "Persons in Situations: Distinguishing New Wine from Old Wine in New Bottles." *European Journal of Personality* 13: 443–53.

—— C. Simmons, A. Jordon et al. (2002). "Rodney King and O. J. Revisited: The Impact of Race and Defendant Empathy Induction on Judicial Decisions." *Journal of Applied Social Psychology* 32: 1208–23.

Jones, W., K. Kugler, and P. Adams. (1995). "You Always Hurt the One You Love: Guilt and Transgressions against Relationship Partners," in *Self-Conscious Emotions: The Psychology of Shame, Guilt, Embarrassment, and Pride.* Ed. J. Tangney and K. Fischer. New York: The Guilford Press, 301–21.

Kamtekar, R. (2004). "Situationism and Virtue Ethics on the Content of Our Character." *Ethics* 114: 458–91.

Kant, I. (1949). "On a Supposed Right to Lie from Altruistic Motives," in *Critique of Practical Reason and Other Writings in Moral Philosophy.* Trans. and ed. L. Beck. Chicago: University of Chicago Press, 1949, 346–50.

—— (2002). *Groundwork for the Metaphysics of Morals.* Trans. A. Zweig. Oxford: Oxford University Press.

Karakashian, L., M. Walter, A. Christopher et al. (2006). "Fear of Negative Evaluation Affects Helping Behavior: The Bystander Effect Revisited." *North American Journal of Psychology* 8: 13–32.

Kashy, D. and B. DePaulo. (1996). "Who Lies?" *Journal of Personality and Social Psychology* 70: 1037–51.

Kaufman, G. (1989). *The Psychology of Shame: Theory and Treatment of Shame-Based Syndromes.* New York: Springer.

Kenrick, D., D. Baumann, and R. Cialdini. (1979). "A Step in the Socialization of Altruism as Hedonism: Effects of Negative Mood on Children's Generosity under Public and Private Conditions." *Journal of Personality and Social Psychology* 36: 747–55.

—— and D. Funder. (1988). "Profiting from Controversy: Lessons from the Person-Situation Debate." *American Psychologist* 43: 23–34.

Kilham, W. and L. Mann. (1974). "Level of Destructive Obedience as a Function of Transmitter and Executant Roles in the Milgram Obedience Paradigm." *Journal of Personality and Social Psychology* 29: 696–702.

Kohlberg, L. (1981). *The Philosophy of Moral Development.* San Francisco: Harper and Row.

—— (1984). *The Psychology of Moral Development: The Nature and Validity of Moral Stages.* New York: Harper and Row.

Konečni, V. (1972). "Some Effects of Guilt on Compliance: A Field Replication." *Journal of Personality and Social Psychology* 23: 30–2.

Krahé, B. (2001). *The Social Psychology of Aggression.* Philadelphia: Taylor and Francis.

Krebs, D. (1975). "Empathy and Altruism." *Journal of Personality and Social Psychology* 32: 1134–46.

Kristjánsson, K. (2008). "An Aristotelian Critique of Situationism." *Philosophy* 83: 55–76.

Krueger, J. (2009). "A Componential Model of Situation Effects, Person Effects, and Situation-by-Person Interaction Effects on Social Behavior." *Journal of Research in Personality* 43: 127–36.

Kugler, K. and W. Jones. (1992). "On Conceptualizing and Assessing Guilt." *Journal of Personality and Social Psychology* 62: 318–27.

Kunda, Z. (1999). *Social Cognition: Making Sense of People.* Cambridge, MA: MIT Press.

Kupperman, J. (1991). *Character.* New York: Oxford University Press.

—— (2009). "Virtue in Virtue Ethics." *The Journal of Ethics* 13: 243–55.

Lamiell, J. (1997). "Individuals and the Differences between Them," in *Handbook of Personality Psychology.* Ed. R. Hogan, J. Johnson, and S. Briggs. San Diego: Academic Press, 117–41.

Landis, S., M. Sherman, R. Piedmont et al. (2009). "The Relation between Elevation and Self-Reported Prosocial Behavior: Incremental Validity over the Five-Factor Model of Personality." *The Journal of Positive Psychology* 4: 71–84.

Larsen, K., D. Coleman, J. Forbes et al. (1972). "Is the Subject's Personality or the Experimental Situation a Better Predictor of a Subject's Willingness to Administer Shock to a Victim?" *Journal of Personality and Social Psychology* 22: 287–95.

Latané, B. and J. Dabbs. (1977). "Social Inhibition of Helping Yourself: Bystander Response to a Cheeseburger." *Personality and Social Psychology Bulletin* 3: 575–8.

—— and J. Darley. (1968). "Group Inhibition of Bystander Intervention in Emergencies." *Journal of Personality and Social Psychology* 10: 215–21.

———— (1970). *The Unresponsive Bystander: Why Doesn't He Help?* New York: Appleton-Century-Crofts.

———— (1976). *Help in a Crisis: Bystander Response to an Emergency.* Morristown: General Learning Press.

—— and S. Nida. (1981). "Ten Years of Research on Group Size and Helping." *Psychological Bulletin* 89: 308–24.

———— and D. Wilson. (1981). "The Effects of Group Size on Helping Behavior," in *Altruism and Helping Behavior: Social, Personality, and Developmental Perspectives.* Ed. J. Rushton and R. Sorrentino. Hillsdale: Lawrence Erlbaum Publishers, 287–313.

—— and J. Rodin. (1969). "A Lady in Distress: Inhibiting Effects of Friends and Strangers on Bystander Intervention." *Journal of Experimental Social Psychology* 5: 189–202.

—— K. Williams, and S. Harkins. (1979). "Many Hands Make Light Work: The Causes and Consequences of Social Loafing." *Journal of Personality and Social Psychology* 37: 822–32.

Leising, D. and G. Müller-Plath. (2009). "Person-Situation Integration in Research on Personality Problems." *Journal of Research in Personality* 43: 218–27.

Levin, P. and A. Isen. (1975). "Further Studies on the Effect of Feeling Good on Helping." *Sociometry* 38: 141–7.

Lewis, H. B. (1971). *Shame and Guilt in Neurosis*. New York: International Universities Press.

Lewis, M. (1995). "Embarrassment: The Emotion of Self-Exposure and Evaluation," in *Self-Conscious Emotions: The Psychology of Shame, Guilt, Embarrassment, and Pride*. Ed. J. Tangney and K. Fischer. New York: The Guilford Press, 198–218.

—— (2008). "Self-Conscious Emotions: Embarrassment, Pride, Shame, and Guilt," in *Handbook of Emotions*. Ed. M. Lewis, J. Haviland-Jones, and L. Barrett. New York: The Guilford Press, 742–56.

Liljenquist, K., C. Zhong and A. Galinsky. (2010). "The Smell of Virtue: Clean Scents Promote Reciprocity and Charity." *Psychological Science* 21: 381–3.

Lindsay-Hartz, J., J. Rivera, and M. Mascolo. (1995). "Differentiating Guilt and Shame and their Effects on Motivation," in *Self-Conscious Emotions: The Psychology of Shame, Guilt, Embarrassment, and Pride*. Ed. J. Tangney and K. Fischer. New York: The Guilford Press, 274–300.

Lindsey, L. (2005). "Anticipated Guilt as Behavioral Motivation: An Examination of Appeals to Help Unknown Others through Bone Marrow Donation." *Human Communication Research* 31: 453–81.

Lord, C. (1982). "Predicting Behavioral Consistency from an Individual's Perception of Situational Similarities." *Journal of Personality and Social Psychology* 42: 1076–88.

Lukes, S. (2009). "Comment: Do People Have Character Traits," in *Philosophy of the Social Sciences: Philosophical Theory and Scientific Practice*. Ed. C. Mantzavinos. Cambridge: Cambridge University Press, 291–8.

Ma, H. (2003). "The Relation of Moral Orientation and Moral Judgment to Prosocial and Antisocial Behaviour of Chinese Adolescents." *International Journal of Psychology* 38: 101–11.

MacIntyre, A. (1984). *After Virtue*, 2nd edn. Notre Dame: University of Notre Dame Press.

Manion, J. (2002). "The Moral Relevance of Shame." *American Philosophical Quarterly* 39: 73–90.

Manley, D. and R. Wasserman. (2008). "On Linking Dispositions and Conditionals." *Mind* 117: 59–84.

Manucia, G., D. Baumann, and R. Cialdini. (1984). "Mood Influences on Helping: Direct Effects or Side Effects?" *Journal of Personality and Social Psychology* 46: 357–64.

Marcus-Newhall, A., W. Pedersen, M. Carlson et al. (2000). "Displaced Aggression Is Alive and Well: A Meta-Analytic Review." *Journal of Personality and Social Psychology* 78: 670–89.

Masters, J. and W. Furman. (1976). "Effects of Affective States on Noncontingent Outcome Expectancies and Beliefs in Internal or External Control." *Developmental Psychology* 12: 481–2.

Mathews, K. and L. Canon. (1975). "Environmental Noise Level as a Determinant of Helping Behavior." *Journal of Personality and Social Psychology* 32: 571–7.

May, J. (2011a). "Egoism, Empathy, and Self-Other Merging." *The Southern Journal of Philosophy Spindel Volume* 49: 25–39.

—— (2011b). "Relational Desires and Empirical Evidence against Psychological Egoism." *European Journal of Philosophy* 19: 39–58.

McCrae, R. (1994). "New Goals for Trait Psychology." *Psychological Inquiry* 5: 148–53.

McDowell, J. (1979). "Virtue and Reason." *The Monist* 62. Reprinted in *Virtue Ethics*. Ed. R. Crisp and M. Slote. Oxford: Oxford University Press, 1997, 141–62.

Meeus, W. and Q. Raaijmakers. (1986). "Administrative Obedience: Carrying Out Orders to Use Psychological-Administrative Violence." *European Journal of Social Psychology* 16: 311–24.

Mendoza-Denton, R., S. Park, and A. O'Connor. (2007). "Toward a Science of the Social Perceiver," in *Persons in Context: Building a Science of the Individual*. Ed. Y. Shoda, D. Cervone, and G. Downey. New York: The Guilford Press, 211–25.

Menesini, E. and M. Camodeca. (2008). "Shame and Guilt as Behaviour Regulators: Relationships with Bullying, Victimization and Prosocial Behaviour." *British Journal of Developmental Psychology* 26: 183–96.

Merritt, M., J. Doris, and G. Harman. (2010). "Character," in *The Moral Psychology Handbook*. Ed. J. Doris and the Moral Psychology Research Group. Oxford: Oxford University Press, 355–401.

Milgram, S. (1963). "Behavioral Study of Obedience." *Journal of Abnormal and Social Psychology* 67: 371–8.

——(1965). "Some Conditions of Obedience and Disobedience to Authority." *Human Relations* 18: 259–76.

——(1974). *Obedience to Authority*. New York: Harper & Row.

Millar, K. and A. Tesser. (1988). "Deceptive Behavior in Social Relationships: A Consequence of Violated Expectations." *The Journal of Psychology* 122: 263–73.

Miller, A. (2004). "What Can the Milgram Obedience Experiments Tell Us about the Holocaust? Generalizing from the Social Psychology Laboratory," in *The Social Psychology of Good and Evil*. New York: Guilford Press, 193–239.

——(2009). "Reflections on 'Replicating Milgram' (Burger, 2009)." *American Psychologist* 64: 20–7.

——B. Gillen, C. Schenker et al. (1974). "The Prediction and Perception of Obedience to Authority." *Journal of Personality* 42: 23–42.

Miller, C. (2008a). "Motivation in Agents," *Noûs* 42: 222–66.

——(2008b). "Motivational Internalism," *Philosophical Studies* 139: 233–55.

——(2009a). "Social Psychology, Mood, and Helping: Mixed Results for Virtue Ethics." *The Journal of Ethics* 13: 145–73.

——(2009b). "Empathy, Social Psychology, and Global Helping Traits." *Philosophical Studies* 142: 247–75.

——(2010a). "Guilt and Helping," in *Advances in Psychology Research*. Ed. A. Columbus. New York: Nova Science Publishers, 117–38.

——(2010b). "Character Traits, Social Psychology, and Impediments to Helping Behavior." *Journal of Ethics and Social Philosophy* 5: 1–36.

——(2011a). "Guilt, Embarrassment, and Global Character Traits Associated with Helping," in *New Waves in Ethics*. Ed. Thom Brooks. Basingstoke: Palgrave Macmillan, 150–87.

——(2011b). "Defining Empathy: Thoughts on Coplan's Approach." *The Southern Journal of Philosophy Spindel Volume* 49: 66–72.

Miller, C. (2011c). "An Overview of Contemporary Meta-ethics and Normative Theory," *The Continuum Companion to Ethics*. Ed. C. Miller. London: Continuum Press, xiv–lii.

—— (2014). *Character and Moral Psychology*. Oxford: Oxford University Press.

Miller, D. and C. McFarland. (1991). "When Social Comparison Goes Awry: The Case of Pluralistic Ignorance," in *Social Comparison: Contemporary Theory and Research*. Hillsdale: Lawrence Erlbaum, 287–313.

Miller, N. and M. Carlson. (1990). "Valid Theory-Testing Meta-Analyses Further Question the Negative State Relief Model of Helping." *Psychological Bulletin* 107: 215–25.

Miller, P. and N. Eisenberg. (1988). "The Relation of Empathy to Aggressive and Externalizing/Antisocial Behavior." *Psychological Bulletin* 103: 324–44.

Miller, R. (1995). "Embarrassment and Social Behavior," in *Self-Conscious Emotions: The Psychology of Shame, Guilt, Embarrassment, and Pride*. Ed. J. Tangney and K. Fischer. New York: The Guilford Press, 322–39.

—— (1996). *Embarrassment: Poise and Peril in Everyday Life*. New York: The Guilford Press.

—— (2007). "Is Embarrassment a Blessing or a Curse?" in *The Self-Conscious Emotions: Theory and Research*. Ed. J. Tracy, R. Robins, and J. Tangney. New York: The Guilford Press, 245–62.

Mischel, W. (1968). *Personality and Assessment*. New York: Wiley.

—— (1973). "Toward a Cognitive Social Learning Reconceptualization of Personality." *Psychological Review* 80: 252–83.

—— (1984). "Convergences and Challenges in the Search for Consistency." *American Psychologist* 39: 351–64.

—— (1999a). "Implications of Person-Situation Interaction: Getting Over the Field's Borderline Personality Disorder." *European Journal of Personality* 13: 455–61.

—— (1999b). "Personality Coherence and Dispositions in a Cognitive-Affective Personality System (CAPS) Approach," in *The Coherence of Personality: Social-Cognitive Bases of Consistency, Variability, and Organization*. Ed. D. Cervone and Y. Shoda. New York: The Guilford Press, 37–60.

—— (2004). "Toward an Integrative Science of the Person." *Annual Review of Psychology* 55: 1–22.

—— (2007). "Toward a Science of the Individual: Past, Present, Future?" in *Persons in Context: Building a Science of the Individual*. Ed. Y. Shoda, D. Cervone, and G. Downey. New York: The Guilford Press, 263–77.

—— (2009). "From *Personality and Assessment* (1968) to Personality Science, 2009." *Journal of Research in Personality* 43: 282–90.

—— B. Coates, and A. Raskoff. (1968). "Effects of Success and Failure on Self-Gratification." *Journal of Personality and Social Psychology* 10: 381–90.

—— and H. Mischel. (1976). "A Cognitive Social-Learning Approach to Morality and Self-Regulation," in *Moral Development and Behavior: Theory, Research, and Social Issues*. Ed. T. Lickona. New York: Holt, Rinehart, and Winston, 84–107.

—— and P. K. Peake. (1982). "Beyond Déjà vu in the Search for Cross-Situational Consistency." *Psychological Review* 89: 730–55.

——and Y. Shoda. (1995). "A Cognitive-Affective System Theory of Personality: Reconceptualizing Situations, Dispositions, Dynamics, and Invariance in Personality Structure." *Psychological Review* 102: 246–68.

————(1998). "Reconciling Processing Dynamics and Personality Dispositions." *Annual Review of Psychology* 49: 229–58.

————(2008). "Toward a Unified Theory of Personality: Integrating Dispositions and Processing Dynamics within the Cognitive-Affective Processing System," in *Handbook of Personality: Theory and Research*, 3rd edn. Ed. O. John, R. Robins, and L. Pervin. New York: The Guilford Press, 208–41.

————and R. Mendoza-Denton. (2002). "Situation-Behavior Profiles as a Locus of Consistency in Personality." *Current Directions in Psychological Science* 11: 50–4.

Mixon, D. (1972). "Instead of Deception." *Journal of the Theory of Social Behavior* 2: 145–77.

Moody-Adams, M. (1990). "On the Old Saw that Character is Destiny," in *Identity, Character, and Morality: Essays in Moral Psychology*. Ed. O. Flanagan and A. O. Rorty. Cambridge, MA: MIT Press, 111–31.

Moore, B., B. Underwood, and D. Rosenhan. (1973). "Affect and Altruism." *Developmental Psychology* 8: 99–104.

Mumford, S. (1998). *Dispositions*. Oxford: Oxford University Press.

Narvaez, D. (2008). "The Social Intuitionist Model: Some Counter-Intuitions," in *Moral Psychology ii: The Cognitive Science of Morality: Intuition and Diversity*. Ed. W. Sinnott-Armstrong. Cambridge, MA: MIT Press, 233–40.

——D. Lapsley, S. Hagele et al. (2006). "Moral Chronicity and Social Information Processing: Tests of a Social Cognitive Approach to the Moral Personality." *Journal of Research in Personality* 40: 966–85.

Nasby, W. and R. Yando (1982). "Selective Encoding and Retrieval of Affectively Valent Information." *Journal of Personality and Social Psychology* 43: 1244–55.

Newberry, B. (1973). "Truth Telling in Subjects with Information about Experiments: Who Is Being Deceived?" *Journal of Personality and Social Psychology* 25: 369–74.

Newman, L. and J. Uleman. (1989). "Spontaneous Trait Inference," in *Unintended Thought*. Ed. J. Uleman and J. Bargh. New York: Guilford, 155–88.

O'Malley, M. and L. Andrews. (1983). "The Effect of Mood and Incentives on Helping: Are There Some Things Money Can't Buy?" *Motivation and Emotion* 7: 179–89.

Orom, H. and D. Cervone. (2009). "Personality Dynamics, Meaning, and Idiosyncrasy: Identifying Cross-Situational Coherence by Assessing Personality Architecture." *Journal of Research in Personality* 43: 228–40.

O'Sullivan, M. (2003). "The Fundamental Attribution Error in Detecting Deception: The Boy-Who-Cried-Wolf Effect." *Personality and Social Psychology Bulletin* 29: 1316–27.

Packer, D. (2008). "Identifying Systematic Disobedience in Milgram's Obedience Experiments: A Meta-Analytic Review." *Perspectives on Psychological Science* 3: 301–4.

Pedersen, W., C. Gonzales, and N. Miller. (2000). "The Moderating Effect of Trivial Triggering Provocation on Displaced Aggression." *Journal of Personality and Social Psychology* 78: 913–27.

Penner, L., J. Dovidio, J. Piliavin et al. (2005). "Prosocial Behavior: Multilevel Perspectives." *Annual Review of Psychology* 56: 365–92.

——H. Hawkins, M. Dertke et al. (1973). "Obedience as a Function of Experimenter Competence." *Memory & Cognition* 1: 241–5.

Petty, R., K. Williams, S. Harkins et al. (1977a). "Social Inhibition of Helping Yourself: Bystander Response to a Cheeseburger." *Personality and Social Psychology Bulletin* 3: 575–8.

——S. Harkins, K. Williams et al. (1977b). "The Effects of Group Size on Cognitive Effort and Evaluation." *Personality and Social Psychology Bulletin* 3: 579–82.

Piliavin, I., J. Rodin, and J. Piliavin. (1969). "Good Samaritanism: An Underground Phenomenon." *Journal of Personality and Social Psychology* 13: 289–99.

Pizarro, D. and P. Bloom. (2003). "The Intelligence of the Moral Intuitions: Comment on Haidt (2001)." *Psychological Review* 110: 193–6.

Pollard, B. (2003). "Can Virtuous Action Be both Habitual and Rational?" *Ethical Theory and Moral Practice* 6: 411–25.

Pomazal, R. and J. Jaccard. (1976). "An Informational Approach to Altruistic Behavior." *Journal of Personality and Social Psychology* 33: 317–26.

Prentice, D. and D. Miller. (1996). "Pluralistic Ignorance and the Perpetuation of Social Norms by Unwitting Actors," in *Advances in Experimental Social Psychology*, xxviii. Ed. M. Zanna. San Diego: Academic Press.

Prentice-Dunn, S. and R. Rogers. (1980). "Effects of Deindividuating Situational Cues and Aggressive Models on Subjective Deindividuation and Aggression." *Journal of Personality and Social Psychology* 39: 104–13.

Prinz, J. (2009). "The Normativity Challenge: Cultural Psychology Provides the Real Threat to Virtue Ethics." *The Journal of Ethics* 13: 117–44.

Purshouse, L. (2001). "Embarrassment: A Philosophical Analysis." *Philosophy* 76: 515–40.

Quiles, Z. and J. Bybee. (1997). "Chronic and Predispositional Guilt: Relations to Mental Health, Prosocial Behavior, and Religiosity." *Journal of Personality Assessment* 69: 104–26.

Rawls, J. (1971). *A Theory of Justice*. Cambridge, MA: Harvard University Press.

Regan, D., M. Williams, and S. Sparling. (1972). "Voluntary Expiation of Guilt: A Field Experiment." *Journal of Personality and Social Psychology* 24: 42–5.

Reisenzein, R. (1986). "A Structural Equation Analysis of Weiner's Attribution-Affect Model of Helping Behavior." *Journal of Personality and Social Psychology* 50: 1123–33.

Rest, J. (1986). *Moral Development: Advances in Research and Theory*. New York: Praeger.

Reynolds, S. and T. Ceranic. (2007). "The Effects of Moral Judgment and Moral Identity on Moral Behavior: An Empirical Examination of the Moral Individual." *Journal of Applied Psychology* 92: 1610–24.

Rick, S. and G. Loewenstein. (2008). "Commentaries and Rejoinder to 'The Dishonesty of Honest People.'" *Journal of Marketing Research* 45: 645–53.

Rigoni, D., S. Kühn, G. Sartori et al. (2011). "Inducing Disbelief in Free Will Alters Brain Correlates of Preconscious Motor Preparation: The Brain Minds whether We Believe in Free Will or Not." *Psychological Science* 22: 613–18.

Roberts, B. (2009). "Back to the Future: *Personality and Assessment* and Personality Development." *Journal of Research in Personality* 43: 137–45.

Roberts, R. (2003). *Emotions: An Essay in Aid of Moral Psychology*. Cambridge: Cambridge University Press.

Robinson, M. and B. Wilkowski. (2010). "Personality Processes in Anger and Reactive Aggression: An Introduction." *Journal of Personality* 78: 1–7.

Rogers, M., N. Miller, F. Mayer et al. (1982). "Personal Responsibility and Salience of the Request for Help: Determinants of the Relations between Negative Affect and Helping Behavior." *Journal of Personality and Social Psychology* 43: 956–70.

Rosenhan, D., P. Salovey, and K. Hargis. (1981). "The Joys of Helping: Focus of Attention Mediates the Impact of Positive Affect on Helping." *Journal of Personality and Social Psychology* 40: 899–905.

——B. Underwood, and B. Moore. (1974). "Affect Moderates Self-Gratification and Altruism." *Journal of Personality and Social Psychology* 30: 546–52.

Rosenthal, R. and L. Jacobson. (1968). *Pygmalion in the Classroom*. New York: Holt, Rinehart, and Winston.

Ross, A. and J. Braband. (1973). "Effect of Increased Responsibility on Bystander Intervention: II. The Cue Value of a Blind Person." *Journal of Personality and Social Psychology* 25: 254–8.

Ross, L. and R. Nisbett. (1991). *The Person and the Situation: Perspectives of Social Psychology*. New York: McGraw-Hill.

Russell, D. (2009). *Practical Intelligence and the Virtues*. Oxford: Clarendon Press.

Rutkowski, G., C. Gruder, and D. Romer. (1983). "Group Cohesiveness, Social Norms, and Bystander Intervention." *Journal of Personality and Social Psychology* 44: 545–52.

Sabini, J. and M. Silver. (1997). "In Defense of Shame: Shame in the Context of Guilt and Embarrassment." *Journal for the Theory of Social Behaviour* 27: 1–15.

————(2005). "Lack of Character? Situationism Critiqued." *Ethics* 115: 535–62.

Salovey, P., J. Mayer, and D. Rosenhan. (1991). "Mood as a Motivator of Helping and Helping as a Regulator of Mood," in *Prosocial Behavior*. Ed. M. Clark. Newbury Park: Sage, 215–37.

——and D. Rosenhan. (1989). "Mood States and Prosocial Behavior," in *Handbook of Social Psychophysiology*. Ed. H. Wagner and A. Manstead. Chichester: Wiley, 371–91.

Schaller, M. and R. Cialdini. (1988). "The Economics of Empathic Helping: Support for a Mood Management Motive." *Journal of Experimental Social Psychology* 24: 163–81.

————(1990). "Happiness, Sadness, and Helping: A Motivational Integration," in *Handbook of Motivation and Cognition*. Ed. E. Higgins and R. Sorrentino. New York: The Guilford Press, 265–96.

Schellenberg, J. and G. Blevins. (1973). "Feeling Good and Helping: How Quickly Does the Smile of Dame Fortune Fade?" *Psychological Reports* 33: 72–4.

Schnall, S., J. Roper, and D. Fessler. (2010). "Elevation Leads to Altruistic Behavior." *Psychological Science* 21: 315–20.

Schroeder, D., J. Dovidio, M. Sibicky et al. (1988). "Empathic Concern and Helping Behavior: Egoism or Altruism?" *Journal of Experimental Social Psychology* 24: 333–53.

Schueler, G. F. (1991). "Pro-Attitudes and Direction of Fit." *Mind* 100: 277–81.

——(1995). *Desire: Its Role in Practical Reason and the Explanation of Action.* Cambridge, MA: MIT Press.

Schwarz, N. (1990). "Feelings as Information: Information and Motivational Functions of Affective States," in *Handbook of Motivation and Cognition.* Ed. E. Higgins and R. Sorrentino. New York: The Guilford Press, 527–61.

Schwartz, S. (1970). "Elicitation of Moral Obligation and Self-Sacrificing Behavior: An Experimental Study of Volunteering to Be a Bone Marrow Donor." *Journal of Personality and Social Psychology* 15: 283–93.

——(1973). "Normative Explanations of Helping Behavior: A Critique, Proposal, and Empirical Test." *Journal of Experimental Social Psychology* 9: 349–64.

——(1977). "Normative Influences on Altruism," in *Advances in Experimental Social Psychology,* x. Ed. L. Berkowitz. New York: Academic Press, 221–79.

——and A. Gottlieb. (1980). "Bystander Anonymity and Reactions to Emergencies." *Journal of Personality and Social Psychology* 39: 418–30.

Shaffer, D. and W. Graziano. (1983). "Effects of Positive and Negative Moods on Helping Tasks Having Pleasant or Unpleasant Consequences." *Motivation and Emotion* 7: 269–78.

Shaw, L., C. Batson, and R. Todd. (1994). "Empathy Avoidance: Forestalling Feeling for Another in Order to Escape the Motivational Consequences." *Journal of Personality and Social Psychology* 67: 879–87.

Sher, G. (1998). "Ethics, Character, and Action." *Social Philosophy and Policy* 15: 1–17.

Sherman, R., C. Nave, and D. Funder. (2010). "Situational Similarity and Personality Predict Behavioral Consistency." *Journal of Personality and Social Psychology* 99: 330–43.

Shoda, Y. (1999a). "Behavioral Expressions of a Personality System: Generation and Perception of Behavioral Signatures," in *The Coherence of Personality: Social-Cognitive Bases of Consistency, Variability, and Organization.* Ed. D. Cervone and Y. Shoda. New York: The Guilford Press, 155–81.

——(1999b). "A Unified Framework for the Study of Behavioral Consistency: Bridging Person x Situation Interaction and the Consistency Paradox." *European Journal of Personality* 13: 361–87.

——and S. LeeTiernan. (2002). "What Remains Invariant? Finding Order within a Person's Thoughts, Feelings, and Behaviors across Situations," in *Advances in Personality Science.* Ed. D. Cervone and W. Mischel. New York: The Guilford Press, 241–70.

——and W. Mischel. (1996). "Toward a Unified, Intra-Individual Dynamic Conception of Personality." *Journal of Research in Personality* 30: 414–28.

————and J. Wright. (1993). "The Role of Situational Demands and Cognitive Competencies in Behavior Organization and Personality Coherence." *Journal of Personality and Social Psychology* 65: 1023–35.

————— (1994). "Intraindividual Stability in the Organization and Patterning of Behavior: Incorporating Psychological Situations into the Idiographic Analysis of Personality." *Journal of Personality and Social Psychology* 67: 674–87.

Sinnott-Armstrong, W. (2005). "You Ought to Be Ashamed of Yourself (When You Violate an Imperfect Moral Obligation)." *Philosophical Issues* 15: 193–208.

Skitka, L., C. Bauman, and E. Sargis. (2005). "Moral Conviction: Another Contributor to Attitude Strength or Something More?" *Journal of Personality and Social Psychology* 88: 895–917.

Slote, M. (2004). "Autonomy and Empathy." *Social Philosophy and Policy* 21: 293–309.

Small, S., R. Shepherd Zeldin, and R. Savin-Williams. (1983). "In Search of Personality Traits: A Multimethod Analysis of Naturally Occurring Prosocial and Dominance Behavior." *Journal of Personality* 51: 1–16.

Smith, A. (2008). "Control, Responsibility, and Moral Assessment." *Philosophical Studies* 138: 367–92.

Smith, D. Livingstone. (2011). *Less than Human: Why We Demean, Enslave and Exterminate Others.* New York: St. Martin's Press.

Smith, K., J. Keating, and E. Stotland. (1989). "Altruism Revised: The Effect of Denying Feedback on a Victim's Status to Empathic Witnesses." *Journal of Personality and Social Psychology* 57: 641–50.

Smith, M. (1994). *The Moral Problem.* Oxford: Blackwell.

Smith, R., Y. Shoda, S. Cumming et al. (2009). "Behavioral Signatures at the Ballpark: Intraindividual Consistency of Adults' Situation-Behavior Patterns and their Interpersonal Consequences." *Journal of Research in Personality* 43: 187–95.

Snow, N. (2000). "Empathy." *American Philosophical Quarterly* 37: 65–78.

——(2009). "How Ethical Theory Can Improve Practice: Lessons from Abu Ghraib." *Ethical Theory and Moral Practice* 12: 555–68.

——(2010). *Virtue as Social Intelligence: An Empirically Grounded Theory.* New York: Routledge.

Snyder, M. and S. Gangestad. (1982). "Choosing Social Situations: Two Investigations of Self-Monitoring Processes." *Journal of Personality and Social Psychology* 43: 123–35.

Sobel, D. and D. Copp. (2001). "Against Direction of Fit Accounts of Belief and Desire." *Analysis* 61: 44–53.

Sober, E. and D. S. Wilson. (1998). *Unto Others: The Evolution and Psychology of Unselfish Behavior.* Cambridge, MA: Harvard University Press.

————(2000). "Morality and 'Unto Others.' Response to Commentary Discussion." *Journal of Consciousness Studies* 7: 257–68.

Solomon, R. (1976). *The Passions.* Notre Dame: University of Notre Dame Press.

——(2003). "Victims of Circumstances? A Defense of Virtue Ethics in Business." *Business Ethics Quarterly* 13: 43–62.

Sorensen, R. (2007). "Bald-Faced Lies! Lying without the Intent to Deceive." *Pacific Philosophical Quarterly* 88: 251–64.

Sosa, E. (2009). "Situations against Virtues: The Situationist Attack on Virtue Theory," in *Philosophy of the Social Sciences: Philosophical Theory and Scientific Practice.* Ed. C. Mantzavinos. Cambridge: Cambridge University Press, 274–90.

Sreenivasan, G. (2002). "Errors about Errors: Virtue Theory and Trait Attribution." *Mind* 111: 47–68.

——(2008). "Character and Consistency: Still More Errors." *Mind* 117: 603–12.

Staub, E. (1974). "Helping a Distressed Person: Social, Personality, and Stimulus Determinants," in *Advances in Experimental Social Psychology*, vii. Ed. L. Berkowitz. New York: Academic Press, 293–341.

Stich, S., J. Doris, and E. Roedder. (2010). "The Science of Altruism," in *The Moral Psychology Handbook*. Ed. J. Doris and the Moral Psychology Research Group. Oxford: Oxford University Press, 147–205.

Stocker, M. (1976). "The Schizophrenia of Modern Ethical Theories." *The Journal of Philosophy* 73: 453–66. Reprinted in *Virtue Ethics*. Ed. R. Crisp and M. Slote. Oxford: Oxford University Press, 1997, 66–78.

——(1981). "Values and Purposes: The Limits of Teleology and the Ends of Friendship." *The Journal of Philosophy* 78: 747–65.

Stocks, E., D. Lishner, and S. Decker. (2009). "Altruism or Psychological Escape: Why Does Empathy Promote Prosocial Behavior?" *European Journal of Social Psychology* 39: 649–65.

Stotland, E. (1969). "Exploratory Investigations of Empathy," in *Advances in Experimental Social Psychology*, iv. Ed. L. Berkowitz. New York: Academic Press, 271–314.

Stuewig, J. and J. Tangney. (2007). "Shame and Guilt in Antisocial and Risky Behaviors," in *The Self-Conscious Emotions: Theory and Research*. Ed. J. Tracy, R. Robins, and J. Tangney. New York: The Guilford Press, 371–88.

————C. Heigel et al. (2010). "Shaming, Blaming, and Maiming: Functional Links among the Moral Emotions, Externalization of Blame, and Aggression." *Journal of Research in Personality* 44: 91–102.

Stürmer, S., M. Snyder, A. Kropp et al. (2006). "Empathy-Motivated Helping: The Moderating Role of Group Membership." *Personality and Social Psychology Bulletin* 32: 943–56.

————and A. Omoto. (2005). "Prosocial Emotions and Helping: The Moderating Role of Group Membership." *Journal of Personality and Social Psychology* 88: 532–46.

Swanton, C. (2003). *Virtue Ethics: A Pluralistic View*. Oxford: Oxford University Press.

Szabados, B. (1990). "Embarrassment and Self-Esteem." *Journal of Philosophical Research* 15: 341–9.

Tangney, J. (1995). "Shame and Guilt in Interpersonal Relationships," in *Self-Conscious Emotions: The Psychology of Shame, Guilt, Embarrassment, and Pride*. Ed. J. Tangney and K. Fischer. New York: The Guilford Press, 114–39.

——(1998). "How Does Guilt Differ from Shame?" in *Guilt and Children*. Ed. J. Bybee. San Diego: Academic Press, 1–17.

——S. Burggraf, and P. Wagner. (1995). "Shame-Proneness, Guilt-Proneness, and Psychological Symptoms," in *Self-Conscious Emotions: The Psychology of Shame, Guilt, Embarrassment, and Pride*. Ed. J. Tangney and K. Fischer. New York: The Guilford Press, 343–67.

——D. Mashek, and J. Stuewig. (2005). "Shame, Guilt, and Embarrassment: Will the Real Emotion Please Stand Up?" *Psychological Inquiry* 16: 44–8.

—— R. Miller, L. Flicker et al. (1996). "Are Shame, Guilt, and Embarrassment Distinct Emotions?" *Journal of Personality and Social Psychology* 70: 1256–69.

—— J. Stuewig, and D. Mashek. (2007a). "Moral Emotions and Moral Behavior." *Annual Review of Psychology* 58: 345–72.

—— —— —— (2007b). "What's Moral about the Self-Conscious Emotions?" in *The Self-Conscious Emotions: Theory and Research*. Ed. J. Tracy, R. Robins, and J. Tangney. New York: The Guilford Press, 21–37.

—— P. Wagner, and R. Gramzow. (1992). "Proneness to Shame, Proneness to Guilt, and Psychopathology." *Journal of Abnormal Psychology* 101: 469–78.

Taylor, G. (2006). *Deadly Vices*. Oxford: Oxford University Press.

Taylor, S. (1991). "Asymmetrical Effects of Positive and Negative Events: The Mobilization-Minimization Hypothesis." *Psychological Bulletin* 110: 67–85.

Tellegen, A. (1991). "Personality Traits: Issues of Definition, Evidence, and Assessment," in *Thinking Clearly about Psychology: Personality and Psychopathology*, ii. Ed. W. Grove and D. Cicchetti. Minneapolis: University of Minnesota Press, 10–35.

Tice, D. and R. Baumeister. (1985). "Masculinity Inhibits Helping in Emergencies: Personality Does Predict the Bystander Effect." *Journal of Personality and Social Psychology* 49: 420–8.

Tilker, H. (1970). "Socially Responsible Behavior as a Function of Observer Responsibility and Victim Feedback." *Journal of Personality and Social Psychology* 14: 95–100.

Toi, M. and C. Batson. (1982). "More Evidence that Empathy is a Source of Altruistic Motivation." *Journal of Personality and Social Psychology* 43: 281–92.

Tracy, J. and R. Robins. (2007). "The Self in Self-Conscious Emotions," in *The Self-Conscious Emotions: Theory and Research*. Ed. J. Tracy, R. Robins, and J. Tangney. New York: The Guilford Press, 3–20.

Trianosky, G. (1990). "Natural Affection and Responsibility for Character: A Critique of Kantian Views of the Virtues," in *Identity, Character, and Morality: Essays in Moral Philosophy*. Ed. O. Flanagan and A. Rorty. Cambridge, MA: MIT Press, 93–109.

Upton, C. (2005). "A Contextual Account of Character Traits." *Philosophical Studies* 122: 133–51.

—— (2009a). *Situational Traits of Character*. Lanham: Rowman & Littlefield.

—— (2009b). "The Structure of Character." *The Journal of Ethics* 13: 175–93.

Valdesolo, P. and D. DeSteno. (2007). "Moral Hypocrisy: Social Groups and the Flexibility of Virtue." *Psychological Science* 18: 689–90.

—— —— (2008). "The Duality of Virtue: Deconstructing the Moral Hypocrite." *Journal of Experimental Social Psychology* 44: 1334–8.

Valentine, M. (1980). "The Attenuating Influence of Gaze upon the Bystander Intervention Effect." *The Journal of Social Psychology* 111: 197–203.

Van Mechelen, I. (2009). "A Royal Road to Understanding the Mechanisms Underlying Person-in-Context Behavior." *Journal of Research in Personality* 43: 179–86.

Vansteelandt, K. and I. Van Mechelen. (1998). "Individual Differences in Situation-Behavior Profiles: A Triple Typology Model." *Journal of Personality and Social Psychology* 75: 751–65.

Vazire, S. and J. Doris. (2009). "Personality and Personal Control." *Journal of Research in Personality* 43: 274–5.

Velleman, J. David. (1989). *Practical Reflection*. Princeton: Princeton University Press.

Vitaglione, G. and M. Barnett. (2003). "Assessing a New Dimension of Empathy: Empathic Anger as a Predictor of Helping and Punishing Desires." *Motivation and Emotion* 27: 301–25.

Vohs, K. and J. Schooler. (2008). "The Value of Believing in Free Will: Encouraging a Belief in Determinism Increases Cheating." *Psychological Science* 19: 49–54.

Vranas, P. (2005). "The Indeterminacy Paradox: Character Evaluations and Human Psychology." *Noûs* 39: 1–42.

Watson, G. (1990). "On the Primacy of Character," in *Identity, Character, and Morality: Essays in Moral Philosophy*. Ed. O. Flanagan and A. Rorty. Cambridge, MA: MIT Press, 449–69.

——and F. Sheikh. (2008). "Normative Self-Interest or Moral Hypocrisy? The Importance of Context." *Journal of Business Ethics* 77: 259–69.

Webber, J. (2006a). "Character, Consistency, and Classification." *Mind* 115: 651–8.

——(2006b). "Virtue, Character and Situation." *Journal of Moral Philosophy* 3: 193–213.

Wegener, D. and R. Petty. (1994). "Mood Management across Affective States: The Hedonic Contingency Hypothesis." *Journal of Personality and Social Psychology* 66: 1034–48.

Weiner, B. (1980a). "A Cognitive (Attribution)-Emotion-Action Model of Motivated Behavior: An Analysis of Judgments of Help Giving." *Journal of Personality and Social Psychology* 39: 186–200.

——(1980b). "May I Borrow your Class Notes? An Attributional Analysis of Judgments of Help Giving in an Achievement-Related Context." *Journal of Educational Psychology* 72: 676–81.

Weiss, R. J. Boyer, J. Lombardo et al. (1973). "Altruistic Drive and Altruistic Reinforcement." *Journal of Personality and Social Psychology* 25: 390–400.

Weyant, J. (1978). "Effects of Mood States, Costs, and Benefits on Helping." *Journal of Personality and Social Psychology* 36: 1169–76.

——and R. Clark. (1977). "Dimes and Helping: The Other Side of the Coin." *Personality and Social Psychology Bulletin* 3: 107–10.

Wicklund, R. (1975). "Objective Self-Awareness," in *Advances in Experimental Social Psychology*, viii. Ed. L. Berkowitz. New York: Academic Press, 233–75.

Wiesenthal, D., D. Austrom, and I. Silverman. (1983). "Diffusion of Responsibility in Charitable Donations." *Basic and Applied Social Psychology* 4: 17–27.

Wiggins, J. (1997). "In Defense of Traits," in *Handbook of Personality Psychology*. Ed. R. Hogan, J. Johnson, and S. Briggs. San Diego: Academic Press, 95–115. Originally Presented in 1973.

Wilkowski, B. and M. Robinson. (2010). "The Anatomy of Anger: An Integrative Cognitive Model of Trait Anger and Reactive Aggression." *Journal of Personality* 78: 9–38.

————and W. Troop-Gordon. (2010). "How Does Cognitive Control Reduce Anger and Aggression? The Role of Conflict Monitoring and Forgiveness Processes." *Journal of Personality and Social Psychology* 98: 830–40.

Williams, B. (1976). "Persons, Character and Morality," in *The Identities of Persons*. Ed. A. Rorty. Berkeley: University of California Press. Reprinted in *Moral Luck: Philosophical Papers 1973–1980*. Cambridge: Cambridge University Press, 1–19.

—— (1985). *Ethics and the Limits of Philosophy*. Cambridge, MA: Harvard University Press.

Williams, L. and J. Bargh. (2008). "Experiencing Physical Warmth Promotes Interpersonal Warmth." *Science* 322: 606–7.

Winter, D., O. John, A. Stewart et al. (1998). "Traits and Motives: Toward an Integration of Two Traditions in Personality Research." *Psychological Review* 105: 230–50.

Winter, M. and J. Tauer. (2006). "Virtue Theory and Social Psychology." *The Journal of Value Inquiry* 40: 73–82.

Wispé, L. (1986). "The Distinction between Sympathy and Empathy: To Call Forth a Concept, a Word Is Needed." *Journal of Personality and Social Psychology* 50: 314–21.

Wolf, S. (1982). "Moral Saints." *The Journal of Philosophy* 79. Reprinted in *Virtue Ethics*. Ed. R. Crisp and M. Slote. Oxford: Oxford University Press, 1997, 79–98.

Wright, J. and W. Mischel. (1987). "A Conditional Approach to Dispositional Constructs: The Local Predictability of Social Behavior." *Journal of Personality and Social Psychology* 53: 1159–77.

Wu, K. and L. A. Clark. (2003). "Relations between Personality Traits and Self-Reports of Daily Behavior." *Journal of Research in Personality* 37: 231–56.

Xu, X., X. Zuo, X. Wang et al. (2009). "Do You Feel My Pain? Racial Group Membership Modulates Empathic Neural Responses." *The Journal of Neuroscience* 29: 8525–9.

Zagzebski, L. (1996). *Virtues of the Mind: An Inquiry into the Nature of Virtue and the Ethical Foundations of Knowledge*. Cambridge: Cambridge University Press.

Zangwill, N. (1998). "Direction of Fit and Normative Functionalism." *Philosophical Studies* 91: 173–203.

Zayas, V. and Y Shoda. (2009). "Three Decades after the Personality Paradox: Understanding Situations." *Journal of Research in Personality* 43: 280–1.

Zemack-Rugar, Y., J. Bettman, and G. Fitzsimons. (2007). "The Effects of Nonconsciously Priming Emotion Concepts on Behavior." *Journal of Personality and Social Psychology* 93: 927–39.

Zhong, C. and K. Liljenquist. (2006). "Washing Away your Sins: Threatened Morality and Physical Cleansing." *Science* 313: 1451–2.

—— B. Strejcek, and N. Sivanathan. (2010). "A Clean Self Can Render Hard Moral Judgment." *Journal of Experimental Social Psychology* 46: 859–62.

Zuckerman, M. and H. Reis. (1978). "Comparison of Three Models for Predicting Altruistic Behavior." *Journal of Personality and Social Psychology* 36: 498–510.

Zuroff, D. (1986). "Was Gordon Allport a Trait Theorist?" *Journal of Personality and Social Psychology* 51: 993–1000.

Index

Printed and bound by CPI Group (UK) Ltd, Croydon, CR0 4YY